MODERN PUBLIC SCHOOL FINANCE

MODERN
PUBLIC SCHOOL
FINANCE

ROBERT J. GARVUE

Florida State University

THE MACMILLAN COMPANY
COLLIER-MACMILLAN LIMITED, LONDON

First Printing

Library of Congress catalog card number: 69–10644

THE MACMILLAN COMPANY
COLLIER-MACMILLAN CANADA, LTD., TORONTO, ONTARIO

Printed in the United States of America

PREFACE

Ralph Waldo Emerson said, "Humanly speaking, the school, the college, society, make the difference between men." Americans generally would agree with Emerson and would add that the survival of a democratic society depends upon educating the mass. A lot of lip service is committed to this assumption, but battered educators who have been on the front lines of the battle between forces promoting mass education and those promoting elite education or the "hold the tax" line would like to see more financial commitment in order that teachers and students may have a reasonable chance for teaching and learning success, rather than being doomed to frequent failures.

This may be news to some Americans, but the doors to equal educational opportunity for attainment have only been partly opened, and even more shocking perhaps may be the news that the most affluent society in the world has not removed the really big dollar bills from its pocketbooks to finance teaching and learning. Public education has survived in spite of meager financial support, primarily because of the personal sacrifices of gallant bands of educators who have had to wage one of the most difficult wars against the old nemesis of ignorance for the sake of even those opposing the aggressors. Thanks to someone (God, if you prefer), economists have emerged as allies of educators by pointing out something that excellent first-grade teachers, for example, have known for decades—that spending for an education is actually an investment in human capital. However, most taxpayers have not been so informed.

As Emerson said, society, too, makes the difference between men, as it makes the difference between a commitment to finance or not to finance adequately the systems of public education. The American society has the processes and the resources available to demand the quality of education it prefers. Free men do make demands rather than merely suggest needs. This understanding plus an understanding of the concept of investment in human capital could turn the tide for society to release the untapped power of the nation's human minds and reap benefits heretofore unknown to so-called civilizations.

Tallahassee   ROBERT J. GARVUE

CONTENTS

LIST OF TABLES

xiii

LIST OF FIGURES

MODERN PUBLIC SCHOOL FINANCE

CHAPTER 1

OPEN SYSTEMS
OF EDUCATION

Introduction

In spite of the fact that man has a brief existence on earth, work is the center of his existence, and he schedules time for activities pertaining to other aspects of life on the periphery of his world of work. One can conjecture in light of impending automation and a near-automatic ability to produce material goods that work in the production of material goods will be on the periphery of a new world of work—the enlightenment of the mind and the heart to provide man with the competencies, attitudes, and values to solve social problems that have plagued him. Yes, man's existence may center around thirty hours of work per week in solving social problems rather than in producing material goods and services. Perhaps existence will center around universities and other educational agencies. Such possibilities, among others, require mankind to analyze change carefully and to formulate new points of view and new institutions.

History teaches us that change is normal, but we have no history of such rapid change brought about by science in the past few decades; the rate of change is no longer normal but abnormal relative to the past. The survival of human life as we know it depends greatly upon man's effective means and

1

ends of adaptability and creativity which are expressed in such institutional forms as the home, church, factory, office, hospital, and civil and educational governments. The adequacy of these institutions will be tested vigorously in future decades.

Currently no institutions are being tested more vigorously relative to the power of adaptability and creativity than the American public school systems. These fifty state systems were adaptable and creative enough in the past to have been a composite fourth force along with the three classical forces of land, labor, and capital in the development of the American society. From the inception of the first American public school systems, theologians emphasized the school's role in teaching people the ability to read the Bible; political scientists stressed its importance in teaching individuals to make intelligent and free choices; sociologists believed in its ability to weld a people of varied ethnic backgrounds into a melting pot of humans; and entrepreneurs realized its power to produce a pool of trained personnel.

Challenges to the Greatest Social Experiment

The American public school systems represent the greatest social experiment conducted by government in the history of the universe, and the idea is being emulated now by other nations. No other nation previously had been so economically able or possibly so humanistic as to attempt to offer education to all educable children of all the people. There are obvious gaps in this attempt, but the United States is rapidly approaching the point of becoming a nation of high-school graduates as is evident by the fact that the median years of schooling completed by adults 25 years old and older increased from 8.4 years to 12 years between 1940 and 1966.

A higher quality of education in the elementary and secondary schools will be essential in the apparent complex world of the future if individuals are to participate intelligently in the varied streams of society. Thus, professional educators and lay citizens must reappraise continuously the educational structures, processes, and functions.

Interest in improving and extending public education has been at an all time high since a globe-shaking event in 1957. Sputnik shook an apathetic American public out of its present and prompted it to wonder about its future, now that a sinister adversary could conceivably throw balls of nuclear energy into and destroy the heart of the United States. A general perception was that the "American way of life" was endangered. Also, the nation's collective pride was hurt. Americans enjoy finishing first in competitive con-tests, and after the initial fear of Sputnik diminished, the 24-hour-a-day question was, "How come the Russians beat us in putting a satellite into orbit?" Scapegoaters that they are, Americans feverishly sought the accountable culprit and in turn spotlighted the nation's military leaders, politicians (particularly those who allowed Russia to recruit more German scientists after World War II than the United States), traitors in the state department, and, finally, the public education systems. Was it not reasonable that our nation's scientists weren't as capable as the Russian scientists because of the public schools' comparatively weak standards? Hadn't American youngsters majored in the "easy" subjects like general math and science, commercial courses, and home economics, instead of the "tough" subjects like advanced mathematics, physics, and foreign language?

The topic of education became controversial, and to whet the readers' insatiable verbal appetite, the nation's publishers responded with a post-Sputnik barrage of literature concerned with "how to improve our schools." The literature was replete with easy answers to solve seemingly complex educational problems relative to teacher training, curriculum, school organization, facilities, and finance. The easy answers included such propositions as the following: eliminate "fuzzy-headed" educationists; require more liberal arts courses in teacher-training programs; work students harder; spend more money for education; pattern our schools after European schools; structure a uniform national curriculum; and fire the superintendent of schools.

A wave of discontent and questioning inundated the nation's 40,000 (reduced to 21,000 by 1968) school districts. Mounting pressure forced local district board members and school superintendents to defend and to probe their internal school operation, probably as they had never done before. Sophisticated financial management became an imperative, for example, as smaller districts merged into larger units for effecting improved educational programs and greater efficiency. In many instances, larger units meant that the school district was the community's largest employer, operated the largest restaurant and transportation service, and implemented the largest budget in either the community's private or public sector. The need for academically talented and experienced fiscal management was obvious as a partial solution to improving the schools.

There is increasing evidence that schools are more innovative during periods of emergencies and, in the case of Sputnik, mounting pressure for change in the United States was probably the result of a myth born of a mistaken belief that what Russia had accomplished was a product of educational superiority. Sputnik probably was more the result of the ability of a totalitarian state to concentrate its resources on a few selected and sensational targets.

Certainly a positive benefit of the harangue has been the formal and in-formal reappraisals of the nation's school systems, although these reappraisals range nationwide on a continuum from a cursory look to a penetrating investigation. It is impossible, of course, to research the comparative effective-ness of school systems during the 1957–1968 period, but one senses the general public's growing confidence that schools are getting better. However, criteria to judge educational effectiveness are not very clear. Regularly, criteria developed by an individual such as Dr. James B. Conant or by a group such as the Educational Policies Commission were used singly or collectively to determine the effectiveness of educational programs.[1]

Openness of a Renaissance

What has been termed *the emerging educational renaissance* is leading the nation to a sovereign and almost fanatical faith in education. Knowledge is recognized for its potential power both in the life of an individual and of a nation, and it appears that education will remain a national topic of concern for an indefinite, but probably lengthy, period of time. One thing for certain is that the interchange between citizens and the educational governments will continue to broaden and to complicate educational policy decisions.

An example of new citizens' involvement and complication of policy-making involves the concept of the community school, whereby a local board of education has contracted out the school's operation to an agency or group. Such a school is the Thomas P. Morgan School, an old institution located in the inner city of Washington, D.C., and made up of poor Negroes, old middle-class families, and a few young prosperous whites.[2]

There has been an active community council in the Thomas P. Morgan School area. In 1967, along with the Institute for Policy Studies, a privately funded group, the council petitioned for the Washington, D.C., School Board to contract out the operation of the school to be jointly run by Antioch College and an elected community school council. The latter consists of eleven Negro members and four white members; seven of the members have children in the school, six are simply community residents, and two are teachers.

The 730 students are divided into groups of 100 to 110 with seven adults for each group. The typical teaching team for each group includes three

[1] James Bryan Conant, *The American High School Today*. New York, McGraw-Hill, 1959; Educational Policies Commission, *An Essay on Quality in Public Education*, Washington, D.C., National Education Association, 1959.

[2] "New Experiment in Education," *Washington Bulletin*. Washington, D.C., Social Legislation Information Service, Oct. 23, 1967, p. 1.

regular licensed teachers, a student teacher, an Antioch intern, and two community interns. Community interns are 18 to 45 years old and have an education ranging from ninth grade to one to two years of college.

In the contractual arrangement, an unanswered question is what relationships will develop between the Washington, D.C., School Board and the community school council. Proponents of the status quo argue that the latter group represents a subtle means of by-passing the established government, similar to by-passing exemplified by federal agricultural committees in the 1930's and community action committees implementing Great Society antipoverty programs today.

As another example of new citizens' involvement in educational affairs and the complication of policy-making, defiant Negro parents and their supporters took over Junior High School 271 in Brooklyn on May 14, 1968, barricading the doors and preventing five "dismissed" teachers from entering. The controversy was touched off when 19 educators—13 teachers, five assistant principals, and one principal—were dismissed by the local governing board of the Ocean Hill-Brownsville School Demonstration District. The district was one of three special units set up in 1967 by the New York City Board of Education as an experiment in school decentralization. The purpose of the project, financed by the Ford Foundation, was to test community control of neighborhood schools. The Brooklyn experiment involves eight schools with 9,000 pupils, most of them Negroes, and 500 teachers, the majority of them whites.

The local governing board charged that the 19 educators had tried to sabotage the experiment or had failed to perform satisfactorily. Claim by the board chairman was that the ouster was legal and that the educators had been transferred out of the district but not dismissed. In September, 1968, New York City's United Federation of Teachers struck because of fear that decentralization would leave teachers vulnerable to the "whims of certain vociferous local citizens."

One senses, in many instances, the professional educators' impatience in dealing with the lay publics and with the publics' representatives in educational government, the 114,000 lay board members. Historically, professed experts in all fields of endeavor have wished away "roadblocks to progress," and, in the case of education, the experts have contended that educational matters should be left to educators, much like medical matters are left to medical doctors. A new group of educational experts is establishing a power base in Washington, D.C., and it is composed of so-called liberal educators, scholars, scientists, and engineers. They, too, seem to be wishing away roadblocks to progress.

Public organizations are not housed in sealed containers but are open subsystems of the broader and total system which is termed *society*. Public organizations are part of this large culture which includes an economic and political system. Public organizations are not only reflections of the total society but may attempt also to have an impact upon improving the whole society. However, since one of the objectives of the society is to maintain itself, ground rules are established for the operation of the subsystem. Thus, a subsystem can make a contribution within so-called tolerable limits established according to wishes of other subsystems.

The open organization depends upon external groups for financial and moral support. The degree of support is determined partially by the external groups' evaluation of the organization's products, particularly when the products are employed after graduation. There is a growing awareness among the professional educators and others leading the movement to strengthen public education that short-term consensus building for the sake of gaining more money for education is insufficient and that it is essential to build long-term moral support and to involve the publics in evaluation of educational products.

The school community, as any social organization, is a "continuing system of differentiated and coordinated human activities utilizing, transforming, and welding together a specific set of human, material, capital, ideational, and natural resources into a unique problem-solving whole engaged in satisfying particular human needs in interaction with other systems of human activities and resources in its environment."[3] It is essential that the participants and outsiders to a social organization have an adequate image of the uniqueness and wholeness of the organization, and this is facilitated through the use of what Bakke terms *the organizational charter*.[4] The charter is not meant to be merely the summation of the organization's parts but rather the interaction and combination of the parts.

A major characteristic of the charter is the reciprocal rights and obligations with respect to each other of the organization, people, and other organizations in the environment. Relative to school organization, there appears to be an intensive movement for the clarification of roles and responsibilities of the publics and the public servant in education. The point is made that so far neither school boards nor administrators seem certain of their limits, as if these limits can ever be determined precisely.

---

[3] E. Wright Bakke, "Concept of the Social Organization," in *Modern Organizational Theory*, Mason Haire, ed. New York, Wiley, 1961, p. 37.
[4] *Ibid.*

New Intergovernmental Relationships

Not only is there a movement for clarification of roles and responsibilities of the publics and the public servant in education, but also among the levels of government. Legally and historically, education in the United States has been a state function with plenary powers in the hands of legislatures. However, states have chosen to delegate varying degrees of operational authority to local school districts, and the federal government has maintained an "interest" in public education. With the passage of the federal Elementary and Secondary Education Act in 1965 and a doubling of the federal government's proportion of financial support from a percentage of 3.9 per cent in 1964–1965 to 8.0 per cent of funds expended for public elementary and secondary education in 1966–1967, it appears that the state and local educational governments will in time gain a full-fledged partner committed to public education beyond that of its past when it only periodically chose to make contributions.

With a more vigorous entry of the federal government in financing education, coupled with its interest in ensuring the elimination of racial discrimination, in redistributing income, and in stabilizing the economy, the delicate balance of local, state, and federal relationships is being disturbed, as can be anticipated in a healthy democracy.

Assessments of the capacity of state and local governments to cope with today's complex social and economic problems and of their proper role in the federal system vary widely. Some authorities call for a new creative federalism and perceive a new era of resurgence and vitality among the state and local governments. Others assert flatly that the states are "sick, sick, sick" and despair of their revitalization short of a major ideological and political transformation.

The debate has been colored by differences of opinion concerning the historic tradition of American federalism. The long-standard view was that throughout the nineteenth century and in most respects until the New Deal, "dual federalism"—in which the functions of the three levels of government were well delineated and in which their administrative activities were kept separate and autonomous—was the prevailing system. Only in the twentieth century did there emerge a new order, termed *cooperative federalism*, in which all the levels of government became "mutually complementary parts of a single governmental mechanism all of whose powers are intended to realize the current purposes of government according to the applicability of the problem at hand."[5]

[5] Subcommittee on Intergovernmental Relations, *The Condition of American Federalism: An Historian's View*, Washington, D.C., U.S. Govt. Printing Office, Oct. 15, 1966, pp. 1–2.

Now there has become popular a new historical view associated mainly with the late Morton Grodzins that dual federalism never characterized the American political scene. Professor Grodzins argued that the system does not resemble a layer cake "of three distinct and separate planes" so much as a marble cake: ". . . there is no neat horizontal stratification," because both policy-making and administrative functions are shared by the federal, state, and local governments. Grodzins went further to say that government does more things in 1963 than it did in 1790 or 1861, but in terms of what government did, there was as much sharing then as today.[6]

Inseparability of Politics and Education

Politics and public education are inseparable in spite of an American tradition to believe in their separateness. The always tentative balance of intergovernmental relationships is determined through political processes, and the balance relative to intergovernmental financing of public elementary and secondary education has not been disturbed drastically for a few decades.

The legislative process at each of the three levels of government, the system of checks and balances among the executive, legislative, and judicial branches of government, procedures for electing and appointing government officials, procedures for forcing or prohibiting the offering of various services by government, and many other governmental processes influence public finance, including educational finance. An assumption of the author is that individuals can affect a social system's preference system if they take the time to become knowledgeable about communication and policy-making channels and become involved in consensus building.

Educational policy-making, like policy-making in other public services, has been dominated by the white, Protestant, rural-minded representatives in the Congress and state legislatures. As was declared by Alan P. Grimes:

> Traditionally, American politics has reflected in its principles the composition of its constituents. For much of our history, the country has been predominantly Protestant and has reflected in its politics a Protestant prejudice, for all the intended separation of religion from the political affairs of men; the country has been predominantly white and has reflected in its politics a pattern of white supremacy; the country has been predominantly rural and has reflected in its politics this rural hegemony.[7]

[6] *Ibid.*

[7] Alan P. Grimes, *Equality in America.* New York, Oxford University Press, 1964, p. 125.

Grimes' thesis is that three decisions of the controversial United States Supreme Court in recent years symbolize the long-delayed challenge of a changing society to the so-called Old Regime. These are the *Brown v. Board of Education* (school desegregation case in 1954), *Engel v. Vitale* (prayer in public school case in 1962), and *Baker v. Carr* (legislative reapportionment case in 1962) decisions. Thus, the emerging "essentially cosmopolitan and urban-oriented" constituency challenged the superiority in race, religion, and politics that the Old Regime enjoyed.[8]

An important development in the politics of educational finance is the growing involvement of big business (assisted by the federal government's "dollars for development") in the production and marketing of educational goods and services entitled by some as package curricula. This places powerful industries in a position that will prompt them to support legislation to increase expenditures for education. In spite of claims of big-business interests for support of public education in the past, educational practitioners on the front lines of education in many areas of the United States have found the strongest opponents to increased financial support for public education to be big-business management. The national labor movement has consistently lobbied for increased funding of public education and, consistent with the President's recent proposal for merging the federal Commerce and Labor Departments, can now merge its efforts with that of big business in the education lobby.

Relative to educational finance, consensus building has to take place. However, there are valid political reasons for serious and dire deliberation of means to finance education. The professionals complain about amateurs dictating policy, particularly schoolboard members (remember that schoolboard members usually are products of public schools) in the case of education. Inadequate finance for education is a roadblock, but if it is hurdled easily such as by fiat by any level of government but particularly by an allpowerful level of government, then the decentralized American public education system will be weakened accordingly.

The American political processes can serve effectively as mechanisms for resource allocation. The alternatives, including the private financing and operating of schools within the regular structure of the marketplace economy, seem flimsy.

There is a new genus of social actors who have been described as something between politicians and technicians, who dream of using scientific social science methods instead of pressure politics to solve the nation's problems. It is most fashionable to be involved in both governmental and social science

---

[8] *Ibid.*, p. ix.

future-planning, and a dozen or so public and private panels and task forces
are so engaged. The Department of Health, Education and Welfare has
assembled a pool of social planners under the leadership of an Assistant
Secretary and a prominent sociologist to explore the possibilities of a so-
called "social state-of-the-union" report. Federal legislation is being
prepared to set up a Council of Social Advisers in the White House.

Elements of old-fashioned central planning are involved in the new futurism
activity, and already an impressive body of economic indicators, goals, and
models has been constructed to describe the nation's economy and to be
used for meeting economic policy objectives. Complaint is that the economic
goals are biased according to economists' values, and emphasis on economic
accounting in governmental planning has excluded crucial social considerations such as involvement of more citizens in governmental and societal
affairs, increasing personal happiness, improving the cultural state of the
nation, and overcoming prejudice.

An example of the use of social indicators by educators is as follows.[9] The
scene is the meeting place of the Administrative Council of the Leon County
School District on a day in the mid-1980's:

> Superintendent Frick is idly watching the local Dow-Jones societal wire
> (formerly the business wire): "Student Indignation Index up .04 per cent. . . .
> Teacher Indignation Index up 8 per cent . . . . Three youths from a Title I
> target area in Tallahassee are accepted at Vassar . . . . Participatory Democracy
> Determinants drops slightly (collapse of a student-faculty teaching team) . . . .
> Local Gross Social Product extrapolated to 789 by December 31."
>
> Suddenly Frick calls excitedly, "Frank, Dick, come here quick. The Native
> Restlessness Index has hit an all-time high!" The Council goes into special
> session, then report their conclusions and recommendations to the chairman
> of the school board, who the next day asks the board for emergency legislation
> to provide a three-hour daily planning period for teachers and free legal
> counseling for students who have been threatened with expulsion from
> school.

Social indicators are meant to quantify the intangibles of quality, feed
them into accounting, and then deal with longer term societal trends that lead
more directly to policy goals. They are needed so that performance standards
can be established and implemented, but one fear is that social indicator
information could become a government monopoly and result in the
termination of social pluralism.

[9] The example is patterned after the model presented by Andrew Kopkind in "The
Future-Planners," *The New Republic*, Vol. 156, Feb. 25, 1967, p. 21.

Critics of central planning perceive social accounting being prepared by a bureaucratic elite that manipulates some reform that is merely sufficient to take care of people's immediate needs. Thus, the planner's role shifts from "the politics of issues to the politics of problems." If this is so, the future is too important to be left to planners, as education is too important to be left to educators.

Under the present political structure, future planning in education could remain primarily decentralized. However, the current emphasis on using economic criteria in evaluating educational input-output relationships and on making schools more efficient could result in sophisticated economists dominating educational decision-making from a central level of government. In the meantime, decentralized units of educational government need to study the concept of social indicators and probe the question of their use in policy-making and evaluating. For some reason, of all the levels of government, it is the federal government which seems most concerned about social indicators and concepts of humanitarianism, democracy, participation, and cultural improvement.

The income tax amendment (Sixteenth Amendment to the Constitution of the United States) was bound to affect intergovernmental relationships because it provided for such a relatively great taxing ability at the federal level. Now that the federal government receives approximately two-thirds of all governmental revenue, there is likelihood of greater involvement of federal authorities in educational decision-making. In addition, unless the decentralized educational governmental units place more emphasis upon intangibles and upon financing quality programs, the nation may be headed for planning by an elite from a central governmental level such as the United States Office of Education and, in the context of the state, from the State Department of Public Education.

The issues of educational control are closely associated with the struggle over tax dollars for education at all levels of government. As the nation heads into a period of "cradle-to-grave" education, when learning will become a way of life for everyone, value systems will change, and one outcome will be a change of citizens' attitudes toward intergovernmental relationships. Perhaps the nation will reach finally a stage when its total resources can be tapped for social progress through a more effective cooperative rather than competitive relationship among the levels of government.

Federal, state, and local governments have shared in the financing of education since the eighteenth century, although the participation of the federal government always has been relatively minor. The federal share in 1968 averages approximately 8 per cent while state and local shares are 40 and 52 per cent, respectively, of the total expenditures for public elementary and secondary education.

At the turn of the twentieth century, only 17 per cent of school funds were provided by the states. Since the economic depression of the 1930's, the amount of state aid has increased significantly. The states doubled their percentage of financial support during the 1930–1950 period but have been on a plateau since. Apparently the states are now having almost as much difficulty as local school districts in locating additional funds for education.

During the first two-thirds of the twentieth century, the gross national product (GNP) multiplied 34 times, but the revenue of all government (federal, state, and local) multiplied 133 times. Expressed in dollars of constant value, the GNP multiplied 8 times and governmental revenue 31 times.[10] Such productivity of the fiscal machinery enabled the nation to build a huge defense establishment, to aid foreign lands, and to expand the range and intensity of the domestic public service. However, cracks are appearing in the gleaming façade as is most evident by the fact that during the past four decades, the federal, state, and local governments have piled up huge debts because public revenue was insufficient to meet expenditure in most years.

There is an inordinate amount of discussion and literature on quantitative economics, systems analysis, operations research, and the so-called scientific management that is to effect efficiency and economies. However, it seems imperative that a new emphasis be given to political economics because educational policies, including the allocation of the nation's resources for education, are going to continue to be made in the political arenas. The delicate balance of intergovernmental relationships is being disturbed, but political rationality appears to be the soundest type of rationality yet devised for resolving public issues as vital as those involving the financing of public elementary and secondary schools.

Assumptions Underlying the Content of This Text

Content of this text includes both descriptive and prescriptive materials. Any normative statements are based upon the following assumptions by the author:

1. The structure of American educational government should remain a delicate balance among all levels of government. However, state legislatures should retain plenary educational power, school systems of reasonable size

---

[10] 1902 and 1966 are used as the earliest and latest years, respectively, for which comprehensive fiscal data are available presently from the U.S. Bureau of the Census and as reported in the *Congressional Record—House*, Dec. 15, 1967, p. H17210.

should operate most schools, and the federal government should continue to serve as an agent of change. In addition, the Constitution of the United States left functions like education not only to the states but to the people. Thus, individual schoolboard members were not elected to run or ruin the schools, nor were superintendents, principals, teachers, parents, tax-paying citizens, governors, legislators, or educational associations and monolithic business enterprises.

2. Even upon receipt of proper information about state and local educational needs and their relevance to the progress of a nation, it is generally possible at any level of government alone to gain political consensus for only a mediocre educational program.

3. Educational progress is deterred by an antigovernmental attitude generated by much of the news media, and by a fanatical faith in the so-called efficiency of the private sector as compared with that of the public sector. The facts are that citizens deal with an imperfect market economy in the private sector and an imperfect government in the public sector.

4. Legislators primarily come from occupational groups with flexible work responsibility—lawyers, farmers, and the business owners. Such disproportionate representation tends to result in creation of economic and political power blocks that support a restricted value set rather than pluralistic sets concerning educational programs.

5. Budget-making is the most concrete evidence of educational planning and should be accomplished through participation of instructional, noninstructional, schoolboard, administrative, and lay personnel. Both short- and long-term educational budgets should be developed through continuing dialogue and hard bargaining during each school year.

6. Statutes mandating schoolboards to negotiate educational matters with its professional employees will promote development of quality education.

7. The quality of an educational program is best determined by education at the margin—that is, the degree to which a school system meets the educational needs of the exceptional child (the brilliant or the disadvantaged)— and is the best criterion of a system's effectiveness.

8. Educational finance must be related to public finance and understood in relation to the concepts of full employment, economic stability, redistribution of income, adequate economic growth, and the promotion of social and economic mobility.

9. The expenditure responsibilities and taxing powers of any particular level of government need not be commensurate.

CHAPTER 2

A THEORETICAL FRAMEWORK FOR DECISION-MAKING IN EDUCATION

Introduction

Purposes of educational government are to determine educational goals and to provide means including fiscal policy and management systems by which the goals can be achieved. The governments, which legally direct the operation of schools, function within a legal structure established through constitutional statements, statutory provisions, court decisions, and board policies, all of which are policy statements of a society. The extralegal forces serve as a composite indirect government which affects education through political influence, advice, or other means.

School districts are governmental units, and because district voters have ultimate responsibility in the operation of schools, board members, school superintendents, and other school officers are involved in politics. School politics include educational decision-making and the activities of individuals and groups to retain or gain decision-making positional authority and power.

The study of politics has been humanized in the most recent decade by greater attention to role players such as superintendents of schools, teachers, and legislators in political situations, rather than emphasis upon the seemingly rigid housing in terms of constitutions and statutes. It is impossible to describe or analyze a political system merely by investigating tables of organization, constitutional doctrines, or practices pertaining to each policy, because the inevitable informal organization emerges as an important behavioral variable. The informal groups cannot be perceived readily by external agencies and are less open to scrutiny than is the formal structure.

Agger defined a political system as follows:

> A political system, however it is bounded in time and space, is a set of relationships, of patterns, perceived by an analyst as characterizing the actions and attitudes of men as they function to effect, to satisfy (or dissatisfy) and to eliminate (or generate) needs of people in a community or society through those institutions symbolized as governmental by the citizens of a polity.[1]

If there were no demands in the form of requests, petitions, commands, and orders for shifts in educational functioning, there would be no politics and no policy-making in education. The political decision-making process, then, is concerned with the disposition of these demands, which can be met, changed, rejected, or suppressed.

The Nature of Policies

Ballinger defined policies as regulative norms "performing the general directive function of providing guidance in particular cases as to what ought (is) to be done."[2] By a policy decision is meant a choice that creates a precedent and thereby determines a course of action over a period of time. It may be intended to effect further decisions or it may influence the choices of others.

Public policies, including fiscal and educational policies, are the selected program of values to be implemented in a unique political setting. They can be considered as regulative, prescriptive, and authoritative. They emerge partially because of an assumption by the policy-maker that the world is

[1] Robert E. Agger, "Political Science and the Study of Administration," in *The Social Sciences and Educational Administration*. Edmonton, Canada, University of Alberta, 1963, p. 45.

[2] Stanley E. Ballinger, *The Nature and Function of Educational Policy*. Bloomington, Indiana University Center for the Study of Educational Policy, Occasional Paper No. 65–101, May, 1965, p. 8.

orderly and knowable, and his intervention of a policy in a situation will lead to a predictable set of consequences. Policies are both the products and instruments of change.

In essence, through policy certain things are made accessible to people while denied to others. Rights and privileges are apportioned, and institutions have varied responsibilities in the apportionment, such as in the distribution of power, respect, authority, and income.

In a pluralistic society such as the United States, to ask which value is in itself preferable leads nowhere, because individuals or groups select preferences that they deem superior based on personal and cultural experiences. Policy results from a vast variety of political activity carried on by both governmental and nongovernmental units. Ideally, too, policy is considered to be a temporary product of an experimental nature. As knowledge changes, policy is to change, thereby leading to a new type of action. Realistically, however, outmoded educational program and fiscal policies remain "on the books" in the fifty states and give an appearance of permanency.

Phases of policy-decision activities have been designated as planning, recommending, innovating, implementing, amending, appraising, and terminating. Implementing is the effective phase of policy because the decision is expressed or operationalized in a series of actions that may result in the consideration and eventual adoption of new policy.

Spiro perceived politics as a process by which a community deals with its problems (problems are defined as obstacles on the road to goals) and issues generated by a problem generally passing through four phases or flow of policy: (1) formulation of issue, (2) deliberation, (3) resolution, and (4) solution of problem.[3]

During the formulation phase of policy-making, a community's awareness of cultural values leads to the recognition of discrepancies between goals and current conditions. The deliberation phase includes consideration of alternative solutions, while the resolution or bid decision means a decision to cut off certain alternatives, and the solution deals with the substance of the problem by bringing to bear short-run power for achievement of the community's long-run goals.

Citizens in the United States ideally favor competition among social forces in building consensus for one or another set of values, to induce one another to engage in the accumulation of values or to enjoy a given value rather than to accumulate it. Individuals and groups in the society, which have conceived or supported solutions to problems, must suggest their ideas to others to

[3] Herbert J. Spiro, "Comparative Politics: A Comprehensive Approach." *American Political Science Review*, Vol. 56, Sept. 1962, p. 580.

gain acceptance and support. If the solutions are capable of solving problems (according to some criteria) and if they are supported by enough members of a society, they will be executed eventually.

Public policies are creatures of their society and are culture-bound. They are the product of a mutual process of education, power, authority, influence, and accommodation between a governmental agency and the various publics. Democratic faith is such that if enough of the facts are presented to John Q. Public, he will concur if the policy is sound fundamentally. The publics generally are more interested in reacting to present policies than in suggesting new ones.

Policy, Values, Ethical Systems, and Institutions

Three elements are of primary importance in the examination of public policies: values, ethical systems, and institutional arrangements. It is within the framework of value systems that the standards of expectation concerning goals, needs, and methods are determined. In a pluralistic society it is difficult to distinguish so-called significant values, not only because of the number of sets, but because of their changing characteristics. In addition, the values reflected in most public policies are not made explicit.[4]

Public policies have changed dramatically within the past few decades merely because of the changing role of government. In addition, the population explosion, technological advancement, increased mobility of the nation's population, and increased labor specialization have forced man into an interdependence that can be mobilized through increased governmental services such as education.

Twentieth century pragmatic realism has replaced eighteenth and nineteenth century ideologies, which consisted of ineffective dogmatic and sterile platitudes as total schemes for the arrangement of societal functions. Political institutions are becoming more accommodating agents. Belief among many professional educators and others is that if public schools do not reduce the number of school drop-outs, elements in the society will resist the gate-keeping-to-the-future function of school personnel and develop other educational institutions that will be more accommodating to the public. Thus, questions regarding policy are more likely to be concerned with whether an agency is meeting people's needs, rather than with their degree of goodness or rightness.

Values are limited to the function of the whole of policy in its environment, whereas ethical standards refer to prescribed actions of individuals and

[4] Morton Kroll, "Hypotheses and Designs for the Study of Public Policies in the United States." *Midwest Journal of Political Science*, Vol. 6, Nov. 1962, p. 366.

groups working within a policy field. The field of ethics is that part of philosophy that is a study of standards for decision-making, and for the past 2,500 years philosophers have investigated ethical questions pertaining to justice, loyalty, and happiness.

The policy arts—which include business and public administration (including educational administration), law, pedagogy, theology, vocational guidance, military science, and social work—are structured to provide a man with the means of effecting a certain action. The literature, particularly in the form of case studies, is replete with fact-oriented guidance, which if followed theoretically will prevent ill-advised action in the specialized areas of work. Many consider this information as much more valuable than an understanding of vague principles of ethics.

There is no sharp contrast between policy and ethics. Students in policy arts—including administrators, lawyers, and engineers—strive for general standards of conduct, although they do not employ the jargon of traditional ethics. There is a tendency to become enmeshed within the occupational matrix of narrow jargon and skills and to ignore related broad-policy issues and philosophical principles. Ethics and policy are not opposites, unless one chooses to identify the words to mean principles and expediency, respectively.

One of the most significant policy changes affecting education is being implemented aggressively by the United States Supreme Court in order to effect further decisions and to influence choices of other people as a result of the Court's decision to outlaw racial segregation in education.[5] This is the greatest administrative undertaking in which the Court has ever engaged and will affect greatly its image. How much individual members of the Court were influenced by philosophy is unclear, but philosophy can assist policy-makers in probing and resolving difficult social issues.

Philosophy and Policies

Philosophy as a set of answerable questions, rather than of questionable answers, can be an organizer of practical thought on policies. For example, Leys has suggested key and practical questions that might be asked concerning decision-making within the framework of ethical systems and has associated them with philosophers as follows:

Utilitarianism (Bentham):
  1. What are probable consequences of alternative proposals?
  2. Which policy will result in greatest possible happiness of the greatest number?

[5] *Brown v. Board of Education*, 74 S. Ct. 686.

Moral Idealism (Plato and Kant):

1. Can you define what you approve? Can you bring various approved practices under a general rule?

2. If there is a conflict of principle, can you find a more abstract principle, a "third principle," which will reconcile conflicting principles?

3. Are you treating humanity as an end and not merely as a means?

4. Are you legislating for yourself?

Semantic Analysis:

1. Is knowledge of fact confused by emotional language?

2. Does language you use prejudge the issues?

3. Are you expecting words to do what words cannot do?[6]

These systems, plus Stoicism, Aristotle's Golden Mean, the ethics of psychologists and others, are not to be construed as mutually exclusive and exhaustive, and a policy-making board such as a state legislature or a local schoolboard should not have to choose only one system within which to operate. However, the classification includes questions that might legitimately be asked by representatives of the varied publics. The alternative questions emerge from a system of underlying assumptions that are not always officially stated and clarified. However, a deliberate attempt by educational administrators and by the nation's 114,000 schoolboard members to consider educational policy via the above set of questions could help to bring about a more rational set of decisions that could be defended and promoted.

Man's institutions, which are developed to play a role in one or more phases of policy-making, have varying degrees of formal and informal sensitivity to their environmental relationships. Institutions tend to change more slowly than do individual components, but they are adaptable in terms of societal needs or they die. Movement is continuous, partly attributable to a gigantic catalyst termed *technology*, and social dynamism is accomplished through consolidating, merging, annexing, developing, hiring, and firing.

The long-term style of leadership in an institution will determine greatly the dynamism of policy. The so-called legalistic style of leadership in education, for example, will be extremely concerned with preordering the entire future by comprehensive and detailed regulations. Thus, a legalistic-type educational administrator might not innovate because the rules would not specify approval, and stability is more prized than change. The pragmatic style will call for such a complete understanding of a situation that weak rules or rules that have unexpected and intolerable implications will be

[6] Wayne A. R. Leys, *Ethics for Policy Decisions*. Englewood Cliffs, N.J., Prentice-Hall, 1952, pp. 189–191.

recognized for what they are. The latter style is built upon a lack of faith in panaceas, universal blueprints, or models to be copied without exception.

Prerequisites of Electorate Decisions

Because of public apathy and popular sentiment for removal of schools from politics, it has not been unusual until the past decade for schoolboards to operate in political vacuums. The degree of citizens' interest in educational matters is an empirical research problem in each of the nation's school systems, but conjecture is that school administrators generally have a lot of autonomy. Evidence is, however, that the public will suspend delegation of policy-making when it is disturbed sufficiently.

Berelson has isolated two requirements in democratic theory that refer primarily to characteristics demanded of the electorate as it initially comes to make a political decision—namely, the personality structure and the factor of interest and participation.[7]

Within a range of variations, Berelson described the character type who can operate effectively in a free society (on a schoolboard or as a member of a teacher professional negotiations team, for example) as having:[8]

> ... capacity to accept moral responsibilities for choices; capacity to accept frustration in political affairs with equanimity; self-control and self-restraint as reins upon gross operation of self-interest; a nice balance between submissiveness and assertiveness; a reasonable amount of freedom from anxiety so that political affairs can be attended to; a healthy and critical attitude toward authority; a capacity for fairly broad and comprehensive identifications; and a fairly good measure of self-esteem and a sense of potency.

Regarding the factor of interest and participation, the electorate is required to possess a degree of involvement and to take an appropriate share of responsibility for political decision-making. There is need also for a fairly strong and continuous involvement of two minorities with extreme competitive viewpoints, and a moderate-to-mild discontinuous interest, but with stable readiness among a larger group to respond in critical situations. Active minority groups in education have included those who emphasize general or technical education, progressive or classical education, and professional or lay control of education. Faith is that their involvement and competitiveness have strengthened the public education movement.

[7] Bernard Berelson, "Democratic Theory and Public Opinion." *Public Opinion Quarterly*, Vol. 16, 1952, p. 315.
[8] *Ibid.*

Democracy and Control of Governmental Leaders

In a society with democratic governments, there is theoretically a high degree of control of the nonleaders over governmental leaders, and leaders must be drawn from the community-at-large rather than from a few social strata. Leadership is thereby selected from a broad base and depends upon active support of the entire community. With few exceptions, every adult is able to have as much to do with the decision-making process as he wants and for which he wins assent of fellow citizens.

There is general consensus that the most competent citizens should provide leadership in education as well as in other public sectors, but a problem is to find agreement on criteria for identification of the most politically competent individuals. Also, once the most politically competent people had been installed as leaders there would be the ever present problem of holding them accountable for their actions and of preventing power corruption.

With exception of a few instances of direct democracy where face-to-face relations among all citizens of a community could be fulfilled, men have been governed always by elites or minorities who had a special claim accorded them by election or appointment to govern. The mass of people in a representative system of government, then, do not rule directly, but the distinguishing feature is that the ruling elite is confirmed in power or else replaced by a new one by the majority of the citizens in periodic elections.

It is an empirical research problem to determine the actual control of nonleaders over governmental leaders in a given setting, but Dahl has proposed the following criteria by which to judge the degree of control, for example, in a school system:

1. Most adults in the organization have an opportunity to vote, with no significant rewards and penalties directly attached;
2. The vote of each member has about the same weight;
3. Nonelected officials are subordinate to elected leaders in policy-making;
4. Elected leaders are subordinate to nonleaders by election;
5. Adults in the organization have several alternative sources of information;
6. Members have opportunity through delegation or direct action to offer rival policies and candidates without severe penalties for doing so.[9]

To the above list, Mayo would add:[10]

[9] Robert A. Dahl and Charles E. Lindblom, *Politics, Economics and Welfare.* New York, Harper Brothers, 1953, pp. 277–278.
[10] H. B. Mayo, "How Can We Justify Democracy?" *The American Political Science Review*, Vol. 56, Sept. 1962, p. 555.

1. Public policies are made by representatives through a process of majority rule;

2. Representatives are elected periodically;

3. Election, policy-making, and politicking in general take place in the framework of political liberties such as free speech, press, assembly, and organization. These liberties are necessary to ensure that policies have popular support.

Thus, not only are policy-makers responsible to the public, but their authorization is ultimately derived from the public. The main point is that democracy provides institutional machinery of popular control. This is certainly true in the area of public education as exemplified by the fact that 95 per cent of the nation's local schoolboard members are elected to office.

Those who are selected to govern depend upon consensus-building to remain in office, and they realize that the consensus that supports them is always tentative and limited. When the government meets opposition, it can retreat, remain mobile, or try to extend the area of agreement by persuasion or force. Consensus is a substitute for official ideology. It is not a codified agreement but rather an informal one among all the major parties to the political competition about the principal issues, the place where discussion will begin, and limits within which any proposed solution must fall.

Both heterogeneous and homogeneous communities have a condition of underlying unity which Cook has conceptualized to include unity by consensus, by agreement, by division of labor, and by spatial proximity. These conditions of unity are effected by social, political, economic, and ecological processes.[11]

Commitment to Rationality

A system of representative government is justified partially on the assumption that through its processes more rational action will occur. An action is rational to the extent that it is correctly designed to maximize goal achievements. Rationality requires coordination or a type of scheduling or dovetailing when several actions are required to attain goals so that net goal achievement is not diminished by unavoidable conflicts among the actions.[12]

The term *rational* has a history of vagueness. *Rational* can be defined as an outcome of rational process decisions (free from blinding loyalties, passion, personal position), awareness of the correct state of affairs and the conse-

[11] Lloyd Allen Cook and Elaine Forsyth Cook, *A Sociological Approach to Education*. New York, McGraw-Hill, 1950, pp. 192–195.

[12] Dahl, *op. cit.*, p. 38.

quence of alternatives, open-mindedness in consideration of political issues, and decisions made in low psychic tension.[13]

The aids to rational calculation include processes for information and discussion, and processes to reduce the number and complexity of variables. The persuasiveness of such customary criteria as class, ethnic group, and ethical superiority is theoretically overcome by deliberate, self-conscious inquiry and the openness of debate, plus the tests of time and competency. That which survives such bitter verbal conflict results not only from an excessively cerebral existence but also from emotional expressions of joy, fun, and anger, risk-taking without calculations for consequences, spontaneity, and human spirit.

Not only are goals to be rational but so are the principles that guide action to the attainment of goals. Different democracies may pursue different goals, and their concept of rationality may vary. The only common element of democracies is the system itself and the effect upon purposes and policies that democratic principles and procedures will have. The purposes pursued could not, except with inconsistency, conflict with operating principles or values of a system. Purposes are worked out in the system itself, and that is what disputes over policy are about—they are not simply disputes regarding alternative means to agreed ends.

Dahl considers a prime goal as a source of satisfaction in itself, while instrumental goals are deemed as having value only because they facilitate attainment of one or more prime goals. His list of prime goals include survival, physiological gratification, love and affection, respect, self-respect, power of control, skill, enlightenment, prestige, aesthetic satisfaction, and excitement. The instrumental goals include freedom, democracy, subjective equality, security, progress, and appropriate inclusion; these govern both the degree to which prime goals of individuals are attained and the manner of deciding who is to obtain his goals when individuals conflict in goal-setting.[14]

In a direct democracy, argument is that each citizen is the best judge of public interest in making policy; in a representative system there is no need to require this assumption to the same extent because voters do not make policies. Representative government does not require that everyone be equally informed on educational fiscal or program policy-making all the time. There is plenty of room for political persuasion. The interplay of politicians and the public does not lead to automatic equilibrium in educational matters but one constantly worked out afresh by conscious efforts of many participants.

[13] Berelson, *op. cit.*, pp. 325–326.
[14] Dahl, *op. cit.*, p. 28.

Part of the defense of democracy and its political-type rationality will rest upon the deficiencies of alternatives because there has never been a choice between ideal systems. It is difficult to relate a political theory to a so-called philosophical basis or to a clear-cut truth-falsehood dichotomy. In addition, at present it is impossible to arrive at principles of political theory by a process of deduction from a philosophical position. Political and everyday reasoning are rarely deduced directly from philosophic or other premises.

Normative justification of a democratic educational government, meaning that democracy is good in itself on a self-evident basis, seems unreasonable without consideration of the educational level, the degree of urbanization, and the technological accomplishments of a society. An underdeveloped area, particularly one that consists of uneducated people, would hardly be a satisfactory setting to establish a democratic form of government.

A reasonable justification of democracy seems to be by reference to social and individual values realized by a democratic system. Good results are in some moral theories (utilitarian) the only moral justification. The social values realized—for example, peaceful adjustment of disputes, peaceful and orderly succession of leaders, adaptability, and peaceful social change—could be its justification. Individual values might include the promotion of rational methods, independence, sympathy, and tolerance.

Governmental effectiveness is determined according to a criteria of actual performance emphasizing the extent to which the government satisfies a basic function as defined by expectations of most members of a society (majority rule) and expectations of powerful groups within it that might threaten the system. Legitimacy of public educational institutions is based on the belief that these existing political entities are the most appropriate ones for society.

The Public Interest

There is no guarantee that the wisest decisions regarding public education will emerge through democratic processes. The theory of democracy is not an ideology that is a handbook of right answers to effect a grand scheme of government, but rather a set of operational principles that allow many ideologies to be expressed and implemented.

The merit of newly emerging political entities is assessed almost wholly in terms of rising standards of living. Such conceptualization of the criteria of effective government stems from the classical economists' view of public interest as the aggregate of individual utilities or consumer satisfactions. However, an emerging model of effective government and of public interest is an awareness of a rational order of justice in terms of the selections of values to be implemented, and of the allocation of resources to serve implementation. Ideally, responsible governmental action will (1) maximize interest satisfaction by being alert to legitimate wants of those it governs and by releasing their initiative and creativeness; (2) be determined by due process and motivated by a desire to avoid destructive social conflict; and (3) respond effectively when requested to be accountable for decisions.

The public interest is best served when the cause of freedom is promoted. Freedom is defined as the high or confident expectation that an individual will continue to have opportunities to achieve his goals. Thus, an individual should have an opportunity not only for access to educational opportunity, but also for attainment of an education. A nation's progress, and more specifically the effectiveness of educational fiscal policy, can be measured by the public's increase in freedom relative to some conception of goal achievement.

The crisis of legitimacy is the crisis of change. Change and movement are functions of all social organisms. Educational administration—itself a society of men operating under man-made laws, fulfilling human needs—is no exception. The terms *passed, appointed, created, satisfied, abolished,* are shorthand for a host of choices, decisions, and other actions of all sorts on educational matters at legislative meetings.

In the context of the nation, the whole logic of government is based on the conception that there is still a national unity and common welfare; democracy is the final organization of common interest.[15] The fragmentation of interests and values in the nation's 50 state educational systems or in the nation's approximately 21,000 local school systems in 1968 does not cause the disunity or upset the stability of the republic, since the overlapping memberships prevent the isolation of groups into opinion centers.

Plato defined democracy as "a charming form of government full of variety and disorder and dispensing a sort of equality to equals and unequals alike." Likewise, Frankel defined democracy as "an arrangement aimed at preventing a society from being locked in by one doctrine—a method of government based on the recognition that men are diverse, ultimate questions are hard to answer, and that all human arrangements are fallible, including its own."[16]

Social pluralism makes bargaining necessary; social pluralism means that groups work through common government and retain some degree of autonomy with respect to one another. In no sector of government is the

[15] Murray S. Stedman, Jr., "A Group Interpretation of Politics." *Public Opinion Quarterly*, Vol. 17, 1953, p. 226.
[16] Charles Frankel, *The Democratic Prospect.* New York, Harper & Row, 1962, p. 29.

concept of social pluralism more evident than in the field of public education. Bargaining in education leads to an educational viability that promotes a dynamic educational government responsive to persistent groups of believers and promoters intending to effect educational policy.

CHAPTER 3

CURRENT
EDUCATIONAL
GOVERNMENT

Introduction

The complexity of the political processes relative to education is compounded by the multilevel legal structure of government, the fragmentation of government at the local level, and by the pluralistic nature of extralegal forces. Unlike most other countries, the United States does not have a national system of public education in which power over schools is concentrated at the national level of government. There is no legal basis for a national system since the Constitution of the United States includes the Tenth Amendment, which states that "The powers not delegated to the United States by the Constitution nor prohibited by it to the states, are reserved to the states respectively or to the people." Thus, if power and authority are not enumerated as national in scope within the Constitution and if not forbidden therein they become state concerns.

The state supreme courts and the United States Supreme Court have consistently held that education is a state function. The American educational

27

structure then consists of fifty American systems of education—one for each state—rather than one national system.

The basic Florida educational statute typifies recognition by the fifty states of their responsibility for public education:

> Public education is basically a function and responsibility of the state. The responsibility for establishing such minimum standards and regulations as shall tend to assure efficient operation of all schools and adequate educational opportunities for all children is retained by the state.[1]

Each state legislature has complete power in providing a school administrative structure, subject to the limitations of the state and federal constitutions, to provide for the educational needs of its populace. The state, for example, may create or abolish school systems at will, either with or without consent of the people living within the area of the system. School buildings are state property even though building funds are provided generally by local bonding or tax programs.

In the exercise of the plenary power of the state legislatures over education, the state constitutions are not construed to be sources of power but merely sources of limitations upon the power of the legislatures. In dealing with constitutional questions, the search of state courts is not for a grant of power to the legislature, but only for a restriction on such power. In contrast, in dealing with federal constitutional questions, the search of federal courts is for a grant of power to the Congress.

State Departments of Public Education

State legislatures vest statewide authority in the central state educational agency for many special and general functions, such as direct operation of educational institutions, administration of state or federally connected educational programs to local systems, certification of teachers, distribution and accounting of state funds allocated to local systems, and supervisory and consultative services to local schools. Progress of the codification of state school laws has been slow, but these laws are the basic source of official state activity in education. Every state legislature has a large reservoir of unused power in the field of education.

The state department of education includes the state board of education, the chief state school officer, and the staff in the state agency that is responsible primarily for state leadership services to local systems and for regulation of public elementary and secondary schools. Organizations and functions of

---

[1] *Florida School Laws*, 1967 Edition, Chapter 229, Section .011.

state departments of education always have been quite different from state to state. State boards of education are tending to become the policy-making bodies for state systems of education, particularly for the public elementary and secondary schools. They are served increasingly by appointed executive officers.

TABLE 3-1. Appointed Chief State School Officers (CSSO), 1967

STATE	TERM OF CSSO	STATE OR JURISDICTION	TERM OF CSSO
Appointed by governor:		Appointed by governor:	
New Jersey	5 years	American Samoa	2 years
Pennsylvania	4 years	Canal Zone	Pleasure of governor
Tennessee	2 years	Puerto Rico	Pleasure of governor
Virginia	4 years	Trust Territory of Pacific	Pleasure of commissioner
		Virgin Islands	Pleasure of governor
Appointed by state board of education:			
Alaska	5 years	Appointed by state board of education:	
Arkansas	Pleasure of board	Nebraska	Pleasure of board
Colorado	Pleasure of board	Nevada	Pleasure of board
Connecticut	Pleasure of board	New Hampshire	Pleasure of board
Delaware	1 year	New Mexico	Pleasure of board
Hawaii	Pleasure of board	New York	Pleasure of board
Iowa	4 years	Ohio	Pleasure of board
Kansas	Pleasure of board	Rhode Island	5 years
Maine	Pleasure of board	Texas	4 years
Maryland	4 years	Utah	Pleasure of board
Massachusetts	Pleasure of board	Vermont	Pleasure of board
Michigan	Pleasure of board	West Virginia	Pleasure of board
Minnesota	6 years		
Missouri	Pleasure of board	Territory of Guam	2 years

As listed in Table 3-1, the chief state school officer is appointed by the governor in four states and in five other jurisdictions. In each of these states and in other jurisdictions with boards of education (American Samoa, Guam, and the Virgin Islands), the state board is appointed also by the governor.

In 25 states and in one other jurisdiction (Guam), the chief state school officer is appointed by the state board of education. In 13 of these the state board is appointed by the governor: Alaska, Arkansas, Connecticut, Delaware, Maine, Maryland, Massachusetts, Minnesota, Missouri, New Hamp-shire, Rhode Island, Vermont, and West Virginia. In 12 other states the board is elected by the voters or by delegations: Colorado, Hawaii, Iowa (convention of local school board delegates), Kansas, Michigan, Nebraska, Nevada, New Mexico, New York (state legislature), Ohio, Texas, and Utah.

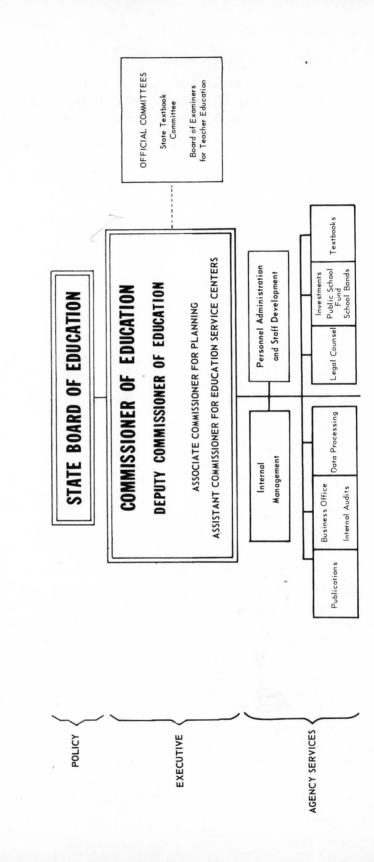

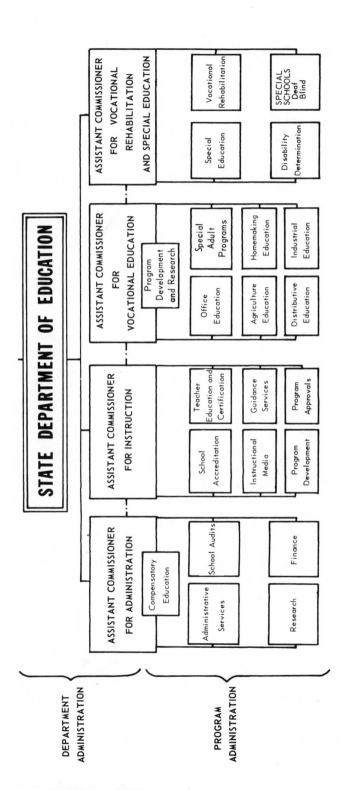

FIGURE 3-1 Texas Education Agency.

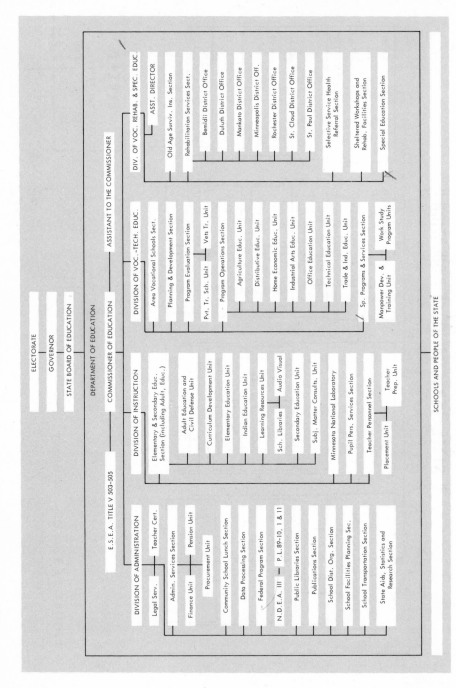

FIGURE 3-2 Minnesota Education Structure.

The following labels appear in the figure:

ELECTORATE
GOVERNOR
STATE BOARD OF EDUCATION
DEPARTMENT OF EDUCATION
COMMISSIONER OF EDUCATION
ASSISTANT TO THE COMMISSIONER
E. S. E. A. TITLE V 503-505

DIVISION OF ADMINISTRATION
Legal Serv.
Teacher Cert.
Admin. Services Section
Finance Unit
Pension Unit
Procurement Unit
Community School Lunch Section
Data Processing Section
Federal Program Section
N.D.E.A. III — P.L. 89-10, I & II
Public Libraries Section
Publications Section
School Dist. Org. Section
School Facilities Planning Sec.
School Transportation Section
State Aids, Statistics and Research Section

DIVISION OF INSTRUCTION
Elementary & Secondary Educ. Section (including Adult. Educ.)
Adult Education and Civil Defense Unit
Curriculum Development Unit
Elementary Education Unit
Indian Education Unit
Learning Resources Unit
Sch. Libraries
Audio Visual
Secondary Education Unit
Subj. Matter Consults. Unit
Minnesota National Laboratory
Pupil Pers. Services Section
Teacher Personnel Section
Placement Unit
Teacher Prep. Unit

DIVISION OF VOC.-TECH. EDUC.
Area Vocational Schools Sect.
Planning & Development Section
Program Evaluation Section
Pvt. Tr. Sch. Unit
Vets Tr. Unit
Program Operations Section
Agriculture Educ. Unit
Distributive Educ. Unit
Home Economic Educ. Unit
Industrial Arts Educ. Unit
Office Education Unit
Technical Education Unit
Trade & Ind. Educ. Unit
Sp. Programs & Services Section
Manpower Dev. & Training Unit
Work Study Program Units

DIV. OF VOC. REHAB. & SPEC. EDUC.
ASST. DIRECTOR
Old Age Surviv. Ins. Section
Rehabilitation Services Sect.
Bemidji District Office
Duluth District Office
Mankato District Off.
Minneapolis District Off.
Rochester District Office
St. Cloud District Office
St. Paul District Office
Selective Service Health Referral Section
Sheltered Workshops and Rehab. Facilities Section
Special Education Section

SCHOOLS AND PEOPLE OF THE STATE

States that have changed from appointment of the CSSO by the governor to appointment by the state board include Massachusetts (1947), Maine (1949), Rhode Island (1951), Ohio (1955), Hawaii (1959), Kansas (1969), and Alaska (1967).

States that have changed from election of the CSSO by popular vote to appointment by the state board are Missouri (1945), Texas and Colorado (1949), Utah (1951), Iowa and Nebraska (1953), New Mexico and West Virginia (1958), Oregon (1961),[2] and Michigan (1963).

TABLE 3-2. States Providing for Election of Chief State School Officer (CSSO) by Popular Vote

STATE	PARTISAN BALLOT	NONPARTISAN BALLOT	TERM OF CSSO (years)
Alabama	X		4
Arizona	X		2
California		X	4
Florida	X		4
Georgia	X		4
Idaho	X		4
Illinois	X		4
Indiana	X		2
Kentucky	X		4
Louisiana	X		4
Mississippi	X		4
Montana	X		4
North Carolina	X		4
North Dakota		X	4
Oklahoma	X		4
Oregon	X		4
South Carolina	X		4
South Dakota		X	2
Washington		X	4
Wisconsin		X	4
Wyoming	X		4

In 21 states the chief state school officer is elected by popular vote. The terms are for two or four years, and the methods of election vary greatly. A few states nominate candidates through political conventions. Sixteen states provide for election using partisan ballots, and five use the nonpartisan approach. Some states use special elections held in the spring rather than in the fall when the political elections ordinarily occur.

[2] In 1965, the Oregon Supreme Court ruled unconstitutional a 1961 law under which the chief state school officer was appointed. Effective November, 1966, the office became elective.

In 13 of the 21 states in which the chief state school officer is elected by popular vote, the state board of education is appointed by the governor: Alabama, Arizona, California, Georgia, Idaho, Indiana, Kentucky, Montana (partially), North Dakota, Oklahoma, Oregon, South Dakota, and Wyoming. In Louisiana, the state board is elected by popular vote, and in South Carolina it is elected by judicial district legislative delegations. In Washington, the state board is elected by schoolboards in convention in each of the congressional districts. State board members are all ex officio in Florida and Mississippi, and some board members are ex officio in North Carolina and Montana.

Wisconsin and Illinois are the only two states without a state board for the administration and supervision of elementary and secondary education. The chief state school officer in both states determines policy and administers the state educational programs.

State-Local Relationships in Education

Typically, state legislatures have chosen to delegate educational authority for operation of schools to local governmental bodies. The relationships are stated in permissive, mandatory, and semipermissive statutes or policies. It is through policy development and implementation that state funds and the skills of human resources at the state level control and influence educational programs throughout a state.

The relationship of a state and its local school systems can be determined to a degree by the extent of financial support provided by the respective governments. In Delaware, for example, 74.4 per cent of elementary and secondary school funds were estimated to be provided by the state government in 1967–1968, whereas in Nebraska, only 3.9 per cent of the funds were estimated to be provided by the state. It is likely that the state provides more extensive educational leadership in Delaware than in Nebraska.

Local initiative and control in education probably depend more upon tradition and practice than upon the character of state statutes and regulations. Everywhere there is legal leeway for much more diversity in local educational programs than now exists. The decisions of the local school about what to teach are related more to college entrance requirements, textbooks used, accreditation, parental demands, and professional opinion than to legal requirements of the states.

Intermediate school administrative units have served as intermediaries between the local school district or system and the state educational agency. An intermediate school system is "an area comprising the territory of two or more basic administrative units and having a board or officer, or both, responsible for performing stipulated services for the basic administrative units or for supervising their fiscal, administrative, or educational functions."[3]

The county was established as a local unit of government when states were first organized in the United States and was regarded as an appropriate area for the general promotion and supervision of public education as well as for other governmental services. Primary concern was with county rural and village schools. As the villages became cities and experienced a rapid growth of population, they were empowered eventually to operate schools that were independent from the rural schools and from the intermediate unit. As a result, the intermediate unit continued to offer leadership predominantly to rural schools.

Intermediate school administrative units generally serve the following functions:

> ... (a) to aid the state central office in exercising general supervision over schools; (b) to provide an organization whereby special supplementary services can be made available on a pooled basis to local districts which, because of small population or other reasons, cannot administer them alone economically; (c) to have responsibility for special phases of the educational program, such as certain vocational training, classes for handicapped children, and so on; and (d) to provide a program of education for post-high school youth who do not attend college.[4]

A number of intermediate units provide excellent services to basic school units or school systems, particularly in the State of California. A new type of a supplementary educational center and service unit as a form of intermediate unit is emerging through encouragement of federal funding under Title III of the Elementary and Secondary Education Act of 1965. Under the terms of this title many services such as guidance, counseling, remedial instruction, school health, psychological, and social work are being provided. The title permits the provision of special educational and related services for persons in or from rural areas or those who are or have been isolated from normal educational opportunities. Also, Title III provides for the establishment of instructional materials centers in the cities and states for the purpose of furnishing modern instructional equipment and materials to the schools in those areas.

[3] National Commission of School District Reorganization, *Your School District*. Washington, D.C., National Education Association, Department of Rural Education, 1948, p. 52.

[4] William P. McLure, *The Intermediate Administrative School District of the United States*. Urbana, Bureau of Educational Research, College of Education, University of Illinois, Feb. 1958, p. 97.

Numbers and Classifications of Local School Systems

Public school systems as defined by the Bureau of Census include two types of government entities with responsibility for providing public schools: (1) those that are administratively and fiscally independent of any other government and are classified as independent school district governments, and (2) those that lack sufficient autonomy to be classified as independent governmental units, each of which is treated as a dependent agency of some other government—a county, municipality, town or township, the state government, or (in the case of Pennsylvania's "joint schools") a group of school district governments. Thus, the Bureau of Census uses the term *school district* solely for the entities considered to be independent, while the more inclusive term *school system* covers not only these but also the school administrative agencies associated with other governments. In this text, the terms *school district* and *school system* will be used interchangeably.

TABLE 3-3. Number and Type of Public School Systems in 1966–1967 and Enrollment in Each Type, as of October, 1966

TYPE OF PUBLIC SCHOOL SYSTEM	NUMBER OF SYSTEMS	PUBLIC SCHOOL ENROLLMENT AS OF OCTOBER, 1966 (THOUSANDS)
United States, TOTAL	23,390	43,842
Independent school districts	21,782	35,342
Other school systems	1,608	8,499
State	3	181
County	495	3,039
Municipal	309	4,113
Township (and town)	747	1,057
Other (Pennsylvania "joint schools")	54	109

SOURCE: Bureau of the Census, *Census of Government 1967—Public School Systems in 1966–67, Preliminary Report.* Washington, D.C., U.S. Govt. Printing Office, Nov. 1967, p. 1.

There was a reduction of 13,629 school systems between the 1961–1962 and 1966–1967 school years as is indicated in Table 3-4. The number of dependent school systems decreased during this same period, but much of the decline was accounted for by a change in census classification to include all Vermont school systems as independent school districts. Before 1967, most Vermont school systems were classed as dependent city or town systems.

Six states each had more than 1,000 school systems in the 1966–1967 school year and accounted for two-fifths of all school systems in the nation: California, 1,240; Illinois, 1,350; Minnesota, 1,287; Nebraska, 2,322; South Dakota, 1,984; and Texas, 1,310. However, Minnesota, Nebraska, and South Dakota participated in the widespread trend toward fewer and larger school systems.

In 25 states responsibility for public schools rested solely with school systems that were independent governmental units. In another 5 states (California, Indiana, Kentucky, Louisiana and Ohio) all school systems that provided education through grade 12 were independent governments. However, each of these states had one or more institutions of higher education operated by a city or county government. A mixed situation was found in 16 states, where the public schools that provided elementary and secondary education were operated in some areas by independent school districts and elsewhere by some other types of government. In the District of Columbia and in four states (Hawaii, Maryland, North Carolina, and Virginia) there were no independent school districts, and all public schools were administered by systems that were agencies of county or city government, or of the state. In Baltimore, Maryland, for example, the education department was one of 38 city departments.

Altogether, 4,422 school systems served an area with the same boundaries as those of some other local government. This coterminous group comprised 80 per cent of all the dependent school systems but included only 14 per cent of all independent school districts.

There were 1,041 countywide school systems enrolling 6.6 million pupils; 1,171 citywide systems with 8.1 million pupils; and 2,210 township systems with 2.1 million. These coterminous school systems accounted for 16.8 million pupils, or 38 per cent of all public school enrollment.

The remaining 18,968 school systems comprised 86 per cent of all independent school districts and 20 per cent of the dependent school systems and served areas that did not correspond directly to those of any other local government. Of these, 298 were classed as "countywide with exceptions," indicating that the entire county was covered except for one or more excluded portions having a separate school system—usually a municipal area, or such an area plus some adjacent territory.

School systems of a countywide or "countywide-with-exceptions" nature were mainly in the South, but were also found in Nevada. All school systems were countywide in three states—Florida, Nevada, and West Virginia. A similar arrangement existed in Maryland and Virginia, because their citywide systems served cities that were geographically separate from any county

TABLE 3-4. Number of Public School Systems in Each State, 1966–1967 and Prior Years

STATE	ALL PUBLIC SCHOOL SYSTEMS		INCREASE OR DECREASE (−) 1961–62 TO 1966–67		INDEPENDENT SCHOOL DISTRICTS				
	1966–67	1961–62	NUMBER	PERCENTAGE	1966–67	1961–62	1956–57	1951–52	1942[a]
United States, TOTAL	23,390	37,019	−13,629	−36.8	21,782	34,678	50,454	67,355	108,579
Alabama	119	114	5	4.4	119	114	112	108	110
Alaska	28	30	−2	−6.7	1	10	8	9	9
Arizona	247	255	−8	−3.1	242	251	250	270	397
Arkansas	402	417	−15	−3.6	402	417	423	422	2,644
California	1,240	1,631	−391	−24.0	1,239	1,630	1,840	2,010	2,809
Colorado	191	312	−121	−38.8	191	312	936	1,352	1,937
Connecticut	178	177	1	0.6	9	38	3	3	14
Delaware	51	91	−40	−44.0	50	90	15	15	14
District of Columbia	1	1	—	—	—	—	—	—	—
Florida	67	67	—	—	67	67	67	67	67
Georgia	194	197	−3	−1.5	194	197	198	187	222
Hawaii	1	1	—	—	—	—	—	—	—
Idaho	120	121	−1	−0.8	120	121	168	305	1,148
Illinois	1,350	1,540	−190	−12.3	1,350	1,540	1,993	3,484	12,138
Indiana	400	885	−485	−54.8	399	884	1,030	1,115	1,182
Iowa	478	1,336	−858	−64.2	478	1,336	3,665	4,653	4,861
Kansas	360	2,261	−1,901	−84.1	360	2,261	3,140	3,984	8,632
Kentucky	202	210	−8	−3.8	200	208	221	232	261
Louisiana	68	68	—	—	67	67	67	67	67
Maine	334	462	−128	−27.7	65	26	8	4	—
Maryland	24	24	—	—	—	—	—	—	—
Massachusetts	398	378	20	5.3	44	29	4	—	—
Michigan	935	1,866	−931	−49.9	935	1,866	3,214	4,845	6,270

State									
Minnesota	1,287	2,355	−1,068	−45.4	1,282	2,343	3,464	6,227	7,673
Mississippi	161	158	3	1.9	161	158	79	93	1,189
Missouri	870	1,649	−779	−47.2	870	1,649	3,234	4,891	8,613
Montana	713	1,015	−302	−29.8	713	1,015	1,149	1,287	1,932
Nebraska	2,322	3,264	−942	−28.9	2,322	3,264	4,942	6,392	7,009
Nevada	17	17	—	—	17	17	17	166	115
New Hampshire	190	230	−40	−17.4	181	221	220	228	231
New Jersey	605	585	20	3.4	522	512	489	481	490
New Mexico	90	91	−1	−1.1	90	91	95	106	105
New York	939	1,248	−309	−24.8	916	1,231	1,664	2,915	6,064
North Carolina	198	173	25	14.5	—	—	—	—	—
North Dakota	539	987	−448	−45.4	538	986	1,998	2,079	2,272
Ohio	713	836	−123	−14.7	710	833	1,168	1,465	1,655
Oklahoma	960	1,225	−265	−21.6	960	1,225	1,643	2,100	4,518
Oregon	398	484	−86	−17.8	398	484	726	1,071	1,844
Pennsylvania	803	2,594	−1,791	−69.0	749	2,179	2,417	2,506	2,546
Rhode Island	40	41	−1	−2.4	3	2	—	—	—
South Carolina	108	110	−2	−1.8	108	109	107	49	1,744
South Dakota	1,984	2,940	−956	−32.5	1,984	2,940	3,288	3,399	3,423
Tennessee	151	153	−2	−1.3	14	14	14	13	11
Texas	1,310	1,481	−171	−11.5	1,308	1,474	1,792	2,479	6,159
Utah	40	40	—	—	40	40	40	40	40
Vermont	267	267	—	—	[b]267	32	16	20	24
Virginia	131	132	−1	−0.8	—	—	—	—	—
Washington	346	411	−65	−15.8	346	411	471	545	1,148
West Virginia	55	55	—	—	55	55	55	55	55
Wisconsin	588	1,827	−1,239	−67.8	519	1,752	3,758	5,298	6,569
Wyoming	177	207	−30	−14.5	177	207	246	318	377

— = Data not available.

[a] The statistics for 1942, based on less intensive and detailed survey efforts than data reported for subsequent years, are subject to limitations of comparability for some states.

[b] Increase reflects change in Bureau of the Census Classification.

SOURCE: Bureau of the Census, *Census of Government 1967—Public School Systems in 1966-67, Preliminary Report.* Washington, D.C., U.S. Govt. Printing Office, Nov. 1967, p. 7.

jurisdiction. The citywide and townshipwide school systems were found primarily in the New England States, but these area patterns were strong also in Indiana, New Jersey, and Pennsylvania.

The noncoterminous school systems included 3,449 classed under the heading *municipal*, for which an enrollment of 16.6 million pupils was reported. These were systems that did not coincide geographically with any entire county, city, or township, but that individually served one or more incorporated places of at least 2,500 inhabitants. Most of these municipal systems included an entire municipal area as well as some adjacent territory, but some embraced only a portion of a municipality.

The remaining other noncoterminous school systems numbered 15,221 and enrolled 8.9 million pupils, or 20 per cent of all public school enrollment. A majority of these were rural systems, although the group included many school systems that served incorporated places with fewer than 2,500 inhabitants. Systems of this nature were especially numerous in the Middle West.

The public school enrollment (43,842,000) reported in Table 3-3 included 992,298 college-grade enrollment in 407 public school systems located in 31 states and the District of Columbia. Most of these 407 systems provided advanced education only at the junior college level, but in 1966–1967 ten of them operated institutions recognized by the United States Office of Education as degree-granting colleges or universities.[5]

Of the 23,390 public school systems in 1966–1967, 5,640 were located in the 227 SMSA's (Standard Metropolitan Statistical Areas). Of these, 5,028 were independent school districts, while 612 were school systems administered by other governments. The school systems in SMSA's represented less than one-fourth of the total number of the nation's school systems but had 28.6 million pupils enrolled or nearly two-thirds of all public school students in the nation.

The metropolitan areas accounted for nearly one-half of all relatively large school systems—3,153 of the total 6,581 systems enrolling 1,200 pupils or more. However, nearly one-fifth of all school systems in SMSA's or 979 systems had fewer than 300 pupils in 1966–1967.

About 8 per cent of all public school systems, or 1,868 systems, did not operate schools. As nonoperating systems they carried out their responsi-

[5] Degree-granting colleges or universities operated by local school systems included the following: Otis Art Institute (Los Angeles County), California; District of Columbia Teachers College, District of Columbia; Washburn University of Topeka, Kansas; University of Louisville, Kentucky; Harris Teachers College (St. Louis), Missouri; Municipal University of Omaha, Nebraska; The City University of New York (4 institutions), New York; Universities of Akron, Cincinnati, and Toledo, Ohio.

TABLE 3-5. Number of Public School Systems of Varied Enrollment Size, 1966–1967 and 1961–1962

ENROLLMENT SIZE (NUMBER OF PUPILS)	NUMBER OF SCHOOL DISTRICTS		PERCENTAGE OF CHANGE, 1961–62 TO 1966–67
	1966–67	1961–62	
United States, TOTAL	23,390	37,019	−36.8
25,000 or more	170	132	28.8
12,000–24,999	350	266	31.6
6,000–11,999	880	671	31.1
3,000–5,999	1,726	1,498	15.2
1,800–2,999	1,819	1,684	8.0
1,200–1,799	1,636	1,587	3.1
600–1,199	2,838	3,157	−10.1
300–599	2,723	3,486	−21.9
150–299	2,091	3,081	−32.1
50–149	2,230	4,214	−47.1
15–49	2,673	6,581	−59.4
1–14	2,386	4,631	−48.5
0 (nonoperating)	1,868	6,031	−69.0

SOURCE: Bureau of the Census, *Census of Government 1967—Public School Systems in 1966–67, Preliminary Report.* Washington, D.C., U.S. Govt. Printing Office, Nov. 1967, p. 3.

bility by providing transportation and paying tuition or reimbursement to other school systems for any public school students who lived in their respective areas.

The 1,400 largest school systems—those having 6,000 or more pupils— accounted for nearly three-fifths (58 per cent) of all public school enroll-ment in the nation, and the 5,181 systems with 1,200 to 6,000 pupils accounted for almost one-third. Thus, only 10 per cent of all public school pupils were in systems with enrollment under 1,200.

Of the 99,644 public schools in operation in 1967, 53,424 or 54 per cent, were under the jurisdiction of the 1,952 school systems that operated 10 or more schools each. At the other extreme, there were 10,918 school systems having a single school. Of the remaining school systems, 2,657 each operated two schools, and 5,995 operated from three to nine schools.

Systems operating 10 or more schools, which comprised only 8 per cent of all school systems, accounted for 62 per cent (27.1 million) of all public school enrollment. On the other hand, the systems operating one or two schools, which represented 58 per cent of all public school systems, reported only 10 per cent (4.3 million) of the total enrollment.

TABLE 3-6. Public School Systems—Size Group by Number of Schools, 1967 and 1962

PUBLIC SCHOOL SYSTEMS	1967	1962	1967 (PERCENTAGE)	1962 (PERCENTAGE)
United States, TOTAL	23,390	34,678	100.0	100.0
Operating systems:	21,522	30,988	92.0	83.7
20 or more schools	630	646	2.7	1.7
10 to 19 schools	1,322	1,182	5.7	3.2
3 to 9 schools	5,995	5,860	25.6	15.8
2 schools	2,657	3,474	11.4	9.4
1 school	10,910	19,826	46.7	53.6
Nonoperating systems:				
0 schools	1,868	6,031	8.0	16.3
Public schools:	99,644	100,339	100.0	100.0
20 or more schools	35,953	29,409	36.1	29.3
10 to 19 schools	17,471	15,449	17.5	15.4
3 to 9 schools	29,988	28,707	30.1	28.6
2 schools	5,314	6,948	5.3	6.9
1 school	10,918	19,826	11.0	19.8

SOURCE: Bureau of the Census, *Census of Government 1967—Public School Systems in 1966–67, Preliminary Report*. Washington, D.C., U.S. Govt. Printing Office, Nov. 1967, p. 4.

Administrative and Teaching Hierarchies at the Local Level

Local school systems continue to play a key governmental role in the operation of public schools according to most state policies. A hallowed tradition has given Americans considerable local autonomy regarding the important matter of educational government. Laymen value local control of schools and tend to interpret this concept to mean control by the system's citizens rather than by professional educators. Conversely, the educators recognize that voters will provide money to finance education, but believe typically that education is too complicated for the average person to understand and that the experts should initiate and implement policy. However, educators seem to recognize the dual role of lay board members in checking the gross abuse of power by the professionals and in building a public consensus for financial support.

Although it is true that local educational government spends considerable time and money to administer state educational policy, much emphasis is given upon what is termed *local leeway for diversity*, or discretionary power in matters of finance, teacher welfare, curriculum, staffing, and organization. Over forty states have a policy to "guarantee," theoretically, a minimum educational program for all youngsters in a state, but the additional policy of *local leeway for diversity* enables local administrative units to develop and operate educational programs of quality consistent with the community expectations, financial capability, and state fiscal policy. Local leeway for diversity is most evident probably in the local organization of schools primarily because of the variable of student population, which will range from no pupils in some systems to over one million students in New York City. Other factors affecting leeway include the qualities of organizational membership, control, power, objectives, and the nature of the administrative and teaching hierarchy.

Policy-making, including implementation, is too great a responsibility for one individual, and a network of individuals is needed to deal with complex social issues. Humans give structure to their organizations through establishment of a hierarchy. The hierarchy is the instrument that enables a governmental organization, for example, to perform its maintenance, adaptive, goal setting, and integrative functions through a formal distribution of workload and allocation of responsibility.

The art of public administration (including educational administration) is the management of the flow of work upward, downward, and laterally within the hierarchy in a political environment. Cooperation among individuals and groups is formalized, and such formalization appears to some to be nothing but provision for red tape, which stifles individual initiative. Users of the term *red tape* are referring probably to the number of hierarchical levels and the seemingly slow and methodical process effected to determine the degree of consensus concerning an activity or idea.

Hierarchies are justified partially on the assumption that role-players in line or staff positions at the successive structural levels have unique vantage points and unique sets of competencies that provide a broader and more probing testing ground as to whether or not an idea is a valid contribution.

In local school systems of adequate size (preferably a bare minimum of 2,000 pupils or more), there are typically four types of personnel in the hierarchy: (1) top-level managers (superintendents and policy-making boards) who are responsible and accountable for the direction of the organization's affairs; (2) a central staff of specialists who provide highly technical services (reading, audiovisual, special education, school business management, etc.); (3) supervisors (principals or department heads) who direct and evaluate the work of teachers; and finally (4), the front-line professionals or teachers who provide direct instructional services to the student population. In addition, nonprofessional personnel, such as custodians, secretaries, and cooks, are assigned positions throughout the hierarchy described.

According to typical normative statements of policy, personnel of the first three types listed have supportive roles to play relative to facilitating the work

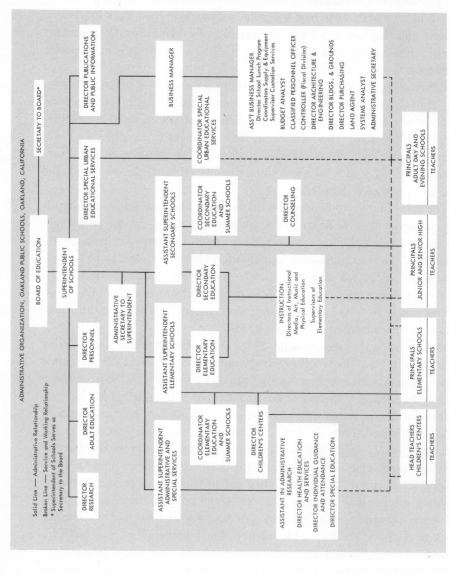

FIGURE 3-3 Administrative Organization, Oakland Public School, Oakland, California.

44

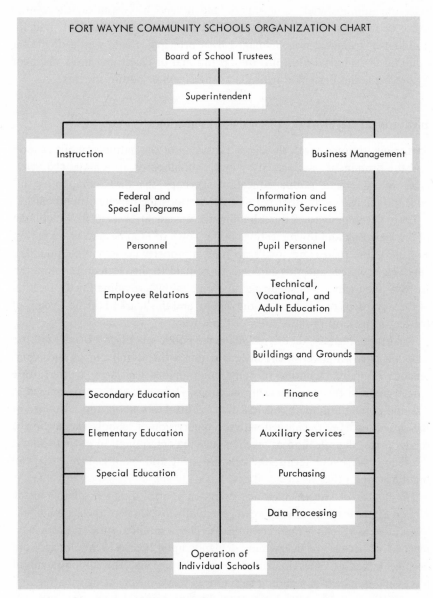

FIGURE 3-4 Fort Wayne Community School Organization Chart.

of teachers. There are school settings, however, in which administration is an end in itself rather than a means through which teachers effect the educational objectives of the school organization.

Within the formal local structure, then, the three levels of local educational management include the institutional level, governed by the board of education and administered by a superintendent and his deputies; the central office or managerial unit, directed by an assistant superintendent; and the building or technical unit, managed by a principal. Some would divide the building or technical unit into the operational or classroom units managed by teachers, and designate teachers as managers or administrators.

Institutional Level—Local Boards of Education

At the institutional level, the decentralization of the nation's public schools and the prominent part played by local schoolboards are unique characteristics of American public education. Perhaps the only comparable lay educational agency in other parts of the world is the private schoolboard.

Early developments of the schoolboard movement evolved from activities of the New England town meetings in the Town of Dorchester, now a part of Boston, in the 1630's and 1640's. In 1639, a property tax levy of 20 pounds a year was assessed, and this sum was to be paid to the elected schoolmaster. In 1645, the town established rules and regulations providing for the election of three wardens or overseers of the school, and this marked the first board of trustees of its kind in the history of the world.

The Massachusetts Act of 1647 made the public schools in Massachusetts a function of town government since it required the establishment and maintenance of public schools. In some communities legislative matters were agreed upon in town or township meetings. However, as towns increased in size and population, there was less direct control of schools and selectmen of the varied towns were charged with the supervision of schools, the levying of school taxes, the selection of teachers and the determination of their salary, the length of school terms, the establishment and maintenance of school buildings, and other related matters.

The boards of selectmen, which exercised control over the schools in the United States for a number of years, gradually lost some of their administrative duties to special school committees. The committee system of management arose because of burgeoning demands upon boards. Schoolboards did become larger as cities increased in population, but the appointment of increasing numbers of standing committees was a means of distributing and expediting administrative duties. Standing committees were appointed to fulfill specific duties such as the employment of teachers, supervision of instructional matters, and selection of textbooks.

The number of standing committees increased, and it became common for boards of education to have 12 to 30 such committees. The boards of education in Cincinnati and Chicago had 74 and 79 different committees, respectively, at a given time in the nineteenth century.

The committee system of schoolboard organization represented the first stage in the process of separating legislative and executive functions of the board of education. When the committee system proved too cumbersome and inadequate, the plan of having a superintendent of schools elected by the board to act as an executive and advisor was inaugurated.

In 1968, the 114,000 members of the local schoolboards in the nation comprised the local district policy-making teams that were responsible for the establishment or adoption of policies that serve as guidelines in the structuring of educational programs. Functions of the schoolboard in addition to policy-making include recruiting and developing personnel, financing and housing the educational program, and interrelating with the varied publics of the community.

Justifications for boards of education are built upon the faith consistent with the theory of representative government that

1. A board of education is more representative of the total population it serves than an individual policy-making agent is.

2. A board of education can make wiser and sounder policy decisions than an individual can.

3. A board of education serves as a safeguard against the abuses of discretionary powers.

4. A board of education serves as a safeguard against the involvement of education in partisan politics and the spoils system.

5. A board of education is a safeguard against needless disruption in the continuity of an educational program.

6. A board of education provides an economical means for management and control of the educational program.

7. A board of education provides a safeguard against fraud and malfeasance.[6]

Viewed in the aggregate, states' statutes concerning local boards of education relative to size of membership, term of office, methods of selection, qualification for membership, nomination procedures, types of elections, area of representation, filling interim vacancies, and compensation are diverse but tend to fall into rather distinct patterns as follows:

1. Size: In 36 states, all boards fall within a range of 3–9 members. A majority of boards consist of an odd number of members.

2. Term of Office: Most school board members are elected for a specified length of term. Members of a few city boards in Alabama may hold office for life. The typical term is for 3–6 years and one or more members are selected each year.

[6] Fred Beach, *The State and Education*. Washington, D.C., U.S. Govt. Printing Office, 1960, p. 4.

3. Methods of Selection: 95 per cent of board members are elected by popular vote.

4. Qualifications for Membership: Most common qualification is that board members are qualified voters. Educational qualifications are found in statutes of 11 states.

5. Nomination Procedures for Elected Boards: Most common method of nomination is by a petition of a small number of qualified voters.

6. Type of Elections: In 32 states all popularly elected boards are selected on a nonpartisan basis and generally in special elections.

7. Area of Representation: Most board members are chosen from the district-at-large, which means that members may be chosen from anywhere in the school system. The term *representation* refers only to selection procedures; a generally accepted principle is that a board member, regardless of how chosen, represents all the people in the school system.

8. Filling Interim Vacancies: Most common method of filling interim board vacancies is by action of the remaining members.

9. Compensation: No compensation is allowed in 22 states.[7]

Appointed or Elected Boards of Education

Much heat can be generated in a discussion of the relative advantages of elected or appointed boards. Proponents of the elected boards claim that an elective board is more democratic and more responsive to the will of the people. Their claim, too, is that an elected board member is more free to act in accordance with what he deems to be in the best interests of the school and the public, than someone appointed who must act in accordance with the wishes of an appointing agency. Claims for the appointed boards are that the appointive method secures many competent people who would not wish to be involved in the business of election and that the average length of service is usually greater under the appointive method, thus providing for more experienced board members.

Consensus is that both good and bad results have come from every known method of selecting board members. However, a premise of representative government is that the policy-adoption board should be subject to the sovereign electoral power of the people, and, as stated previously, this is a way of life in the United States as exemplified by the fact that 95 per cent of the nation's school board members are elected by popular vote.

[7] Morrill M. Hall, *Local Boards of Education.* Washington, D.C., U.S. Govt. Printing Office, 1957, p. 66.

Policy-Making Role of Local Schoolboards

As was stated in Chapter 2, written policies are the legislative enactments of boards of education and are an important factor in achieving effective school administration, delineation of responsibility, and the working relationships of all who work in a school system. They also speed orientation of both new school board members and instructional and noninstructional personnel. In addition, they save time and effort by eliminating the necessity of having to make a decision each time a recurring situation develops.

Written policies are not necessarily all-inclusive, since for one reason or another, unwritten guidelines exist in numerous school systems. The degree of the number of unwritten policies is one criterion for determining whether a system is administered "according to law" or "according to man." Policies represent the official position of a schoolboard on important educational matters and foster continuity, stability, and consistency of board action. An alternative to management according to policy is management by expediency and the corresponding type of administration that reacts to crisis after crisis as would a fire brigade to fire after fire.

Like good policy in any organization, educational policies must be narrow enough to designate direction for an administrator, but broad enough to allow for unique administrative interpretation and implementation. Guidelines for policy development include the following:

1. Written school board policies should be keyed to the needs of the local school district and be the product of local effort.

2. Written policies should be developed and periodically revised by co-operative action reflecting the efforts and points of views of the board of education, the school administration, the school staff, and the public.

3. Written policies should be conveniently and efficiently arranged in a handbook or manual in such a way as to make them easy to locate and use. Areas covered could include educational philosophy, school operation and program organization, board of education, administration, business and operational procedures, certificated personnel, non-certificated personnel, students, instruction, and school-community relations.

4. The written policies of the board of education should be comprehensive, covering the major areas with which school boards are concerned.

5. School board organization, school operation, and the organization of the school program should be explained clearly in policies which are placed near the front of the policy manual.

6. School boards should adopt a system which distinguishes between policies, rules, and regulations.

7. The format of the policy manual should be carefully planned.

8. Abridged policy manuals should be utilized to supplement the comprehensive policy manual in meeting the informational needs of special groups such as parents, teachers, and pupils.

9. Copies of policy manuals should be strategically distributed.[8]

Rules or regulations are sometimes differentiated from policies. Rules or regulations are defined as the detailed directions that are concerned with putting policies into practice. They give specific directions telling how, by whom, where, and when things are to be done, and are executive in nature. The chief educational administrator is responsible for statements of rules and regulations that he and other professional staff members structure to ensure policy implementation.

Policy-Making Role of Educational Administrators

When the first textbooks in public administration appeared in the United States approximately forty years ago (Leonard D. White's *Introduction to Study of Public Administration*, Macmillan, 1926; and W. F. Willoughby's *Principles of Public Administration*, Johns Hopkins Press, 1927), they were based upon premises and concepts about the executive branch and its administrative agencies that had been half a century in the making. They synthesized premises, concepts, and data resulting from Woodrow Wilson's *Essay on Public Administration* in 1887; the civil service reform movement beginning in the late 1860's and culminating in the Pendleton Act of 1883; scientific management in the commercial world; and the work of municipal research bureaus, particularly concerning budgeting and accounting.

A main element of this synthesis was the policy-making and administration dichotomy, and it was not until the post-World War II period that a strong enough dissent occurred to destroy the dichotomy. Sayres has summarized the new premises that have arisen in the field of public administration since World War II as follows:

1. Public administration is inescapably culture-bound;
2. Public administration is one of major political process;
3. Organizational theory is a problem of political strategy;
4. Management techniques and processes have costs as well as benefits. Initial contributions to rationality decline as they become the vested interest of a group;

[8] *How to Develop Written Policies—A Guide to Procedures*, Washington, National School Boards Association and National Education Association Joint Committee, 1960, p. 8.

5. Public administration is ultimately a problem in political theory; the fundamental problem is responsibility to popular control; the responsibility and responsiveness of administration to elected officials (executive and legislative) is of central importance in a government based increasingly on exercise of discretionary power by agencies of administration.[9]

Again, it is an open empirical research problem to determine the political activities of the 19,000 superintendents of local school systems in the United States. However, in the units of adequate size, it is probable that a main function of the superintendent is to work within a framework of political considerations and to use his status, influence, and power to effect an educational program through policy recommendation, evaluation, innovation, modification, deletion, and implementation. The mere legal approval by the policy-making board may be the most elementary step in the policy process, and a politically effective superintendent could be the agent who developed the policy except for the official signatures.

Agger includes administrators as a part of a political system as follows:[10]

A demand or a decision-making process is deemed administrative if it is regarded by the maker, or by participants therein, as involving relatively routine implementations of a prior, more generally applicable decision, or implicating relatively minor values of a relatively few people at any one time, or as having technical criteria available to guide the technically-trained expert in his selection from one or another from a set of alternative outcomes. A political demand or political decision-making process, in contrast, is conceived by the maker or participants therein as involving relatively extraordinary review of an existing decision or an entirely new decision, implicating relatively large numbers of persons, with value judgments or preferences rather than technical criteria as the major factors in determining the selection by policy-makers of one or another set of alternative outcomes.

Operationally, those who work at successive levels in a bureaucratic hierarchy tend to look upon everything decided at their work level to be policy and everything left to a lower level as administration. Whether the administrator is involved in political and/or administrative decision-making is an empirical question in each unique political setting. One cannot decide properly whether popular government prevails until he examines the nature of the process by which influential decisions are made.

[9] Wallace S. Sayres, "Premises of Public Administration, Past and Emerging." *Public Administration Review*, Vol. 18, 1958, pp. 102–105.

[10] Robert E. Agger, "Political Science and the Study of Administration," in *The Social Sciences and Educational Administration*. Edmonton, Canada, University of Alberta, 1963, p. 45.

TABLE 3-7. Estimated Professional Staff and Per Cent Distribution, 1966–1967

	Enrollment Grouping				Total, All Operating Systems
Position	25,000 or More	3,000–24,999	300–2,999	1–299	
	Number of Staff				
Professional staff assigned to individual schools	529,853	864,508	518,922	57,183	1,970,466
Teachers	484,259	782,813	471,344	51,789	1,790,205
Principals (supervising and assistant)	22,062	38,289	26,104	4,146	90,601
Counselors	8,391	14,844	6,056	119	29,410
Librarians	6,855	13,809	7,699	475	28,838
Other[a]	8,286	14,753	7,719	654	31,412
Central-office administrators	9,733	25,739	15,683	3,784	54,939
Superintendents, and associate and assistant superintendents	1,037	5,293	9,693	3,249	19,272
General administration officers[b]	1,485	3,579	1,109	119	6,292
Administrators for finance, business, and school plant	1,324	2,973	856	119	5,272
Officers for instructional administration and supervision	2,769	6,890	2,088	119	11,866
Administrators for special subject areas[c]	2,165	4,935	1,321	178	8,599
Other[d]	953	2,069	616	…	3,638
Total—All professional staff	539,586	890,247	534,605	60,967	2,025,405

	ENROLLMENT GROUPING				TOTAL, ALL OPERATING SYSTEMS
POSITION	25,000 OR MORE	3,000– 24,999	300– 2,999	1–299	
	PER CENT DISTRIBUTION				
Professional staff assigned to individual schools	98.2%	97.1%	97.0%	93.8%	97.3%
Teachers	89.7	87.9	88.2	84.9	88.4
Principals (supervising and assistant)	4.1	4.3	4.9	6.8	4.5
Counselors	1.6	1.7	1.1	0.2	1.5
Librarians	1.3	1.6	1.4	0.8	1.4
Other[a]	1.5	1.6	1.4	1.1	1.5
Central-office administrators	1.8	2.9	3.0	6.2	2.7
Superintendents, and associate and assistant superintendents	0.2	0.6	1.8	5.3	1.0
General administration officers[b]	0.3	0.4	0.2	0.2	0.3
Administrators for finance, business, and school plant	0.2	0.3	0.2	0.2	0.2
Officers for instructional administration and supervision	0.5	0.8	0.4	0.2	0.6
Administrators for special subject areas[c]	0.4	0.6	0.3	0.3	0.4
Other[d]	0.2	0.2	0.1	...	0.2
Total—All professional staff	100.0%	100.0%	100.0%	100.0%	100.0%

[a] Includes directors of guidance, head counselors, social workers and visiting teachers, psychologists, psychometrists, and heads of departments.

[b] Includes administrative assistants to superintendent, administrators of employed personnel, administrators for research, food services, health services, pupil transportation, and community relations.

[c] Includes central-office supervisory personnel for art, home economics, industrial arts, music, vocational education, physical and health education, mathematics, science, and foreign languages; excludes special teachers.

[d] Includes administrators for pupil personnel services, attendance officers, and guidance personnel.

SOURCE: *NEA Research Bulletin*, Washington, D.C., National Education Association, March, 1968, p. 19.

TABLE 3-8. Estimated Enrollment and Per cent Distribution, All Operating Public School Systems, October, 1966

	ENROLLMENT GROUPING				TOTAL—ALL OPERATING SYSTEMS
ITEM	25,000 OR MORE	3,000–24,999	300–2,999	1–299	
Estimated enrollment	12,281,483	19,019,917	10,363,336	940,997	42,605,733
Estimated number of operating systems	159	2,736	9,075	9,727	21,697
Percent of total enrollment	28.8	44.7	24.3	2.2	100.0
Percent of total systems	0.8	12.6	41.8	44.8	100.0

SOURCE: *NEA Research Bulletin*, Washington, D.C., National Education Association, March, 1968, p. 19.

Educational administrators have policy-making functions, particularly in recommending policy changes to the legislative body. Likewise, legislative bodies may provide administrative procedures to guide implementation of policy. Even though public policy is regarded as the exclusive work of the representative legislative body, the executive (which theoretically executes policy only) and the judicial body (which theoretically reviews enforcement) may "fill in details" whenever policy is indefinite. Thus, a superintendent of schools, other educational administrators, and teachers can be policy-makers in effect.

Appleby stressed the flexibility and dynamism of institutions which result from the political nature of the governmental business when he stated:

> Policy-making may take place with reasonable public safety at many levels in executive government because the order of any decision is always subject to political determination and arrived at in a political environment . . . . order of a particular decision is preliminary and tentatively determined within the executive branch by political, administrative, procedural, technical or factual and social evaluations. These evaluations constitute a more or less rough consensus of horizontal and perpendicular associations, individuals and groups participating in constitutional and environmental context. The level at which a decision is to be made, therefore, may be shifted upward or downward as evaluations point to more or less controversy or to more or less importance.[11]

Branches of government may have preponderant but not exclusive responsibilities. Each branch uses discretion in making decisions, but in representative government the decision as well as the order of the decision-making

[11] Paul H. Appleby, *Policy and Administration.* University, Ala., University of Alabama Press, 1949, p. 13.

is always subject to a final determination in a political arena of varied complexities. To a great extent, final determination is based upon the importance of the decision, the related public interest, as well as the competencies of members of the government and the historical precedents.

The author is aware of a superintendent in a major school system who is known to "run a tight ship," even to the degree that at board meetings, which are attended regularly by representatives of the mass media, board members are handed statements of new policy commitments prepared in advance by the superintendent and his central staff. Undoubtedly, some board members would be overwhelmed by the complexity of educational policy-making and would feel much more secure being directed by such a powerful top-administrator who superimposes a positive sense of direction.

Examples of Educational Policy and Administrative Plans for Policy Implementation

On April 28, 1965, the New York City Board of Education adopted a statement of policy governing a program of excellence for the city schools. The policy became a framework within which the superintendent and the staff were to administer the public school educational program. Included in the policy statement was an outside limit of time, 1972 to 1973, for the complete reorganization of the school system to accomplish the policy objectives.

The following are examples of the policy statement sections and the respective administrative plans to implement policy:

[Policy statement: Human relations] An essential aspect of our educational program is the continuing improvement of human relations. . . . The school system will intensify its efforts at developing public understanding and appreciation of the essentiality of integration as a component of excellence in education. [Administrative plan]:

1. During the past year, there has been an energetic and sustained program to develop and assemble materials concerning human relations and the contributions of minority groups to American culture. Since the ground work has already been laid, it is expected that with continuing efforts there will be a substantial increase in the use by schools of appropriate text books, library books, films, and other supplementary materials.

2. Additional materials will be developed, such as "Call Them Heroes," a series of 48 short biographies of people living in New York. Existing materials, such as "Puerto Rican Profiles," will be revised; and teachers' guides will be developed for the effective use of such materials as "The Negro in American History."

3. A basic list of books dealing with the role of minorities in American History and culture has been developed and sent to each school, while a traveling exhibit is being sent to each district. Principals have been asked to use this list as a minimal requirement to achieve a balanced textbook and library collection.

4. The offices of the field assistant superintendents, the Human Relations Unit, Office of the Education Information Services and Public Relations, and other divisions and units have been instructed to expand and intensify programs of public information with reference to the new policies of the Board of Education, particularly as they relate to integration. It is evident that this area requires a planned, systematic and energetic effort to explain to the public the meaning of these new policies, the reasons for them, and the positive effects upon excellence of education. The best of plans may well founder on the shoals of public indifference, misunderstanding, or neglect. The campaign to enhance public information and to gain public support is a most crucial aspect of the total program. It will be developed jointly by the Human Relations Unit and the Office of Education Information Services and Public Relations.

[Policy statement: Continuing programs] The educational program of our city must be geared to excellence. This excellence must reach every child in every school. The capable pupil is entitled to a program of studies which will challenge his abilities to the utmost. At the same time, the child who finds learning more difficult should be helped by every service at our command to achieve his potential.

An essential aspect of our educational program is the continuing improvement of human relations, which can only be completely effective in an integrated school situation.

[Administrative plan]: The free choice–open enrollment transfer program for elementary and junior high schools will be continued with a number of improvements:

1. Parents will be asked to designate areas or clusters of schools to which they wish to send children. This will result in more equitable distribution of children and greatly decreased travel time.

2. Services to "receiving" schools will be increased. The sum of $2,500,000 has been included for this purpose in the 1965–1966 budget request.

3. More Effective Schools will be designated as "receiving" schools for "other" pupils. The objective is to have at least one such "receiving" school in each borough, similar to the one which is now in operation.

The sum of $6,110,250 has been requested for 1965–1966 to extend the More Effective Schools program from ten to twenty schools. In addition, great weight was given to the possibility of maintaining and extending the integration program.

It is proposed to add what has become known as "Prong II" to the College Discovery and Development Program. Its purpose is to identify the potentially able from among the disadvantaged early enough in their school career (grade 9) to enable a special program of studies, remediation, enrichment, and tutoring to release their academic potential. Those selected will be admitted to one of five high schools designated as "College Development Centers" where a special staff will conduct a program to enable these young people to meet the requirements for graduation and college admission. In September 1965, 120 students will be admitted to the tenth grade of each of five academic high schools, one for each borough, Jamaica, Seward Park, Port Richmond, Jefferson, and Roosevelt.

Admission will be open to graduates of all junior high schools in the borough.

The cost to the Board of Education for staff, equipment, and supplies will be $150,000.[12]

Undoubtedly there has been a serious dialogue between the New York City Board of Education and its administrative network concerning both policy and its implementation. However, in New York City and throughout the nation another potent policy-developing force is emerging—the teaching profession.

Emerging Policy-Developing Role of Teachers

Through processes of professional negotiations or collective bargaining, teachers are beginning to play a more prominent role in developing school policy, particularly pertaining to teacher welfare and fiscal policy at the local, state, and national levels. Because of a certain teacher insistence for being involved, teachers are described as being militant, which is an unfair emotional description of a profession striving for status and power to influence policy in an area where its members are the most knowledgeable in the society.

There are school communities, of course, where teacher participation in policy development has been effected over a long period of time. However, under paternalistic leadership or under conditions of teacher apathy or powerlessness, there are thousands of school settings where teacher involvement relative to policy development has been nil.

In most states, school boards undoubtedly have the authority under their specific powers of contract to negotiate with teachers collectively. Teachers, however, are insisting upon specific legislation state by state in order to be ensured of their rights. As of November, 1967, professional negotiation laws— with varying names—were on the books in 14 states: Alaska, California, Connecticut, Florida, Massachusetts, Michigan, Minnesota, Nebraska, New

---

[12] *Implementation of Board Policy on Excellence for the City's Schools*, submitted to the Board of Education, City of New York, by Dr. Bernard E. Donovan, Acting Superintendent of Schools, April 28, 1964.

York, Oregon, Rhode Island, Texas, Washington, and Wisconsin. Eight states mandated teacher-schoolboard negotiations if a majority of the teachers in a given system indicated a willingness for such an arrangement: Massachusetts, Connecticut, Rhode Island, Wisconsin, Michigan, California, Washington, and Oregon. This movement is consistent with the growing organization and the increased complexity of society, which has become a society of pressure groups. There is no reason for teachers not to use the vehicle of a pressure group while it is being used so effectively by almost all adults in the society.

The nature of public service has changed during the latter half of the twentieth century. Society is demanding a high caliber of professional, technological, and scientific service, and, of course, the caliber depends upon the recruitment of highly competent people for whose service private industry bids vigorously in order to meet its personnel needs. The increased level of preparation and competence of teachers, for example, plus the increasing trend of persons to devote their lifetime to education has resulted in the development of education more nearly as a true profession. The fact that 92 per cent of public elementary and secondary teachers in 1967 had college degrees as compared with the year 1946 when 32 per cent had degrees is evidence enough that the individual and collective competency of the profession has increased dramatically.

The American Association of School Administrators (AASA) finds the reasoning for a rather broadly construed concept of negotiation most persuasive.[13] The AASA believes negotiations in good faith may well encompass all or some aspects of policy governing such items as the following:

1. Curriculum
2. Inservice education
3. Personnel policies
4. Teaching assignments
5. Transfers and promotions
6. Recruitment of teachers
7. Discharge and discipline of teachers
8. Provision of physical facilities for teachers
9. Grievance procedures
10. Recognition of the negotiating team
11. Lunch and rest periods
12. Salaries and wages
13. Welfare benefits
14. Class size
15. Leaves of absence
16. Expiration date of negotiation agreements
17. Other mutually agreed upon matters that directly affect the quality of the educational program

[13] *School Administrators View Professional Negotiation.* Washington, D.C., American Association of School Administrators, 1966, pp. 38–40.

An NEA official summarized effects of teacher negotiations by saying that negotiations are:

1. *Productive* in terms of benefits and understandings;
2. *Vital* in breaking the financial stranglehold that has choked public education;
3. *Catalytic* in getting teachers to assume their full professional responsibility;
4. *Therapeutic* in getting all participants to see the opportunities and challenges of their new roles;
5. *Stimulating* in moving state legislatures to a positive posture with regard to their responsibility for public education;

But . . .
6. *Traumatic* to the superintendent who sees no need for sharing his negotiating role.

The shape of things to come from teacher negotiations with school boards is not clear and it will probably change form many times. The impact of negotiations on school budgets will depend on such factors as the availability of funds, the effectiveness of the strike or sanction threat and implementation, the capabilities of the teacher representatives, and the readiness of local teacher organizations to assume negotiation responsibilities. Teachers' concerns are going beyond those of self-interest, but there will be an initial concentration on salaries and fringe benefits because of the teacher perception of their long-term subsidizing of American public education.

The Federal Government and Education

Although an average of only 8.0 per cent of elementary and secondary school revenue came from federal sources in 1966–1967 (compared with 4.4 per cent in 1959–1960), the federal government has maintained an active interest in public education for over 175 years as exemplified by the fact that more than 150 federal laws for support of education have been passed. Federal appropriations are regularly made for support of college housing, practical nurse training, school lunch programs, language development, vocational education, veterans education, and other programs.

The federal government does not operate according to any unified body of educational policies and historically has played a limited role in the determination of policies for the state systems of education. However, an ambitious policy objective is outlined in the United States Office of Education's recent report on the Office's role in the future:

As national concern and activities in the field of education have grown rapidly in recent years, the role of the Office as an advisor on educational policies and programs has likewise expanded. The Office is regularly called upon to review and evaluate legislative proposals affecting education, as referred through the Bureau of the Budget and the Department. In this climate of expanding federal educational interest, greatly increased demands for service to the Congress on behalf of the Executive Branch seem virtually certain.

Specific policy areas in which the Office should have an increasingly important role in the next decade include the educational aspects of our foreign policy and of programs to implement that policy. Active cooperation by the Office in programs affecting education carried on by other federal agencies is also an essential requirement of balanced national and international policy in education. This aspect of the office role needs to be further developed and strengthened.[14]

An additional quotation from the same report stresses relationships of the federal, state, and local levels of educational units:

In addition to the federal level of public policy determination, the Office has much concern with policy matters at the state and local levels and in higher education institutions. Active leadership by the Office to encourage constructive consensus on particular problems or issues in American education helps to crystallize public policy at all levels. This development of consensus is encouraged in a number of ways. The Office calls national conferences focused on identified problems and issues; it participates in cooperative programs to develop voluntary national standards; and it exerts a continuous stimulating effect through its daily operational contacts in categorical assistance programs.[15]

The federal government has served public education as a change agent for the state school systems. For example, the Morrill Act of 1862, the Smith–Hughes Act of 1917, and the National Defense Education Act of 1958 were enacted to provide financial incentives for states to overcome respective program deficiencies in college technical education, secondary school vocational education, science, mathematics, foreign language, and guidance. Through financial incentives, the federal government typically offers to match a dollar with a dollar raised through state and/or local effort.

The United States Office of Education

Upon the recommendation of the National Association of State and City School Superintendents, which is now called the American Association of

[14] *A Federal Education Agency for the Future*, Washington, D.C., U.S. Govt. Printing Office, April, 1961, p. 51.
[15] *Ibid.*, p. 52.

School Administrators (AASA), Congress enacted into law in 1867 the establishment of a Department of Education, to be directed by a Commissioner appointed by the President. The Department was to be responsible for

> ... collecting such statistics and facts as shall show the condition and progress of education in the several states and territories, and of diffusing such information respecting the organization and management of schools and school systems, and methods of teaching, as shall aid the people of the United States in the establishment and maintenance of efficient school systems, and otherwise promote the cause of education throughout the country.

The U.S. Department of Education operated as an independent agency until 1869, when it became an office attached to the Department of the Interior. In 1870 the title was changed from Office of Education to Bureau of Education, but its former title was restored in 1929. In 1939 the Federal Security Agency was created and the Office of Education was placed under its jurisdiction, and in 1953 the Office of Education became one of the units in the Department of Health, Education, and Welfare, which replaced the Federal Security Agency.

The major functions of the U.S. Office of Education today are very similar to those prescribed in 1867: educational research, educational services, and the administration of the various educational grants. The Office employs specialists in such areas as elementary, secondary and higher education, international education, vocational education, library education, health and visual education, and educational administration, including school finance, housing, business administration, and allied fields. These specialists provide consultative services and general leadership in their respective areas in addition to conducting research.

The Office of Education has had a field network for many years, which functioned mostly as "eyes and ears." Now the field offices have been upgraded with a regional assistant commissioner to head each one, and they have been given substantive program responsibilities with additional staff to conduct the expanded activities. Atlanta was the first regional office to go into full operation on the new basis and was followed by Dallas, Chicago, Denver, Charlottesville, San Francisco, Kansas City, New York, and Boston.

Over the past hundred years, the staff of the Commissioner of Education has grown from three to more than 2,600 employees. Appropriations for OE have risen from 18,592 dollars in 1867 to nearly four billion dollars in 1967.

The recent trend toward strengthened decentralization was initiated by President Lyndon Johnson in a speech at the University of Michigan in 1964 when he said:

> The solution to our problem does not rest on a massive program in Washington, nor can it rely solely on the strained resources of local authority. It requires us to create new concepts of cooperation—a creative federalism—between the national capital and the leaders of the local communities.

The regional organizational blueprint was developed by a White House task force headed by Dwight A. Ink, one of the federal government's top administrative experts. The so-called Ink Report pointed out the administrative difficulties involved in a program disbursing some four billion dollars a year and recommended strengthening the regional staffs to maintain closer contact with the school authorities and institutions served by the Office.

Eventually all regional offices will have delegated responsibility for reviewing and approving state plans and projected programs of activities for state grant programs and for project approval in certain others. They will continue to give professional help in each program area. They will have primary responsibility for grant awards, maintaining prime records, and reporting on the use of grant funds.

Extralegal Educational Forces

The United States is a nation of a legion of organizations and individuals interested in playing a role in the development of educational policy in addition to the role played by legal bodies. Organizations range from those of two or more members in an informal neighborhood coffee group to the formal one million-member National Education Association. Chances are good at the local level that the coffee club with its membership solidarity may be more powerful relative to influencing a local school board than the federated NEA with its less-than-enthusiastic membership consisting primarily of women (described by one wit as "mobile masses of maidens meditating matrimony") who are not contemplating a long-term career in teaching.

Voluntary organizations no longer exist to provide only entertainment or physical or emotional outlets for their members, but rather to exert a force in the satisfactory resolution of problems of most concern to the group. The forces are complex, contradictory, complete, and, in many instances, controlling in the determination of the effectiveness of public school systems.

It is a mistake for one to think of "the public" as one homogeneous mass. Yet, it is rather common for administrators or schoolboard members to state that "the public won't stand for it." One question might be, "Which public?" Perhaps a vociferous minority can convince a board that the minority represents an entire community.

There are a number of publics that are composed of individuals who have common interests. Individuals form themselves into publics in many ways— economically into trade unions or chambers of commerce, politically into parties or leagues of voters, and educationally into PTA's, for example. When the consequences of a decision become critical for those who are not directly involved in making it, publics will emerge and decisions that produce indirect consequences can no longer be regarded as private. The informal and extra-legal publics form a functional part of the nation's governmental system.

Thus, the Farm Bureau demands vocational agriculture, the American Legion laments the lack of teaching patriotism, the Conservation Club requests a course requirement in conservation, the DAR worries about the teaching of Communism, the Chamber of Commerce conceives a new course in the economics of free enterprise, sports writers push for a new fieldhouse and the firing of a team of coaches, the American Federation of Labor fights programs that may release youngsters into the labor market too soon, the local mayor resents competition for tax funds, college professors in each academic discipline propose the addition of at least one more course, the state teachers' association legislates for a duty-free lunch period for teachers, the ministerial association preaches against the removal of God from the schools. The listing of forces and their demands could continue endlessly.

From the essential maze of interaction with organizations or publics, the local schoolboard members and their administrative team must determine the school system's reasonable tasks. A first function is to structure an organization to meet the system's task objective, which is instruction primarily, and at the same time to help ensure the maintenance of the system.

American Governmental Structure in the Future

Moynihan stated recently that "The past is never so clear as the future, save possibly with respect to the structure of American government. Prolonged war, economic malaise, and racial stalemate will make for a more centrally directed system; peace, growth, and assimilation will make for a more related and permissive one. But the structure of the system is likely to continue to be much the same." [16] The federal system provides a rich range of opportunities for participation and is apt to be valued for just that reason, particularly by the evolving class of formally educated middle-class electorate.

[16] Daniel P. Moynihan, "The Relationship of Federal to Local Authorities." *Daedalus*, Summer, 1967, p. 801.

Although the structure of American government probably will remain the same, themes for the last third of the twentieth century are developing and appear to include a new kind of federalism (Moynihan termed it *wedding cake federalism*), new varieties of special-purpose government, metropolitanism in education, national social accounts, the quest for community, and the rediscovery of the market.[17]

Federalism will become a multitiered system of bureaucracies and governmental units surmounted by the person of the President. The lines of authority and communication within the federal system are more likely to assume a triangular form in which each government has direct relations with the other two clusters of public activity.

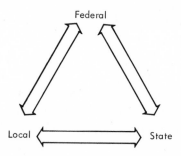

Central-city Negro areas and the white suburbs will merge into metropolitan educational units that will bring an end to racial isolation of Negroes in public schools and provide a broader and more equitable tax base to remove the disparity between per-pupil costs that exists now in central cities and their peripheral areas. Social indicators will produce more information about society that result in attempts to do more for society. Conscious priority will be given to promote a sense of community exemplified by the Ford Foundation recommendation to the City of New York Board of Education to decentralize the school system and provide for subdistrict neighborhood or community schools with their own school board.

Finally, social problems are likely to be approached more often by means of an income strategy rather than by a services strategy, whereby the poor are given money to purchase housing, medical care, or whatever else they need. One conceptualization is that where results are more important than processes the private sector can contract for a profit-making organization to run a chain of educational institutions, for example.

Local control of education in the United States relative to educational programming and financing is a myth if the term *control* is defined as com-

[17] *Ibid.*, pp. 804–807.

mand, since the local, state and federal governments are involved in educational control processes. With the development of a national-level society, including a national labor market and a mobile population resulting greatly from a communications and transportation revolution, strong arguments can be made for a more centralized organization of education. There was little argument for the framers of the Constitution of the United States to provide for anything but a decentralized educational system, because communication problems then made it impossible to institute centralized control. In addition, labor problems were local in nature, and most lifetimes were spent in residing and working within the boundary of a few square miles.

However, it is a basic fact that education legally is a state function, and it is the state that must lead in the development of adequate educational and financial programs. A leading weekly periodical described the United States Commissioner recently as the "master of United States schools in 1967." This is a ridiculous description in light of both the small federal contribution in financing education and the *de jure* organization of schools. In addition, it is inconceivable that the federal government is likely to become the master of public education during the next decade because of the strengthening of state departments of education, the complexity in changing the legal structure of education, the emergence of organizations like the Compact for Education and the eight-state project entitled Designing Education for the Future, the probable movement from categorical to general aid from the federal government primarily through implementation of a revenue-sharing plan, and growing realization of the need for multiple leadership.

CHAPTER 4

THE ALLOCATION
OF RESOURCES
FOR EDUCATION

Introduction

Public policy-making centers around the processes of acquiring and allocating resources for the public sector. Each process is a political one, partially effected by a public response or demand which political leaders interpret.

The rational process of public policy-making includes the determination of social objectives and identification of needs; estimation of required resources to meet the needs; and effecting a revenue program to implement policy. The scientist seeks refinement in methods and tools of analysis for each of these processes and endeavors to improve the definition of objectives as well as the methods of measuring needs and estimating resources, plus adding on an input-output evaluation dimension. An assumption is that increases in the quantity and quality of education offered will result in increasingly more rational decisions in both the private and public sectors.

The United States has been described as an undeveloped country when it comes to planning for the so-called efficient allocation of national resources.

At the federal level there is neither a central planning board nor a central statistical agency to gather data. Rationale for current planning status in the nation includes the private-enterprise ethos; decentralization of educational authority; and a reluctance to effect social planning requiring specific information about individuals, which would be an invasion of privacy.

Historically, guidelines for allocating resources for public schools at local, state, and federal levels have been ambiguous and nonscientific. Currently, there is growing confidence among those who concern themselves with the spending of public money that masses of data now can be digested and analyzed by computers, leading hopefully to more rational (equated with scientific) types of decision-making relative to resource allocation. Time will determine the validity of the basis for such optimism, but at present the political type of rationality continues to seem most valid. Assumption is that educational programs that can stand the rigid test of time and of the scrutiny of the competent, plus the decentralized hammering out of educational and fiscal policy, deserve to be considered as rational.

A magical percentage of funds is to be distributed neither to education and other governmental services, nor to sectors within the field of education. The piece-meal financing of public education and of government in general reflects the complexity of both. Few individuals, for example, understand the comprehensive nature of education, and as a result there are multiple demands for segments. Various pressure groups seek power to implement their favored educational value segment or segments, as was exemplified in the discussion on extralegal educational forces in Chapter 3 of this text.

Governmental budgets are dollar translations of programs and include revenue and expenditure plans to implement public programs provided through policy. The practice of budgeting was developed in England and is considered a part of the movement toward representative or popular control of the public purse. Budgeting in United States' governmental units is a twentieth-century concept and emerged from pioneer work of the National Municipal League and of an impetus given by President Taft, who requested a commission "to inquire into the methods of transacting the public business." The Federal Budget and Accounting Act of 1921 brought reasonable order out of resource allocation chaos at the federal level.

The nation's 114,000 public school board members serving in the 21,000 school systems in 1968 are budget-conscious, as are certain lay citizens—at least those who are taxpayers in the systems. In enlightened educational circles, the budgetary process, which will be considered in the next chapter, is considered to be a continuous process of presentation and adoption, administration, and appraisal. Financial administration, then, is a dynamic process that assists in resource allocation, particularly by recording and analyzing dollar facts about programs.

Rationale for Allocation of Resources to Education

No advanced society leaves education to the individual, or even to the family. Courts of record in the United States have held consistently that provision of public education is necessary for the maintenance of a democratic society. However, the provision of education through the private sector has not been discouraged, and courts have held that children cannot be compelled to gain an education in public schools, rather than in private or so-called protest schools. Approximately 14 per cent of the students attending elementary and secondary schools are enrolled in private schools, 90 per cent of them in Roman Catholic schools.

Not only is there a mixture of public and private efforts in education, but also in the fields of health, national defense, recreation, research and development, and in other areas. Health, however, tends to be administered mainly in the private sector, and national defense is administered mainly in the public sector.

The interrelationship of public and private sectors is evident by the production of goods for the public sector by the private sector. In addition, the public sector is providing funds to private enterprise for development of projects such as the supersonic transport and electronic instructional media.

Decisions of educational governments are considered in relation to the demands of other functions, and all functions possess common factors such as purpose, organization, process, and resources. However, the criteria for evaluating each function relative to these factors may differ.

In education, purpose is defined in terms of the well-being of the individual and society, relative to economic and noneconomic goals. A difficulty always arises in translating general goals into measurable needs and standards.

As a factor, the type of organization may modify purpose, alter the nature of the educational program and the methods of instruction, affect the quantity of resources needed, and shape the outcome. Justification for reorganization of school units into larger units is based upon the faith that a new type of organization can facilitate positive change and improvement. Not only is size of a school system considered important, but also the arrangement of pupils, staff, facilities, and program.

Obviously, the processes of education, and the available resources to be expended for education, are going to be determinants of the nature of the education function. Educational resources and processes are inputs whose adequacy and efficiency must be related to purposes, organization, and to each other.

The justification for allocation of resources for education at the local, state, or federal levels is based currently on one or more of the following criteria:[1]

1. *Average practice.* The federal government and state governments have attempted to equalize financial resources among the state and local governments by assuring that each school unit (state or local) of an expenditure level equal to that of the average unit in the nation or state. Assumption is that this improves educational conditions in the laggard districts and perpetually acts to create an increasingly higher level for the average district. The concept average serves as an incentive for citizens to excel beyond the ordinary since there are communities that are not satisfied with the ordinary in education.

2. *Operational efficiency.* States have justified varied levels of expenditures to different local school units by assuming that certain kinds of administrative organizations are more efficient than others. Thus, in the State of Wisconsin, so-called basic units receive $30 per pupil state aid, while integrated (integrated in terms of program) units receive $44 per pupil.

3. *Educational outcomes.* Belief is that particular personal or social outcomes will result from varying expenditures of resources. The outcomes have relative values; for example, the social benefits resulting from requiring high school students to complete a course in United States Government, and the personal benefits resulting from a student completing a course in advanced music composition, although social benefits can be derived also from the latter.

4. *Economic returns.* Economists have advanced the concepts of marginal utility, economic stabilization, redistribution of wealth, economic welfare, and productivity, as forming the basis of justification for allocation of resources for education. The Federal Employment Act of 1946 is an attempted interrelationship of these concepts, and serves as an economic theory underlying recent federal educational policy.

Alternate Proposals for Analysis of Resource Allocation

The process of decision-making regarding allocation of resources for education is not analogous to the price-demand schedule in the market system of material goods. The process differs in that it is a political one, and in part an involuntary one, by which a public response or demand is interpreted by

---

[1] William P. McLure, "Allocation of Resources," *The Theory and Practice of School Finance*, Warren E. Gauerke and Jack R. Childress (eds.), Chicago, Rand McNally and Company, 1967, pp. 64–65. Comments after each *italicized* criterion are those of the author.

politicians at all levels of government and then translated into educational and corresponding fiscal programs.

McLure's thesis is that education suffers in competing for public funds with other services such as highways, conservation of natural resources, and the health services in the public domain, since much knowledge about man and his education does not become a part of the political or decisional process.[2] In addition, automobile owners paying a gasoline tax perceive a direct benefit in improved highways, sportsmen perceive a direct benefit in sports opportunities when buying a hunting license, while nonparents may not perceive any benefits when paying property taxes for the education of children unknown to them.

McLure points out that some of the knowledge concerning education is technical, esoteric, and difficult to communicate widely to the laymen. Admittedly, some of the knowledge cannot be demonstrated simply and dramatically, and it borders on the presumptive. For example, there is recent evidence to indicate that the experiences of preschool children may be more determinative in the development of the individual than the first few years of primary education under current formal education arrangements. As knowledge increases, it may be found that most families cannot or will not provide alone experiences of adequate positive contribution and minimal deprivation to the child in his early years. It is conceivable, then, that activities in this area will be developed in the public sector in the form of universal or mandated programs of counseling services and organized instruction for children of earlier than current school entrance ages. The new programs may be considered rational by governments, but not by laymen, including parents and certain other taxpayer units.

Even though the public schools are not research-oriented generally, the educational enterprise in the public sector has characteristics of organization through which such new programs can be developed. There are established procedures of data collection, measurement, estimation, data collation, and reporting, and more sophisticated information systems are being created. As a result, trends on enrollments, pupil achievement, expenditures, facilities, and many other characteristics are available.

Research has begun to reveal relationships between resource inputs and educational outputs. The scholarly studies of Professor Paul R. Mort and his colleagues on cost-quality relationships have been revealing on the input-output formulation, and other studies are referred to later in this chapter. Unfortunately, similar studies on education in the private sector have been nonexistent for lack of any data collected over a period of time. Government

[2] *Ibid.*, p. 66.

has been hesitant to pry into the status of private education, so the study of allocation of resources to education has become restricted to public education only. This limitation seriously restricts the scope of an allocation analysis and prevents the serious consideration of reasonable allocations of resources to private and public schools, respectively.

Some traditional approaches to the analysis of resources for allocation to education have included the following:

1. Reliance upon budget proposals and justifications advanced by governing bodies. This has been true particularly in higher education. The practice of budget padding in initial requests has become ubiquitous. The process of political negotiation seeks out the hard line of defense where the alternatives in utilization of resources and the estimation of educational demand are clearly defined.

2. Biennial estimates of demand and the corresponding resource needs. This short-term estimation has been commonplace among states for public elementary and secondary schools.

3. Occasional surveys conducted on the crest of a growing school crisis. These have been used at local district levels in conjunction with school bond issues, and on statewide bases for public schools and higher education.[3]

Recent deviations from the traditional approaches indicate the possibility of more sophisticated analyses through development of strong research departments in state education offices working in conjunction with research departments in colleges and universities; the practice of almost continuous analysis and projection rather than an infrequent, crisis-based type; and the increase in the scope of analysis.[4]

Friedman's Proposals for Educational Financial Support

Friedman has challenged the accepted role of government in education, and proposed that it is probably desirable and feasible for a great bulk of American families to meet education costs directly.[5] His theme is familiar and developed around a faith in a market place pricing system of a so-called free economy.

Friedman laments the unbalanced growth of educational responsibility in education. He appreciates the financing of elementary and secondary education by government, but particularly protests the governments' administra-

[3] McLure, *op. cit.*, p. 67.

[4] *Ibid.*, p. 68.

[5] Milton Friedman, "The Role of Government in Education," *Economics and the Public Interest*, Robert A. Solo, ed. New Brunswick, N.J., Rutgers University Press, 1955.

tion of the schools that provide such education. He holds that the governmental administration of schools is neither required by the financing, nor is governmental monopoly justified in its own right in a predominantly free-enterprise society.

Friedman understands that government has been concerned appropriately with widening the opportunity for young men and women to receive professional and technical training, but objects to the "inappropriate means" of subsidizing such education, largely in the form of making it available free or at a low price in governmentally operated schools.

Friedman would provide that (1) the government give each parent of a school-age child a specified sum (in voucher form) to be used solely in paying for general education; (2) the parents be free to spend this sum and any additional sum at a school of their own choice, provided it met certain minimum standards laid down by the appropriate governmental unit; and (3) schools be conducted under a variety of auspices, including private enterprises operated for profit, nonprofit institutions established by private endowment, religious bodies for value teaching, and by governmental units.

For vocational education, Friedman argued that the government should deal directly with the individual student, who would receive a subsidy, but would obligate himself to pay the state a specified fraction of his earnings upon graduation. Such a self-financing program would, according to Friedman, eliminate existing imperfections in the capital market and thus widen the opportunity for individuals to make productive investments in themselves, while at the same time assuring that the costs are borne by those who benefit most directly rather than by the citizenry at large.

It is Friedman's claim that the greater amount of private enterprise in education would tend to make schools more efficient, promote a healthy variety of schools, and develop the educational enterprise into a more flexible one. Public operation of schools would not be eliminated but would exist along with increasing numbers of privately operated schools.

Proper Scope of Governmental Activity

Friedman's proposals remind one of the perennial question of the proper roles of the private and public sectors. Most Americans agree on the proper scope of government, but there is always a controversial shifting border area between the private and public sectors. Agreement is that government must provide certain collective goods and other goods not suitable for market processes. The controversial area is concerned with matters of electric power, insurance, commercial activities of the Defense Department, communications satellites, and other cases such as the government's role in providing needed expansion for outdoor recreational facilities.[6] The provision for public support and operation of educational institutions has not been very controversial. Most Americans treasure the unique educational system that is so vital in maintaining opportunities for social, economic, and political mobility.

Benson has emphasized that, in the economics of the case, public support of elementary and secondary education must be defended in terms of the generalized benefits to all households in the country. His basic reason is the "inapplicability of the exclusion principle."[7] The exclusion principle refers to private transactions in which a buyer of a piece of goods is excluded from a commodity if he does not pay the market price. In the case of common defense and education, among other services, the service would fail largely of support, since there undoubtedly would be only sporadic donations of extremely public-spirited citizens if government did not compel households to make contributions.

Benson argued that the Friedman plan would increase sharply social stratification, and that the public schools would become the dumping grounds for problem children. He feared, too, that through advertising some sharp operators might gain an initial market advantage. In addition, he called the market principle of "let the buyer beware" inappropriate when something as important as a child's preparation for life is at stake.[8]

According to Benson, the fragmentation of education, which is implied by Friedman's proposal, could result in the increase of costs, since it is clear that small schools are expensive to operate. Relative to claims of educational diversity under the Friedman plan, Benson stated that it was hard to show that existing private schools have been responsible for important advances in instructional methods.

However, proposals such as Friedman's will be given more attention if there continue to be serious public school inadequacies, inequities, and resistance to change. Wealthy citizens have alternatives now to a public school education for their children: private schools or a move to better public schools in suburban areas. The poor do not have this choice.

Competitive educational programs already suggested include community-operated public schools independent of a citywide board of education; specialized schools of art, music, and science; apprenticeship programs sponsored by private industry; and state-chartered experimental schools.

[6] Otto Eckstein, *Public Finance.* Englewood Cliffs, N.J., Prentice-Hall, 1964, pp. 16–17.
[7] Charles S. Benson, *The Economics of Public Education.* Boston, Houghton Mifflin, 1961, p. 318.
[8] *Ibid.,* p. 330.

Financial support suggestions comprised federal tuition grants, a combination of private and public funds, and public funds channeled to private or semiprivate boards of directors.

In 1967, a Task Force on Economic Growth and Opportunity of the United States Chamber of Commerce stated:

> Competition with existing public school systems offers a promising means of improving both public and private education. If all parents, at every income level, could choose between sending their children to public schools and sending their children to approved private schools at public expense, both public and private education would improve as schools attempted to attract and hold pupils. Businessmen should press for the fullest possible consideration of proposals designed to enhance competition in education. Local, state and federal governments should consider legislation which would enable communities to adopt programs establishing a public-private option for all children.[9]

Reasons for such a statement may stem from a mistrust in government and a fanatical faith in the free enterprise system or a fear that an educational monopoly, which serves as a gatekeeper to roads of success, has been established. Those minorities not passing through the gates by "adjusting to the system" are then denied certain kinds of futures.

The major differences in the decision-making machinery of the private and public sectors are as follows: (1) governmental decisions involve an element of compulsion; (2) without the test of the market, there can be no assurance that a public service will actually render benefits greater than its cost; (3) the voter has to register his preference about a package of issues, whereas in the marketplace he can decide about each piece of goods separately; (4) decisions made by the political process reflect the distribution of political power among pressure groups, regions, and the like, and the groups that are well organized receive more benefits than the rest.[10]

Eckstein pointed out that in the marketplace dollars are votes, but that the political process represents a safety valve for our capitalistic system by modifying the income distribution generated through the marketplace. Eckstein stated, too, that for true collective goods there is no alternative to collective action. He emphasized that "the relevant comparison is not between perfect markets and imperfect governments, not between faulty markets and all-knowing, rational, benevolent governments, but between inevitably imperfect institutions."[11]

[9] Peter Schrag, "Competition for the Public School." *Saturday Review*, April 15, 1967, p. 75.

[10] Eckstein, *op. cit.*, pp. 17–18.

[11] *Ibid.*

There are individuals and groups who would permit government action only when the private market cannot do the job, such as the provision for collective goods (a piece of goods is private if someone who does not pay can be excluded from its use, as discussed in Benson's rebuttal to Friedman). Other Americans take a different philosophical position and see the government in a role as a competing source of initiative, an agency to reject some decisions of consumers in the market economy and thus change the pattern of consumption, and an agency to redistribute income.[12]

The role of the discount rate as arbiter of the allocation of resources between private and public enterprise is critical. For clarification, the term *discount rate* as used in the monetary world is the rate established by the Federal Reserve System governing the cost of member bank borrowings from the System. On the other hand, the discount rate to be used in judging the economic feasibility of governmental programs reflects the availability of capital.

The right discount rate becomes that number which indicates correctly when resources should be transferred from one sector to another. In an economy in which the level of employment is high, if resources are made available to the government they must be transferred out of the private sector. If any resources used by a government project would otherwise be totally unemployed, their use obviously incurs no opportunity cost in the private sector. In an economy such as that of the United States since World War II, employment of resources usually has been so high that this consideration is quite irrelevant to the facts of the matter.

A rather obvious criterion to test the desirability of a proposed resource transfer is that if the resources in question produce a rate of return in the private sector, which society evaluates at r per cent, then the resources should be transferred to the public sector if a project in the latter sector yields a return greater than r per cent. The logic of this criterion is self-evident pertaining to the minimal dictate of efficiency.

The standard is the concept economists call opportunity cost. A governmental project is desirable if and only if the value of the net benefits that it promises exceeds the cost of the lost productive opportunities which that investment causes. Economists generally agree that the appropriate discount rate to use in evaluating public programs is the opportunity cost of capital in the private sector. That is, the discount rate should reflect the rate of return that a given amount of resources employed by the government could earn in the private sector. This rate varies over time and largely reflects the credit market conditions. In December, 1967, the opportunity cost of capital in the private sector was judged to be at least 10 per cent.

[12] *Ibid.*, pp. 14–15.

The federal government has been using a variety of discount rates, the determination of which has had little to do with opportunity costs. For example, public works projects undertaken by the Corps of Engineers and the Bureau of Reclamation have been applying the historical coupon rate at the date of issue of long-term government securities, or about 3.25 per cent; many highway projects involving federal funds use a zero interest rate, and a majority of highway projects that employ positive interest rates utilize discounts that vary from .1 per cent to 6 per cent; poverty program evaluations have used interest rates of both 5 per cent and 7 per cent.

If rates used in evaluating government projects were raised to reflect economic opportunity costs, unquestionably this would have a profound effect on budget priorities. A low-rate structure has been used to justify many large public works programs to the point where there undoubtedly has been overinvestment in that area. A more realistic discount rate would have doubtless led to increased government investment in human resource programs.

Trends of Resource Allocation to Public Services

It is important in the study of resource allocation for education to consider the distribution of expenditures for all public services, since educational finance is a part of public finance, and since data on all services give a perspective of the total resources devoted to the public sector over a given period of time. Educators generally are so committed to the potential of education that they seem intolerant of the needs of other important services such as health, safety, highways, and others. The emotional appeal of more assistance "for our kids" is resented by civil government officials who may be pressured to lower tax rates, while school authorities continue to raise tax rates for school purposes.

A 24-year trend of eleven categories of governmental services at all levels (federal, state, and local) is shown in Table 4-1. Total expenditures rose from 43.5 billion dollars in 1942 to 189.4 billion dollars in 1966. All publicly supported educational expenditures increased from 2.7 billion dollars to 34.8 billion dollars in that period. If national defense were excluded, the noneducational functions increased approximately 7 times over this period, as compared to nearly 13 times for public education. The ultimate test of rationality for expenditure in each category depends on evaluation of absolute figures in terms of economic and noneconomic criteria, which remain unclear and diversified among individuals and groups.

In Table 4-2, a trend in the use of tax resources for thirteen categories of governmental services at the state and local levels (excluding federal, which

TABLE 4-1. Trend in Distribution of Tax Resources for Selected Functions of All Government (Federal, State, and Local) (General Expenditures in Billions of Dollars)

FUNCTION	1942 AMOUNT	1942 PERCENTAGE OF TOTAL	1950 AMOUNT	1950 PERCENTAGE OF TOTAL	1960 AMOUNT	1960 PERCENTAGE OF TOTAL	1965 AMOUNT	1965 PERCENTAGE OF TOTAL	1966 AMOUNT	1966 PERCENTAGE OF TOTAL
TOTAL	$43.5	100.0	$60.7	100.0	$128.6	100.0	$174.0	100.0	$189.4	100.0
National defense and international relations	26.6	61.14	18.4	30.31	47.5	36.93	55.8	32.06	60.8	32.10
Education	2.7	6.20	9.6	15.81	19.4	15.08	30.0	17.24	34.8	18.37
Natural resources	2.5	5.74	5.0	8.23	8.4	6.53	11.0	6.32	10.3	5.43
Highways	1.8	4.13	3.8	6.26	9.5	7.38	12.3	7.06	12.9	6.81
Interest on general debt	.2	0.45	4.9	8.07	9.3	7.23	11.4	6.55	12.3	6.49
Health	.9	2.06	.7	1.15	1.0	0.77	1.8	1.03	2.1	1.10
Hospitals	.5	1.14	2.0	3.29	4.2	3.26	5.9	3.39	6.3	3.32
Postal system	.9	2.06	2.3	3.78	3.7	2.87	5.3	3.04	5.7	3.00
Public welfare	1.3	2.98	3.0	4.94	4.5	3.49	6.4	3.67	7.0	3.69
Police protection	.4	0.91	.9	1.48	2.0	1.55	2.8	1.60	3.0	1.05
All other	5.7	13.10	10.1	16.63	19.1	14.85	31.3	17.98	34.2	18.05

SOURCE: *Statistical Abstract of the United States.* Washington, D.C., Bureau of the Census, 1967.

TABLE 4-2. Trend in Distribution of Tax Resources for Selected Functions of State and Local Governments (General or Direct Expenditures in Billions of Dollars)

	1942		1950		1960		1965		1966	
FUNCTION	AMOUNT	PERCENTAGE OF TOTAL	AMOUNT	PERCENTAGE OF TOTAL	AMOUNT	PERCENTAGE OF TOTAL	AMOUNT	PERCENTAGE OF TOTAL	AMOUNT	PERCENTAGE OF TOTAL
TOTAL	$9.2	100.0	$22.8	100.0	$51.9	100.0	$74.5	100.0	$82.8	100.0
Education	2.6	28.2	7.2	31.5	18.7	36.0	28.6	38.3	33.3	39.1
Natural resources	.2	2.1	.7	3.0	1.2	2.3	1.7	2.2	2.0	2.4
Highways	1.5	16.3	3.8	16.8	9.4	18.1	12.2	16.3	12.3	14.8
Health	.2	2.1	.4	1.7	.6	1.1	.8	1.0	.9	1.0
Hospitals	.4	4.2	1.4	6.1	3.2	6.1	4.5	6.0	5.0	6.0
Public welfare	1.2	13.0	2.9	12.7	4.4	8.4	6.3	8.4	6.8	8.2
Police	.4	4.2	.8	3.5	1.9	3.6	2.5	3.3	2.8	3.3
Fire protection	.2	2.1	.5	2.1	1.0	1.9	1.3	1.7	1.4	1.8
Sanitation and sewage	.2	2.1	.8	3.5	1.7	3.2	2.4	3.2	2.6	3.1
Housing and urban renewal	.2	2.1	.5	2.1	.9	1.6	1.3	1.7	1.4	1.8
Local parks and recreation	.1	1.1	.3	1.3	.8	1.5	1.1	1.4	1.2	1.4
Interest on general debt	.6	6.5	.5	2.1	1.7	3.2	2.5	3.3	2.7	3.2
All other	1.3	14.1	3.1	13.6	6.5	12.5	9.3	12.4	10.1	12.2

SOURCE: *Statistical Abstract of the United States.* Washington, D.C., Bureau of the Census, 1967, p. 423.

was included in Table 4-1) is indicated. Again, educational expenditures and noneducational expenditures increased approximately 13 and 7 times, respectively, during the period between 1942 and 1966.

The expenditure of $60 billion on defense programs means that the nation must forego $60 billion of nondefense goods and services. The transfer of productive resources to defense purposes takes place partly by reducing government spending on nondefense programs and partly by reducing civilian spending on consumer and capital goods through tax rates that are higher than they would otherwise be.

There are tangible and occasionally significant incidental benefits that flow from the defense program to the civilian sector (peaceful uses of military technology, training of personnel, and the "spin-off" of new science-based enterprises). However, there can be little doubt that the nation could have obtained these same benefits at substantially lower costs and with more certainty if comparable research and training resources had been devoted directly to civilian purposes.

If a reduction of international tensions or an improvement in the efficiency with which defense dollars are used should permit a curtailment of the amount spent for defense, the society would be better off. With appropriate public and private policies, a reduction of the defense budget can and should be a source of increased material welfare for all our citizens and a source of rapidly increasing investments in human capital through educational channels.

Rationale for Future Allocation of Resources to Education

Socialization goals of education including the fulfillment of the personality, development of good citizenship and patriotism, preparation for a wholesome family life, and the development of good work habits have been held in high esteem by professional educators, but more pragmatic members of the society have emphasized education's economic rewards in the past decade. It is now apparent from the nation's emphasis upon economic criteria for justification of resource allocation that educational decisions are vocational in essence—that is, students are in school to receive the correct preparation for the right job for them. If it is true, however, as suggested in Chapter 1, that the principal work of the future will be education for solving social problems or for learning for the sake of learning, then other criteria besides economic ones will have to be isolated for decision-making.

The so-called scientific allocation of resources promised by experts in such fields as systems analysis or operations research was exemplified by a scientifically oriented individual in discussing the merits of the alternatives of investing $20,000 in driver education or in special education programs. His rationale in choosing to invest in driver education was that he had data indicating the probability of the death of youngsters in automobile accidents and comparative data suggesting the number of lives saved because of driver education programs. Further rationale was that since those whose lives would be saved from automotive deaths would make greater contributions to society than youngsters in special education who were suffering from abnormalities, justification could be made for selecting the driver education investment. An alternative solution and a more humanitarian one, of course, would have been a political solution—that is, the provision of both programs. It is true, however, that because resources are scarce in a point of time, it becomes necessary to consider what relative shifts can be made between programs in an effort to raise total benefits. Ideally there is an optimum mix of all economic quantities that would produce maximum economic and noneconomic benefits relative to private and social costs and values.

Beginning with the Smith–Hughes Vocational Act of 1917, federal legislation has tended to stress the economic efficiency aspect of vocational education as described in a part of the Act:

> ... The controlling purpose of such education shall be to fit for useful employment; ... and shall be designed to meet the needs of persons ... who are preparing for a trade or industrial pursuit or who have entered upon the work of a trade or industrial pursuit; ....

This goal was reaffirmed by the Vocational Education Act of 1946, an amendment to the George–Barden Act of 1936. However, both acts in terms of the monies appropriated tended to emphasize home economics heavily, and the traditional home economics stressed the socialization goal. A noticeable change in home economics occurred through passage of the Vocational Act of 1963, which provided funds for fitting individuals for gainful employment, and which contained no explicit statement of the socialization function of courses in home economics.

From statements of educational goals at the state and local levels, it is quite clear that the socialization goal is a necessary and major function of a primary school. However, there is a definite emphasis upon the economic returns of education to individuals and to society in justifying investments in education at the secondary and postsecondary levels of education.

Growing proof of education as a factor in economic welfare seems assured, as was exemplified in the Employment Act of 1946. A continuing problem, however, is the determination of a central analytical concept of economics upon which to develop a set of criteria to measure welfare. Currently the central concept appears to be maximum economic welfare through maximizing production, efficiency, and income. Relative to education, continuing emphasis is being given to the relationship between economic goals of the society and the educational systems. Intellectual preparation for its own sake has been relegated to a position lower than that of a series of economic goals—redistribution of income, economic stabilization, and increased productivity—as a rational goal for which to allocate resources for education.

Marginal utility is an economic concept that has been useful in determining the point at which an additional amount of resources slated for production of certain material goods will yield equivalent values and satisfactions if transferred and spent on other goods. The futility of investigating the use of this concept in education seems evident unless educational output is measured only in the degree of a student's feedback of factual material, and unless priorities of values can be established to make possible a measurement of satisfactions realized from one investment to another. However, in the area of vocational education, it is probable that such questions as whether or not to spend more or less funds on training metal workers vis-à-vis airplane mechanics can be answered by marginal analysis of relative cash benefits.

There may be an analogy in the economic theory of "factor price determination" in the marketplace, which is of value to the process of allocation of resources for education, if Friedman's plan for financing and operating schools were adopted. Thus, in the private economy the price of each factor in the productive enterprise is adjusted to the level at which the amount of the factor used is equal to the amount demanded by the productive process, and at the point of equilibrium the price of a factor must equal the marginal revenue or product return for a firm. This theory of the distribution of income could be applicable relative to teacher salaries if the Friedman idea were implemented.

The traditional supply and demand analysis of the determination of wages is still appropriate for the partial explanation and prediction of behavior in the labor market. However, the old market forces and the administrative wage-setting procedures operate alongside each other.

Resources that are allocated to education make a most important contribution to the national and state redistribution of income, and great reliance has been placed in this belief as indicated by the massive antipoverty programs. Fiscal policies of government do affect the distribution of income among households. Subsidies, for example, for farm products, payments to veterans, public housing, and retirement benefits, tend to reduce inequality of income among households. Humane governments would conscientiously accomplish this redistribution, and others would be driven to it eventually, if those in power are to prevent a revolution from occurring.

The goal of redistribution of income tends to conflict with that of economic efficiency in economic terms. Training the educationally, psychologically, and physically handicapped will invariably result in a relatively lower marginal return per dollar invested for society, especially when a large pool of un-trained people who are not so handicapped exists. Economic justification for training the handicapped likely would be that the recipients of training would become taxpayers rather than societal parasites, and that they would no longer be supported by governmental direct-transfer payments. A society that ignores humanitarian goals and sticks to cold economic principles might find direct-transfer payments the more economical.

Fiscal policies of government are not economically neutral, and intention-ally or otherwise they influence the level of economic activity. They have effects on employment, prices, and business activity in general. Taxes are known to differ in their effects upon consumption, investment, and saving. According to Shultz and Harriss, taxes influence in four ways: (1) purchasing power; (2) propensities to spend and to save; (3) investment; and (4) in-centives to work.[13]

Timing of governmental activity to effect economic stabilization is crucial. However, educational leaders have not advocated heavy governmental spend-ing only in time of recession except for construction of school facilities. They have argued for spending to meet educational needs independently of business cycles, because educational expenditures are predominantly of investment character and generate future income through increased productivity of individuals. Only to a limited extent can education affect economic stabiliza-tion in the short-run, and that is through technical programs that could educate unemployables or underemployables for employment.

McLure deemphasized the role of education in effecting immediate economic changes:

> Resources for education are more closely associated with the "educative population" which fluctuates first in terms of numbers of students, and second in terms of changes in the nature of education resulting from occupational changes. The child goes through school only once, and his needs cannot be deferred without harm. The adult who needs re-education at a particular time and place suffers if his opportunity is non-existent or if it is deferred. It would seem, therefore, that education is one of the services in society which along

[13] W. J. Shultz and C. L. Harriss, *American Public Finance*. Englewood Cliffs, N.J., Prentice-Hall, 1959.

with national defense, should be evaluated primarily in terms of the principle of the long term basic social need and only incidentally for the immediate effect of expenditure on the economy.[14]

According to a Department of Commerce analysis of 86 industries, a $1-billion increase in state and local expenditures for current operation and school construction would lead to a total output of $1.3 billion among the industries studied, as well as an aggregate increase in employee compensation throughout the economy of $851 million. Of this increase, $624 million would go directly to teachers and other personnel. Direct and indirect sales would add $75 million to new construction, $54 million to retail trade, $42 million to heating, plumbing, and structural metal products industries, and $40 million to the food product industry.[15]

The fourth concept upon which rationale for maintaining and increasing the expenditures for public education appears to be developing is that of productivity. Benson discussed the possible use of the analogy of industrial indexes of productivity in evaluating utilization of resource effectiveness in education.[16] The concept has potential in education, but an index is impossible until educational productivity can be defined more adequately. In addition, part of educational output is for consumptive purposes, while part has deferred value and cannot be measured currently. Relative to the consumptive goal of education, emphasis upon it may lead to a pursuit of training and an expenditure of funds, which might have little market relevance.

As a society tools up its educational system to educate citizens for a white-collar technological society as contrasted with a blue-collar one, manpower demands of the society may necessitate an additional number of years of formal education for prospective employees. An alternative would be a radical increase in efficiency (achievement of highest possible outputs for a given cost) of the educational institution, so that greater output is produced in an original period of time.

Promising means of increasing educational productivity according to qualitative criteria include adoption of advanced teaching instruments, the extension of the school-year length, an increase in the number of staff per 1,000 students, and employment of teachers skilled in motivating students to perform better.

There is no clearcut method to estimate the portion of resources that constitutes investment in future productivity. Some preliminary studies of

[14] McLure, *op. cit.*, p. 80.
[15] Lawrence C. McQuade, "The New Tycoon." *American Education*, Vol. 2, Oct. 1966, p. 27.
[16] Benson, *op. cit.*, pp. 336–338.

Schultz,[17] Miller,[18] Becker[19] and others on lifetime earnings of individuals with given levels of education give clues that may lead to better knowledge about educational investment in future productivity. In a recent article containing more current data than the previous studies cited, McQuade stated that men between 25 and 64 years of age with less than eight years of schooling earn an annual income of nearly $3,641, those with a high-school education earn about $6,700 a year, and those who have completed four or more years of college earn over $10,000 a year.[20] During his lifetime, the man with four or more years of college can expect to earn about $360,000, while the man with less than eight years of schooling can look forward to about $125,000.[21]

Hidden costs of education are being considered now by economists in computing input-output relationships and include foregone earnings of students as well as employee consumption of time that might be used in the production and distribution of goods and services. McQuade estimated the $41 billion expended for formal education in 1965 would increase to $100 billion if informal and peripheral aspects were added.[22] He arrived at the figure by adding the following: the money that would be realized if school property were commercially developed, the foregone income of students, the taxes supporting our tax-exempt educational facilities, and all the money spent on commercial schools, classes, and seminars held by unchartered institutions. In addition, financing the knowledge industry—including research and development, publishing and printing, television, and other communication machinery that spreads information, training, and knowledge throughout our society—would add another $100 billion and mean a national educational investment total of $200 billion in 1965.

Educational Output and Its Measurement

Belief is that in education a fairly good job in measuring such inputs as the dollars spent, facilities built, teachers hired, pupils enrolled, etc., has been effected, but that there is a problem of not only measuring but of not knowing what to measure relative to outputs. The difficulty is that students are not only

[17] Theodore W. Schultz, "Investment in Human Capital." *The American Economic Review*, Vol. 51, March, 1961, pp. 1–17.

[18] Herman P. Miller, "Annual and Lifetime Income in Relation to Education: 1939–1959." *The American Economic Review*, Vol. 50, Dec. 1960, pp. 962–982.

[19] Gary S. Becker, "Underinvestment in College Education." *The American Economic Review*, Vol. 50, May, 1960, pp. 346–354.

[20] McQuade, *op. cit.*, p. 27.

[21] *Ibid.*

[22] *Ibid.*

to achieve certain test scores, but to attain certain attitudes and competencies in dealing with new situations among other outputs.

A budgetary dilemma is how to allocate resources among competing agencies, both inter- and intrasectoral. For example, how can a rational decision be reached relative to allocations dealing with severe present problems and with prevention of future problems?

In order to choose one alternative over another, decision-makers must have a criterion or test. In the private sector, the criterion may generally be the optimization of profit, whereas in the public sector, such as in education, there are not such clear-cut and tangible objectives.

One problem in determining allocation and a satisfactory input-output ratio for budgeting purposes in education is commensurability. Competing or alternative programs must be measurable in comparable cost-benefit terms. It is true that an input of bricks versus an input of salaries of a number of teachers in a governmental project can be determined through the price market, but many outputs of government are not sold ordinarily in the marketplace. Thus, output prices comparable to input costs cannot be so determined.

Some approximation of ideal criteria is all that can be accomplished in most educational analyses. Estimated guesses pertaining to educational output will have to be employed, tested, and revised. It is possible, however, to record types of output or return on educational investment, including relationship of education and earning, rate of return on investment in education, and the contribution of education to economic growth.

For example, it has been determined that those of a prior generation who remained in school beyond the twelfth grade earned 30 per cent more than high-school graduates, while those who completed a four-year college program earned 60 per cent more than the high-school graduates. This type of data can provide partial documentation for support of an educational program and its corresponding budgetary plan. However, there are serious limitations to this documentation, since it is impossible thus far to portion out the contribution of educational attainment, family background, sex, discrimination on basis of age, race, or sex, and industrial composition of relevant labor markets or the nature of intelligence to earnings.

Table 4-3 includes the best data available relative to mean annual income for males 25 years old and over by level of school completed. The income estimates are undiscounted and are not adjusted for taxes, but do reflect an adjustment for expected mortality. The data for 1939 are wages and salaries, data for 1946 are earnings, and data for 1949, 1956, and 1958 are for total income. The data differentiations are the result of changes in conceptualiza-

TABLE 4-3. Mean Income (or Earnings) by Level of School Completed, for Males 25 Years Old and Over, for the United States—1939, 1946, 1949, 1956, 1958, and 1967

YEAR	ELEMENTARY-HIGH SCHOOL DIFFERENTIAL (AVERAGE INCOME)			HIGH SCHOOL-COLLEGE DIFFERENTIAL (AVERAGE INCOME)		
	ELEMENTARY-SCHOOL GRADUATE	HIGH-SCHOOL GRADUATE	DIFFERENCE (PERCENTAGE)	HIGH-SCHOOL GRADUATE	COLLEGE GRADUATE	DIFFERENCE (PERCENTAGE)
1939	—	$1,661	—	$1,661	$2,607	57
1946	$2,327	2,939	26	2,939	4,527	54
1949	2,829	3,784	34	3,784	6,179	63
1956	3,732	5,439	46	5,439	8,490	56
1958	3,769	5,567	48	5,567	9,206	65
1967	3,641	6,700	84	6,700	10,000 plus	49 plus

— Data not available.

SOURCES: The data for 1939, 1946, 1949, 1956, 1958 are from Herman P. Miller, "Annual and Lifetime Income in Relation to Education: 1939–1959," *The American Economic Review*, Vol. 50, Dec. 1960, p. 969. The data for 1967 are from Lawrence C. McQuade, "The New Tycoon," *American Education*, Vol. 2, Oct. 1966, p. 27.

tion of income by statisticians during the period. In addition to the data differentiations, there is not a common price basis, so that 1958 income reflects some price increases relative to the earlier years, for example.

With all the above-listed methodological restraints, Miller's data showed that on the average a 1958 male high-school graduate annually earned 48 per cent more than the average elementary-school graduate, while the 1958 average college graduate earned 65 per cent more than the average high-school graduate. McQuade's data referred to earlier in this chapter included comparative earnings in 1967 and was added to Miller's data for certain previous years to comprise Table 4-3.

The most comprehensive empirical work completed in estimating the expected internal rates of return to education was done by W. Lee Hansen. Hansen used 1949 census data in estimating rates of return on the basis of both total and private resource costs and calculated both average and marginal rates of return. Table 4-4 includes his results.

The bold figures that form a diagonal line in Table 4-4 are the marginal

TABLE 4-4. Internal Rates of Return to Total Resource Investment in Education for United States Males, 1949[a]

FROM			(1)	(2)	(3)	(4)	(5)	(6)	(7)
To	AGE		6	8	12	14	16	18	20
		GRADE	1	3	7	9	11	13	15
(1)	7	2	**8.9**	—	—	—	—	—	—
(2)	11	6	12.0	**14.5**	—	—	—	—	—
(3)	13	8	15.0	18.5	**29.2**	—	—	—	—
(4)	15	10	13.7	15.9	16.3	**9.5**	—	—	—
(5)	17	12	13.6	15.4	15.3	11.4	**13.7**	—	—
(6)	19	14	11.3	12.1	11.1	8.2	8.2	**5.4**	—
(7)	21	16	12.1	12.7	12.1	10.5	10.9	10.2	**15.6**

[a] All rate-of-return figures are subject to some error, because the estimating to one decimal place had to be made by interpolation between whole percentage figures.
SOURCE: W. Lee Hansen, "Total and Private Rate of Returns to Investment in Schooling." *Journal of Political Economy*, Vol. 71, April, 1963, p. 134.

rates of return (extra benefit gained by incurring extra cost), and the other figures in the columns are the average rates of return. Thus, the marginal rate of return for a person 12 years old who leaves the seventh grade to complete his eighth-grade education is 29.2 per cent. For the same 12 year old, his average rate of return for completing college is only 12.1 per cent as is included as the bottom figure in column 3. It is evident that the marginal rate

of return tends to be higher at terminal stages such as eighth grade, high
school, and college graduations. There is also a declining value of the
marginal rate of return from eighth grade to college graduation.

Limitations of Hansen's study are similar to those of Miller's study. In both
studies, only monetary benefits are being estimated, and it is certain that
nonmonetary benefits such as extended occupational and cultural opportunity, additional competency to be involved in community decision-making,
and psychological advantages such as a positive state of self-esteem exist.

The studies of Schultz and Denison have concluded that a better educated
labor force has contributed significantly to the nation's economic growth.
Schultz estimated the increase to be 16.6 to 32.2 per cent of growth during
the 1929–1957 period, and Denison estimated the growth rate attributable to
increased education for the same period to be 23 per cent.[23]

There has been an increasing trend to gear educational expansion to
specific economic objectives, such as maximizing the rate of growth of income.
Stated another way, educational plans have been geared to specific economic
objectives. Having isolated the economic objectives of educational planning,
one might think that one could proceed directly to consider the application
of cost-benefit analysis to investment decisions in education. This has not
been the case, however, since the issue has been contested by two opposing
schools of thought (with numerous subvarieties thereof) the manpower-
forecasting approach and the rate-of return approach.

The manpower-forecasting approach tells the educational planner to tailor
the expansion of the educational system to quantitative forecasts of the
demand for highly qualified manpower. The rate-of-return approach advises
the planner to calculate the internal rate of return on investment in education
and to supply just enough schooling to equalize the yield of investment in
human capital with the yield of investment in physical capital.

Basic to both approaches is the problem of forecasting the productivity of
labor. In addition, there are difficulties encountered in translating labor
requirements by occupation into labor requirements by educational qualifications. The simplest method of converting occupation into education is to
apply the mean number of years of schooling currently observed in each
occupation or job cluster. Such a scalar as the mean, however, does not
express adequately the concept of minimum educational attainment for
satisfactory job performance because performance is a complicated function
of native ability, psychomotor skills, work experience, on-the-job training,
and probably formal education. The problem for the educational planner is

---

[23] Jon T. Innes, *et al.*, *The Economic Returns to Education*. Eugene, The University of
Oregon Center for the Advanced Study of Educational Administration, 1965, p. 41.

that of specifying a vector that depicts the combination of varying amounts and types of formal education required in different occupations.

Except for the professions such as medicine and teaching where custom and tradition impose a minimum entrance qualification, there appears to be no unique relationship in the labor force between educational background

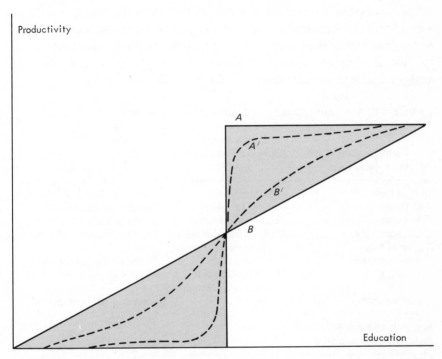

FIGURE 4-1 Hypothetical Relationships Between Education, Occupation, and Productivity.

SOURCE: Mark Blaug, *A Cost-Benefit Approach to Educational Planning in Developing Countries*, a paper prepared as Report No. EC–157, The International Bank for Reconstruction and Development, December 20, 1967, p. 11. The report does not necessarily represent the view of the bank and its affiliated organization.

and occupational affiliation. In addition, the manpower forecaster cannot seize upon simple patterns or trends of productivity among sectors in the American economy.

If the real world is correctly depicted by *A'* in Figure 4-1, the relationship between occupation and education is purely technical and can be determined by "job analysis," that is, analysis of the skill content of a job. If *B'* is representative of the real world, there is no such thing as a minimum educational requirement for the job; there is an optimum amount of education for the job, but it cannot be determined without introducing the earnings of workers, a variable that so far has been steadfastly ignored by manpower forecasters. In the case of B', the task of translating forecasts of numbers in different occupations into numbers with certain amounts of education, conceived as a purely physical relationship, is doomed at the outset: worker A with 12 years of schooling may be twice as productive in job X as worker B with 8 years of schooling, but if A costs three times as much as B, the optimum amount of education for job X is nevertheless 8 years. A rate-of-return analysis does not include forecast of manpower demand or supply.

TABLE 4-5. Burkhead's Model of Education as a Production Process

INPUT VARIABLES (LAND, LABOR, CAPITAL)	PROCESS VARIABLES (CURRENT EXPENDITURE POLICIES)	OUTPUT VARIABLES (BENEFITS TO THE INDIVIDUAL AND SOCIETY)
Student time In the classroom At home Extracurricular Personnel time Administrative Teaching Clerical Maintenance Auxiliary Materials and supplies Buildings and equipment	Class size Size of the school Teacher-pupil ratio Ratio of administrative and clerical personnel to students Use of personnel for guidance or remedial instruction	Increased intellectual curiosity Social adaptation Development of creativity Increase in skills and earning ability Increased lifetime earnings Growth of informed electorate Increased national growth

NOTE: Professor Burkhead emphasizes that this table does not show the whole range of possible input, process, and output variables. Meaningful measures are not always available, but the planning framework suggested here may be useful in the development and improvement of school programs.

SOURCE: *Education in the States*, New York, National Committee for Support of the Public Schools, p. 29.

The nonmonetary benefits of an educational investment such as those included among output variables in Table 4-5 are more difficult to measure. In addition, economic criteria are not the only criteria to be applied to the allocation of resources and the distribution of program outputs. Analyses as part of the planning-programming-budgeting (PPBS) process do not constitute a prepackaged instant decision-maker to replace judgment, common sense, and compassion, or to leave resource allocation to computers. Public sentiment and tradition will be a strong criterion of resource allocation also.

Cost-Benefit Analytical Studies

Since early in 1966, the Department of Health, Education, and Welfare (DHEW) has undertaken a series of analytical studies of its programs and possible programs. One study that was still in process at the time of this writing focused on alternative ways of improving the education of disadvantaged children. Title I of the Elementary and Secondary Education Act provides substantial funds to improve the educational opportunities of children from low-income families. Head Start and other federal programs also contributed to this end, but remarkably little is known about the effective ways of reaching these children. The study that was in progress was an attempt to see what can be learned about the relative effectiveness of spending money in different ways. A team of analysts were visiting 12 major cities over a period of several months trying to determine exactly how Title I money was spent—what programs were mounted and what kinds of services were received by what kinds of children. The teams also were looking at test scores, attendance, and dropout rates, and other evidence of impact of the compensatory education program. The analysts were looking at evidence, too, relating to preschool programs and to compensatory education programs financed from sources other than Title I.

The type of study described is difficult and must be undertaken with caution and humility. Test scores are often poor measures of what children know. Immediate changes in the behavior or achievement of severely deprived children should not be expected to result from moderate increases in school expenditures. There is a danger that very little if any improvement will be found and that the study will be used—perhaps erroneously—to justify the cutting back of promising and exciting programs whose real impact cannot be measured quantitatively or will not be apparent for many years.[24]

In reviewing the DHEW's analytical studies before a congressional committee in the first session of the Ninetieth Congress, a spokesman for the DHEW stated:

> Let me hasten to point out that we have not attempted any grandiose cost-benefit analyses designed to reveal whether the total benefits from an additional million dollars spent on health programs would be higher or lower than that from an additional million spent on education or welfare. If I was ever naïve enough to think this sort of analysis possible, I no longer am. The benefits of

[24] *The Planning-Programming-Budgeting System: Progress and Potentials.* Hearings before the Subcommittee on Economy in Government of the Joint Economic Committee, Washington, U.S. Govt. Printing Office, 1967, p. 8.

health, education, and welfare programs are diverse and often intangible. They affect different age groups and different regions of the population over different periods of time. No amount of analysis is going to tell us whether the nation benefits more from sending a slum child to preschool, providing medical care to an old man or enabling a disabled housewife to resume her normal activities. The "grand decisions"—how much health, how much education, how much welfare, and which groups in the population shall benefit—are questions of value judgments and politics. The analyst cannot make much contribution to their resolution.[25]

The New York City Budget Director stressed that evaluation of cost and effectiveness is very difficult in the area of education. One possible measure of effectiveness being considered in the city is the number of lower income youngsters—perhaps the number of Negroes or Puerto Ricans that actually matriculate in the university system—on the theory that the rationale for the city's expenditure of $150 million a year on a system of higher education is largely in the area of social and economic mobility.[26]

One of the issues at stake in New York City is the More Effective Schools (MES) program, which has been in effect for two years. The program was structured to provide smaller classes and specialized personnel in slum-area schools and has been particularly supported by the American Federation of Teachers.[27] Evaluation shows that some of the control group schools are "outrunning the More Effective Schools, although the results are very murky." It costs about $578 more per pupil on the More Effective Schools program than for the education of those pupils in the control groups, and it "may well be that PPBS and adequate program evaluation to the contrary, the city may ultimately be driven to accept an expansion of the program that the evaluation will not support."[28]

Cost-Benefit Studies in Vocational Education and Training

One could guess reasonably that a most fruitful area for cost-benefit studies in education would be that of vocational education and training because of specificity of purpose and of relative ease in follow-up studies. However, the research done in vocational education has been described as quite fragmentary and diverse. Apparently, only a few studies on vocational education

---

[25] *Ibid.*, p. 5.

[26] *Ibid.*, p. 92.

[27] Bernadette S. Julian, "The AFT in Caucus and Convention: New Style for 1967." *Monthly Labor Review*, Vol. 90, Nov. 1967, p. 20.

[28] *The Planning-Programming-Budgeting System: Progress and Potentials, op. cit.*, p. 93.

have been done in which costs, training time, and benefits have been simultaneously related, and these were local case studies rather than a national-scale type.[29]

Much reliance has been placed upon the M.A. or Ph.D. thesis for research in evaluating the benefits of vocational education. Stromsdorfer cites the typical error in such studies is to argue that X per cent of graduates of Y vocational program entered the skill for which they were trained, and on the basis of this gross placement ratio the training is designated as a success.[30] There is no recognition of the need for a control group and seldom any awareness that only net and not gross placement ratios are critical, since some proportion of people trained in an area would have entered the work regardless of training.

Stromsdorfer assessed the cost-benefit study of Arthur J. Corazzini as the best done.[31] Corazzini made a case study based on cost and earnings data taken from vocational programs and graduates in Worcester, Massachusetts. In it the costs and benefits of vocational high-school and post-high-school vocational training as well as technical training were contrasted.

Corazzini investigated the question of whether to invest in two additional years of vocational schooling after high-school graduation from an academic curriculum or to invest in vocational training during the first twelve years of schooling. He found that the graduate of a post-high-school vocational training program was a poor investment if he chose to train in the same skilled trades open to vocational high-school graduates, but a good investment if the academic graduate entered a technical or semiprofessional area in the thirteenth and fourteenth years of formal schooling.

Independently conducted surveys of the cost-effectiveness of programs of the type incorporated in the "War on Poverty" are now beginning to appear. Ribich, after examining the "pay-off rates" of various educational measures and the related questions as to whether these are sufficient to justify a considerable emphasis on education in the poverty program, concluded that:

> Vocationally oriented training, at least in the form of recent manpower training programs, exhibits a higher rate of payoff than does general education. The rates are sufficiently in excess of those computed for improvements in general education that it is difficult to dismiss this result as an accident due

[29] Ernst W. Stromsdorfer, *A Developmental Program for an Economic Evaluation of Vocational Education in Pennsylvania.* University Park, Pa., Institute for Research on Human Resources, 1967, p. 23.

[30] *Ibid.*, p. 24.

[31] Arthur J. Corazzini, *When Should Vocational Training Begin?* A mimeographed paper prepared for a conference sponsored by the Center for Studies in Vocational and Technical Education, University of Wisconsin, June 10–11, 1966.

entirely to the particular estimating techniques used. . . . With the exception of
the job training programs, benefit-cost ratios were found to be generally less
than unity. And, as suggested [by Ribich's earlier analysis] . . . unweighted
benefit-cost ratios would have to be something in excess of unity before it can
be argued that education is clearly superior to transfers or other forms of
direct help.[32]

Similarly, the Institute for Defense Analyses, in its report on federal
poverty programs, asserted that "it appears that education and training
programs, except for older workers, are quite promising for alleviating
poverty . . . [and] training programs are a relatively inexpensive way to raise
the incomes of lower income families."[33]

Those cost-benefit analysts who have evaluated training schemes have continued in the tradition of most other empirical investigators of the returns to
education; they pay lip-service to the presence of indirect or nonmonetary
benefits, but do not attempt to measure them. However, there is less need to
be defensive about the failure to measure these effects in cost-benefit analyses
of antipoverty training schemes because indirect effects are thought to be
particular advantages flowing from a general education rather than from
vocational training, and secondly, the aim of the war on poverty is essentially
an economic one.

Summary of Cost-Benefit Conceptual and Methodological Problems

Because of the complementarity among the benefits that fulfill the varied
goals of education, and because of the fact that benefits spill over to third
parties often in an unmeasurable form, benefits are conceptually more
difficult to measure than costs. Because education has both investment and
consumption aspects, it is difficult to separate these two aspects. Education is
an enjoyable process of consumption, and, to this extent, investment costs
are overstated, and the internal rate of return to education is likely to be
understated. In essence, the whole problem in education is one of joint costs
creating joint outputs where outputs relating to efficiency, consumption,
income redistribution, and socialization are being produced in varying mixes
over a period of time.[34]

[32] Thomas I. Ribich, *Education and Poverty*. To be published by The Brookings
Institution, Washington, D.C., and quoted in "A Critique of Cost-Benefit Analyses of
Training," *Monthly Labor Review*, Vol. 90, Sept. 1967, p. 45.
[33] *Federal Poverty Programs—Assessment and Recommendations*, Report R-116,
Arlington, Virginia, Institute for Defense Analyses, 1966, as included in "A Critique of
Cost-Benefit Analyses of Training," *Monthly Labor Review*, Vol. 90, Sept. 1967, p. 45.
[34] Stromsdorfer, *op. cit.*, pp. 47–48.

Indices of benefit measures in terms of economic efficiency goals appear to be among the easiest of educational benefits to be isolated. Shifts in relative earnings and incomes, length of job search, employment and unemployment are indices that can be developed for both pre- and posteducational experiences. Indices for socialization goal measurement are more difficult to isolate, although participation in civic affairs, including voting behavior, juvenile delinquency rate changes, and general knowledge of current events, are concrete enough for measurement.

Cost data are currently more profuse than benefit data. A perennial cost problem is that empirical data indicates variations because of the size of school population, class hours of instruction, quality of equipment and materials, and these factors must be controlled in order to derive valid cost-benefit information.

As was pointed out by Prest and Turvey, one practical value of the cost-benefit analysis is that it causes questions to be raised. It uncovers unsuspected problems, implicit assumptions, and preconceptions that would not ordinarily be revealed. Finally, "even if cost-benefit analysis cannot give the right answers, it can sometimes play the purely negative role of screening projects and rejecting those answers which are obviously less promising."[35]

[35] A. R. Prest and Ralph Turvey, "Cost-Benefit Analysis: A Survey." *The Economic Journal*, Dec. 1965, p. 730.

CHAPTER 5

BUDGETARY
CONCEPTS AND
PROCESSES

Introduction

The belated nationwide interest in governmental allocation of resources and in the budgetary processes is to a large extent the result of rising prices, full employment, and frequent governmental budget deficits, which have impressed legislative bodies and so-called conservative citizens generally with the need for restraints. The continuance of "full employment" as national policy, which is being implemented reasonably well in the 1960's, has paradoxically been accompanied by a more critical attitude towards governmental intervention in the economy. In addition, there is a growing critical attitude towards the size of governmental employment and expenditure at all levels. This is in contrast to the 1930's when mass unemployment and idle resources prompted action in the public sector.

Between fiscal 1965 and fiscal 1968, the national income accounts budget—the budget viewed by economists as the most relevant for gauging economic impact—has increased over $50 billion, about one-half of which can be

96

attributed to Vietnam war costs. In 1967, the federal government was spending about $155 billion in an economy of $785 billion. The increases at state and local levels have been equally large. From March, 1964, to March, 1967, there was a 30 per cent rise in state and local tax revenues and a proportional advance in the rate of expenditures. Faced with this situation, it is of utmost importance that policy-makers be armed with the best possible tools for evaluating the effectiveness of public programs and expenditures.

Historically, Americans have prized the so-called efficiency of the private sector and have been critical of the perceived inefficiencies of government. An antigovernment feeling has persisted primarily because of a mistrust of politicians and of the intangible nature of governmental output.

The author recently had a face-to-face confrontation with a leading insurance executive who insisted that if public schools would teach less basket-weaving and ceramics there would be plenty of money available for important aspects of education. Implication of the remarks was that public schools were spending too much money for frills. The author countered with a remark that, on the contrary, there were not enough basketweaving and ceramics courses because investment in fine arts programs was meager and investment in special education programs was similarly meager.

When the author inquired whether insurance premiums spent for an executive suite (including a sophisticated bar-restaurant complex in which the author-insurance executive dialogue occurred) in a new insurance sky-scraper was considered a frill, the executive stated that private funds were expended for the suite. The author questioned whether premiums paid by the public were private, but the dialogue terminated with the unanswered question.

There appear to be dual standards relative to actual behavior in the private sector and the latter's expectations and demands of behavior of personnel in the public sector. As another example, consultants from the private sector are persistently recommending implementation of a planning-programming-budgeting system (PPBS) in government. In the meantime, PPBS implementation is in its infancy in the private domain.

The Development of Program Budgeting

An impetus to more considered treatment of the subject of allocation of resources at all levels of government has been given by the Johnson Administration at the federal level in its emphasis upon PPBS development and implementation. The "quiet revolution" is providing linkage between program planning and budgeting. The proposed sequence of activities includes:

1. Identification of goals with precision and on a continuing basis;
2. Choosing among goals the most urgent;
3. Searching for alternative means of reaching goals most effectively at the least cost;
4. Informing selves about costs for the next year, the following year, and the ones following that.

At the federal level of government, it has been traditional for the budget to be developed from estimates prepared by executive departments and their subdivisions. The departments have submitted budget estimates to the chief executive and his central budgetary staff, and the latter ordinarily have scrutinized exceptions to the previous year's budget—exceptions in terms of increases or decreases in objects of expenditure, with emphasis on personnel, supplies, and equipment.

The inadequacies of the traditional system were recognized as early as 1912 by President Taft's Commissions on Economy and Efficiency, which stated what the function of a budget should be:

> The best that a budget can do for the legislator is to enable him to have expert advice in thinking about policies to be determined. His review of the economy and efficiency with which work has been done should be based on facts set forth in the annual reports of expenditures which would supplement the budget.
>
> To the administrator (i.e., the head of an executive department) the advantage to be gained through a budget is the ability to present to the legislature and to the people, through the Chief Executive or someone representing the administration, a well-defined, carefully considered, lucidly expressed welfare program to be financed, and in presenting this, to support requests for appropriation with such concrete data as are necessary to the intelligent consideration of such a program.
>
> To the Executive (i.e., the President) the advantage to be gained lies in his ability to bring together the facts and opinions necessary to the clear formulation of proposals for which he is willing actively to work as the responsible officer. To the people the advantage is the fact that they are taken into the confidence of their official agents. Therein lies the practical use and purpose of the budget.

The Taft Commission then proposed a comprehensive budget with a classification based on the distinction between current and capital items and in terms of programs or functions. A systematic review of the budget after the fact was also recommended.

Change in budgetary procedures at the federal level was not effected until the passage of the Budget and Accounting Act of 1921, which required the President to submit a comprehensive executive budget and created the Bureau of the Budget as a staff agency.

The introduction of the planning-programming-budgeting system can be traced back to the Dupont Corporation in 1915. Development was slow until the innovation of the War Production Board control system in 1942. The WPB developed the Reproduction Requirements Plan (which established priority needs and allocations) and the Production Requirements Plan, the first federal program budgeting effort.[1]

Further budgetary improvement was delayed until 1949 when the Hoover Commission recommended that the "whole budgetary concept of the federal government should be refashioned by the adoption of a budget based upon functions, activities, and projects: this we designate a 'performance budget.'" The Hoover Commission recommendation was made a legislative require-ment by the Budgeting and Accounting Procedures Act of 1950. The Second Hoover Commission recommended a "program budget" and corresponding improvements in the governmental accounting system to facilitate cost analysis.

In connection with weapons system analysis for the U.S. Air Force during 1949–1960, the Rand Corporation used PPBS, and then the Department of Defense implemented the system in 1961. Since 1965, the President has instructed 21 nondefense departments to institute a similar planning technique.

Partial implementation of the program budget idea is evident in recent messages on the budget given by the President. Major programs listed in the message cut across departmental lines. However, it is unlikely that decisions are made through interdepartmental conferences and coordination, or that information is shared in a way to limit the strictly departmental decision-making. In addition, the present federal budget is primarily concerned with estimated expenditures for a succeeding fiscal year and lacks the long-term estimated costs of an ideal program budget.

Purposes of Program Budgeting

The budget is an agency's plan of operations, which is expressed normally in words, numbers, and dollars. The budget expresses the "conclusions reached by an agency regarding one segment of time and the action to be taken during

[1] Henry De Vos, et al., "Planning-Programming-Budgeting Systems (PPBS)—What Value to Business?" The Journal of Accountancy, Dec. 1967, p. 77.

that time in pursuance of matters that have been studied, planned, and programmed. The course of action requires the expenditure of human effort and
the utilization of physical and material resources."[2]

Programs are "combinations of activities that produce distinguishable
products."[3] For example, a community education program could include the
activities of unemployment retraining, summer playgrounds, school extension
and community educational centers.

Program budgets focus on the outputs of programs, whereas traditional
budgetary approaches tend to emphasize expenditure inputs. Through program budgeting policy-makers have an opportunity to assess as fully as
possible the total costs and benefits, both current and future, of various alternatives. It endeavors to determine rates of return for programs, as well as the
rate of return to be foregone when one program is chosen over another.

Program budgeting is a system that will develop and communicate in
financial terms the cost of programs designed to accomplish the stated
objectives of school units, enabling the management of schools to compare
program proposals, relate them to current activities, evaluate them in terms
of priority, and then to increase or decrease allocations of resources to them.[4]

Information such as is included in Figure 5-1 would enable decision-makers
to understand comparative input and output, program by program. Further
sophistication in the budgetary system exemplified in Figure 5-1 could be
gained by adding descriptive dimensions of: program orientation and history;
estimated magnitude of program in 1970–1975; prospective changes in program orientation; coordination and cooperation systems; laws and regulations;
and the economic classification of program expenditure.

Programs and budgets should be consistent with each other so that departures of the budget from the program call for revisions of the program
and vice versa.[5] Revisions of either should be continuous and comprehensive.
Comprehensiveness is vital in that elements of a program are frequently
highly interdependent. A disadvantage of an emphasis upon comprehensiveness is that aggressive and competent units may experience a slow-down in
program development and change because of the need to interrelate with
other units, which will require cost in time, effort, and probable confusion.

[2] *Program-Oriented Information: 1. Analysis and Proposals.* Baltimore, Maryland State
Department of Education, 1966, p. 9.

[3] Charles J. Hitch and Roland N. McKean, *The Economics of Defense in the Nuclear
Age.* Cambridge, Mass., Harvard University Press, 1963, p. 49.

[4] *Final Report of the Advisory Committee on School Budgeting and Accounting,*
Sacramento, Calif., Assembly Interim Committee on Education, Oct. 1966, p. 44.

[5] David Novick, ed., *Program Budgeting: Program Analysis and the Federal Budget,*
Cambridge, Mass., Harvard University Press, 1965, p. 44.

ADULT EDUCATION PROGRAM (Reg. & S.S.)

Objectives:
Provide classes for adult students to develop knowledge, skills and attitudes necessary to meet the individuals', communities', and nations' immediate needs, and prepare for the future.

Services:
The program includes counseling and guidance, academic classes leading to a high school diploma, elementary classes for high school entrance, vocational classes, English and citizenship classes, and fine art classes. Registration fees are charged as follows: $1.00 for all high school graduates, $3.00 for P.B.X. classes; $5.00 for lapidary classes; and $24.00 for driver education and training.

DIR. COSTS ONLY	RESOURCES OR "INPUT"			"OUTPUT" Evaluation
	NO. of EMPS.	DIR. COSTS ONLY 1966 — 67	EST. DIR. COSTS 1967 — 68	
Principals' Salaries	2	$ 30,176.	$ 31,946.	6,964 students enrolled in adult education classes during 1966 — 67; 177 earned high school diplomas; 150 completed the nurse's aid program; 55 earned American citizenship certificates; and 7 earned high school entrance certificates
Director of A/E	1	18,012.	18,849.	
Teachers' Salaries	125	149,448.	167,160.	
Other Cert. (Part-time)	5	2,175.	600.	
Class'd. (Part-time)	20	34,188.	40,126.	
Class'd. (Full-time)	5			
Textbooks		1,070.	16,500.	
Other Books		706.	1,000.	
Instructional Supplies		5,520.	16,184.	
		TOTAL $241,295.	TOTAL $292,365.	

Comments:
Regular state aid income for 1966 — 67 adult education was $144,545, and Federal funds were $63,685, for a total income of $208,230.

FIGURE 5-1 Excerpt of a Sample Program Budget—El Monte Union High School District.

Central Concepts of Program Budgeting

The principle of rationality in choosing among alternative courses of action is central to effective program budgeting. However, the meaning of program budgeting is broader than this and embraces structural, analytical, informational, and hard bargaining elements.[6]

Relative to structural aspects, programs are functional and end-product oriented and composed of all cost associated with their attainment. Short-range specific decisions that have to be made are made within a framework of sophisticated long-range planning.

The heart of the analytical process is emphasis on a systematic examination of alternative courses of action and their implications, and this process has been equated with systems analysis, operations research, cost-benefit, or cost-effectiveness studies. Although it is recognized that most major long-range planning decision programs are resolved primarily on the basis of intuition and judgment, faith is that the techniques of analysis can sharpen the intuition and judgment through more objective evaluations of the possible cost of alternative programs in relation to their values.

The informational element of program budgeting is vital for the accomplishment of the two functions just discussed—namely, determination of objectives and the relative costs of meeting the objectives. In addition, the information system must provide progress reports and expenditure control.

A strong advantage of the program budgeting plan is the emphasis upon hard bargaining, which requires a mixture of political, economic, social, technical, and fiscal considerations. As discussed in previous chapters, special interest groups are active at varied stages of the educational decision-making, particularly at budget-making time, which in many instances is short-term rather than long-term.

Program Budgeting and Relationship to Accounting

The concept of programs in education is not new, but budgeting and accounting for them as separate entities have not been common practice. For example, the U.S. Office of Education's Handbook II, entitled *Financial Accounting for Local and State School Systems*, which has been the nation's bible of school accounting, is primarily a presentation of appropriation categories in which the emphasis is on not overspending the array of estimates,

---

[6] *Ibid.*

rather than on relating the achievement of objectives to the dollar spent.[7] For decision-making purposes, the information yielded has limited value. Following the counsel of representatives of several national educational organizations, staff members of the Handbook Program in the U.S. Office of Education are exploring research and practice as they relate to program planning, budgeting, and accounting in school systems. Draft copies of a revised Handbook II (Handbook II-A) have been placed in the hands of reviewers for their criticism.

In Handbook II-A, most of the Handbook II functions (administration, instruction, operation of plant, maintenance of plant, auxiliary services, fixed charges, etc.) will exist but will be shifted around to meet the taxonomical needs of the new program-oriented accounting structure. The proposed school finance accounting will provide for four major purposes or component parts, including legislative management (board of education), instruction, supporting services, and ancillary services and transactions. These will be the major "things" that will be happening that will enable a school district to meet its objectives. The structure of accounts will provide for the following areas for coding school finance transactions: (1) object purchased, (2) fund, (3) source of revenue, (4) service area, (5) area of responsibility, (6) scope, (7) activities assignment, (8) grade span, (9) pupils served, (10) subject matter, and (11) location (physical). The first six categories relate to finance per se, whereas the others come from pupil, staff, property, and instructional program handbooks.

The establishment of an information system as proposed is vital to provision for program budgeting at all levels of educational government. Because a program is made up of the elements involved in the achievement of what is believed worth accomplishing, a number of files of information must be established and appropriated. For example, if a program is to raise the level of reading ability of a number of children, an important step would be the creation of an informational file for each youngster. Next the curriculum file would be created and would include a schedule of activities for the children. The staff file would include the assignment of staff members such as teachers, teachers' aides, librarians, and others to the reading program. Facilities, plus equipment and supply files, must be designated for the program as well. When the salaries of staff members and the cost of things are allocated to the program, at least part of the finance file is established, and the sum of these

---

[7] This section of the publication includes many of the conceptualizations stated in a paper prepared and read by Allan R. Lichtenberger of the U.S. Office of Education at the National Education Association Committee on Educational Finance meeting in St. Louis, Missouri, on April 4, 1967.

activities is a great part of the program-budgeting process.

As the program is established and operated, it is traced through record-keeping, and program accounting is accomplished. At the termination of a program sequence, the total cost of activities, materials, and services can be identified through a type of cost accounting.

There can then be an assessment of how well objectives of the program are being met, even though measurement capabilities may be limited. Whatever the gain in reading ability is the value added or the benefit. The cost in dollars associated with the benefit can then be related in a cost-benefit ratio.

The reading program will have gone through a cycle, and through feedback from the experience of that cycle there can be a closing of the loop to re-planning, rebudgeting, reoperating, reaccounting, and re-evaluation. A body of important knowledge in relating achievement to dollars spent is developed in this way.

All program-oriented budgeting, accounting, and reporting components will be built upon the identification and use of a set of cost centers. A *cost center* is defined as the smallest segment of program that is separately re-cognized in the school system's records, accounts, and reports. The total budget for a program will be the sum of the budgetary provisions made for all the cost centers that are deemed to comprise a program.

The revision of Handbook II plus the use of Handbook III dealing with property information, Handbook IV with staff records, Handbook V with pupil data, and Handbook VI with standard terminology for instruction will provide the nation with comparable educational terminology that will provide decision-makers with a common core of data dimensions and categories. Such information will provide much about the analytic elements of PPBS—objectives, alternatives, costs, and effectiveness.

A Critique of Program Budgeting in Education

PPBS is not a substitute for the experience, the intuition, and the judgment of educational decision-makers. Its aim is to sharpen that intuition and judgment by stating problems more precisely, by discovering new alternatives, and by making explicit the comparison among alternatives.

Decisions in and about education will continue to come from the political process, influenced by value judgments, and from the pressures coming from the various interested parties as well as from the process of systematic analysis. Most problems of importance are not susceptible to solution merely by highly abstract mathematical or economic techniques. Likewise, numbers cannot be assigned to every element of a problem. Good systematic analysis does not ignore the intangibles nor rule out subjective evaluation and the appropriate use of judgment, as long as these are made explicit. Also, the name *cost-benefit analysis* reminds one that the question of who benefits and who bears the cost is a question involving values as well as analysis.

The governmental budget is the key instrument for public planning, and in its expenditure portion it represents the most direct point of contact between a governmental unit and the marketplace. In the expenditure portion, public decisions concerning labor, land, capital, and material needs are translated into dollars and then the governmental unit must compete with the private sector for scarce resources.

There is new emphasis upon using the budget as a planning tool and as an analysis document rather than strictly as an accounting system designed principally to categorize cost breakdowns, such as by people employed and by supplies purchased. Administrators of school systems have used some principles of program budgeting in justifying bond issues for major capital programs and by providing corresponding long-term payment schedules to indicate methods of financing the programs. The long-term emphasis contrasts with the typical year-to-year operating budget determination.

An important justification for use of program budgeting is that it forces consideration of the relationship between individual projects and the programs of which they are a part. However, the cost-effectiveness aspect is more appropriate in the private than in the public sector as a decision-making tool because the tool is an approach to lower the average, total, and marginal cost curves for given output rather than an attempt to change positions on any given cost curve. In the private sector, a change in output to maximize profits would be effected when appropriate. However, governments are not geared to maximize profits, and the citizens' willingness to pay taxes does not allow for construction of demand curves, which are so important in marketplace analysis.

The human being is more than a resource, and cost-benefit analysis should therefore always overestimate intangible output when considering resource allocation. Hopefully, cost-benefit analysts will recognize the limitations or analytic relevance of their tools.[8]

Educational Budgets—Multipurpose Tools

In spite of the problems in developing a so-called rational budget, school systems and other educational administrative units such as state departments of public education and the U.S. Office of Education make judgments about

[8] Leslie E. Carbert, "Cost Effectiveness Analysis at the State Level." *Tax Digest*, Sacramento, California Tax Payers Association, Third Quarter, 1966, p. 73.

allocations of resources and prepare budgets on a regular basis. Ideally, budgets are the culmination of many months of executive planning and evaluation and are the plans for meeting educational needs. The budgets are an important instrument of social, political, and economic policy, because they influence input and output of these segments of our society. In addition, budgets are financial reports to the citizens on how the educational units are spending funds, and at the same time they are requests for legislation, since legislative sanction—whether it be a local schoolboard, the state legislature, or the federal Congress—is needed before proposals can be translated into action.[9]

Oregon was the first state to enact a law requiring every schoolboard in the state to prepare and publish a school budget. This law was enacted in 1915, and since then nearly every state has established requirements relative to a school budget. The early conceptualization of the school-budget function was that publication of budgets would require school officials to justify the educational program, and that the lay citizens who attended required legal hearings might initiate an action to reduce expenditures and lower taxes. As described above, the budget now is conceptualized as being a multipurpose tool to (1) determine the educational program, (2) translate the educational program into estimated dollar costs, (3) provide the necessary funds for a school systems' operation, and (4) control expenditures. These elements will be discussed in succeeding chapters.

Legal Budgetary Controls

Legal provisions in every state control varied aspects of public school budgetary procedures including mandates for preparation of budgets; prescription of budget forms and the fiscal year for the school budget; mandates for filing of budgets, such as filing date; and mandates for review of school budgets by nonschool agencies. Legal controls over expenditures, revenues, and indebtedness for school purposes have developed in varied forms, too, from state to state.[10]

The many constitutional, statutory, and regulatory measures in most states probably have had a positive impact in systematizing procedures for planning and controlling programs, expenditures, and revenues.[11] It is the claim in

[9] This statement on the budget as a multipurpose tool is an adaptation of part of the introductory statement included in *The Budget in Brief, Fiscal Year 1967*, Executive Office of the President of the United States, Bureau of the Budget, January 24, 1966.

[10] See *Public School Finance Programs of the United States*, Washington, D.C., U.S. Govt. Printing Office, 1960.

[11] Leon Ovsiew, *et al.*, "Budgeting," in *The Theory and Practice of School Finance*, Warren E. Gauerke and Jack R. Childress, eds. Chicago, Rand McNally, 1967, p. 210.

Florida, for example, that for the purpose of "promoting economy and efficiency in the financial operations of the public schools, and for the purpose of keeping all school expenditures within the estimated receipts, transfers, and balances, as provided herein, there is established a budget system for the control of the finances of county boards." [12] The important role of the superintendent of schools in the preparation of the local school budget plus a listing of other legal budgetary controls are typified by financial procedures authorized in the *Florida School Code*, as partially prescribed below:

> Duties and responsibilities of superintendent—The superintendent shall exercise all powers and perform all duties listed below and elsewhere in the law provided, that in so doing he shall advise and counsel with the board of education.
>
> The recommendations, nominations, proposals and reports required by law and regulation to be made to the board by the superintendent shall be either recorded in the minutes or shall be made in writing, noted in the minutes and filed in the public records of the board. . . .
>
> (12) Finance—[the superintendent shall] recommend measures to the board to assure adequate educational facilities throughout the school system, in accordance with the financial procedure authorized in Chapters 236 and 237, and as prescribed below:
>
> (a) Plan for operating all schools for minimum term. . . .
>
> (b) Annual budget—[the superintendent shall] prepare the annual school budget to be submitted to the board for approval according to law; submit this budget, when approved by the board, to the state superintendent on or before August first of the year, on forms required under regulations of the state board; provided, that the tentative school district budget shall be open to examination by the trustees before such budget is included in the budget to be submitted to the board of education. . . .
>
> (13) School Districts—
>
> (a) . . . .
>
> (b) Budgets and expenditures—[the superintendent shall] prepare, after consulting with the principals of the various schools . . . tentative annual budgets for the expenditure of district funds for the benefit of public school pupils. . . .[13]

The Budget Calendar

A typical state department of public education manual pertaining to local district budgets directs local boards of education to adopt a policy that

[12] *Florida School Code*, Chap. 237, Sect. .05, 1965 Ed., p. 121.
[13] *Florida School Code*, Chap. 230, Sect. .33, 1965 Ed., pp. 34–39.

authorizes the administrator to make and implement a budget calendar "to expedite the determination of the educational program and the preparation of the budget."[14] Briefly, a budget calendar sets forth the procedures to be followed in the preparation of a budget. It designates the official who is responsible for various procedures and at what period of time each step is to be taken. The Kansas *School Budget Manual* states that the suggested budget calendar consists of two parts and that "all schools follow part I, while part II is applicable to schools under a board of education and [the schools or the boards are] to use Budget Form Number 4." The manual continues:

> Schools that use Budget Form Number 1, that is common school districts, and rural high school districts, shall prepare a proposed budget of expenditures for the ensuing year and post it with notice of the annual meeting. In common school districts the budget should be prepared and posted ten days prior to the first Friday in June and in rural high school districts the budget is to be prepared and posted eleven days preceding the first Friday in June. At the annual meeting the total amount of the budget is to be determined and within ten days the clerk of the board shall certify a copy of the budget to the county clerk.[15]

In Kansas, the budget calendar is defined as follows:

Date	Procedure	Responsibility of
PART I		
January 1	Conference to discuss program, services, and budgeting	Superintendent
February 1	Project enrollment for next school year	Superintendent
March 1	List of new teachers needed next school year	Superintendent and principals
April 1	Submission of list: (a) New equipment (b) Equipment to be replaced (c) Supplies (d) Books (e) Repairs and remodeling,	Principals
May 1	Completed working budget including the line items and expenditure for each item	Superintendent and clerk
On or before May 15	Evaluation of the budget by those who prepared it	Superintendent and staff

[14] *School Budget Manual: A Guide for Preparing and Managing School Budgets in Kansas.* Topeka, Kans., State Department of Public Instruction, Sept. 1964, p. 8.
[15] *Ibid.*

PART II

As soon after July 1 as possible	Present budget to the board	Superintendent
On or before August 5	Board must approve and publish a proposed budget; at least ten days must lapse between date of publication and date of hearing	Board of Education
On or before August 25	Board adopts final budget, certifies budget and proof of publication to the county clerk [16]	Board of Education

Directions to Kansas school districts include the following additional statements:

The use of the budget calendar in different size schools and types of districts necessitates some variations and adjustments in procedure. Several variations are noted briefly as follows:

(1) The work of making estimates for instructional supplies may be facilitated by the use of a system of blanks on which the needs of each teacher and principal are entered. These are compiled and supplemented by the superintendent or his office staff. Estimates of materials and supplies should be based on accepted standards of quality approved by the school board.

(2) Some items, janitorial supplies, library books and replacement of equipment can be budgeted on a per pupil basis. Non-recurring items can be listed, coded and carried as special line items in the budget.

(3) Budgeting for repair and remodeling can be handled in several ways by: (a) using a fixed amount per year per building adjusted for fluctuations in price level; or (b) by obtaining estimates of the cost from architects or contractors.[17]

In any district where a judicious plan of budgeting expenditures is followed, the detailed budget is a sizeable document. The budget in this form is very valuable to the board, administrators, instructional and noninstructional staffs, and lay citizens. It is the basis for answering questions that may be raised at budget hearings, and for the budget officer and others to implement once the budget is approved.

Interrelationships of Calendars

The existing interrelationship of the school budget calendar, the assessment calendar, and the fiscal year hampers good educational planning in most of the nation's school districts. The element of uncertainty it imposes on governing boards throughout the budget-planning cycle extends to interested

[16] *Ibid.*, pp. 8–9.
[17] *Ibid.*

citizens and taxpayers, making it difficult for them to evaluate the annual school budget prior to its adoption. The major defect of the arrangement is that it requires school officials and schoolboard members to make important decisions about educational expenditures on the basis of incomplete and highly tentative information concerning the amount of revenue that will be available to cover such expenditures.

For example, the California public school fiscal year, like that of all other public agencies in California, commences on July 1 of one year and ends on June 30 of the next succeeding calendar year. The assessment calendar begins on the first Monday in March, when the taxable status of all property is determined, and ends on the third Monday in August, when the state assessed roll is transmitted to the county auditor. Although school budget planning commences early in the school year and proceeds on an approved schedule, only three dates on a California school budget calendar have a legal significance. They include:

1. July 1 (on or before). A tentative budget must be filed with the county superintendent of schools.
2. July 20 (on or before). A publication budget must be filed with the county superintendent of schools, with a copy to the county auditor.
3. August 8 (or August 10 in districts of 10,000 or more ADA). The final school district budget must be adopted.

An understanding of the problems imposed on California public school districts as a result of the existing interrelationship of calendars can be gained by reviewing the dates listed in Table 5-1, all of which are of legal significance in the development of the annual school budget. The sequential arrangement of these dates reveals several important facts:

1. For more than a month at the beginning of each fiscal year, California school districts are obliged to operate without an officially adopted budget.
2. Reasonably reliable information relative to the value of taxable property assessed by the county assessor is not available until a few days before the publication budget must be adopted and filed with the county superintendent of schools.
3. Final information concerning taxable property assessed by the State Board of Equalization is not filed with the county auditor until after the final school budget has been adopted.

The fact that school districts are required by law to adopt both a tentative and a final budget before firm information is available concerning the assessed valuation of all taxable property within their boundaries presents special problems for those districts entitled to equalization aid from the state. Without reliable assessed evaluation figures, school district officials have no way of determining what their income will be from either the local property

TABLE 5-1. Interrelationship of Fiscal Year, School Budget Calendar, and Assessment Calendar, State of California

March (first Monday)	Taxable status of all property is determined. (Revenue and Taxation Code Section 751)
May 1 through 15	All teachers to be re-employed for the next school year must be so employed by the governing board; probationary teachers whose services may not be required must be given written notice. (Education Code, Sections 13258 and 13443)
July 1 (on or before)	Tentative budget must be filed with the county superintendent of schools. (Education Code, Section 20601)
July 1	Beginning of fiscal year. (State Constitution, Article 20, Section 5)
July (first Monday)	Assessor must complete local property tax roll. (Revenue and Taxation Code, Section 616)
July (third Monday)	Local roll equalized by the county board of equalization. (Revenue and Taxation Code, Section 1603) Special laws apply to Los Angeles County only.
July 20 (on or before)	Publication budget must be filed with county superintendent of schools, with a copy to the county auditor. (Education Code, Section 20606)
August 8 (August 10 in districts of 10,000 ADA or more)	Final school district budget must be adopted. (Education Code, Section 20651)
August (first Monday)	Assessment period ends for state-assessed property. (Revenue and Taxation Code, Section 753)
August (third Monday)	State-assessed roll is transmitted to the county auditor. (Revenue and Taxation Code, Section 756)
September 1	County board of supervisors sets the tax rate. (Education Code, Section 20705)

tax or from the state school fund. The reason is that state property equalization aid formulas are based on local assessed valuation to reflect the difference between the local and the statewide ratio of assessed value to full value of all taxable property.

The California Advisory Committee on School Budgeting and Accounting recommended in October, 1966 that:

1. The present fiscal year (July 1 to June 30) be retained. Justification was that (a) it spans the natural school year; (b) contracts for teachers are

more conveniently made for the academic year; (c) budget planning and preparation of annual reports to the federal and state government would become complicated if the fiscal year were to be changed.

2. The Revenue and Taxation Code be amended so that all taxable property was assessed as of the first day of January, with local and state roll to be delivered to the county auditor on the first day of May.

3. School districts be notified of the assessment adjusted ratio during the ensuing fiscal year by May 1.

4. The Revenue and Taxation Code be amended so that the school tax rate would be computed on the basis of the completed roll rather than the equalized roll. Justification was that the normal difference of less than one per cent between the rolls was likely to be offset by additions to the roll that came about as a result of adjustments caused by discovery of properties inadvertently omitted by adjustments from postaudits.

5. The Education Code be amended to provide for the adoption of the tentative school budget on or before May 15, a public hearing between June 1 and June 15, and adoption of the final budget on or before June 30.

Complicating the interrelationships between local and state calendars is the addition of the federal fiscal calendar. This complication will be discussed in Chapter 10.

Local School System Budgeting

The budget is a school system's plan of operations that is expressed in words, numbers, and dollars. It expresses the conclusions reached by the system in pursuance of matters that have been studied, planned, and programmed in one segment of time. Implementation of a course of action requires the expenditure of human effort and the utilization of physical and material resources.

Money is the focal point in a budget because the human effort must be compensated and the physical and material resources must be acquired, distributed, and maintained through expenditures of money. The budget document includes a separate treatment of the revenue and expenditure sides, respectively but to a lesser degree also correlates particular sources of revenue and specified items of expenditure.

Sophisticated school systems generally develop several types of budgets including (1) a current budget (pertains to operations in a fiscal year); (2) a long-term budget (a plan comprising a community's educational aspirations for a future period of five to ten years); (3) a capital budget (capital outlay plans of several years); (4) a building budget (revenues and expenditures of a building project); and (5) a special project budget (projects omitted or separated from current expenditures). Special consideration is given to the current budget in this section because it entails typically from 80 to 90 per cent of a system's expenditures. However, Appendix A includes methodology for predicting or projecting expenditures of any school budget into the future.

Budget preparation takes many forms in the different school systems. The simplest and least effective is the lump-sum (in a top-down sequence in the hierarchy) procedure whereby the chief school administrator puts together a series of figures based on previous expenditures. The administrator makes a determination of how much an increase the public will tolerate, and his

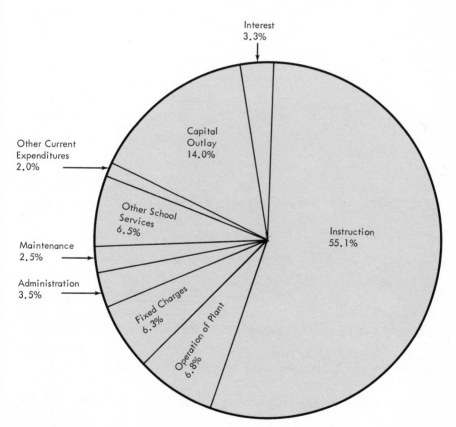

FIGURE 5-2 Summary of Per Cent of Expenditure by Function, Public Elementary and Secondary Schools: United States, 1965–1966.

SOURCE: "Digest of Educational Statistics 1966," United States Department of Health, Education and Welfare, Office of Education.

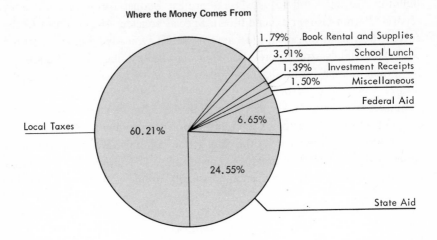

Where the Money Comes From

1.79% Book Rental and Supplies
3.91% School Lunch
1.39% Investment Receipts
1.50% Miscellaneous
Federal Aid
6.65%
Local Taxes   60.21%
24.55%
State Aid

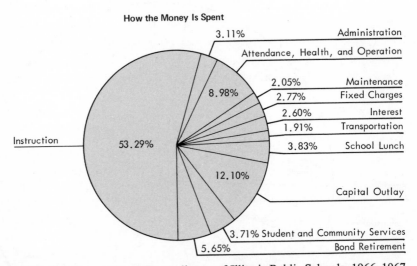

How the Money Is Spent

3.11%   Administration
Attendance, Health, and Operation
2.05%   Maintenance
8.98%   2.77%   Fixed Charges
2.60%   Interest
1.91%   Transportation
Instruction   53.29%   3.83%   School Lunch
12.10%
Capital Outlay
3.71% Student and Community Services
5.65%   Bond Retirement

FIGURE 5-3 Receipts and Expenditures of Illinois Public Schools, 1966–1967.

SOURCE: "Special Issue, Public School Support," *Fact Sheet*, Office of the Superintendent of Public Instruction, State of Illinois, May 10, 1968, p. 4.

budget-making primarily becomes one of "last year's plus 5 per cent," for example.

A far more satisfactory method of budget preparation is that of preparing the program or performance budget (a bottom-up sequence in the hierarchy), which depicts the educational need and includes the translation of the program into dollar costs. This type of budget should be developed by the practitioners who will render the service or who will use the supply or equipment to be budgeted. Many proponents of educational reform believe that a first order of business is a drastic decentralization of school administrative organizations in urban America and the extension of authority to school principals for hiring, for budget development, and for the development of curriculum, with advice from teachers and families served by the school.

The preparation of the current or annual operating budget ideally is a year-round job. Needs are expressed by the practitioners and these expressions are reviewed by supervisory and administrative personnel. Requests or estimates are then consolidated by the business office and reviewed again by the administration, instructional and noninstructional personnel, and by the board of education. Revenue estimates are made and compared with the expenditure needs, revenues and expenditures are balanced, public hearings are held, and final adoption by the board of education is made.

All these procedures are time-consuming, and completion of one budget means the beginning of another and the relating of it to the long-term operating budget. School budgeting is not only time-consuming, but requires a great deal of diligence on the part of all involved. However, all the effort is justified if the educational program purchased through a well-planned budget is even a trifle better than one purchased through lump-sum budgeting procedures.

Assuming that the fiscal year is July 1 to June 30, budget forms should be distributed to the principals and other instructional as well as noninstructional staff personnel early in September. Three or more types of budget information should be requested from the school and departmental organizations:

1. Staffing needs should be expressed. These should be based upon anticipated enrollment, changes in instructional programs, desired teacher-pupil ratios, and noninstructional staff needs. Ideally, these needs should express not only the judgment of the principal, departmental chairmen and their respective staffs, but also the lay public.
2. Equipment needs should be expressed as well as indication as to whether the equipment is additional or a replacement.
3. Building or school plant needs should be categorized as additions, alterations, or renovations.

It should not be necessary for the decentralized operational units to request routine maintenance because this should be scheduled by the centralized maintenance personnel. Normally, instructional or office supplies have been budgeted on a uniform unit basis for the entire school system. However, there is growing realization of the need for varying the amount of expenditures per pupil dependent upon the nature of the educational problem relative to each.

Operational units should spend the months of September and October in preparing data to be forwarded to the school system's budget officer by November 1, prior to the beginning of the new fiscal year on July 1. The budget officer and the appropriate administrative-instructional team then review the budgetary requests. Each request should be reviewed carefully, and if one is questioned by the reviewing team, the initiator should be given an opportunity to justify his report.

It is quite likely that as professional negotiation procedures are legalized more clearly there will be an increasing amount of schoolboard-teacher negotiating team face-to-face confrontations on budgetary requests, particularly when an impasse is reached early in administrator-teacher negotiations pertaining to budgetary matters. At a time when prospective teachers are being instructed in the "new math," the "new English," the "new social studies," etc., it is difficult to include a course in school finance in their undergraduate programs. However, it seems imperative for teachers to receive formal instruction in finance if they are to be involved in procedures relative to the allocation of resources in the public sector.

Eventually, the budget officer must consolidate requests into an appropriate budget document, incorporating into the document those items that must be included because of existing laws, regulations, or prior contracts. The latter items encompass expenditures such as debt service, payment of interest, reduction on the principal of bond issues, premiums for insurance, the employer's share of social security or other retirement program costs, and transportation costs. The budget is then ready for review by the board of education.

After the board of education has reviewed the budget, made such alterations as it sees fit, and is satisfied that the document reflects the educational program it proposes to finance, a public budget hearing should be held. Faith is that if the public is sufficiently convinced that the budget reflects the type of educational program the community desires, the means will be found to finance the program within constraints of constitutional and statutory law.

Most school systems prepare their budgets in two separate documents. The first is the formal budget, which is detailed and intended mainly for a limited audience generally consisting of the board of education and any review board. This document becomes a decision-making instrument. The same document, after having been amended or altered, serves as the basis of accounting activity during the coming year. Generally, the document includes the superintendent's message, which is a statement of educational goals, a review of the current status of the school, and a description of the programs that the budget will finance. It includes a summary of the receipts and expenditures, a detailed statement of receipts and expenditures, and statistical data with comparisons pertaining to previous budgets or pertaining to other school systems in the state or nation.

After adoption of the formal budget, a second budget document—the public budget—generally is prepared. This budget is prepared for distribution to the public and is less detailed and in more readable form than the formal document.

In the meantime, long-range financial planning requires that a budget for a period of at least five years be developed and that it should be subject to revision annually. It is not essential that the long-range budget be as accurate as the annual operating budget. It should reflect such elements as enrollment forecasts, class-size policy, additional school facilities needed, course offerings, maintenance and operation policies, auxiliary services, equipment needs, salary schedules, local tax bases, assessment practices, state and federal programs, the costs of borrowing money, and inflationary influences. It should reflect the trends of the past and the educational objectives of the future. The public should have a part in the long-range planning for schools. Such involvement of the public in planning for education logically should thwart apathy and enhance support.

The capital improvement budget is a long-range budget and should reflect the capital needs for the school system for a period of at least five years. This budget should be revised annually in light of changing needs. It should depict the physical plant needs, including new buildings, building additions, site needs, and equipment needs. It should show each proposed capital project and reflect the proposed annual expenditure for each project. If the long-range budget is kept continuously before the public, it will tend to ease the shock when proposed bond issues are announced.

The building and special project budgets are short term and developed primarily for internal use. However, even on a short-term basis, such budgets provide the most concrete instruments for planning and controlling.

Examples of Installing a Planning-Programming-Budgeting System at the Local School System Level

At least eight states and many major cities already employ PPBS techniques. The Ford Foundation has given its support to the movement by funding a joint program (the 5–5–5 program) with five states—Wisconsin, California, Michigan, Vermont, and New York; five counties—Los Angeles County;

Wayne County, Detroit; Dade County, Miami; Davidson County (greater Nashville), Tennessee; and Nassau County, New York; and five cities— San Diego, Denver, Dayton, New Haven, and Detroit. School systems—state and local—are involved in these areas studying application of PPBS to state and local governments.

In addition, there are isolated examples of other PPBS installations in local school systems. For example, a Chicago suburban area system's board of education requested their administrative agency to prepare a proposal for PPBS implementation in 1968–1969. Interest was created through the two-year investigatory work done in the school system by an associate professor of industrial engineering, who is employed in a nearby university.

Initial efforts are being made at the administrative level, and much of the preliminary and tentative planning was to be done by the professor, the superintendent of schools, and the school system business manager. An assistant business manager was to be employed to free the business manager for work in development of the new program budget. In addition, graduate students from the same university employing the professor were to do detailed studies.

Four different budgets, each organized on a unique basis, were to be prepared: (1) the legal budget; (2) a budget based on totals expended for objects (travel, textbooks, teachers' salaries, etc.); (3) a grade-level budget for coordinators who administer the instructional program; and (4) a program budget.

The sequence of activities for development of a program budget included (1) development of initial planned programs; (2) determination of resources required to achieve program objectives; (3) development of a data-processing system in order to have a continuing program of analysis, planning, programming and budgeting; (4) preparation of the 1968–1969 budgets; and (5) development of a continuing implementation plan for use of program planning and budgeting, including a cost effectiveness analysis applied to program budgeting itself to determine whether or not it is effective.

Through such budgetary procedures, educational communities can come to grips on a regular basis with the difficult problem of gaining rational decision-making pertaining to the allocation of resources. Because the budget document represents a community's effort to select and implement educational values for a sequential fiscal and academic year, one wonders how any rationality in decision-making could be effected without implementation of a PPBS or comparable system, allowing for output as well as for input considerations. However, implementation throughout the nation remains very scattered.

Even under PPBS, it is difficult for educational administration to arrange for communication with those forces which have something to contribute toward improving an educational program, to analyze and synthesize these communications, to translate alternatives into dollars, and to make choices for implementation. Most difficult of all is the goal setting and corresponding program formation. In fact, the education profession is as vulnerable to attack as it is because of an inability to state goals as clearly as do engineers, doctors, and other professionals. However, contrasted with traditional budgeting, PPBS forces a concentration on goal setting, which could lead to a reduction of professional vulnerability.

CHAPTER 6

EDUCATIONAL PROGRAMMING AND BUDGETING

Introduction

Budget preparation begins with a determination of an educational program or alternative programs. A suitable curricula set, acceptable teaching and guidance services, suitable facilities, and the internal allocation of material and human resources are some of the minimum requirements to be evolved.

The process of determining the educational program ideally involves the schoolboard, professional and nonprofessional personnel, and in many instances representative lay people. Making major policy decisions relative to the educational program is the responsibility of the schoolboard. Making policy recommendations to the board, filling in details of board policy, and implementing policy is the function of the school staff.

Some major schoolboard policies pertaining to the educational program are not expressed in writing, but are understood generally to be in effect. Others are recorded in the minutes of the board or in prepared statements of board policies.

Among the program determinants will be the following:

1. The scope of the program to be provided. For example, should policies provide for:

    a. Maintenance of nursery school or kindergarten?
    b. Organization of classes for exceptional children?
    c. Provision for adult education work?
    d. Offering summer school courses?
    e. Providing junior college classes?
    f. Area vocational schools?

2. The quality of teaching that the community and the board require, and the salary schedule (in other words, determination of the teachers' standard of living) that must be implemented to obtain and retain good teachers. The board may have, for example, a policy that requires all teachers to have a master's degree and to meet certain other academic and experiential requirements.

3. Board policy relative to pupil-teacher ratios. This determines the number of teachers required and has a very important influence upon the educational costs.

4. Board policy relative to furnishing supplies and textbooks and equipping laboratories or libraries. (It is probable that no other professionals have received less "supply" support than teachers over a long period of time.)

5. Board policy relative to providing special services such as transportation, health and dental services, and the school lunch program.

6. The requirements of the state department of public education and the regional association of colleges and universities.

The superintendent and his staff must plan the program in accordance with policies determined by the board. But evaluation of the educational program is a continuous process, and periodically schoolboard policies and the educational program should be re-examined. School budgets function to enforce such re-examination on a regular basis.

Leeway for Diversity

Complaint throughout the nation is that public school programs are so "middle class" in content and in instruction. Most teachers, administrators, and schoolboard members are members of the middle socioeconomic class. Youngsters and adults from lower socioeconomic cultures, particularly in the central city of our nation's metropolitan areas, can be at a great disadvantage when taught by individuals with foreign value systems. Those

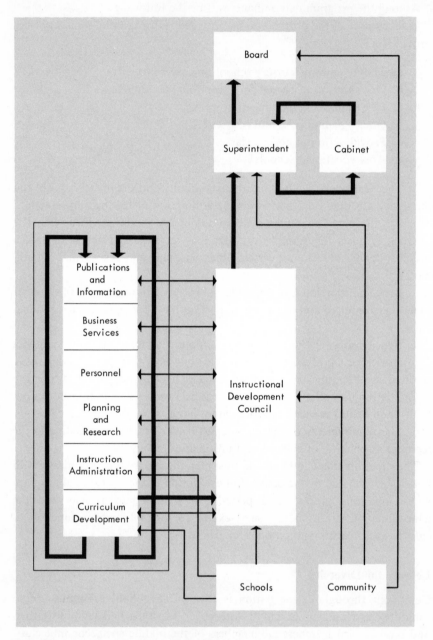

FIGURE 6-1 Organizational Structure for Planning.

SOURCE: *A Guide to Systems Planning*, Seattle, Washington, Public Schools, 1966, p. 16.

values identified with the middle class include priority to deeds and emphasis on effort, optimism, individualism, and equality of individuals; morality—citizens judge legislative statutes or schoolboard rules and regulations in terms of high natural law; pluralism—no single dogma prevails; and an abundance of natural goods.[1]

More than feeble attempts are being made now in some school systems to implement the concept of leeway for diversity pertaining to meeting needs of students with diverse cultural value systems. In spite of a number of educational directives in the form of constitutions, statutes, and board of education regulations, there is legal leeway for much more diversity in local educational programs than now exists. State mandates pertaining to curricula and teacher salaries, for example, are bare minimum requirements in terms of the nation's educational needs. In addition, local school systems participate in federal educational programs on a strictly voluntary basis.

There is more than a feeble cry for states to endeavor to develop finer articulation in curriculum to facilitate transition from one state school system to another. Leeway for diversity among the states is exemplified by the fact that in 1966 the State of Hawaii prescribed no curriculum courses while the States of Iowa and California prescribed 34 and 33, respectively.[2] Twenty-seven states prescribed 0 to 10 courses while the remainder provided 11 to 34.

The leeway described results partially from noncontrollable variables (noncontrollable by local boards of education), including the influence of human resources in the local community as well as influences of both state and federal governments. Swanson has described the local influence as including human resources, economic resources, and the decision-making process.[3] Human resources include the size of the community, the kind and distribution of work skills among the population, and the tradition of the community with respect to education. Mort termed the latter as educational climate, while James described it as expectations.[4]

Children of school age are an important human resource and are the

[1] E. S. Mengert, et al., The Study of Administration. Eugene, University of Oregon Press, 1961, pp. 41–43.

[2] George D. Marconnit, "State Legislatures and the School Curriculum." Phi Delta Kappan, Jan. 1968, p. 272.

[3] Austin D. Swanson, The Cost-Quality Relationship. A mimeographed paper delivered to the National Education Association Committee on Educational Finance meeting at St. Louis, Missouri, April 4, 1967, p. 8.

[4] Paul R. Mort, "School and Community Relationships to School Quality," Teachers College Record, Vol. 55, Number 4, Jan. 1954, pp. 201–214. H. Thomas James, et al., Determinants of Educational Expenditure in Large Cities of the United States, Cooperative Research Project Number 2389, Stanford, Calif., School of Education, Stanford University, 1966.

principal input into the school system. Public schools have little control over the selection of their pupils. Economic resources are those accessible to taxation by the school board—usually real estate—and those not accessible— ordinarily, for example, personal or corporate income—which determines the demand or willingness to pay for education.

There are few empirical data regarding the influence of the decision-making process as a noncontrollable variable in determination of educational pro- gramming. The process includes selection of schoolboard members, the geographic boundaries of school districts, the relation between the business and instructional functions of the board, the board's taxing, and budgetary powers, etc.

The effectiveness of school districts would vary greatly if left strictly to local influences, some of which are uncontrollable as described, but variation is moderated generally by state and federal governmental influences. Manip- ulation of resources by the board is confined to local tax levy, allocation of resources, and the levy on student time.[5]

The Pennsylvania studies in the 1930's under Mort's supervision pointed out the limit on discretionary powers of local districts, boards, and adminis- trators in resolving local educational problems.[6] A conclusion was that general supervision by state authorities and increased state financial support were essential if local school programs were to be improved.

Concepts of Quality, Equal Opportunity, Holding Power, and Vocational Education

Who is to determine whether or not a given local school system has met any standard of quality education? It seems reasonable under our legal structure that state departments of public education should assist schools in meeting whatever standards are to be met. Typically throughout the nation, state departments of education are staffed inadequately to perform this vital function. It is clear that the state governments are ultimately accountable for educational quality, but that they have taken a laissez-faire position toward the question of how well the local systems have performed.

The degree to which a local school government uses its leeway for diversity in educational programming and financing will determine its relative standard of quality education until state departments become more aggressive in assuming their responsibility. Likewise, state legislatures should become as

[5] Swanson, *op. cit.*, p. 9.
[6] Paul R. Mort and Frances G. Cornell, *American Schools in Tradition.* New York, Bureau of Publications, Teachers College, Columbia University, 1941.

interested in manpower or management audits as they have been in financial audits.

The concepts of quality, equality of educational opportunity, holding power, and vocational education are discussed in the next several pages as educational objectives to be considered by local school governments in implementing the principle of leeway for diversity.

1. QUALITY OF EDUCATION

The phrase *quality of education* does not mean the same to each person. An evaluator's own set of educational values underlies his description of a quality school. Thus, one person will refer to a quality school that he attended by statements such as, "They just don't learn kids today like they did when I went to school." Others claim a school has quality when it emphasizes the "three R's," provides a good college background, or offers broad technical training leading to employment. Some persons emphasize fact-memorization abilities of students, and others emphasize the critical-thinking and problem-solving abilities.

What one considers a frill will be considered a life's necessity by another. Driver education may be a frill to one who in the meantime supports public school ballet instruction. The problem of developing, standardizing, and using appropriate criteria of determining what is essential learning and what is quality education plagues professional educators and makes them vulnerable to so-called efficiency experts. Many of the latter measure quality only in terms of high teacher-pupil ratios or low current expenditures per pupil.

There is no simple classification system to describe the quality of a total school program. Thus, the quality of a school must be described in terms of the quality of its parts. One school will be better in achieving certain educational goals, while it will be inferior to other schools in achieving another set of goals. Some schools do a better job with boys than with girls.[7]

In the New York Quality Measurement Project conducted by the New York State Education Department for over a decade, researchers assumed that it was possible to measure the achievement level of pupils through the use of standardized achievement tests and that a variation of a school district's mean score from the average of the total groups of schools could be a measure of the effectiveness of the school. Of the 100 school systems in the project sample, 12 were identified as being almost universally good (in grades 4, 5, 6, 7, 8, 10, and 11) in their effectiveness in teaching the basic skills, while 12 others were identified as being almost universally poor. Certain staff charac-

[7] William D. Firman, "Which Schools Are Better?" *NEA Research Bulletin*, Washington, D.C., National Education Association, Oct. 1963, p. 87.

teristics, expenditures, and administrative data were examined for these districts to determine whether or not important differences might be identified.[8]

The excellent schools were two-thirds the size of the poor schools, nearly twice as wealthy, and their median expenditure was about 25 per cent more per child. The better schools had nearly five more professionals per 1,000 pupils (53.2 and 48.5), and had staffs that had traveled more extensively and were generally younger. There was a larger percentage of the staffs of the good schools at higher salary levels than in the poor schools (80 per cent to 65 per cent), although the poor schools had a slightly higher average salary, probably associated with the fact that the poor schools had more hometown teachers and kept them longer. The good schools recruited on a nationwide basis while the poor schools recruited their staffs locally.

Bloom used the Armed Forces General Educational Development Test scores as a criterion in research conducted in 1955 and discovered a marked variation in the general level of achievement by residents of the various states.[9] The correlation was .75 between expenditure for education and achievement.

Military rejection rates based upon the percentage of young men from six army areas in the United States who failed the Armed Forces Qualification Test (AFQT) in the calendar year 1965 were related to what the schools in each of the areas were providing for current expenditures per pupil in average daily attendance (ADA) in the school year 1964–1965. Averages were 20.9 per cent mental test failures nationally and $483 current expenditures per pupil in ADA. Results by the grouping of states are included in Table 6-1. Failure rates on the AFQT and related tests ranged from a low of 6 per cent in the state of Washington to a high of 55 per cent in the District of Columbia. The highest rejection rate by region was for that area including the states of Alabama, Florida, Georgia, Mississippi, North Carolina, South Carolina, and Tennessee. This region spent $323 per pupil for current expenditures, and its rejection rate was 36.7 per cent. The region with the lowest rejection rate (12.6 per cent) spent $504 for current expenditures per pupil.

The Kentucky Quality Education Study reported in March, 1968, was a system analysis of 197 Kentucky public school districts based on their socio-economic and educational characteristics.[10] Using multiple regression analysis

---

[8] *Ibid.*, pp. 88–89.

[9] Benjamin S. Bloom, "The 1955 Normative Study of the Test of General Educational Development." *The School Review*, March, 1956.

[10] William J. Diamond, Charles F. Martin, Sr., and Richard I. Miller, *Quality Rankings of Kentucky School Districts*, Lexington, a Service Report of the Bureau of School Service, College of Education, University of Kentucky, Vol. VII, March, 1968, No. 4, 225 p.

and computer technology, Diamond, Martin, and Miller examined relationships that existed in Kentucky among (a) community socioeconomic factors,
(b) instructional factors, and (c) several measures of student achievement.

Over 300 factors were identified from various studies as possibly influencing
quality education and 19 were selected as input, process, or output variables
according to the following criteria: their prevalence and reliability in other
studies of quality education; their applicability to Kentucky schools based
upon the state's economic, social, geographic, and educational conditions;
and the availability of data.

The profile of quality ranking for Jefferson County in Figure 6-2 was
determined (as it was for each school district in Kentucky) as follows: For

TABLE 6-1. Military Rejection Rates for Each Army Area, Based on Armed Forces
Qualification Test (AFQT) Failures in 1965 and Related to Current
Expenditures Per Pupil in Average Daily Attendance (ADA) in School
Year 1964–1965

Army Area	Military Rejection Rates (Percentage)	Current Expenditure per Pupil
Area 1		
Connecticut, Maine, Massachusetts, New Hampshire, New Jersey, New York, Rhode Island, Vermont	18.0	$667
Area 2		
Delaware, District of Columbia, Kentucky, Maryland, Ohio, Pennsylvania, Virginia, West Virginia	19.7	443
Area 3		
Alabama, Florida, Georgia, Mississippi, North Carolina, South Carolina, Tennessee	36.7	323
Area 4		
Arkansas, Louisiana, New Mexico, Oklahoma, Texas	25.8	393
Area 5		
Colorado, Illinois, Indiana, Iowa, Kansas, Michigan, Minnesota, Missouri, Nebraska, North Dakota, South Dakota, Utah, Washington	12.6	504
Area 6		
Arizona, California, Idaho, Montana, Nevada, Oregon, Wisconsin, Wyoming	13.1	532

SOURCE: Richard de Neufville and Caryl Conner, "How Good Are Our Schools?" *American
Education*, Vol. 2, Oct. 1966, p. 6.

each variable, the mean was calculated by adding the value of the variable for each district and dividing by the number of districts. The standard deviation for each variable was calculated as was a Z score for each variable for each district. From standard tables of the normal distributions, Z scores were converted to the percentage of the entire population for plotting on the profile sheets. For each district, the Z scores for all variables were added together and divided by the number of variables. This computed value was

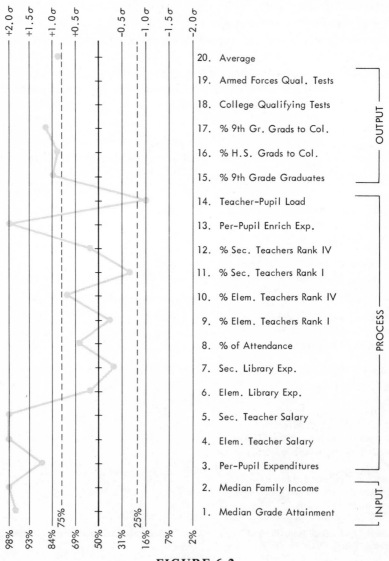

FIGURE 6-2

therefore the average Z score for the district over all 19 variables. The first-ranked district (Ft. Thomas) was therefore the district with the highest average Z score.

It should be noted that equal weight was given to each variable in these rankings. Thus, each input variable was given equal weight with regard to every other input variable and also to each variable in the process or output category.

A major conclusion from the study was that the rankings suggest that community wealth and expenditures largely determine the rank of school districts. In addition, school size alone was not the determining factor in school quality because many larger systems with adequate financial resources were inferior, suggesting that other factors in addition to those used in the research were responsible for large school districts ranking low in quality. Causes may include lack of community interest and support, poor administrative leadership, or the influence of a number of other socioeconomic and cultural factors combined with these to affect the quality of school systems.

In studies now underway models of financial allocations are being developed by multiple regression analysis techniques using school-affected pupil achievements as the dependent variable and expenditures per unit for various categories of educational service as the independent variables. The measure of school-affected achievement will be the school district median residual value, whereby a residual is computed for each pupil by subtracting from his actual achievement score on a standardized test the achievement score predicted from his socioeconomic rating. Samples used are from the New York Quality Measurement Project and from Project Talent.[11]

The general theory of instruction that has dominated the educational scene in the United States has been built upon the premise that the primary task of the teacher was to select and organize information for forwarding to the learner. The emphasis in measurement and evaluation has been upon transmission of information relevant to the cognitive domain of learning—that is, the objectives that deal with the recall or recognition of knowledge and the development of intellectual abilities and skills. The purpose of American education goes far beyond student achievement in the cognitive domain to include concern for areas such as:

The affective domain—attitudes, motivations, interests, adjustment, anxieties;

Social development—acceptance, recognition, belonging, leadership, interaction;

[11] John C. Flanagan, *A Survey and Follow-up Study of Educational Plans and Decisions in Relation to Attitude Patterns: Studies of the American High School.* Pittsburgh, University of Pittsburgh, 1962.

Physical development—general health and ability, speech, motor skills, dexterity, and

Academically related problems—reaction of employers, continuing professional development of teachers.[12]

Attitude scales, personal evaluation, sociometric devices, speech pathology surveys, audiological surveys, physical examinations, participation in recreation program surveys, and many other instruments and devices should be used (but are not being used) with professional observations of behavior to collect evidence about the total educational endeavor.

One of the pitfalls in evaluation of American education has been the failure to allocate sufficient funds and human talent. Other pitfalls have included:

1. Failure to use a sufficiently sensitive instrument to reflect change.
2. Too short a period for change in behavior to occur.
3. Failure to obtain baseline data or initial measurements.
4. Tendency to state objectives in terms of available measuring instruments.
5. Failure to avoid the influence of biased ratings.
6. Failure to consider the analysis of evaluation data in the planning stages of an educational program.
7. Failure to involve participating professionals in planning.
8. Failure to consider the impact of an educational experience on broad educational outcomes.[13]

Legislative bodies, including state legislatures and local boards of education, are becoming more and more vehement in their demands that the education profession clarify outputs, thereby mandating the development and implementation of PPBS. There is a natural and laudable absolutism in the basic philosophy of educators, which holds that the only legitimate aim of educational policy is to provide as much education to each person as he can benefit from—that is, until its marginal utility is zero. Education is considered by the profession to be an end in itself and measures production in terms of inputs rather than outputs. Thus, it is implied that progress is proportional to the volume of inputs used. Economists argue that procedures that measure production in terms of inputs rather than outputs has a built-in bias towards the inefficient use of resources.[14]

[12] *Guide to Evaluation of Title I Projects*, Draft Information Copy, Washington, D.C., U.S. Office of Education, Oct. 1966, p. 33.

[13] *Ibid.*, pp. 81–84.

[14] Excerpt from *Cost-Benefit Analysis of Social Projects*, Report of a meeting of experts held in Rennes, France (Sept. 27–Oct. 2, 1965), Report No. 7, Geneva, April, 1966, p. 123.

2. EQUALITY OF EDUCATIONAL OPPORTUNITY

A second concept worth consideration in implementation of a policy of leeway for diversity is that of equality of educational opportunity. A California State Senate Fact-Finding Committee on Revenue and Taxation in a study reported in March, 1965,[15] considered three possible meanings of "equality of educational opportunity":

1. Each child shall be offered opportunities to develop his own inborn talents to the fullest degree of which he is capable.
2. Each child is provided with schooling in accordance with his "age, aptitude, and ability."
3. A and B have equality of educational opportunity when they live under conditions that do not provide either person with any material advantage over the other in selecting or pursuing his educational goals.

The committee concluded that these goals could not be reached in the foreseeable future because (1) some children know more than others know when they enter school, and others have a strong motivation to learn; (2) not all children can receive instruction from the one teacher who is best for them in a given school year; (3) children learn from each other, but not every child can be put with one group from whose presence he will profit most; and (4) schools cannot cater to all individual vocational educational needs.

Knowledge about how people learn and about what combinations of school resources are most efficient in promoting their learning is limited. A benchmark for a state to use in judging whether departures from equality of educational opportunity are sufficiently serious to warrant the state's taking action to correct them is the expenditure per pupil expressed in dollars. An assumption, then, is that those school districts spending an equal amount per pupil are essentially offering equal educational opportunities. However, it is only a good approximation if the districts have approximately the same proportion of children who are inexpensive and expensive to educate, respectively, and similar hiring advantages relative to teachers recruited.

Expanding the concept of "equal educational opportunity" to "equal educational opportunity of attainment" would mean a significant shift in educational programming and financing. Implementation of the expanded concept would place the school system in the role of an accommodating agent rather than in the role of a gatekeeper. Emphasis would be placed upon the school systems' acceptance of full responsibility to reduce the differences in

[15] *State and Local Fiscal Relationships in Public Education in California*, Sacramento, Senate Fact-Finding Committee on Revenue and Taxation, March, 1965, p. 17.

quality of students' achievements that exist today primarily because responsibility for achievement has been delegated to students.

3. HOLDING POWER OF SCHOOLS

The increased holding power of schools is evident in the summary shown in Table 6-2. Note that at the beginning of the twentieth century approximately 6 of each 100 persons 17 years of age were high-school graduates. The number graduating per 100 persons 17 years of age increased to approximately 77 by 1964, although an estimate was that the figure dropped to 73 in 1965.

The increase in holding power can be accounted for partially by legislative extensions of the compulsory education age requirements and by the fact that young people stayed in school because of limited job opportunities for the nongraduates. Undoubtedly, however, more interesting educational opportunities, better instruction in terms of meeting needs of individuals, and more

TABLE 6-2. Number of High-School Graduates Compared with Population 17 Years of Age, United States, 1869–1870 to 1964–1965

| SCHOOL YEAR | POPULATION 17 YEARS OLD[b] | HIGH-SCHOOL GRADUATES[a] | | | NUMBER OF PERSONS 17 YEARS OLD GRADUATED (PERCENTAGE) |
		TOTAL	BOYS	GIRLS	
1869–70	815,000	16,000	7,064	8,936	2.0
1879–80	946,026	23,634	10,605	13,029	2.5
1889–90	1,259,177	43,731	18,549	25,182	3.5
1899–1900	1,489,146	94,883	38,075	56,808	6.4
1909–10	1,786,240	156,429	63,676	92,753	8.8
1919–20	1,855,173	311,266	123,684	187,582	16.8
1929–30	2,295,822	666,904	300,376	366,528	29.0
1939–40	2,403,074	1,221,475	578,718	642,757	50.8
1949–50	2,034,450	1,199,700	570,700	629,000	59.0
1951–52	2,040,800	1,196,500	569,200	627,300	58.6
1953–54	2,128,600	1,276,100	612,500	663,600	60.0
1955–56	2,270,000	1,414,800	679,500	735,300	62.3
1957–58	2,324,000	1,505,900	725,500	780,400	64.8
1959–60	2,862,000	1,864,000	898,000	966,000	65.1
1961–62	2,768,000	1,925,000	941,000	984,000	69.5
1963–64[c]	3,001,000	2,302,000	1,129,000	1,173,000	76.7
1964–65[c]	3,670,000	2,668,000	1,315,000	1,353,000	72.7

[a] Includes graduates of public and nonpublic schools.
[b] Data from the Bureau of the Census.
[c] Preliminary data.
SOURCE: *Digest of Educational Statistics, 1965 Ed.* Washington, D.C., U.S. Govt. Printing Office, 1965, p. 53.

effective counseling have been important factors in increasing the holding power of the schools.

A program alternative for a schoolboard is to maintain its system's holding power relative to the past, or to attempt to increase the power annually by some percentage. A commitment to an increase could mean extension of such offerings as remedial reading, vocational education, reduction of the teacher-pupil ratio, and a nationwide teacher-recruiting drive.

4. RENEWED INTEREST IN VOCATIONAL EDUCATION

The fourth and final concept to be considered relative to implementation of leeway for diversity is that of renewed interest in vocational education. Even though there has been a dramatic increase in the holding power of the American public schools, approximately 750,000 youngsters of high-school age were dropping out of high school each year during the 1960's. The projected figure of 7.5 million drop-outs in the 1960–1970 decade represents social dynamite and an unmeasurable loss of economic and noneconomic productivity.

Many educators realize that there are few truly comprehensive high schools in the nation, and that most high schools are geared best to serve college-bound youngsters. There is a renewed interest in the improvement and expansion of vocational education programs, particularly those in the area of technical education.

In the 1963 report of the Panel of Consultants on Vocational Education, the following facts and corresponding questions were included:

. . . . Of every 10 students now enrolled in the elementary grades, 3 will probably not attain high school graduation. How will these three earn a living in the world of the 1980's without a high school diploma? How can the schools help them before and after they drop out? Of the other seven boys and girls, who will finish high school in this decade, three will not go on to college. What will these three high school graduates do for a living? How well will their high school education prepare them to earn a living or, in the case of many of the girls, to perform the duties of housewife or mother? Of the remaining four students who will eventually enter college, only two will receive baccalaureate degrees. What are the employment prospects of the two who do not complete four years of college? How will high school and post-high school study help them earn a living?[16]

There will be 100 million Americans working in the 1970's, a number equal to the entire population of the United States in 1915. An important question

[16] *Education for a Changing World of Work.* Washington, D.C., U.S. Govt. Printing Office, 1963, p. 3.

is how well the educational system of the United States will prepare these citizens to enter the shops, stores, factories, homes, offices, farms, and service establishments of the nation, change occupations if need be, and progress in their chosen tasks.

It is recognized that, in its broadest sense, all education contributes to vocational competency. For example, the physician, the lawyer, and the teacher receive occupational preparation in specialized undergraduate and graduate schools. Liberal education and vocational education are both essential aspects of the problem of preparing an individual for living and for earning a living; they cannot be thought of as hostile or mutually exclusive enterprises. Greene recognized value in both liberal and vocational education for the attainment of future individual and national goals when he stated:

> What is obviously needed is a truly liberal academic community in which the study of art and typewriting, of philosophy and accounting, of theology and medicine, of pure and applied are, though admittedly very different, judged to be equally honorable and valuable in their several ways. In such a community the so-called liberal disciplines would indeed be liberal because they would be studied and taught with an eye to the total enrichment of the life of responsible members of a free society; and in such a community the acquisition of the vocational skills, from the simplest to the most complex, would be equally liberal because they would be taught not in a spirit of predatory egoism, but in a spirit of deep social concern for the needs of others and for the common good.[17]

A basic general education is the best foundation for entering upon a vocational education program, and it is essential for the schools to increase their efficiency in teaching the fundamental school subjects to all students. It is obvious that the early school quitter who has not acquired the basic skills (reading and mathematics) is not only unable to find satisfactory permanent employment, but also is handicapped greatly in acquiring specific vocational training as an adult.

The dramatic new federal interest in public education, especially in compensatory education, has brought a great variety of programs and services aimed toward aiding many of the children in deprived communities. The effect in general was to give the child and adult more and better educational services of all kinds. Features have included increased counseling of children and parents, mental and physical health services, and adult education. Content for the high-school academically slow student was beginning to be oriented toward the reality of work experience as distinct from unrealistic

[17] *Ibid.*, p. 7.

academic expectations. Youngsters in such a program could expect to be graduated and to realize a respectable way of life in the world of work.[18]

Recent shifts in the structure of the labor market have imposed increased demands upon public education to prepare young adults and experienced workers alike for changing work careers. The shift from production-oriented occupations to service occupations alluded to earlier has increased the need for cognitive and social skills in addition to the more familiar manipulative skills. Many of the more traditional entry-level occupations have become unavailable to the high-school or junior-college graduate.

Unfortunately, much of what has been taught in the public schools was the result of a failure of many to recognize that technology has generated profound changes in the nature of work. As muscle power continues to give way to brain power, each person needs to understand and master to some extent the man-made environment that surrounds everyone. The tendency in the past to separate general and vocational education has penalized both those who are collegebound and those who plan to terminate their formal education at the end of high school or junior college. Those who plan to go on to college have not been prepared to cope with the possibility of their dropping out of college; about half the students entering college have been dropping out before completion. Seven out of each ten students in high school have been receiving little, if any, specific vocational training. Of the 10 per cent exposed to vocational programs, many have been graduated with already-obsolete skills.

The use of educational television, videotapes, teaching machines, and simulators has opened new avenues of approach to vocational educational problems. New textbooks that gear the information to the background and reading level of the student have been appearing. Experiments with tutorial programs involving older students or subprofessionals offer hope for giving more intensive attention to those requiring it, while at the same time helping to counter the spiraling cost of education.

In Richmond, California, a major effort was made to integrate the vocational and general educational curricula. This was accomplished by redesigning the content of traditionally taught subjects so that it related as much as possible to job-training programs. Mathematics was taught by means of job-related examples and problems. Communication skills were related to performance requirements on the job. What were at one time judged to be potential dropouts in the tenth grade became by their senior year in high school candidates for technical training at nearby junior colleges.

[18] See, for example, *The Quest for Racial Equality in the Pittsburgh Public Schools*, The Annual Report for 1965, Board of Public Education, Pittsburgh, Pa.

Although most of the research and development efforts in curriculum have been small and fragmented—that is, directed to the improvement of a particular subject matter area—recent pilot efforts to an integrated design of an entire curriculum are much in evidence.

It is a black mark against American public education that many poor persons have negative attitudes toward the public school system. In fact, it has been recommended that the Community Action Agency (established under provision of the Economic Opportunity Act) should hold basic education classes for both adults and teen-age dropouts in nonschool settings, such as neighborhood centers, settlement houses, and skill-training centers.[19] Negative attitudes toward public schools developed because of irrelevant curricula, as well as the students' history of failure to meet the school systems' standards, standards that became ends in themselves.

A prime reason for the passage of the federal Economic Opportunity Act has been the failure of the public schools to "meet the needs and interests of students and to develop students to their capacity." The main purpose of the Economic Opportunity Act is well known. The principal means of eliminating "the paradox of poverty in the midst of plenty" is stated to be "opening to everyone the opportunity for education and training, the opportunity to work . . . ." Emphasis is on youth employment, and Title I of the Act deals with "Youth Programs."[20]

The Job Corps is aimed at a particular hard-core of disadvantaged youth who need a "change in surroundings and associations" in order best to receive "education, vocational training, useful work experience" that will increase their employability and prepare them "for the responsibilities of citizenship."[21] The Neighborhood Youth Corps (NYC), designated as "work-training programs" in the Economic Opportunity Act, has the purpose of increasing employability of jobless youth and the resumption or continuation of school attendance of high-school dropouts or potential dropouts. Socially useful jobs on either public or nonprofit private projects are to be combined with "vocational training and educational services."

The Community Action Programs (Title II-Part A of the Economic Opportunity Act) were established to help "urban and rural communities

[19] *Community Action for Employment: Manpower Development.* Washington, D.C., Office of Economic Opportunity, July, 1966, p. 10.

[20] "The major part of the war on poverty . . . is that part which involves the problem of finding jobs for young people, especially those who have been born into the world of poverty, and have no way out save through education, training and a decent job." . . . Willard Wirtz, Secretary of Labor at the House Education and Labor Committee Hearings on Economic Opportunity Act, March 19, 1964.

[21] *Economic Opportunity Amendments of 1965*, House Committee on Education and Labor, Report No. 428, May 27, 1965, p. 2.

mobilize their resources to combat poverty." A "Community Action Program" was defined as one that, among other things, "provides services, assistance, and other activities . . . [that] give promise of progress toward elimination of poverty or a cause or causes of poverty through developing employment opportunities, improving human performance, motivation, and productivity . . . ." In outlining the components of a CAP program which justified the OEO Director in making CAP grants to "appropriate public or private nonprofit agencies," the Act listed "employment, job training and counseling, health, vocational rehabilitation, housing, home management, welfare, and special remedial and other noncurricular educational assistance . . . ."

In addition to the Economic Opportunity Act, Congress approved the Vocational Education Act of 1963, which modernized and enlarged federal financial support to state vocational education to subsidize all nonprofessional occupations training that was "realistic in the light of actual or anticipated opportunities for gainful employment." It introduced new attention to training of disadvantaged youth and provided a program of part-time employment to youths who needed such income supplement to continue vocational education.[22]

The Vocational Education Act of 1963 authorized financial support for high-school classes, for full-time vocational education of those out of school, for up-grading employed workers, for construction of facilities, for education of "persons who have academic, socioeconomic, or other handicaps that prevent them from succeeding in the regular vocational education program," and for "ancillary services and activities to assure quality in all vocational education programs. . . ."

As a result of recent legislation described, a great deal of educational leadership has been provided other than through the traditional formal school structure. Perhaps the nation is realizing what Ataturk meant when he assumed the Turkish presidency in 1924 and announced, "Our nation is going to be one big schoolhouse. We're all going to learn and we're all going to teach." Early in America's history, youngsters received an education in the larger community laboratory. As the cult of childhood was promoted, youngsters were withdrawn from the "real world" and placed in educational cubicles until they were ready for adulthood, and currently they are being

[22] The Federal Vocational Education Assistance Program had, prior to 1963, been based on the Smith–Hughes Act of 1917 and the George–Barden Act of 1946. Federal Aid was limited to training for specified occupations, and almost two-thirds was for agriculture and home economics. See U.S. Department of Health, Education, and Welfare, Office of Education, *Digest of Annual Reports of State Boards of Vocational Education*, 1961, Table 3, p. 7.

placed again into the larger community laboratory, thereby completing an educational cycle as exemplified by a listing of agencies that may be involved in a comprehensive manpower (and educational) program:[23]

Locating the Unemployable and Underemployed (Outreach and Recruitment)
    CAA Neighborhood Service Centers and Employment Centers
    State Employment Services, including their Youth Opportunity Centers and Rural Mobile Units
    Welfare Departments
    Schools
    Private Social Service Agencies
    Police and Courts
Intake Interview
    CAA Neighborhood Service Centers and Employment Centers
    Schools (for dropouts)
    Community Centers
    Public Housing
    State Employment Services
    Youth Opportunity Centers
    Settlement Houses
    Welfare Departments
    Other Private Social Service Agencies
Evaluation
    CAA Neighborhood Service Centers and Employment Centers
    State Employment Service
    Public and Private Rehabilitation Agencies
Prevocational Training
    Federal Programs of Assistance to Communities for Basic Education
    Adult Basic Education Program (Title II-B, Economic Opportunity Act)
    Title I, Elementary and Secondary Education Act
    Neighborhood Youth Corps (Title I-B, Economic Opportunity Act)
    Manpower Development and Training Act
    Work Experience Program (Title V, Economic Opportunity Act)
    Community Action Program (Titles II-A and III-B, Economic Opportunity Act)
Vocational Training—Institutional
    Community Colleges
    Schools
    Private Vocational Schools
    Employers' or Union Training or Educational Programs
    Colleges
    Adult Educational Programs

[23] *Community Action for Employment: Manpower Development, op. cit.,* pp. 22–23.

    Technical Institutes
    Skill Centers
    Private Agencies (CAA, YMCA, etc.)
    Indigenous Groups (OIC, Blazer Council, etc.)
    Work Study Programs
Vocational Training—On-the-Job
    Employers
    Trade Associations
    Tribal Councils
    Subcontract to public or private agency
    Unions
    Civil Service
Placement
    CAA Neighborhood Service Centers
    Employment Services
    Rehabilitation Agencies
    Civil Service Personnel Office
    Employment Centers
    Newspaper Ads donated by Newspapers, Civic Groups, etc.
    Urban League
    Unions
    Private, nonprofit employment programs
    Trade Associations
    Employer Groups
    Businessmen's Clubs
Follow-Up
    Neighborhood Service Center
    Volunteers
    Placement Personnel
    Youth Opportunity Center
    Trainees
Job Development
    Employment Service
    Community Action Agency
    Universities
    Economic Development Agencies
    Management Consultant Firms
    Union Research Divisions
    Trade Associations

The Feasibility of School Evaluation

Evaluation is the process of determining the extent to which specified objectives have been reached. Stated in another way, evaluation is the process of assessing the extent and direction of change resulting from an educational experience.

The steps in evaluating educational outcomes can be enumerated as follows:

1. Identification of an educational need in terms of a deficiency, a gap in required competencies, or the absence of some desired behavior.
2. Definition of educational objectives to be achieved through the experience to be evaluated. These objectives should reflect the need which the educational experience is designed to alleviate.
3. Translation of the educational objectives into behavior which will be displayed if the objectives are achieved.
4. Identification of situations in which the presence or absence of the designated behavior can be observed and recorded.
5. Establishment of standards, norms, or units which can be used as interpretive values to reveal absolute or relative amounts of behavior displayed.
6. Selection and consequent application of an evaluation device or devices derived from steps four and five to all those participating in the educational experience.
7. Analysis of evidence yielded by the evaluation device in terms of progress toward the defined objectives.
8. Statement of conclusions regarding effectiveness in terms of the extent to which objectives were achieved.[24]

(Dividing the evaluation process into eight steps is purely arbitrary. The total number of steps is a function of step size and could be three to thirteen, depending on the condensation or expansion of the steps as presented.)

Assessing progress toward objectives is of central concern to educators. Evaluation applies to all areas of educational endeavor—curriculum, instructional methodology, pupil personnel services, public relations, physical plant construction, finance, research, and others. To evaluate is to judge the worth, rate, or value of something. Evaluation has taken place anytime something is judged good or bad, better or worse, worth continuing or discontinuing. In education, evaluation is a concern of administrators, teachers, specialists, boards of education, state and federal offices, parents, legislators, taxpayers, and all those who carry any responsibility whatsoever for the educational process.

Examples of such decision-making include diagnosing learning difficulties, revising curricular content, granting tenure, and selecting instructional

[24] *Guide to Evaluation of Title I Projects, op. cit.,* pp. 8–9.

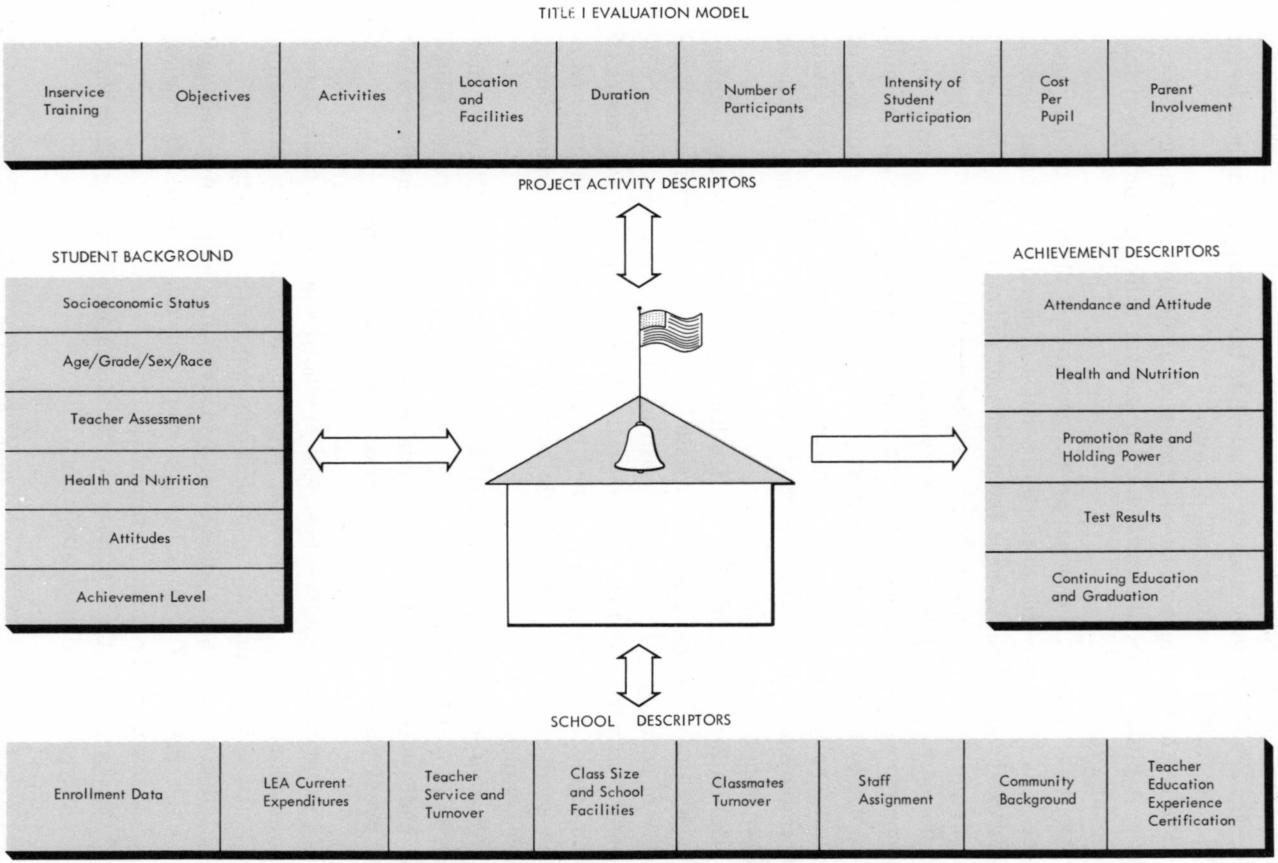

TITLE I EVALUATION MODEL

STUDENT BACKGROUND

Socioeconomic Status
Age/Grade/Sex/Race
Teacher Assessment
Health and Nutrition
Attitudes
Achievement Level

PROJECT ACTIVITY DESCRIPTORS

Inservice Training
Objectives
Activities
Location and Facilities
Duration
Number of Participants
Intensity of Student Participation
Cost Per Pupil
Parent Involvement

ACHIEVEMENT DESCRIPTORS

Attendance and Attitude
Health and Nutrition
Promotion Rate and Holding Power
Test Results
Continuing Education and Graduation

SCHOOL DESCRIPTORS

Enrollment Data
LEA Current Expenditures
Teacher Service and Turnover
Class Size and School Facilities
Classmates Turnover
Staff Assignment
Community Background
Teacher Education Experience Certification

FIGURE 6-3 Title I Evaluation Model.

materials. Although there are many possible bases for making decisions, such as custom and tradition, appeal to authority, logic, and personal experience, the concept of collecting evidence on which to base decisions has been by far the most fruitful for educational progress.

The key to the total evaluation process is an effective statement of objectives. A project without clearly stated objectives is like the proverbial ship without a rudder.

Objectives for an educational project grow out of observed needs. Sometimes it is barely possible to recognize that a need exists; at other times, a need can be sensed but is vague and undefined; and at still other times, many needs are readily apparent. Needs can be determined from "felt needs" expressed by pupils, from discrepancies in performance when some group is compared with other pupils at the same level, from interferences with learning as noted by teachers or other observers, or from demands on "graduates" of educational programs at any level made by teachers at higher grade levels, by employers, or by other members of society such as community leaders or other responsible citizens.

During the summer of 1964, the Trustees of the Martha Holden Jennings Foundation subsidized a preliminary study designed to determine the feasibility of developing a "yardstick" instrument or process by which school-boards and administrators could measure the strengths and weaknesses of their schools. The study was directed to two questions: "What material is now available?", and "What might be done?" once the preliminary study was completed.

An advisory committee comprised of men from the Greater Cleveland area hired Leonard M. Britton, an educator, to conduct the study.[25] Britton visited or made other contacts with educational leaders and institutions throughout the country and summarized his reports under four headings:

1. Subjective evaluators—those who evaluated schools and made recommendations for improvement primarily upon collected information assembled on the basis of professional experience and judgment;
2. Objective evaluators—those who made evaluative judgments based upon the analysis of data collected through the use of tests, observation forms, and other such instruments;
3. General evaluators—those who exhibited a very broad or generalized interest in school evaluation; and

[25] Leonard M. Britton, *Operation Yardstick: A Study of Feasibility of School Evaluation.* Cleveland, financed by The Martha Holden Jennings Foundation, Summer 1964, 121 p.

4. Operations researchers—those who showed interest in utilizing the techniques of operations research, or systems analysis, in the process of school evaluation and improvement.

Subjective evaluators included distinguished professors throughout the nation, Dr. James Bryant Conant, the Educational Policies Commission, the New England School Development Council, and the Association for Supervision and Curriculum Development. Objective evaluators named were the New York Quality Measurement Project, the Educational Testing Service, the National Merit Scholarship Corporation, the National Citizens Council for Better Schools, the Brookings Institution, the Great Cities Program for School Improvement, and others. Operations researchers included representatives of the Case Institute of Technology, Ernst and Ernst Management Services, Purdue University, the Rand Corporation, and the System Development Corporation.

No generalizations could be made from the Britton report. The following ideas generating from Britton's discussion with a private management consultant and operations researcher certainly sums up the problem of educational evaluation with no key to answers:

1. Before any purposeful measurement and evaluations can take place, the development of a clear and precise statement of educational objectives must be accomplished;

2. The instrumentation for recognizing and measuring the degree of attainment of these objectives must be available;

3. The techniques for being able to perform discriminative analysis on the collected data must be available in such a manner that it is possible to see what is good and effective, and what is bad and inefficient.[26]

To this, experienced educators, schoolboard members, and others involved for many years in educational development would say to the scientifically oriented, "Amen!", "Welcome aboard," and "Good luck."

In the meantime, school communities developing educational programs and educational budgets could use criteria of excellence as developed by subjective evaluators, as follows:

1. Evaluation should be based on stated objectives.

2. Evaluation should be based on intimate and comprehensive knowledge of the community.

3. Evaluation should be a continuous activity.

4. Evaluation should be comprehensive.

5. Evaluation should be a cooperative process involving many people.

[26] *Ibid.*, pp. 112–113.

6. Evaluation should identify strengths as well as deficiencies.

7. Evaluation should involve many instruments.

8. Evaluation should be based on knowledge of children and youth.

9. Evaluation requires the board to look at itself.

10. Evaluation should appraise existing practices affecting the staff.

11. Evaluation is based on the belief that what people think makes a difference.

12. Evaluation should culminate in self-improvement.[27]

In addition, the Institute of Administrative Research, Teachers College, Columbia University, has worked closely with the Metropolitan School Study Council (70 school communities in and around New York City), the Associated Public School Systems (school communities throughout the United States), and the Central School Boards Committee for Educational Research (an organization of central school communities in New York State), in so-called action improvement of school systems. One of the instruments of educational quality measurement developed by the IAR includes *The Growing Edge*.[28] This instrument is available in two forms, one each for the elementary and secondary schools, and uses the measure of school adaptability as an indicator of quality. The process is based upon the observation of school practices that reflect the "growing edge" of American education. The specific practices included in the instrument were organized around four major areas of educational purpose—that is, (1) the teaching of the basic skills, (2) the teaching of the areas of knowledge, (3) the discovery and development of special aptitudes of individuals through test and tryout, and (4) the development of gross behavioral patterns like citizenship, character, and thinking.

Observers using *The Growing Edge* visit classrooms and check off practices found present or substituted adequately in an alternative manner. Supposition is that the more practices present, the more adaptable the school and the better the institution.

A great number of variables have been correlated with the adaptability criterion, and the following four findings are of particular interest:

There is a correlation of .60 between adaptability and per pupil expenditures; .44 with the per cent of business and professional workers who are residents of the community; .30 with the per cent of the staff who have five or more years of training; and .57 with the average salary of staff.[29]

[27] *Judging Schools With Wisdom*. Washington, D.C., American Association of School Administrators and the National School Boards Association, 1959, pp. 1–2.

[28] Paul R. Mort, *et al.*, *The Growing Edge*. New York, Metropolitan School Study Council, 1957.

[29] Britton, *op. cit.*, p. 49.

The Budget and Program Evaluation

The process of evaluation is a vital one in the set of administrative processes, and, of course, the budget is a useful instrument. A suggested list of pertinent questions relative to the budget and the evaluation process includes the following:

1. Can the organization meet its objectives on the basis of present budgetary provisions?
2. Does the budget give a high enough priority to the crucial problems or difficulties of the organization?
3. What activities can be curtailed or eliminated without materially affecting educational opportunities?
4. Would expansion of present activities improve educational opportunities?
5. What present activities are contributing their full measure to a realization of the objectives?
6. Is the educational program balanced?
7. Are budgets being adjusted upward to meet declining dollar values?
8. Are there social changes which have made aspects of the educational program obsolete?[30]

Unfortunately, at least from an educator's point of view, it is typical for schoolboards to understand money better than intangible values such as "meeting the needs of individuals," "better teachers," "new programs," or "expanding educational services." As a result, schoolboards have tended to begin the budgeting process with the determination of the amount of funds to be expended and with a direction to the superintendent to spend it so that the citizens "get the best for their money." However, there are numerous communities in the United States where the superintendents have played leadership roles to the effect that steady increases in allocations and in the educational expectations for a school community have been committed.

The following is a suggested list of recommendations for improving school budgeting that seems dominated by evaluation activities, which if implemented should strengthen local school government and programming:

1. An organized plan for school budgeting should be developed adequately step by step, by the superintendent of schools with the assistance of his professional staff. Full use should be made of all persons and groups who can help to expedite the process of developing an adequate school budget.
2. A budget calendar or time schedule should be utilized.

[30] Leon Ovsiew, et al., "Budgeting," in The Theory and Practice of School Finance, Warren E. Gauerke and Jack R. Childress, eds. Chicago, Rand McNally, 1967, pp. 213–214.

3. The current school budget should be prepared within the framework of a long-term budget covering a period of at least five years.

4. Good public relations should be maintained on a day-to-day basis in order to keep the entire electorate, as well as official bodies, properly informed as to the actual educational needs of the people and how they may be met. A special campaign seeking support of the school budget is a poor substitute for the continuous day-to-day plan just recommended.

5. From time to time, brochures or leaflets giving pertinent data on all phases of the school program should be prepared and distributed to the public.

6. Great care should be exercised to see that both income and expenditures are not over-estimated.

7. An adequate unencumbered cash balance or operating surplus should be maintained from year to year in each school system which needs such funds to make revenues available as needed to pay current operating expenses. (For example, during the period between July 1, or the beginning of the fiscal year, and November 1, when local property taxes begin to be collected.)

8. Once the school budget is adopted, it should be executed in a business-like manner to the end that every dollar will purchase 100 cents worth of value for the public schools. [Author's note: Florida's Governor was elected on such a platform in 1966. He termed it bringing the "tools of management in the private sector to solve problems in the public sector"—whew!!!]

9. Good budgetary control through an encumbrance system and a system of providing monthly reports to the local board of education on funds available for use should be maintained.

10. A copy of all budget amendments or revisions should be furnished to the State Commissioner of Education.

11. Among other items the school budget document should include supporting statistical data such as population trends where school plant expansion is involved, enrollments, average daily attendance, number of positions, and average salary trends.[31]

Problems Encountered in Budgeting

Weston and Brigham have isolated four major problems encountered in the use of budget systems in any type of enterprise.[32] First, budgetary programs can become so detailed and so complete that they become meaningless, unduly expensive, and cumbersome.

Second, enterprise goals may be replaced by budgetary goals. However, budgets are ideally to be considered as means rather than ends, and enterprise

[31] *Accounting Manual for Tennessee Public School Systems.* Nashville, Tennessee State Department of Education, 1961, pp. 37–38.

[32] J. Fred Weston and Eugene F. Brigham, *Managerial Finance*, Second Ed. New York, Holt, Rinehart & Winston, 1966, pp. 218–219.

goals (educational ones, for example) should by definition supersede subsidiary plans of which budgets are a part. In addition, since budgets are based on future expectations that may or may not be realized, there is no acceptable reason for neglecting to alter budgets as circumstances change.

Third, organizational inefficiencies can be hidden in a sequence of budgets by a continuation of initial expenditures without proper evaluation. Budgets growing from precedent should not be used as umbrellas under which slovenly, inefficient management can hide. Consequently, provision must be made for re-examination of standards in the budgetary processes, and attention must be given to other bases of planning by which policies are translated into numerical terms.

Finally, there is some case study evidence that the use of budgets as an instrument of tyranny or as a pressure device can cause resentment and frustrations that lead to inefficiency. To counteract this effect, top management should increase the participation of subordinates during the varying stages of budget development.

An excellent set of educational budgets can represent the epitome in planning, the excitement of the interrelationship of multiple educational forces, the dynamism of an adaptable organism, the most tangible plan for decision implementation, and the best indication of a community's commitment to improvement of mankind. Teacher professional negotiation or collective bargaining laws will bring a new excitement and dynamism to educational budget-making at the state and local levels, leading to a further opening of the public educational systems and a more excellent set of programs and budgets. However, a most difficult problem remains, and that is the difficulty in projecting long-term budgetary needs. Appendix A, entitled "Expenditure Projections and Elements of Trend Fitting," includes in-depth explanations of mathematical tools showing promise as projection instruments.

7

GOVERNMENTAL
REVENUE SYSTEMS

Introduction

Because provision for public education is a state responsibility, each state must provide the means for financing its educational system through constitutional and statutory provisions. School finance is a branch of public finance, and school lobbyists compete through political processes for public funds with lobbyists for other deserving public services such as welfare, police, fire, general government, hospitals, and highways. Much of the substance of politics at the state level is constituted in the policy areas of taxation, education, welfare, and highways.

The history of public school finance in the United States reflects many methods of finance. During the nation's colonial period, reliance was placed upon church and private support. The notion that education was a public matter was founded on the conceptualization that maintenance of religious orthodoxy was a primary duty of government. Reinforcement of church training through a system of compulsory education was not difficult to accept in a homogeneous religious community. Thus, in 1642 and in 1647 when the Massachusetts General Court directed parents to educate children and when Massachusetts towns were required to establish schools, respectively, religious motives were dominating.

148

At the time of the establishment of the federal government, the new state governments did not accept responsibility for schools, and financial support for education came in the form of lotteries, rate bills (charges to parents of pupils), contributions, private school societies, and, of course, again from church support. Much reliance was begun to be placed upon funds received from the sale of land to support schools. It had become the national policy, beginning with the Ordinance of 1787 and implemented by the Ohio Act of 1802, to provide federal grants of land for public schools to all new land states. The original thirteen states, which were not public-land states, along with Maine, Vermont, West Virginia, Tennessee, Kentucky and Texas, were not recipients of land. The other 29 states of the 48 existing prior to the admission of Hawaii and Alaska received a total of over 70 million acres as an outright gift.

Under the land-grant provisions, one or more sections of land in each Congressional Township were, under the so-called Ohio plan, "granted to the inhabitants of each township for the use of school," while under the Illinois and Michigan plans, respectively, grants were made to "the state for the use of the inhabitants of such townships and for the use of schools," and "to the state for the use of the schools." At the time of the admission of Ohio to statehood a question had arisen as to whether the state ought to have the right to tax public land owned by the United States but included in the prospective state's boundaries. The Ohio legislature agreed not to tax land owned by the federal government, and in return the Congress provided Ohio with the sixteenth section of each township for purposes of education.

The Michigan plan of 1836, which did not limit the use of funds to the township level, became the standard method of making school land grants to all states admitted after that year. Money received from the sale of land-grant property proved to be insufficient for public school support, as did funds received by chance from lotteries or from the sporadic tax support during the first half of the nineteenth century.

The first state school systems established in New York in 1812, Maryland in 1816, New Jersey in 1824, and in Illinois and Massachusetts in 1827, did not require the local operation of schools. Something revolutionary and unique was included in the statutes pertaining to the establishment of schools in New York, however, by the stipulation that local schools had to match the financial support from the state. A permanent school fund was created out of legislative appropriations and from funds derived from the sale of public lands. Interest earned on the fund was to be distributed annually on the basis of population.

State after state gradually required the operation of local district schools, and permissive local tax support tended to become mandatory during the first half of the nineteenth century. Initial mandatory tax support came from taxes on property of parents whose children were in school.

Regional differences in educational structure and finance had developed in the 1790's and early 1800's, primarily because of the influence of varied religious influences. Because of the congregational structure of the dominant religious groups in New England, for example, there was a lack of centralized authority to establish schools, and governmental authority was invoked to implement goals of the Puritan ideal. In the South, the Church of England dominated both secular and religious education. Only orphans or others unable to utilize private schools were sent to public schools. The growth of public schools found relatively easy acceptance in the West, where Jacksonian democracy took root more easily.[1]

The district schools eventually included grade divisions such as exist in elementary schools today, but, as you will recall, it was not until the famous Kalamazoo court case in 1874 that high schools were clearly eligible for public tax support.[2] Prior to this case, secondary schools were principally private, although there had been an increasing demand and interest for the establishment of public high schools after the establishment of the first one in Boston in 1821.

By 1880 all thirty-eight states had established a position of chief state educational officer and other state educational regulatory and leadership personnel. The concept of educational quality and its relationship to the expenditure of public money stimulated states' efforts to develop educational standards. However, in the post-Civil War era the South was not only confronted with a weaker tradition than the remainder of the country relative to public education, but with two other inhibiting factors—dire poverty and the race problem.[3]

By the beginning of the twentieth century, the states had accepted responsibility for public education, but the operation of schools and much of the tax support had been delegated to the local school systems, including intermediate school administrative units. Development of the public schools during the century has not been the same in all states, since each has had different goals at varied times. As the nation has moved through the Industrial Revolution and into a scientific revolution, the educational system in each

[1] Robert H. Salisbury, "State Politics and Education," in *Politics in the American States*, Herbert Jacob and Kenneth N. Vines, eds. Boston, Little, Brown, 1965, pp. 332–333.

[2] *Stuart v. School District No. 1 of Kalamazoo*, 30 Michigan 69, 1874.

[3] Salisbury, *op. cit.*, p. 335.

state has had to undergo varying adaptations to the changing economic and social conditions in order to best serve the educational needs of individuals and the society.

The Industrial Revolution, including advances in transportation and communication, changed the United States from an agrarian nation to a major industrial power. Huge industrial centers were established, there was a mass migration from the farms to cities, wealth tended to be centered in urban areas, and many governmental services such as highways and hospitals were administered by centralized governmental agencies.

As the period of the scientific revolution or nuclear age developed in the 1950's, suburban areas mushroomed, tax bases were upset when industrial organizations decentralized and industrial plants were moved from populous areas to sites in the middle of sparsely populated areas in the country, and thousands migrated to new industrial centers. State legislatures were placing more and more demands upon the public schools in areas such as guidance, adult education, special education, and vocational education, in many instances without providing the necessary means to finance the added programs and services. Wealth was being concentrated in the urban areas, and the property tax was becoming less reliable as an indicator of wealth.

State and Local Sharing of Educational Costs

The concept of state and local sharing of educational costs did not develop rapidly until the depression years of the 1930's, when property owners were unable to pay taxes. State support increases since then have been attributable to the fact that the states are in a position to levy nonproperty taxes for statewide financial needs and to distribute revenue where needed. A substantial portion of both federal and state spending for education in Fiscal Year (FY) 1966, for example, was in the form of intergovernmental payments, as shown in Table 7-1.

State funds have been used to (1) help communities establish the operation of a school system; (2) provide relief to those districts unable to provide sufficient local funds; (3) encourage new programs; (4) provide payments in lieu of taxes through property lost by local districts to new state parks or to new industry which received tax exemptions; and (5) provide general support for schools through a foundation program.

More than forty states have developed state foundation programs, and leading programs will be described in Chapter 9. These programs designate the amount of money that must be made available to all administrative units to support the basic instructional program defined as essential for all young-

TABLE 7-1. Government Expenditures for Education, Fiscal Year 1966
(Dollars in Millions)

ITEM	FEDERAL	STATE	LOCAL
TOTAL education expenditure	$4,564	$17,749	$25,750
Intergovernmental expenditure	3,014	10,177	35
Direct expenditure	1,550	7,572	25,715
Local schools	—	231	24,860
Institutions of higher education	—	6,353	855
Other	1,550	989	—

SOURCE: *Governmental Finances in 1965–66*, Series GF-No. 13, Washington, D.C., U.S. Govt. Printing Office, 1967, p. 8.

sters in a state. Typically, funds are disbursed from general funds appropriated by the state legislature, rather than from restricted earmarked funds. Local leeway is advisable so that a local school district has power to tax itself to support a better program than provided through the foundation program.

Total Governmental Revenue

The nation's present tax systems developed a little at a time, and in 1965 all levels of government received approximately 27 cents of every dollar of the nation's gross national product (GNP). There is much controversy concerning the maximum proportion of the GNP that can be allocated to governmental functions, as discussed previously. Economists do not agree on the maximum percentage, although the literature is replete with proposals for limits of 25 to 30 per cent of the GNP. Information in Table 7-2 indicates that all the leading Western European nations spend a greater proportion of their GNP for government than does the United States of its own.

The federal government collected approximately two-thirds, or 62.6 per cent, of the $225 billions in total governmental revenues produced in FY 1966, while the state and local governments collected 19.1 per cent and 18.4 per cent, respectively. A somewhat different distribution appears if allowance is made for the effect of intergovernmental transfers. In terms of the final recipient level of government, public revenue was distributed in FY 1966 as shown in Table 7-3.

Revenue and expenditure, respectively, comprise all amounts of money received or paid out by a government and its agencies (net of correcting transactions such as recoveries or refunds), with the exception of amounts for

TABLE 7-2. Taxes in Major Nations—How the Burden in U.S. Compares

	INCOME TAXES, OTHER "DIRECT" TAXES (PERCENTAGE)	SALES TAXES, OTHER "INDIRECT" TAXES (PERCENTAGE)	SOCIAL SECURITY TAXES (PERCENTAGE)	TOTAL TAXES (PERCENTAGE)
Taxes as a percentage of total output of goods and services, or gross national product				
France	6.7	17.6	14.2	38.5
Sweden	19.6	12.8	6.0	38.4
Norway	13.1	15.0	6.8	34.9
Austria	12.0	15.6	7.2	34.8
Germany	10.4	14.2	9.8	34.4
Netherlands	12.7	10.1	11.3	34.1
Denmark	13.6	14.3	1.8	29.7
Italy	6.6	12.6	10.4	29.6
Britain	10.7	13.5	4.4	28.6
United States	13.8	9.3	4.2	27.3
Canada	10.7	14.6	1.8	27.1

NOTE: Tax figures are for all levels of government in each country. Percentages are for 1965, latest year available for all countries.
SOURCE: *U.S. News and World Report*, Feb. 27, 1967, p. 63. Copyright 1967 U.S. News and World Report, Inc.

debt issuance and retirement and for loan and investment, agency, and private trust transactions. Subject to some relatively minor exceptions, governments' internal transfers from fund to fund are excluded, and aggregates for groups of governments exclude intergovernmental transactions among the governments involved.

Because government is defined to include all public agencies, corporations, and funds, revenue and expenditure totals include amounts of revenue and expenditure (on a gross basis) of government-operated enterprises, utilities, and public trust funds.

TABLE 7-3. Distribution of Public Revenue, Fiscal Year 1966 (in Terms of Final Recipient)

LEVEL OF GOVERNMENT	AMOUNT	PERCENTAGE
TOTAL REVENUE	$225,641,000,000	100.0
Federal	128,022,000,000	56.7
State	38,851,000,000	17.2
Local	58,768,000,000	26.0

SOURCE: Governmental Finances in 1965–66, Series GF-No. 13, Washington, D.C., U.S. Govt. Printing Office, 1967, p. 2.

Relative to tax revenue, there are marked differences in tax structure among the three levels of government.[4] The federal government relies primarily on income taxes—corporation and individual—to supply the major portion of all federal tax revenue. The property tax yields most of the tax revenue for local governments, while no one type of tax is so predominant for state governments. However, sales and gross receipts taxes—including not only those of general application, but also selective taxes on sales of motor fuel, liquor, tobacco, and other particular commodities or services—altogether provide more than half of all state tax revenue.

TABLE 7-4. Governmental Revenue for Fiscal Year 1966 by Percentage from Sources and by Percentage Increase from Prior Fiscal Year

	PERCENTAGE				PERCENTAGE OF INCREASE FROM FISCAL YEAR 1965	
ITEM	ALL GOVERN- MENTS	FEDERAL	STATE	LOCAL	FEDERAL	STATE AND LOCAL
Revenue from all sources	100.0%	100.0%	100.0%	100.0%	12.2%	12.0%
Intergovernmental revenue	—	—	22.2	30.0	—	17.8
Revenue from own sources	100.0	100.0	77.8	70.0	12.2	10.1
General revenue from own sources	83.5	84.0	62.5	59.7	11.1	11.0
Taxes	71.3	73.8	53.2	46.2	11.1	10.7
Charges and miscellaneous general revenue	12.2	10.2	9.3	13.6	11.1	12.3
Current charges	8.5	7.0	6.5	9.7	6.2	11.6
All other	3.7	3.3	2.8	3.8	23.2	14.3
Utility revenue	2.2	—	—	8.6	—	3.3
Liquor stores revenue	0.7	—	2.5	0.3	—	7.1
Insurance trust revenue	13.5	16.0	12.9	1.4	18.2	7.3

NOTE: Because of rounding out of numbers, detail may not add up to totals.

SOURCE: *Governmental Finances in 1965–66*, Series GF-No. 13, Washington, D.C., U.S. Govt. Printing Office, 1967, p. 4.

[4] Taxes are intended to comprise all "compulsory contributions exacted by a government for public purposes, except employer and employee assessments for retirement and social insurance purposes, which are classed as insurance trust revenue."

TABLE 7-5. Tax Revenue for Fiscal Year 1966 by Percentage from Sources and by Percentage Increase from Prior Fiscal Year

| ITEM | PERCENTAGE | | | | PERCENTAGE INCREASE FROM FISCAL YEAR 1965 | | |
	ALL GOVERN-MENTS	FEDERAL	STATE	LOCAL	ALL GOVERN-MENTS	FEDERAL	STATE AND LOCAL
TOTAL TAXES	100.0	100.0	100.0	100.0	11.0	11.1	10.7
Income	57.4	82.2	21.5	1.7	15.0	15.2	12.9
Individual	37.4	53.3	14.6	1.7	13.8	13.6	16.4
Corporation	20.0	28.9	6.9	—	17.2	18.1	5.7
Property	15.3	—	2.8	87.1	9.2	—	9.2
Sales, gross receipts, and customs	21.0	14.1	58.0	7.5	2.5	−7.3	11.5
Customs duties	1.1	1.7	—	—	22.5	22.5	—
General sales and gross receipts	5.7	—	26.8	4.9	15.6	—	15.6
Selective sales and gross receipts	14.1	12.4	31.2	2.5	−3.2	−10.2	7.9
All other	6.3	3.8	17.6	3.7	10.1	7.2	12.1

NOTE: Because of rounding out of numbers, detail may not add up to totals.
SOURCE: *Governmental Finances in 1965–66*, Series GF-No. 13, Washington, D.C., U.S. Govt. Printing Office, 1967, p. 5.

Nontax general revenue of governments consists mainly of current charges —that is, amounts received for performance of specific services benefiting the person charged and from sales of commodities and services other than from utility and liquor stores sales. Nearly one-half of federal revenue from current charges in FY 1966 was from postal receipts. Sales by the Commodity Credit Corporation accounted for another substantial portion of such revenue. Other federal current charges revenue included rental receipts from federal housing projects; insurance premiums for housing insurance; reimbursement of appropriations from proceeds of sales; charges for subsistence and quarters collected from government personnel; advances from foreign governments for purchase of military and other supplies, equipment, and services; and many other items.

General revenue from interest earnings consists of interest on governmental loans and on securities held by governments, other than such investments held by employee retirement and social insurance funds. A major portion of all investments of state and local governments is in the form of interest-bearing federal securities and securities of state and local governments, including those of the investing government. The federal government also holds large amounts of its own securities, as well as a relatively minor amount of securities issued by state and local governments. Therefore, a significant portion of gross governmental revenue from interest received in FY 1966, for example, came from governments rather than from other sectors of the economy.

Sales receipts of state and local liquor stores and local water, electric, gas, and transit utilities were largely offset in FY 1966 by the cost of purchasing and producing the commodities and services sold, and only any net excess of sales revenue over the cost of producing this revenue was available for financing other types of governmental services. In FY 1966, local expenditures for utility purposes (including capital outlays and interest on utility debt, as well as current operation expenditure) were somewhat more than the total of local utility revenue.[5] However, for both state-operated and locally operated liquor stores sales revenue exceeded expenditures.

The external transactions of governments with respect to social insurance and employee retirement systems were listed in Table 7-4 as insurance trust revenue. This heading covered amounts for the federal system of Old Age, Survivors, and Disability Insurance and for systems relating to unemployment compensation, employee retirement, workmen's compensation, and the like. Insurance trust revenue altogether represented about one-eighth of all governmental revenue. The major portion of such revenue was from contributions from employers and employees and other ultimate beneficiaries, and the remainder was from earnings on investments of insurance trust systems administered by state and local governments.

Tax Overlapping

Tax overlapping—the practice of two or more governments (local, state, and federal) levying on the same subject or object—is as old as the United States itself. All local governments and the states have always, or nearly always, levied property taxes. The federal income tax that was enacted during the Civil War and repealed in 1872 overlapped the income taxes of Southern and some Eastern states. During the Civil War and again during the Spanish-American War, Congress enacted death duties, which overlapped some state levies.

A checklist of the different kinds of taxes used in the United States in 1967 shows a significant number used simultaneously by both federal and state governments and, not infrequently, by local governments. This was true of

[5] *Governmental Finances in 1965–66*, Series GF, No. 13, Washington, D.C., U.S. Govt. Printing Office, 1967, p. 26.

individual and corporation income taxes, death and gift taxes, and taxes on motor fuels, alcoholic beverages, tobacco products, amusements, and public utilities. The principal exceptions were customs duties, which were levied only by the federal government, and property, general sales, and motor vehicle license taxes, which were levied only by the state and local governments. Examples of tax overlapping are included in the tax summary for FY 1968 below:

Income—federal government, 38 states (personal income), 40 states (corporate income), and 3,000 local governments

General sales—44 states and more than 3,000 localities

Property—taxes in all 50 states, largely for revenue in 70,000 local governmental units, and applied to real estate, personal property, or both

Payrolls—employees, employers, and self-employed

Death—federal and 49 states

Gifts—federal and 12 states

Liquor, beer, wines—federal and 50 states

Cigarettes—federal and 49 states

Gasoline—federal and 50 states

New automobiles—federal excise, plus many states

Admission—federal tax has been repealed; states and local governments still tax admissions

Tires and tubes—federal, plus state and local sales taxes

Telephones—federal, plus state levies, usually under general sales tax

Air travel—federal excise

Occupation or business fees—50 states and many local governments

Real estate—transfers subject to federal taxes, 30 states and many local taxes

Stock transfers—4 states, including New York

Mortgages—most counties tax recording of mortgages

Automobile tags—49 states plus a county tax in Hawaii

Auto operator's licenses—49 states

Boat registration—most states

Sewers and water—use charges are general

Hunting and fishing—50 states

Although tax overlapping is widespread in the sense that often a tax category providing the major part of the revenues at one level is used also, if only to a minor degree, at another level, the system is characterized by a substantial degree of revenue separation. Over half of the states have abandoned the property tax, which the federal government is prohibited from using, and have left it exclusively to their local governments. About fifteen years ago, the federal government repealed its electrical energy tax, in which local governments were interested. In more recent years, it has largely eliminated its admissions taxes. However, the objective of Congress in repealing these federal taxes was quite unrelated to tax simplification and coordination and had other more politically compelling motivations.

As a result of the transformation that has occurred in the national tax structure since the turn of the century, the property tax is now one of the very few major taxes involving little or no tax overlapping among the three levels of governments—federal, state, and local. Apart from customs duties, the only other taxes that are substantially the province of a single level of government are the income and the motor vehicle and operator's license taxes. The federal government accounted for 93 per cent of income tax collections in FY 1966 and the states for 98.5 per cent of the motor vehicle and operator's license taxes.[6]

Under a federal system of government, the federal government and state-local governments are largely free to choose any tax they please, and they have generally chosen differently. Beyond the very few strictures prescribed by the Constitution of the United States, each of the 50 states is fiscally autonomous and enjoys a kind of tax sovereignty, as in a sense do also the many local governments operating under home rule or liberal charter provisions. Their theoretical tax autonomy is limited, however, by practical political considerations, interjurisdictional tax competition, and problems of tax administration.

Each state guards jealously its right to shape its own tax policies, and this handicaps the realization of a master design for the division of tax sources between the federal and state governments. The interstate variety is considered by many to be the strength of the governmental system. The affinity for different solutions is not solely a desire for variety and independence. With the wide differences in economic, social, and political circumstances in this country, a tax structure design favorable to some governments at any given time is certain at any given time to be unfavorable to others.

Freeman complained that a federal fiscal system long ago ceased to be that in everything but name:

> The term "system" implies an intelligently planned and orderly scheme. But no one planned our intergovernmental financial arrangements—and nobody would possibly have planned them the way they are. There is, at the least, room for doubt whether they should be called intelligent. It is certain that they are not very efficient.

[6] *Ibid.*, pp. 15–16.

.... To our foreign observer's eye the present overlapping of hundreds of taxes will seem to impose an unnecessary and excessive burden on the taxpayers. He may hold the parallelism, duplication or conflict among a myriad of expenditure programs, run simultaneously by numerous agencies which compete against each other in fierce campaigns of violent noncoordination, to be a state of confusion, disorder and disarray. And he is likely to regard the hundreds of intricate devices by which one level of government pretends to aid, but actually aims and manages to control, others as chaos.[7]

Freeman yearns for a neat arrangement for allocation of assignments and resources among governments. His antifederal bias is clear, but like numerous other specialists Freeman has chosen to ignore the value of applying criteria other than that of his own discipline in evaluating events.

State Tax Sources

At the turn of the twentieth century, the federal government obtained most of its revenue from customs and excises on liquor and tobacco, while state and local governments depended primarily on property taxes. Property taxes continued to be the major state tax source through the 1920's. Between 1902 and 1927, state property taxes quadrupled in yield, and this increase in collections coincided with substantial increases in local property taxes. There was a groundswell of complaints produced against property taxation, and in response to this criticism the base of state property taxes was gradually whittled away by tax-rate limitations, homestead exemptions, and the abolition of property taxes on intangibles. Gradually the states relinquished property taxation to local governments and sought revenues in other tax areas. This development in state taxation coincided with the efforts of the federal government, first under pressures of World War I and then under the stimulus of the Great Depression, to broaden its own revenue system. In the process, both federal and state governments had recourse to some of the same tax areas as discussed previously in this chapter.

The percentage distribution of state tax collections by source for selected years between 1902 and 1968 is given in Table 7-6. Table 7-7 designates the states increasing tax rates and enacting new taxes during the 1959–1968 period. Since 1959, the 50 states had enacted about 269 increases in the rates of their major taxes and imposed 26 new taxes, including 11 new retail sales taxes.

[7] Roger A. Freeman, "What Federal Fiscal System?" A paper presented at the Tax Institute of America Symposium in Washington on Nov. 29, 1967 and included in *The Congressional Record*, Dec. 15, 1967, p. H17210.

TABLE 7-6. Percentage Distribution of State Tax Collections by Source for Selected Years Between 1902 and 1968

YEAR	TOTAL, EXCLUDING EMPLOYMENT TAXES	INDIVIDUAL INCOME	CORPORATION INCOME	DEATH AND GIFTS	GENERAL SALES[a]	MOTOR FUEL	ALCOHOLIC BEVERAGES	TOBACCO	AMUSEMENT	PUBLIC UTILITY	PROPERTY	MOTOR VEHICLE AND OPERATORS LICENSES	ALL OTHER
1902	100.0	—	—	4.5	—	—	—	—	—	—	52.6	—	42.9
1913	100.0	—	—	8.6	—	—	.6	—	—	—	46.5	1.7	42.5
1922	100.0	4.5	6.1	7.0	—	1.4	—	—	—	—	36.7	16.1	28.3
1927	100.0	4.4	5.7	6.6	—	16.1	—	—	—	—	23.0	18.7	25.5
1932	100.0	3.9	4.2	7.8	.4	27.9	—	1.0	—	—	17.3	17.7	19.7
1936	100.0	5.9	4.3	4.5	13.9	26.2	4.8	1.7	—	—	8.7	13.8	16.3
1940	100.0	6.2	4.7	3.4	15.1	25.3	5.8	2.9	—	—	7.8	11.7	17.0
1944	100.0	7.8	10.9	2.8	17.7	16.8	6.6	3.9	1.4	3.1	6.0	9.7	13.5
1948	100.0	7.4	8.7	2.7	21.9	18.7	6.3	5.0	2.0	2.3	4.1	8.8	12.2
1952	100.0	9.3	8.5	2.1	22.6	19.0	4.5	4.5	1.6	2.3	3.7	9.4	12.4
1956	100.0	10.3	6.7	2.3	22.7	20.1	4.1	3.9	1.7	2.2	3.5	9.7	12.9
1960	100.0	12.2	6.5	2.3	23.9	18.5	3.6	5.1	1.6	2.0	3.4	8.7	12.1
1962	100.0	13.3	6.4	2.5	24.9	17.8	3.6	5.2	1.5	2.0	3.1	8.1	11.6
1966	100.0	14.6	6.9	2.8	26.8	15.8	3.4	5.2	—	1.9	2.8	7.6	12.2
1967	100.0	15.4	7.0	2.5	28.0	15.2	3.3	5.0	—	1.9	2.7	7.2	11.8

a Includes the collections from the business and occupation taxes levied by Washington and West Virginia.

SOURCES: Bureau of the Census, *Historical Summary of Governmental Finances in the United States*, 1957 Census of Governments, Vol. IV, No. 3; *Compendium of State Government Finances in 1962*, 1963; *Governmental Finances in 1965–66*, August, 1967; and *State Tax Collections in 1967*, Series GF—No. 16, 1967.

A large part of the expenditure increase of the past decade was financed by consumer and income taxes. The general sales tax has proved to be the most responsive state levy. Several factors have accounted for this, including the fact that there is no national sales tax to impinge in this area. In addition, the volume of retail sales rose 45 per cent in a decade. Increase in the sales tax receipts also was influenced significantly by the addition of 11 states that introduced the tax for the first time.

Among the selective excises, the gasoline and cigarette taxes have been most active. The favorable matching provision of the federal highway grants, particularly the 90:10 provisions of the Interstate Highway Program, exerted pressure on the states to find matching money, including increases in gasoline taxes.

Local Tax Problems

Financing local government in the years ahead poses one of the more pressing intergovernmental problems. The revenue requirements on many local governments have outpaced their resources because many functions of civil government that have expanded most rapidly are traditionally local. Despite substantial increases in the amount of state and federal aid (federal aid now constitutes about one-sixth of total state and local revenues), many cities, counties, and school districts have been able to finance their burgeoning activities only by recourse to taxes not well suited for local use.

The revenue requirements of local governments will continue to mount as the quality and quantity of their programs are brought into better conformity with the further growth and urbanization of the population, with the increasing exacting requirements of business for community services and facilities, and with rising living standards. Significant adjustments in state-local fiscal relations will be required to prevent the aggravation of disparities between local needs and local resources.

It is a state responsibility to realign fiscal resources at the local level. Realignment is a continuing process and embraces adjustments in the state-local division of functional responsibilities as well as intergovernmental financial aids and taxing powers.

The realignment of fiscal resources takes different forms and takes place at different times nationwide, reflecting interstate variations in institutional arrangements and preferences. It probably will be necessary in the future, as in the past, to relieve the local units of some functional responsibilities, and to increase state financial aid in states where the imbalance between needs and resources is of significant proportions and widespread among local jurisdictions. Increasing state financial aid is likely to be the more frequent

TABLE 7-7. States Increasing Tax Rates and Enacting New Taxes, Selected Taxes, 1959–1968

STATE	SALES	PERSONAL INCOME	CORPORATION INCOME	MOTOR FUEL	CIGAR-ETTES	ALCOHOLIC BEVERAGES
Alabama	x[a]	—	x	—	xxx	x
Alaska	—	x	—	xx	x	x
Arizona	x	xx	xx	xx	x	x
Arkansas	—	—	—	x	x	—
California	x	xx	xx	x	Nx	xx
Colorado	x	x	x	x	Nx	x
Connecticut	x	—	x	—	xxx	x
Delaware	—	x	—	xx	xx	x
Florida	—	—	—	—	x	xx
Georgia	—	—	x	—	x	x
Hawaii	x	x	x	—	x	x
Idaho	N[a]	xx	xx	x	xxx	xxx
Illinois	xxx	—	—	x	xxx	x
Indiana	N	N	N	—	xx	—
Iowa	x	xx	xx	x	xxxx	xx
Kansas	x	x	x	—	xx	xx
Kentucky	N	—	—	—	—	—
Louisiana	—	—	—	—	—	—
Maine	xx	—	—	—	xxxx	x
Maryland	—	x	x	x	x	—
Massachusetts	N	x	x	x	x	x
Michigan	x	N	N	x	x	x
Minnesota	N	xxx	xxx	xx	xxx	x
Mississippi	x	—	—	x	xx	N
Missouri	x	—	—	x	x	x
Montana	—	xxx	xx	x	—	x
Nebraska	N	N	N	x	xx	x

avenue of local fiscal relief. Pressures to increase locally raised revenues inevitably will persist, however, because intergovernmental fiscal institutions are slow to change, tax diversification has much appeal, the inclination to exercise home rule is strong, and the need for additional financial resources at the local level is immediate and pressing.

Growth is not peculiar to local governments, and increasing government costs have not been confined to a single level of government nor limited to the postwar years. Growth in the volume of governmental activity has been a general occurrence throughout most of the past thirty years. The behavior of governmental activity has not differed materially from that of other phases of national economic life. Production, employment, consumption, savings, and economic activity generally have attained levels anticipated by few as recently as ten years ago.

TABLE 7-7. (*Contined*)

STATE	SALES	PERSONAL INCOME	CORPORATION INCOME	MOTOR FUEL	CIGAR-ETTES	ALCOHOLIC BEVERAGES
Nevada	x	—	—	—	x	x
N. Hampshire	—	—	—	x	xx	—
New Jersey	N	<u>N</u>	x	x	xxx	x
New Mexico	x	x	x	xx	x	xx
New York	N	x	—	x	xx	x
N. Carolina	—	—	—	—	—	x
N. Dakota	xx	—	—	—	x	x
Ohio	x	—	—	x	xx	x
Oklahoma	—	—	—	—	xx	N
Oregon	—	—	—	x	N	—
Pennsylvania	xxx	—	x	x	xxx	x
Rhode Island	xxx	—	x	x	xx	—
S. Carolina	—	x	—	—	x	x
S. Dakota	x	—	—	—	xxx	x
Tennessee	—	—	xx	x	xx	xxx
Texas	Nx	—	—	—	xx	x
Utah	xx	x	x	—	x	—
Vermont	—	—	—	—	xxx	—
Virginia	N	—	—	x	N	x
Washington	xxx	—	—	xxx	xxx	x
W. Virginia	x	N	<u>N</u>	x	x	—
Wisconsin	N	xxxx	—	x	xxx	xxx
Wyoming	xx	—	—	x	xx	—
Dist. of Col.	x	x	—	x	x	xx

[a] Each x indicates a tax increase enactment and each N indicates a new tax. 1967 enactments are underlined.

SOURCE: Advisory Commission on Intergovernmental Relations, *State and Local Taxes, Significant Features 1968*, Washington, D.C., U.S. Govt. Printing Office, January 1968, p. 10.

National economic growth, of which rising local expenditure is but one manifestation (and to which it contributes), generates part of its own fiscal solution. It automatically increases the revenue yield under existing tax rates. However, a substantial revenue gap remains because local requirements are increasing faster than the economy, while the revenue yield of local taxes can keep pace with requirements only with the benefit of some tax-rate increases or intergovernmental transfers from state or federal levels.

In 1966 when local governments spent $53.6 billion on general governmental services, they raised $35.4 billion from their own general revenue sources.[8] They depended for one-third of their total financing requirements

[8] *Governmental Finances in 1965–1966, op. cit.,* pp. 20–21.

on intergovernmental aids. To state this fact is not to imply that it is cause for concern in itself, since this could be affirmed as cooperative federalism, or so-called creative federalism, in which the adjustment of functional responsibilities and intergovernmental aids is a continuing process. It serves to give financial balance to the family relationship between states and their political subdivisions and to the interdependence of the federal, state, and local governments. Creative federalism will be discussed further in Chapter 10, which is devoted primarily to federal financial support of public elementary and secondary education.

Although all governments—federal, state, and local—have shared and will continue to share in expenditure increases, the financing of these increases poses particularly difficult problems for local governments. They have only such taxing powers as their respective state constitutions and legislatures grant them. For example, local governments do not commonly have the power to levy nonproperty taxes with the exception of home-rule powers granted in charter provisions or by general municipal power to levy license taxes.

A number of other basic constraints on local tax decision-making include the facts that, first, the mobility of persons and business makes it impractical for one locality to impose tax burdens that differ significantly from those found in neighboring communities; and second, size and considerations of administrative efficiency and cost preclude local use of most tax sources.

The satisfactory resolution of the revenue needs of local governments and their ability to function in a manner compatible with state and national interests will involve more than tax mechanics. It will depend on progress in many directions, including the reorganization of local governmental units themselves into structures more appropriate for present and prospective requirements. Another area requiring attention is the intergovernmental division of functional responsibilities and intergovernmental financial aid.

Local Revenue Sources

Local governments finance their activities from locally raised revenues, state and federal aid, and borrowing. Generally, they may not engage in deficit financing of operation and maintenance costs and may borrow only for capital outlay purposes. Some resort to short-term borrowing in anticipation of tax collections.

Approximately 33 per cent of the current revenue of local governments in FY 1967 was state and federal aid, chiefly the former. State aid includes, of course, some funds that originated in federal assistance to states.

TABLE 7-8. Percentage Distribution of Local Government General Revenue by Source for Selected Years, 1927–1966

FISCAL YEAR	INTERGOVERNMENTAL REVENUE (PERCENTAGE)		LOCAL SOURCES (PERCENTAGE)			TOTAL GENERAL REVENUE (PERCENTAGE)
	FROM FEDERAL GOVERNMENT	FROM STATE GOVERNMENT	PROPERTY TAXES	OTHER TAXES	OTHER GENERAL REVENUE	
1927	0.2	10.1	73.9	2.0	13.9	100.0
1932	0.2	14.1	73.1	2.0	10.6	100.0
1936	3.7	22.9	62.6	3.5	7.3	100.0
1940	4.0	23.8	60.1	4.7	7.3	100.0
1944	0.4	25.1	59.4	4.7	10.4	100.0
1948	1.9	28.9	51.4	6.6	11.2	100.0
1952	1.4	29.8	48.9	7.0	13.0	100.0
1956	1.3	28.5	48.8	7.4	14.0	100.0
1960	1.8	28.5	48.1	6.9	14.7	100.0
1962	2.0	28.5	48.0	6.6	14.9	100.0
1966	2.6	30.8	44.9	6.6	15.1	100.0

SOURCES: U.S. Bureau of the Census, *Historical Summary of Governmental Finances in the United States*, 1957 Census of Governments, Vol. IV, No. 3; and *Governmental Finances* (annually since 1958).

Local government general revenue by percentage of source for selected years from 1927 to 1966 is given in Table 7-8.

In FY 1966, local governments raised about 67 per cent of their general revenue from local sources divided between taxes and other sources approximately in the ratio of 3.5 to 1. The latter include user charges, sale of commodities, service and real estate, special assessments for public improvements, and interest earnings.

Taxation at the local level in most parts of the country has continued to be largely synonymous with property taxation. With few exceptions, it has been the most important single producer in local jurisdictions. Although the property tax has been the object of severe criticism for decades, it has been putting on a remarkable performance in terms of productivity. Criticism since the depression years has been based on inequities as well as economic grounds. However, among all local taxes the property tax accounted for 97 per cent during the 1920's and until 1934, after which it declined gradually to 88 per cent, where it has remained for nearly two decades. In 1966, property taxes produced $24.3 billion for local governments, more than twice the amount collected in 1956. These receipts represented 87 per cent of local tax collections in 1966.

This comparatively strong performance of the property tax has been in part a product of rapid urbanization—that is, growth in new construction and rising land values—and in part a result of substantial increases in rates and higher assessments.

Under pressure for new revenues, localities have in recent years attempted to broaden and strengthen their tax bases through the imposition of sales taxes—usually on a sharing basis with their state government—and through the addition of new taxes on earnings. Although these taxes have increased substantially in percentage terms over the decade, they were still relatively small revenue producers in 1966—$2 billion for sales taxes and $0.6 billion for income taxes. Other local taxes—permits, licenses, special assessments, fines, etc.—have increased very little since 1956.

Seventeen states permit local general sales taxes and about 3,000 localities now levy general sales taxes with the largest numbers (about 1,300) in Illinois. California is second with over 400 local sales taxes, and Alabama, Mississippi, Utah, and Virginia follow with well over 100 each.

There is now widespread use of local income taxes in five states (Kentucky, Maryland, Michigan, Ohio, and Pennsylvania). Over 3,000 local jurisdictions levy income or payroll taxes, the great majority of them in Pennsylvania.

The pressure for nonproperty tax revenues has been particularly strong in states where the property tax base is shared by more than two overlapping jurisdictions. In these cases the pressure has come in the jurisdictions with greater tax autonomy, mainly the cities. The single-purpose jurisdictions, notably school districts, typically rely almost wholly on the property tax, and this has obliged cities serving the same taxpayers to look to other taxes and to nontax revenue sources.

There are various motivations for the reluctance to leave the entire burden of the increasing local tax revenue requirements to the property tax. The appeal of tax diversification for its own sake is one of them. Another is the tendency to judge tax rates in terms of the levels of earlier years and to confuse the contributions to the increases in property tax bills made by changes in tax rates with that of higher property values reflected in higher assessed valuations. The consideration of tax equity also plays a part, in that the base of the property tax consists largely of only one form of wealth—real property. It burdens property owners regardless of their income status, including retired homeowners with reduced incomes, and leaves untouched those with large amounts of wealth in other forms.

Political resistance to property tax increases stems also from concern with its effect on the location of businesses. Business property frequently accounts for a third or even more of the real property tax base, and repeated expression of fear that high property taxes will deter new business has a restraining influence on local governing bodies.

Citizens' committees, chambers of commerce, promotional groups, and scholars have examined the relationship between state and local taxes and industrial location and growth. Some have argued that state and local taxes are such a minor item of business costs that they cannot significantly influence business decisions, and others have retorted that business threats to locate or move elsewhere were merely ill-advised attempts to win special concessions.

In the *Ninth Annual Report* of the Advisory Commission on Intergovern-mental Relations, dated January 31, 1968, pursuant to Public Law 86-380, which requires the submission of a report on or before January 31 of each year, the Commission stated (page 18) in its study of state-local taxation and industrial location that:

1. The relative importance of the tax differential factor in industrial location decisions appears to increase as the location process narrows down to a particular jurisdiction within a general region.

2. Differences in tax levels among widely separated states exert little influence on plant locations. As between regions, non-tax factors such as access to markets, and labor, and supply costs are decisive.

3. Only among local governments within a state, and especially within a met-ropolitan area, do "low" tax loads exert some discernible pull on plant location.

4. Because states generally have been careful not to get "too far out of line" with their neighbors, tax differentials among states within the same region usually appear too small to have a strong plant location influence.

Property tax criticisms have centered on the tax's sins against the cardinal rules of uniformity, of equality, and universality of taxation. Critics have complained that the tax puts a premium on dishonesty and debauches the public conscience when it is applied to intangibles as well as tangibles.

A related factor is public dissatisfaction with the administrative short-coming of the tax. Recent widespread efforts to improve tax assessment procedures—some locally, some prescribed by state legislatures—have not yet enhanced the national reputation of the tax.

Property Taxes—Their Administration and Need for Reform

Property taxes were applied to 74,832,000 pieces of property in the United States and a locally taxable assessed valuation of $491.8 billion in 1966, provided seven-eights of all locally raised revenue, and were second only to personal and corporation income taxes in the hierarchy of productive single

TABLE 7-9. Estimated Revenue and Nonrevenue Receipts for Public Elementary and Secondary Schools, 1966–67

| Region and State | Revenue Receipts by Source (in Thousands) | | | | Percentage of Revenue Receipts by Source[a] | | | Nonrevenue Receipts (in Thousands) | Total Receipts (Cols. 5 and 9) (in Thousands) |
| | Federal[b] | State | Local and Other[c] | Total | Federal[b] | State | Local and Other[c] | | |
1	2	3	4	5	6	7	8	9	10
50 states and D.C.	$2,148,908	$10,689,559	$13,983,019	$26,821,486	8.0%	39.9%	52.1%	$3,373,422	$30,194,908
New England	100,762	355,104	847,779	1,303,645	7.7	27.2	65.0	102,551	1,406,196
Connecticut	21,000	142,000	250,000	413,000	5.1	34.4	60.5	40,000	453,000
Maine	12,000	33,700	67,000	112,700	10.6	29.9	59.4	14,000	126,700
Massachusetts*	53,000	130,000	378,000	561,000	9.4	23.2	67.4	N.A.	561,000
New Hampshire	4,500	7,619[d]	65,279	77,398[d]	5.8	9.8[d]	84.3	24,000	101,398[d]
Rhode Island	7,000	28,289	52,500	87,789	8.0	32.2	59.8	18,000	105,789
Vermont	3,262	13,496	35,000	51,758	6.3	26.1	67.6	6,551	58,309
Mideast	410,434	2,659,555	3,403,407	6,473,396	6.3	41.1	52.6	717,700	7,191,096
Delaware	4,500	71,000	17,000	92,500	4.9	76.8	18.4	5,000	97,500
Maryland	39,934	170,631	324,407	534,972	7.5	31.9	60.6	106,000	640,972
New Jersey	60,000	308,000	677,000	1,045,000	5.7	29.5	64.8	130,000	1,175,000
New York	188,000	1,453,000	1,539,000	3,180,000	5.9	45.7	48.4	473,000	3,655,000
Pennsylvania	91,000	656,924	750,000	1,497,924	6.1	43.9	50.1	1,700	1,499,624
District of Columbia	27,000	—	96,000	123,000	22.0	—	78.0	—	123,000
Southeast	579,477	2,494,097	1,591,899	4,665,473	12.4	53.5	34.1	443,695	5,109,168
Alabama*	46,000	225,000	79,000[e]	350,000	13.1	64.3	22.6	25,000	375,000
Arkansas	35,469	86,833	70,730	193,032	18.4	45.0	36.6	30,000	223,032
Florida	40,858[f]	328,965	338,318	708,141	5.8	46.5	47.8	16,695	724,836
Georgia	68,700	283,868	129,851	482,419	14.2	58.8	26.9	43,000	525,419
Kentucky	42,000	158,000	102,000	302,000	13.9	52.3	33.8	35,000	337,000
Louisiana	49,073	306,028	125,000	480,101	10.2	63.7	26.0	60,000	340,101
Mississippi	43,000	111,000	66,000	220,000	19.5	50.5	30.0	16,000	236,000
North Carolina	76,377	333,903	113,000	523,280	14.6	63.8	21.6	70,000[g]	593,280
South Carolina	41,000	152,000	66,000	259,000	15.8	58.7	25.5	11,000	270,000

Tennessee	45,000	188,500 [h]	142,000 [l]	375,500	12.0	50.2	37.8	38,000	413,500
Virginia	65,000 [j]	225,000	290,000	580,000	11.2	38.8	50.0	90,000	670,000
West Virginia	27,000	95,000	70,000	192,000	14.1	49.5	36.5	9,000	201,000
Great Lakes	323,337	1,674,043	3,307,206	5,304,586	6.1	31.6	62.3	891,400	6,195,986
Illinois	90,000	332,585	1,075,000 [k]	1,497,585	6.0	22.2	71.8	381,400	1,878,985
Indiana	42,669	276,587	394,206	713,462	6.0	38.8	55.3	60,000	773,462
Michigan	70,000	607,000	595,000	1,272,000	5.5	47.7	46.8	220,000	1,492,000
Ohio	88,000	318,000	858,000	1,264,000	7.0	25.2	67.9	150,000	1,414,000
Wisconsin	32,668	139,871	385,000	557,539	5.9	25.1	69.1	80,000	637,539
Plains	172,713	584,163	1,349,300	2,106,176	8.2	27.7	64.1	237,000	2,343,176
Iowa	19,000	55,000	285,000	359,000	5.3	15.3	79.4	35,000	394,000
Kansas	26,000	99,298	196,000	321,298	8.1	30.9	61.0	20,000	341,298
Minnesota	35,000 [l]	220,000	320,000	575,000	6.1	38.3	55.7	100,000	675,000
Missouri	54,313	166,765	300,000	521,078	10.4	32.0	57.6	45,000	566,078
Nebraska	16,500	8,600	134,800	159,900	10.3	5.4	84.3	19,500	179,400
North Dakota	7,500	20,500	49,500	77,500	9.7	26.5	63.9	7,500	85,000
South Dakota	14,400	14,000	64,000	92,400	15.6	15.2	69.3	10,000	102,400
Southwest	211,000	907,750	844,000	1,962,750	10.8	46.2	43.0	241,500	2,204,250
Arizona	25,000	91,000	107,000	223,000	11.2	40.8	48.0	47,000 [m]	270,000
New Mexico	29,000	114,000 [n]	40,000	183,000	15.8	62.3	21.9	9,500	192,500
Oklahoma	38,000	73,750	170,000	281,750	13.5	26.2	60.3	25,000	306,750
Texas [o]	119,000	629,000	527,000	1,275,000	9.3	49.3	41.3	160,000	1,435,000
Rocky Mountain	59,669	251,141	395,431	706,241	8.4	35.6	56.0	76,576	782,817
Colorado	30,000	77,500	187,500	295,000	10.2	26.3	63.6	43,000	338,000
Idaho	7,000	31,641	37,200	75,841	9.2	41.7	49.0	6,800	82,641
Montana [p]	9,400	34,000	75,000	118,400	7.9	28.7	63.3	12,600	131,000
Utah	11,269 [q]	86,000	65,731	163,000	6.9	52.8	40.3	9,176	172,176
Wyoming	2,000	22,000	30,000	54,000	3.7	40.7	55.6	5,000	59,000
Far West	261,516	1,655,100	2,199,500	4,116,116	6.4	40.2	53.4	635,000	4,751,116
California	200,000	1,260,000	1,800,000	3,260,000	6.1	38.7	55.2	550,000	3,810,000
Nevada	7,516	34,100	21,500	63,116	11.9	54.0	34.1	22,000	85,116
Oregon	23,000	84,000	204,000	311,000	7.4	27.0	65.6	27,000	338,000
Washington	31,000	277,000	174,000	482,000	6.4	57.5	36.1	36,000	518,000

TABLE 7-9. (Continued)

REGION AND STATE	REVENUE RECEIPTS BY SOURCE (IN THOUSANDS)				PERCENTAGE OF REVENUE RECEIPTS BY SOURCE[a]			NONREVENUE RECEIPTS (IN THOUSANDS)	TOTAL RECEIPTS (COLS. 5 and 9) (IN THOUSANDS)
	FEDERAL[b]	STATE	LOCAL AND OTHER[c]	TOTAL	FEDERAL[b]	STATE	LOCAL AND OTHER[c]		
1	2	3	4	5	6	7	8	9	10
Alaska	16,000	33,606	13,497	63,103	25.4	53.3	21.4	20,000	83,103
Hawaii	14,000	75,000	31,000	120,000	11.7	62.5	25.8	8,000	128,000

* Estimated by NEA Research Division.

N.A. = Not available.

[a] Percentages may not add up to 100.0% because of rounding.

[b] Includes all federal grant programs to state and local systems including aid to federally impacted areas, school lunch and milk, National Defense Education Act, Manpower Development and Training Act, vocational education, Economic Opportunity Act, Elementary and Secondary Education Act, etc. Estimates of federal revenues under Title I of ESEA have generally been included on the basis of expected expenditures for the 1966–1967 school year.

[c] Includes revenues from local and intermediate sources, gifts, and tuition and fees from patrons.

[d] Excludes state's share of teacher retirement and social security.

[e] Includes funds not handled by custodian of school funds.

[f] Federal revenues are probably underestimated because of state law which prohibits a county from budgeting receipts or expenditures for federal programs until the projects are actually approved and funds committed.

[g] Includes approximately $40,000,000 from sale of state bonds for school construction.

[h] Includes $169,100,000 in state revenue to local school systems, $15,000,000 for teacher retirement, and $4,400,000 for operation of state department of education.

[i] Includes local funds for debt retirement.

[j] ESEA revenues reported on a "cash receipts" basis.

[k] Excludes receipts from students, etc., for athletics, book rentals, and other student and community services.

[l] Includes $5,500,000 from federal funds paid to districts too late to be included in 1965–66 receipts.

[m] Includes proceeds from county bond issues.

[n] Includes revenues for operation of the Public School Finance Division which is not a part of the state department of education.

[o] Excludes revenues for kindergartens; also excludes revenues for public junior colleges which are no longer under local school systems.

[p] NEA Research Division estimates confirmed by the Montana Education Association.

[q] Adjusted to include estimated deficit in School Lunch Program.

SOURCE: *Estimates of School Statistics, 1966–67*, Research Report 1966–R20, Washington, D.C., National Education Association, 1966, Table 10, p. 32.

TABLE 7-10. State and Local Government Receipts, Selected Years, 1929–1966

	BILLIONS OF DOLLARS				PERCENTAGE OF DISTRIBUTION			
	1929	1948	1956	1966	1929	1948	1956	1966
State and local government receipts	7.8	18.4	36.4	87.9	100.0	100.0	100.0	100.0
Total tax revenues	6.4	13.7	27.0	58.7	82.4	74.8	74.1	66.8
Income taxes	.1	.6	1.6	5.4	1.8	3.1	4.3	6.2
Corporate profits tax accruals	.1	.7	1.0	2.3	1.9	3.7	2.9	2.6
Property taxes	4.7	6.1	11.8	25.1	60.1	33.4	32.3	28.6
General sales taxes[b]	(c)	2.0	4.1	10.4	(c)	10.8	11.3	11.9
Gasoline taxes	.4	1.3	2.8	4.7	5.3	7.2	7.7	5.4
Liquor taxes	(c)	.4	.6	1.0	(c)	2.4	1.6	1.1
Tobacco taxes	(c)	.4	.5	1.6	(c)	2.0	1.5	1.8
Death and gift taxes	.2	.2	.3	.8	2.1	1.0	.9	.9
Motor vehicle licenses	.3	.6	1.3	2.2	4.4	3.4	3.6	2.5
Other taxes	.5	1.4	2.9	5.1	6.9	7.8	8.1	5.8
Receipts other than taxes	1.4	4.6	9.4	29.2	17.6	25.2	25.9	33.2
Nontaxes	.9	1.2	2.4	6.2	11.6	6.3	6.6	7.1
Contributions for social insurance	.1	.7	2.0	4.9	1.5	3.9	5.5	5.6
Federal grants-in-aid	.1	2.0	3.3	14.8	1.5	10.8	9.2	16.9
Surplus of government enterprises	.2	.8	1.7	3.3	3.0	4.3	4.6	3.7
State government receipts[d]	2.4	9.8	18.8	48.0	100.0	100.0	100.0	100.0
Taxes	1.9	7.1	14.1	30.9	82.4	73.2	74.7	64.4
Receipts other than taxes	.4	2.6	4.8	17.1	17.6	26.8	25.3	35.6
Nontaxes	.2	.4	.7	2.3	9.0	3.6	3.8	4.9
Contributions for social insurance	(a)	.5	1.3	3.4	1.5	4.8	6.8	7.2
Federal grants-in-aid	.1	1.5	2.1	9.8	4.3	15.3	11.2	20.5
Local payments	.1	.1	.3	.5	2.0	1.0	1.4	1.1
Surplus of government enterprises	(a)	.2	.4	.9	.7	2.0	2.1	1.9
Local government receipts[d]	5.9	11.6	23.5	55.5	100.0	100.0	100.0	100.0
Taxes	4.5	6.6	12.9	27.8	76.2	56.6	54.9	50.1
Receipts other than taxes	1.4	5.0	10.6	27.7	23.8	43.4	45.1	49.9
Nontaxes	.7	.8	1.7	3.9	11.7	6.9	7.1	7.0
Contributions for social insurance	.1	.2	.7	1.4	1.4	2.0	3.2	2.6
Federal grants-in-aid	(a)	.5	1.2	5.0	.3	4.3	5.2	9.0
State payments	.4	2.9	5.7	15.0	6.8	25.1	24.1	27.1
Surplus of government enterprises	.2	.6	1.3	2.4	3.7	5.1	5.5	4.3

[a] Less than 0.05 billion dollars.

[b] Includes local sales taxes.

[c] Small amount included in other taxes.

[d] Total state receipts include local payments to states, and total local receipts include state payments to localities; neither type of intergovernmental payment is included above in total combined state and local receipts.

NOTE: Detail may not add up to total because of rounding.

SOURCE: Office of Business Economics, U.S. Department of Commerce.

TABLE 7-11. Relation of Selected Items of State and Local Government Finances to Personal Income, 1965–1966

STATE	GENERAL REVENUE PER $1,000 OF PERSONAL INCOME						GENERAL EXPENDITURE PER $1,000 OF PERSONAL INCOME					
	TOTAL	FROM FEDERAL GOVERNMENT	ALL STATE AND LOCAL GENERAL REVENUE SOURCES	TAXES TOTAL	TAXES PROPERTY ONLY	CHARGES AND MISCELLANEOUS GENERAL REVENUE	ALL GENERAL EXPENDITURE	EDUCATION TOTAL	EDUCATION LOCAL SCHOOLS ONLY	HIGHWAYS	PUBLIC WELFARE	HEALTH AND HOSPITALS
United States average	156.04	24.65	131.38	106.63	46.36	24.75	155.67	62.55	47.15	23.99	12.69	11.10
Median state	165.04	30.22	132.43	105.32	45.20	26.40	167.88	67.69	50.02	32.27	11.76	9.93
Alabama	179.34	49.56	129.77	95.97	17.42	33.80	180.38	71.02	47.27	35.51	19.26	12.16
Alaska	268.69	119.25	149.44	91.68	21.94	57.76	294.90	88.21	54.01	87.15	8.65	9.04
Arizona	200.78	40.76	160.01	128.38	59.71	31.63	201.63	91.11	62.76	34.97	10.24	7.44
Arkansas	175.75	48.27	127.47	102.25	26.70	25.22	176.28	67.01	50.19	34.95	19.67	10.65
California	179.78	29.50	150.27	124.71	62.58	25.55	184.06	69.13	53.09	21.72	18.82	11.09
Colorado	194.63	37.75	156.88	125.26	58.47	31.62	192.37	87.72	61.20	27.60	19.66	11.80
Connecticut	126.77	16.00	110.77	94.29	48.21	16.47	127.75	45.06	39.49	22.15	10.20	7.63
Delaware	155.59	23.15	132.43	96.66	19.41	35.76	173.62	68.46	49.57	41.94	7.44	8.55
District of Columbia	137.52	36.95	100.57	84.41	29.64	16.15	140.62	32.61	31.96	14.10	11.80	21.83
Florida	162.37	22.95	139.42	106.16	41.56	33.26	160.53	61.76	48.54	24.37	9.28	14.87
Georgia	160.42	32.95	127.47	96.89	28.94	30.57	156.73	62.26	48.92	24.47	13.38	17.34
Hawaii	202.45	41.12	161.33	129.21	27.98	32.12	199.52	66.35	46.22	19.93	9.82	14.49
Idaho	186.36	36.90	149.46	119.98	47.42	29.48	176.49	67.82	50.48	42.69	12.01	10.67
Illinois	123.19	15.25	107.94	90.97	46.15	16.96	117.20	49.84	38.55	14.64	9.91	9.05
Indiana	141.16	16.53	124.62	100.55	49.32	24.07	135.62	69.06	50.49	20.68	5.57	9.35
Iowa	168.24	23.99	144.24	117.83	60.60	26.40	161.32	73.92	54.15	35.64	12.02	10.00
Kansas	165.04	24.65	140.39	114.89	56.19	25.50	152.75	65.07	45.78	31.67	10.83	9.89
Kentucky	161.65	39.05	122.59	94.76	25.38	27.83	167.51	63.69	46.14	34.54	16.60	10.41

State												
Louisiana	209.29	45.38	163.91	120.07	25.87	43.84	203.61	72.83	55.00	36.22	28.32	12.02
Maine	160.81	31.24	129.57	110.83	54.53	18.73	151.50	52.97	40.78	37.14	14.25	7.74
Maryland	136.22	17.00	119.21	98.03	41.23	21.17	141.12	58.87	47.88	18.64	7.17	12.49
Massachusetts	146.42	19.97	126.45	110.34	62.42	16.10	141.57	43.90	36.94	17.36	16.21	12.67
Michigan	148.79	18.85	129.94	103.68	45.20	26.26	149.60	69.05	47.39	17.66	8.59	12.71
Minnesota	187.71	30.22	157.49	124.94	62.24	32.54	179.28	74.48	55.25	32.86	15.53	12.47
Mississippi	201.28	47.79	153.48	115.46	31.55	38.02	204.42	73.86	52.32	45.03	19.82	17.40
Missouri	141.01	28.35	112.65	92.39	36.38	20.26	135.31	54.98	42.45	23.43	14.03	9.93
Montana	202.77	50.04	152.72	118.73	66.54	33.98	201.47	78.02	56.87	59.64	11.76	7.99
Nebraska	145.61	23.63	121.97	94.08	67.41	27.89	148.33	62.79	46.01	32.27	9.34	8.91
Nevada	181.63	40.40	141.23	108.59	43.42	32.63	208.95	67.28	55.35	45.81	6.31	15.75
New Hampshire	137.03	22.78	114.24	95.25	60.31	18.99	149.82	54.10	41.93	36.93	11.07	8.45
New Jersey	120.28	12.53	107.75	90.46	58.45	17.29	118.25	46.30	41.07	15.03	6.69	7.81
New Mexico	248.25	73.57	174.69	120.10	27.70	54.59	234.51	109.09	74.39	49.74	16.49	12.26
New York	162.53	14.02	148.51	126.11	51.32	22.39	163.08	58.40	48.90	15.65	14.21	16.68
North Carolina	154.61	27.31	127.30	102.92	26.81	24.37	149.32	68.08	50.02	22.48	11.61	11.24
North Dakota	208.57	37.88	170.68	113.43	56.69	57.25	208.41	83.53	59.42	45.60	14.37	6.91
Ohio	127.19	18.61	108.57	86.38	44.72	22.18	130.10	55.70	43.69	23.33	9.52	7.65
Oklahoma	185.05	43.50	141.54	105.32	34.09	36.21	184.79	73.74	51.82	30.87	30.84	10.68
Oregon	183.03	40.88	142.14	109.28	51.77	32.85	183.25	81.58	57.89	34.24	11.44	8.59
Pennsylvania	131.46	18.20	113.26	94.95	31.95	18.31	131.29	55.02	45.35	19.61	10.44	7.63
Rhode Island	143.03	26.06	116.96	103.68	45.64	13.27	153.77	54.62	43.67	23.40	17.31	8.99
South Carolina	153.95	28.87	125.07	99.33	21.74	25.73	147.08	64.82	53.04	25.68	8.79	12.58
South Dakota	197.27	42.70	154.56	123.82	68.92	30.73	195.87	84.58	62.27	57.54	12.98	5.06
Tennessee	158.41	36.17	122.23	96.80	28.63	25.42	167.88	60.92	43.97	37.40	11.54	14.58
Texas	150.56	25.29	125.26	95.32	43.41	29.93	148.84	65.32	51.11	27.53	10.60	8.67
Utah	201.05	49.47	151.58	121.29	50.41	30.29	213.57	110.08	75.20	41.23	12.85	8.11
Vermont	204.46	54.78	149.68	128.75	50.27	20.93	201.57	72.18	45.44	58.61	15.97	9.65
Virginia	139.32	26.73	112.58	89.04	31.82	23.54	146.37	61.76	50.34	33.68	5.82	8.80
Washington	181.05	29.93	151.11	115.49	35.97	35.62	168.65	71.53	49.32	28.14	13.04	7.46
West Virginia	174.79	47.33	127.45	101.90	26.64	25.54	174.32	67.69	51.39	45.58	17.63	8.86
Wisconsin	166.97	17.34	149.62	126.38	56.39	23.24	172.39	77.14	53.43	28.66	11.08	10.98
Wyoming	262.32	88.51	173.81	124.60	66.20	49.20	271.80	107.35	67.19	89.19	10.10	16.70

173

NOTE: Because of rounding, detail may not add up to totals. These data are estimates subject to sampling variation.
SOURCE: *Governmental Finances in 1965–66*, Series GF-No. 13, Washington, D.C., U.S. Govt. Printing Office, 1967, p. 50.

sources of tax revenues in the country.[9] The property tax is a tax generally conditioned on ownership of property, regardless of any liens against it, and measured by its value. In some cases it is levied on leaseholds. In four states (Delaware, Hawaii, New York, and Pennsylvania) it is a real estate tax on land and improvements. In the other 46 states and the District of Columbia, the property tax base, although consisting mainly of real estate, includes varying mixes of tangible and intangible property, such as household goods livestock, motor vehicles, stock-in-trade, machinery and fixtures, money and credit, and stocks and bonds.

The property tax is far from a comprehensive tax on property because in many states partial exemptions ($14.9 billion in the United States in 1966) are allowed such as for homesteads, veterans, senior citizens, and fallout shelters. In addition, billions of dollars worth of church, educational, and governmental real estate are exempted from property taxation, and the value of most of these exemptions are unrecorded. Untold billions of dollars worth of tangible and intangible personal property likewise are not entered in the assessment records.

The exemption of household goods, entirely or partially, is allowed in most states, and intangibles—money, stocks and bonds, accounts receivable, etc.— are exempt from general property taxes in most states. Even in states such as Illinois, where the property tax is legally intended as a comprehensive tax on substantially all private wealth, vast amounts of personal property escape ad valorem taxation because of the difficulty in locating personal property, the complexity of appraising some kinds of personalty, and the tendency to allow the taxpayer to assess his own property.

Among the classes of local government, school systems rely most heavily upon property taxes, obtaining almost all their tax revenue and over half of their total revenue from that source in 1967. Table 7-9 includes school revenue and nonrevenue receipts by source and by state as estimated for 1966–1967. Local receipts, primarily from local property taxes, accounted for nearly $14 billion of a total $26.8 billion in revenue receipts.

The property tax is the most productive single source of revenue in the combined state and local tax structure. Of the $58.7 billion collected by state and local governments in the form of tax revenue in 1966, property taxes accounted for 28.6 per cent or $25.1 billion. The general sales tax followed in second place, accounting for 11.9 per cent and $10.4 billion.[10]

[9] Bureau of the Census, *Census of Governments, 1967—Assessed Valuation for General Property Taxation*, Preliminary Report, Washington, D.C., U.S. Govt. Printing Office, Feb., 1968, p. 1.

[10] *Survey of Current Business*, Washington, D.C., Office of Business Economics, U.S. Department of Commerce, October, 1967, Table 5, p. 26.

Individual states and their local governments vary considerably in their reliance on property taxation, ranging in FY 1966, for example, from 14.6 per cent of all general revenue from their own sources in Delaware to 55.2 per cent in Nebraska.[11] State variations in the amount of property taxes as a proportion of total revenue collected per $1,000 of personal income are given in Table 7-11.

There have been periodic outcries throughout the history of the property tax that property bears too large a share of the tax burden and that tax rates have reached their saturation point. These cries have had their effect, usually during depression periods, and are reflected in most states in the form of constitutional or statutory property tax rate limitations. These limitations and their effects on local governments were examined in some detail by the Advisory Commission on Intergovernmental Relations. The Commission found that although property tax restrictions might have had some initial impact in limiting tax rates, local governments have in the long run contrived to expand their property tax revenue in spite of the limitations. On balance, the limitations have had damaging effects on the structure and fiscal operation of local governments that far outweigh any presumed benefits from them.[12]

Property tax restrictions have stimulated the creation of special districts for the primary purpose of gaining additional taxing authority and thus have aggravated the proliferation of local governments. They have necessitated recourse to short-term financing to cover operating deficits, which ultimately had to be funded. They have encouraged long-term borrowing for activities that might have better been financed out of current revenue. They have necessitated extensive special legislation in some states to relieve individual jurisdictions, thereby in effect shifting the local governing bodies' appropriating function to state legislatures. They have impaired the ability of local officials to budget effectively where specific limitations apply to particular governmental functions. They have imposed onerous burdens on administrative agencies and added to the already overcrowded dockets of the courts. Where property tax limitations are especially rigid and communities have reached their tax limit, assessors are often subjected to conflicting pressures from governing bodies seeking additional property tax revenue and from taxpayers who wish to prevent property taxes from rising. They are thus forced into policy-making positions with control over the level of local governmental spending.

---

[11] Computed from data in *Governmental Finances in 1965–66, op. cit.*, pp. 31–33.

[12] Advisory Commission on Intergovernmental Relations, *State Constitutional and Statutory Restrictions on Local Taxing Powers*, Washington, D.C., U.S. Govt. Printing Office, Oct. 1962.

Administration of the property tax is governed by the state constitutional and statutory provisions, which usually spell out in considerable detail the rules under which property taxation operates. Although the states have virtually relinquished the property tax as a state revenue source, they have considerable influence on its administration. The states decide how the assessment and collection machinery is organized, including the divisions of responsibility between state and local officials.

State action can limit or narrow the property tax base, and every state legislative session deals with many bills aimed at reducing property taxes. These efforts generally take the form of allowing or increasing exemptions, such as those for homesteads, veterans, and, of late, senior citizens. Almost invariably these exemptions—the property tax "giveaway system," as it has been called—are imposed upon local governments by state law (particularly in Florida, Georgia, Louisiana, Mississippi, and Oklahoma) without revenue being provided to them to replace the tax loss. Property taxpayers not eligible for such exemptions then find their rates increased. As has been mentioned, even the amount of revenue local governments can raise from property taxation is restricted by state constitutional and statutory provisions, usually in the form of rate limits.

Property tax administration involves three basic operations: (1) assessment, or setting the taxable property values; (2) determination of the amount of revenue to be raised from the property tax, or setting the levy; and (3) collection of the tax.

Assessed values are determined usually by both state and local government officials. In most states, the taxable value of operating railroads and other utility property is set by a state agency. As a rule, the state agency arrives at a unit value on the entire operating property of a public utility company and then distributes the valuation in some proportional basis among the taxing units in which its properties are located. In some states, the state agency appraises other kinds of business property, such as mines, liquor, business inventories, and the like. In Oregon, for example, timber is appraised on behalf of the local assessors by the state tax agency.

Local assessors determine the assessed value of all other taxable real and personal property under their jurisdiction. Local assessment organization differs considerably from state to state, varying from that in 28 states in which the county is the primary assessing unit to that in 12 states with hundreds of city, village, and township assessors. Hawaii is the only state that provides for completely centralized administration of the property by a state agency.

In the 28 states with primarily county assessment, there is considerable overlapping of the assessment function. Ten permit cities to do their own assessing, even though the county also determines the taxable value of the property, and assessors may be part-time elected officials covering very small jurisdictions, or they may be full-time, well-paid appointed officials. The local assessor usually has a great deal of discretion as to the value he can set on an individual piece of property, although a taxpayer who is dissatisfied with his assessment can appeal to an administrative body (usually a local board of equalization) and finally to the courts.

The amount of the individual's property tax bill is determined by the legislative body of the jurisdiction or jurisdictions in which his property is located. Each of the local governments—county, city, school system, etc.—decides how much it will need to provide its services. Having determined how much money will be needed, the chief executive with his finance officer adds up the amount of money available from all sources except the property tax—state and federal revenue sharing, local nonproperty taxes, service charges, etc. The amount that remains to be financed from the property tax is then divided by the total assessed valuation to arrive at the tentative rate, usually expressed as a number of mills, or dollars per hundred dollars of assessed valuation. The determination of the actual tax rate and, therefore, the level of expenditures is a political decision vested in the local governing board. Because almost all states have constitutional or statutory tax-rate limitations, often in terms of particular governmental purposes, setting the tax rate is complicated further. In many states, state-imposed limitations hamstring local officials in budgeting their funds.

When the tax rate (or levy) is finally set, the assessment roll containing the assessed valuation of each piece of taxable property in the jurisdiction is turned over to the tax collector. The collector (or some other official) multiplies the assessed valuation by the rate (extends the tax) to arrive at the amount of tax liability that attaches to each parcel of property.

In 20 states, property tax collection is exclusively a county function, and the county collector bills the taxes for all jurisdictions in the county—municipalities, school systems, and special districts, as well as the county.[13] Another eight states provide for centralized county collection but allow cities to do their own collecting with the option of contracting with the county for collection services.[14] In the New England states and Michigan, New Jersey, New York, Pennsylvania, and Wisconsin, the property taxes are collected by

[13] The 20 states are Arizona, Arkansas, Colorado, Idaho, Indiana, Iowa, Kansas, Minnesota, Montana, Nebraska, Nevada, New Mexico, North Dakota, Ohio, Oklahoma, Oregon, South Dakota, Utah, Washington, and West Virginia.

[14] The 8 states are Alabama, California, Florida, Louisiana, Maryland, Mississippi, North Carolina, and Tennessee.

cities, towns, villages, and boroughs, and in the case of New York, by school districts. The counties have little or no tax-collecting function in those states and obtain their own taxes from the cities and towns that collect for them.

Except in Michigan and New York, there is little or no overlapping of tax collection; in almost all other states a taxpayer is billed by only one governmental unit to meet its own levy and that of the county and the school system in which he resides. In New York a taxpayer may be confronted with separate property tax bills from the township collector, the village collector, and the school system collector. Even the billing dates may differ for each local government.

Many states now are taking some of the steps necessary to improve the administration of their property tax systems. With the advice and encouragement of such organizations as the National Association of Tax Administrators and the International Association of Assessing Officers, there is a continuing trend toward the training and professionalization of personnel. The geographic organization for property assessment has been moving toward centralization at the county level and elimination of overlapping assessment districts. More than half the states conduct assessment-ratio studies, using sampling techniques to reveal variations in assessment levels among assessing jurisdictions and among property classes within assessing jurisdictions.

Relative to revenue factors, the states have compelling reasons for a new look at the property tax. Their views as to its proper role in their overall tax systems are bound to vary, but none of them can afford to disregard its potential value for the demanding years ahead. Those states that place substantial dependence on the property tax can increase its reliability by raising the quality of administration. The few states that have not found it necessary to put much dependence on this tax can turn to it for a better-balanced revenue system. The states that have permitted it to decline to a minor position through pressure or neglect, or have reduced its productivity through maladministration or fear to put more reliance on it because its management is defective, have weakened their financial outlook.

Aside from being a good revenue producer, the property tax has the dependability and adjustability that local governments need. The required revenue yield can be obtained from year to year with a convenient range of flexibility and a satisfactory degree of precision, and the collectability of most classes of property taxes is assured by enforceable lien on the property. These merits are vitiated in practice, however, if highly restrictive tax-rate limits combined with serious underassessment relegate the property tax to an inflexibly minor role in local governmental finance.

Characteristics of a High-Quality State-Local Tax System

With the fiscal reality in mind that new and expanding public services at the state and local government levels require the effective use of both consumer and income taxes and that 30 states now impose both levies, the Advisory Commission on Intergovernmental Relations has identified the characteristics of a "high-quality" state-local tax system. Emphasis is upon the following concerning sales, income, and property taxes:[15]

State sales and use tax.—States can make effective and fairly equitable use of a sales tax if three prime conditions are met:

—*To insure productivity*, the tax base employed covers most personal services as well as retail sale of tangible items;

—*To insure fairness*, some provision is made for "pulling the regressive stinger" —either an outright exemption of food and drug purchases or a system of income tax credits and cash refunds to shield subsistence income from the sales tax collector's reach; and

—*To promote taxpayer convenience and administrative simplicity*, States must credit their taxpayers for sales and use taxes paid to other states; eliminate charges for audit of multistate firms; exchange audit and other information with one another; and permit local governments to "piggy-back" (local rate is added to the state rate and is administered by the state) their levy on the state sales tax.

State personal income tax.—A State can make effective and equitable use of the personal income tax if it meets at least three critical tests:

—*To insure fairness*, provides for personal exemptions at least as generous as those under the federal income tax;

—*To promote taxpayer convenience and administrative simplicity*, employs withholding at the source and confirms the technical provisions of its law to federal provisions; and

—*To insure productivity*, makes effective use of the income tax as evidenced by state collections equal to at least 20 percent of the federal personal income tax collections in that state.

The Commission calculated that only 11 of the 33 states with broad-based personal income taxes (excluding the newly enacted Michigan and Nebraska

[15]*Fiscal Balance in the American Federal System*, Vol. I, Chap. 4 (in press); and as reported in Advisory Commission on Intergovernmental Relations, *State and Local Taxes Significant Features 1968*, Washington, D.C., U.S. Govt. Printing Office, January, 1968, pp. 5–9.

taxes) met this last requirement in terms of the ratio of their collections to
federal tax receipts:

Alaska	25.3%	New York	20.6%
Delaware	21.7	North Carolina	21.1
Hawaii	26.5	Oregon	31.5
Idaho	25.4	Utah	21.4
Minnesota	29.0	Vermont	32.8
		Wisconsin	32.8

A conclusion relative to the income tax was that a graduated rate was not
a requirement because a broad-based flat rate tax can be productive and still
provide a substantial degree of progression when combined with personal
exemptions.

Local property tax.—Any effort to create a more effective and equitable
revenue system for state government must also come to grips with local
property tax overburdens. By all odds, this $26 billion revenue producer
stands out as the "sick giant" of our domestic revenue system—a fiscal
pathology that can be traced to *individual* and *group* property taxpayer overburden situations.

Individual property taxpayer overburden situations can be traced to either:

(a) Over-assessment due to the lack of uniform valuation practices—an
administrative matter; or

(b) Below average family income that raises an ability to pay issue.

Property owners as a *group*—those representing an entire local jurisdiction—
can also be relatively overburdened by:

(a) Unusually high governmental costs due to poor management practices;

(b) An underdeveloped tax base due to the political fractionation of the
metropolitan economic entity; or

(c) An anemic tax base or extraordinary expenditure demand or both caused
by the heavy concentration of poor people within the jurisdiction.

To facilitate a more uniform assessment of property, the advisory Commission in a report on *The Role of the States in Strengthening the Property Tax*
offered 29 policy recommendations based upon the following major assumptions:

1. That the prevailing joint state-local system for administering the property
tax can work with a reasonable degree of effectiveness only if the state
tax department is given sufficient executive support, legal authority, and
professional stature to insure local compliance with state law calling for
uniformity of tax treatment.

2. That professionalization of the assessment function can be achieved only if
the assessor is removed from the elective process and selected on the basis
of demonstrated ability to appraise property.

3. That the perennial conflict between state law calling for full value assessment and the local practice of fractional assessment can be resolved most expeditiously by permitting local assessment officials to assess at any uniform percentage of current market value above a specified minimum level provided this policy is reinforced with two important safeguards:

   a. *A full disclosure policy*, requiring the state tax department to make annual county assessment ratio studies and to give property owners a full report on the fractional valuation policy by county assessors, and

   b. *An appeal provision* to specifically authorize the introduction of state assessment ratio data by the taxpayer as evidence in appeals to review agencies on the issue of whether his assessment is inequitable.

Recognizing that if the local assessor could equalize all property tax assessments at full value, or at some uniform percentage thereof, the collection of this tax would still create special hardships for property owners with low income, the Commission cited a Wisconsin tax credit plan as a reasonable solution. The plan created in 1964 rebates to low income elderly persons—both homeowners and renters—that part of their property tax payment in excess of 5 per cent of household income. Because this tax relief program is financed from state funds and administered by the Wisconsin State Tax Department, it neither erodes the local tax base nor interferes in any way with the local assessment process.

Fiscal Future of State and Local Governments

As Heller has suggested, ". . . under the whiplash of prosperity, responsibilities are outstripping revenues."[16] A number of recent studies have pointed out a possible "fiscal mismatch" between needs and resources. Under nonwar conditions, the supply of readily available federal revenues appears to rise faster than current demands as discussed earlier in this publication, but the state-local situation is the reverse; expenditure demands on state and local governments rise faster than readily available revenue supply.

Over the 1956–1966 decade, for example, state and local purchases rose 134 per cent to reach $77.2 billion in 1966. This rise was faster than the growth in GNP, and, therefore, the share of the nation's current dollar output taken by states and localities rose from 7.9 per cent in 1956 to 10.4 per cent in 1966.[17]

A significant part of this increased share can be attributed to rising prices. The prices paid by state and local governments rose more than twice as fast

---

[16] *Revenue Sharing and Its Alternatives: What Future for Fiscal Federalism?* Vol. II, Washington, D.C., U.S. Govt. Printing Office, July, 1967, p. 736.

[17] *Survey of Current Business, op. cit.,* p. 21.

as in the private sector and almost 25 per cent faster than in the federal sector. If state and local purchases were measured in constant 1958 dollars, growth was less pronounced. The rise from 1956 to 1966 was 68 per cent, and the share of GNP rose from 8 per cent to 9.2 per cent.

Much of the 68-per-cent rise in real state and local purchases was a result of the growth in the nation's population and its shift to urban areas. The population grew 16.5 per cent during the 1956–1966 decade; if real purchases were measured on a per capita basis, the rise in spending was 44 per cent. This increase in real per capita purchases was associated mainly with intensified demands for more and higher quality public services, and these in turn stemmed from the rise in living standards. In addition, the most rapid population advances were concentrated in groups requiring the most costly services; the school-age population rose 32 per cent and the population age 65 and over rose 24 per cent.

By far the largest component of state and local purchases is compensation of employees. This component increased 150 per cent from 1956 to 1966 and accounted for 57 per cent of total state and local purchases in 1966. About three-fifths of the increase in compensation resulted from the rise in the number of state and local employees, which totaled 5 million in 1956 and reached 8.3 million in 1966. The 8.3 million employees in 1966 represented 11 per cent of the 1966 civilian labor force (as compared with 7.5 per cent in 1956) and put the number of state and local employees at more than three times the civilian employment of the federal government.

The average annual earnings per full-time state and local employee rose 55 per cent over the decade, as compared with increases of 50 per cent for federal employees and 46 per cent for employees of private industry. In addition, new construction put in place by state and local governments doubled over the decade to reach $20 billion in 1966. This constituted about one-fourth of total state and local purchases and represented an equal proportion of construction outlays for the nation as a whole. Roughly two-fifths of state and local construction activity was devoted to highways and one-fourth to education, while the remainder was allocated among hospitals, water, sewers, and other public facilities.

All other goods and services purchased by these governments amounted to $13.3 billion in 1966 and covered office supplies, motor vehicles, equipment, furniture, and other items used in the routine execution of state and local functions. Also, transfer payments—almost all of which were devoted to public assistance programs and to beneficiaries of government pension funds —more than doubled in the decade since 1956 and amounted to $7.5 billion, or roughly 9 per cent of total state and local spending.

After a lengthy study projecting the detailed components of state and local finance to 1975, a prime conclusion was that the financial outlook for state and local government in the decade of 1965–1975 was considerably more favorable than had generally been realized. According to the projection results, general revenues of state and local governments (including federal grants) would exceed general expenditures by nearly $5 billion in 1975. Looking at the still broader financial operations, chiefly extending the scope to include borrowing and debt retirement, the excess of availability of funds over outlays would increase slightly. These governments typically borrow about one-half of the amounts they spend for capital investment. If this practice continued, total debt would rise from $100 billion in 1965 to $169 billion in 1975. However, the average increase of about $7 billion annually would represent a slackening in the relative growth rate in debt, as well as a decline in outstanding debt in relation to revenues.

Expenditures were projected to rise from $75 billion in 1965 to $142 billion in 1975. This represented continued high growth, but at a relative pace more nearly consistent with that of the first half of the 1960's than with the faster

TABLE 7-12. Source and Use of Major State and Local Government Funds,[a] Actual and Projected, Fiscal Years 1965 and 1975 (Dollars in Billions)

	ACTUAL 1965	PROJECTED 1975
Sources of funds		
General revenue	$74.3	$146.9
Profit on liquor stores	.3	.3
New long-term borrowing	11.2	16.1
Other borrowing[b]	1.1	1.0
TOTAL funds available	86.9	164.2
Use of funds		
General expenditures	75.0	142.0
Long-term debt retirement	5.0	8.8
Employee retirement systems	1.8	3.0
Deficit on utility operations	1.0	.5
Additions to liquid assets	4.8	3.6
TOTAL funds required	87.5	157.9
Funds available less funds required	−.6	+6.4

[a] Excludes transactions of social insurance systems. Utility and liquor store operations are entered on a net basis.

[b] Net increase in total debt outstanding minus difference between long-term debt issued and retired.

SOURCE: Actual data from Bureau of the Census, U.S. Department of Commerce, Projections by Tax Foundation, and as reported by Elsie M. Watters, "Fiscal Outlook for State and Local Governments," a paper presented at the Tax Institute of America Symposium, Washington, Nov. 30, 1967, Table 1, p. 2.

rate recorded in earlier postwar years. For the decade, the indicated rise was 89 per cent, in comparison with a 123-per-cent advance in the decade ending in 1965.

TABLE 7-13. State and Local General Expenditures, Actual and Projected, Fiscal Years 1955–1975 (Dollars in Billions)

| | ACTUAL | | PROJECTED | PERCENTAGE OF CHANGE | |
FUNCTION	1955	1965	1975	1955–1965	1965–1975
TOTAL, general expenditures	$33.7	$75.0	$142.0	+122%	+89%
Education	11.9	29.0	52.9	164	83
Highways	6.5	12.2	16.6	89	36
Public welfare	3.2	6.3	17.1	99	170
Health and hospitals	2.5	5.4	10.6	112	97
All other	9.7	22.1	44.8	128	103

SOURCE: Actual data from Bureau of the Census, U.S. Department of Commerce, Projections by Tax Foundation, and as reported by Elsie M. Watters, "Fiscal Outlook for State and Local Governments," a paper presented at the Tax Institute of America Symposium, Washington, Nov. 30, 1967, Table 2, p. 5.

Relative to education, outlays of $52.9 billion (for elementary and secondary schools plus colleges and universities) were projected for 1975, representing an increase of 83 per cent in the decade between 1965 and 1975, in comparison with a 164 per cent rise during the previous decade. Enrollment gains will average out at 162,000 per year in the public elementary and secondary schools in contrast with the experience of the 1955–1965 period, when additions averaged 1,187,000 a year. With per-pupil standards rising as in the first half of the 1960's, operating costs per pupil would reach $852 by 1975, about three-quarters higher than in 1965, or a total of $37.1 billion in 1975 for public elementary and secondary education. A comparison of the Tax Foundation projections with the projections of the Council of State Governments and of the Department of Health, Education and Welfare is shown in Table 7-14.

There is relatively little difference among the three sets of projections in 1970. A relaxation in enrollment pressures in the 1965–1975 decade was expected to exert a moderating influence on future spending trends. Thus, local elementary and secondary school spending, as projected by the Tax Foundation at $37.1 billion in 1975, was to be up 66 per cent over the decade, in contrast to a rate of growth almost twice that rate (121 per cent) in the decade ending in 1965.

Relative to revenue increases, conservative estimates of the automatic

TABLE 7-14. Comparison of Projected Enrollments and Expenditures for Education in Several Studies, 1970 and 1975[a]

| | | PUBLIC ELEMENTARY AND SECONDARY SCHOOLS | | | | |
| | | 1970 | | | 1975 | |
SERIES	UNIT	CSG	HEW	TF	HEW	TF
School age population	Millions	53.0	53.0	53.0	55.3	51.7
Enrollments	Millions	44.8	44.8	44.2	47.1	43.0
Average daily attendance	Millions	41.2	41.4	41.1	43.8	40.0
Current expenditures per pupil in ADA	Hundreds	$672	$659	$650	$806	$852
Total current expenditures	Billions	27.7	27.3	26.7	35.3	34.1
Capital expenditure	Billions	3.3	3.7	3.7	4.2	3.0
TOTAL expenditures	Billions	31.0	31.0	30.4	39.5	37.1
Additional classroom construction	Thousands, rooms	65.3	68.8	68.8	67.4	48.4

[a] Initials in column headings refer to Council of State Governments (CSG); U.S. Department of Health, Education, and Welfare (HEW); and Tax Foundation (TF). Projections published by HEW in constant 1963-1964 dollars have been converted to current dollars according to the assumptions of the TF study (98 per cent of the population aged 5 through 17 will attend school; 85 per cent of them will enroll in public schools; per pupil expenditures in constant dollars will increase at the same rate as in the period from 1959 to 1964—4 per cent annually). Calendar year for CSG; school year for HEW and TF. HEW data are on a different basis from the Bureau of the Census concept used in the other two studies. For local schools the differences are small.

SOURCE: *Fiscal Outlook for State and Local Government to 1975*, New York, Tax Foundation, Inc., 1966; Selma Mushkin and Eugene McLoone, *Local School Expenditures: 1970 Projections*, Chicago, Council of State Governments; and reported in *Federal, State, Local Fiscal Projections*, Vol. III of *Revenue Sharing and Its Alternatives: What Future for Fiscal Federalism?*, July, 1967, p. 1331.

response of taxes to rising incomes point to a 75 per cent rise in yields from existing (1965) taxes in the decade ahead. State and local tax systems will yield about $100 million in taxes, both on the average and at the margin for every billion dollars of personal income. The kind of moderate growth on which the projections are based—substantially less than the 5.5 per cent real growth reported in 1967—would add annual increases averaging $4 billion to revenues in the years ahead, producing $90 billion in tax resources in the year 1975. The 1955 tax structure, if left in effect, would have produced only $70 billion by 1975.

Funds from federal grant-in-aid programs existing in 1965 are estimated to rise from $11 billion in 1965 to $30 billion by 1975. State-local taxes per capita would rise by 50 per cent to $400, but the amounts would not change in relation to income.

TABLE 7-15. State and Local General Revenue Actual and Projected, Fiscal Years 1955–1975 (Dollars in Billions)

	Actual		Projected	Percentage of Change	
Source	1955	1965	1975	1955–1965	1965–1975
Total, general revenue	$31.1	$74.3	$146.9	+139%	+ 98%
Total from state and local sources	27.9	63.3	116.9	127	85
Taxes	23.5	51.6	90.2	120	75
Current charges	3.0	8.4	18.8	183	124
Miscellaneous	1.5	3.3	7.8	124	134
Total from federal grants	3.1	11.0	30.0	252	172

Source: Actual data from Bureau of the Census, U.S. Department of Commerce, Projections by Tax Foundation, and as reported by Elsie M. Watters, "Fiscal Outlook for State and Local Governments," a paper presented at the Tax Institute of America Symposium, Washington, Nov. 30, 1967, Table 3, p. 11.

The Tax Foundation study tends to dispel the gloom with which state and local finance has come to be viewed in the United States over the past few decades. Projections published by the Council of State Governments in the so-called "Project '70," and those published by the Committee for Economic Development (*A Fiscal Program for a Balanced Federalism*, June, 1967) resulted in conclusions similar to those of the Tax Foundation study.

Concerning the use and interpretation of projection results, Heller stated critically:

> Statistical projections, then, are essential for planning, for defining problems. But projections are not forecasts, and forecasts are not goals . . . . The question . . . is not *whether* states and localities can make ends meet, but *on what terms*. On terms that just cover the irresistible minimum or that meet our aspirations? . . . .[18]

As the aspirations of a free people tend to be perceived more and more as demands rather than as needs, projections made at the beginning of such a transitional stage are bound to be even ultraconservative. The projections cited were effected primarily before the glaring stage of demands manifested in widespread rioting in the nation. Undoubtedly, the projections are conservative, and realities will require additional tax revenues than those projected, plus an extension of borrowing power, and a very flexible system of intergovernmental system of finance and management. These matters, particularly as they pertain to public elementary and secondary schools, will be discussed in the next three chapters.

[18] Walter W. Heller, *New Dimensions of Political Economy*. Cambridge, Mass., Harvard University Press, 1966, p. 135.

CHAPTER 8

A GOVERNMENTAL
NONREVENUE
SYSTEM— MUNICIPAL
BONDING

Introduction

In the two decades between 1946 and 1966, state and local governments expended approximately $220 billion for capital outlays, or about $1,135 per person, using 1966 population figures. About half of the $220 billion expenditure was financed by borrowing.

During recent years, capital outlays have accounted for about one-fourth of all expenditures by state and local governments. About four-fifths of these outlays was for new construction, about 12 per cent for the purchase of land and existing structures, and the remaining 8 to 9 per cent involved equipment purchases (including replacements). Slightly over 40 per cent of the outlays has been for highways, including urban streets, local roads, and toll facilities, and nearly one-fourth has been for educational facilities. Although expenditures for highways and education have generally paralleled the overall

187

growth of state and local government capital outlays, the capital expenditures for health and hospitals have lagged considerably.

At the present time there are no internally consistent statistics relating to state and local government capital outlays, bond sales, and outstanding indebtedness. Instead, there are independently compiled series on (1) capital outlays and construction expenditures (collected by the Governments Division, Bureau of the Census, on a fiscal-year basis); (2) construction put in place (collected by the Construction Statistics Division, Bureau of the Census, on a calendar-year basis); and (3) bond sales and refundings (two different series, both on a calendar basis, one compiled by the Bond Buyer and the other by the Investment Bankers' Association), and debt outstanding, new debt issued, and retirements (collected by the Governments Division, Bureau of the Census, on a fiscal-year basis).

The estimated indebtedness of state and local plus federal governmental debt was estimated to be $427.0 billion at the end of FY 1966.[1] The estimated indebtedness of state and local governments alone was approximately $107 billion, or about six times that of 20 years before. Of the $110.1 billion borrowed during the 14 fiscal years, 1952–1966, $101.4 billion, or 92 per cent

TABLE 8-1. Indebtedness and Debt Transactions of State and Local Governments, Fiscal Year 1966 (Dollars in Millions)

ITEM	TOTAL	STATE GOVERN- MENTS	LOCAL GOVERN- MENTS	PER CAPITA
TOTAL debt outstanding	$107,051	$29,564	$77,487	$546.57
Long-term	101,000	28,504	72,497	515.68
Full faith and credit	59,800	12,709	47,091	305.32
Nonguaranteed	41,200	15,795	25,405	210.36
Short-term	6,051	1,060	4,991	30.89
Net long-term debt outstanding	91,202	24,488	66,714	465.66
Long-term debt by purpose:				
Local schools	24,851	2,522	22,329	126.88
Local utilities	16,917	—	16,917	86.37
All other	59,232	25,982	33,250	302.42
Long-term debt issued	12,129	3,597	8,532	61.92
Long-term debt retired	5,641	1,367	4,274	28.79

NOTE: Because of rounding out, detail may not add up to totals. Local government amounts are estimates subject to sampling variation.

SOURCE: *Governmental Finances in 1965–66*, Series GF-No. 13, Washington, D.C., U.S. Govt. Printing Office, 1967, p. 28.

[1] *Governmental Finances in 1965–66*, Series GF-No. 13, Washington, D.C., U.S. Govt. Printing Office, 1967, p. 11.

was used for capital outlays. Over the 8 fiscal years, 1958–1966, long-term debt issued financed about 50.4 per cent of state and local government capital outlays. About one-fifth of the capital outlays has, in recent years, been financed by federal grants-in-aid, and the balance has been financed by state and local governments from taxes and other current revenue.

In a study prepared for the Subcommittee on Economic Progress of the Joint Economic Committee, Congress of the United States, and reported in December, 1966, three chapters provided an overview of the state and local public works sector of the economy.[2] The first analyzed and projected state and local public works expenditures in relation to GNP; the second examined the materials requirements for such expenditures; and the third examined their labor requirements. A summary of the findings is discussed in the next few paragraphs.

Since 1958 the ratio of real state and local government expenditures for structures and equipment to real GNP has fluctuated within a relatively narrow range—between 2.8 and a little over 2.9 per cent. If one assumes the average annual growth rate in real GNP to be nearly 4.5 per cent from 1965 to 1975, the unemployment rate to be 3 per cent and a 2-per-cent increase per year in the GNP price deflator, and taking into account other factors, GNP is projected at $940 billion in 1970 and at $1,275 billion in 1975 (assumption A). Assuming an average annual growth rate in real GNP of a little over 4 per cent from 1965 to 1975, a 4-per-cent unemployment rate, and a 1.5 per cent increase per year in the GNP price deflator, coupled with other factors, GNP is projected (in current prices) to rise from $676 billion in 1965 to $905 billion in 1970, and to $1,180 billion in 1975 (assumption B).

From these GNP projections, it is prolected that state and local government purchases of structures and equipment (net of residential buildings), which amounted to $19.5 billion in 1965, would rise to $28.5 billion in 1970 and to $39.1 billion in 1975 under assumption B, and to $29.9 billion in 1970 and $44.2 billion in 1975 under assumption A.[3]

After surveying the components of the construction and building materials industries, the authors of Chapter 2 of the government report concluded that:

> To meet future increases in construction demand in both the private and public sectors it is expected that the construction and building materials industries will increase their productive capacities. Prefabrication and pre-finishing have been and will continue to be important sources of promoting innovation and labor-saving devices on construction sites. . . . When one

[2] *Public Facility Needs*, Vol. 1, Washington, D.C., U.S. Govt. Printing Office, Dec. 1966, pp. 35–91.
[3] *Ibid.*, p. 11.

considers all the factors, it is difficult to avoid the conclusion that the construction materials industries should be able to meet the needs of future construction —as they have in the past—through innovation, product development, and increased productive capacity.[4]

The authors of Chapter 3 estimated that allowing for increased productivity, 2,802,000 full-time workers will be needed in 1975 for the $41.7 billion of public construction projected under assumption A and 2,744,000 for the $36.6 billion on construction projected under assumption B. Thirty-eight per cent of these (1,070,000 and 1,048,000, respectively) would be needed in the construction industry and the balance in sectors supplying the necessary materials and service.

State and local public agency capital requirements for public facilities have been estimated at $328 billion for the decade of 1966–1975. For 1970, these capital requirements are estimated at $32 billion, and for 1975 they are estimated at $41 billion, which compares to the $20 billion of capital outlays expended by state and local public bodies in 1965. As shown in Table 8-2, over 40 per cent of the anticipated capital requirements are for transportation facilities, and nearly 20 per cent each are accounted for by education and water and sewer facilities.

TABLE 8-2. Summary Comparison of Public Facility Capital Outlays of State and Local Public Agencies in 1965 with Estimated Capital Requirements for 1966–1975 (Dollars in Billions)

	ACTUAL	ESTIMATED		
GROUP OF FACILITIES	1965 [a]	1970	1975	1966–1975
Water and sewer	$2.7	$5.5	$6.8	$56.5
Electric and gas	.8	1.3	1.4	12.8
Transportation	8.9	13.5	17.7	141.1
Education	4.9	5.9	7.8	62.0
Health	.8	1.3	1.7	13.1
Recreation and culture	1.5	3.4	4.4	35.0
Other public buildings	.5 [b]	.7 [c]	.9 [c]	7.3 [c]
TOTAL	20.1	31.6	40.7	327.8

[a] Adjusted to reflect facility categories where data are not available.

[b] Excludes publicly owned industrial plants.

[c] Includes police stations with estimated capital requirements assumed to be $1 billion during 1966–1975.

SOURCE: *Public Facility Needs*, Vol. 1, Washington, D.C., U.S. Govt. Printing Office, Dec. 1966, p. 14.

[4] *Ibid.*

Educational Construction Activity, 1946–1965

In the first post-World War II year, 1946, the physical volume of new construction, both private and public, was more than double that of each of the preceding two war years. Federal, state, and local construction constant dollar outlays in 1946 were about 15 per cent of total new construction. With demobilization, federal government construction dropped off somewhat, but state and local outlays followed the pattern of private construction, and many categories showed an enormous spurt between 1945 and 1946. For example, the value of public educational construction activity in constant dollars jumped by almost 50 per cent in one year's time.

Educational construction increased fourfold between 1947 and 1949 and then began to slow down as the wartime backlog was eliminated partially. However, the growing school population, as well as a high rate of population mobility, and housing development in suburban areas continued to stimulate school building. By the mid-1950's, expenditures reached a physical volume peak (not surpassed until 1965), which was more than double the 1949 rate of outlays. Average annual growth over the 20-year period for new public educational facilities was the highest among all state and local construction categories, as shown in Table 8-3.

TABLE 8-3. State and Local Construction Activity, 1947–1965[a]

	ACTIVITY (MILLIONS OF 1957–1959 DOLLARS)		AVERAGE ANNUAL RATE OF INCREASE (PERCENTAGE)
	1947	1965	
TOTAL state and local	$3,279	$13,396	8.2%
Nonresidential building	635	4,351	11.3
Educational	363	3,042	12.5
Hospital and institutional	75	397	9.6
Administrative and service	57	414	11.6
Other nonresidential	140	498	7.3
Nonbuilding construction	2,644	9,106	7.1
Sewer	329	954	6.1
Water	286	699	5.1
Highways	1,631	6,543	8.0
All other	398	910	4.7

[a] The statistics for 1947 and 1965 are prepared by Business and Defense Services Administration on a comparable basis by using the "old" Bureau of the Census series that terminated with 1965.
SOURCE: *Public Facility Needs*, Vol. 1, Washington, D.C., U.S. Govt. Printing Office, Dec. 1966, p. 57.

Capital outlay for local schools increased less rapidly than other state-local outlays in the 1952–1958 period, so that the fraction of the total applied to schools dropped from about one-fifth in the early 1950's to about one-sixth in 1964–1965. However, with the stronger-than-average rise in capital outlay for institutions of higher education, the fraction of all capital expenditure of state and local governments going to education as a whole has been relatively unchanged. The percentage of distribution of capital outlay of state and local governments for education and for selected years, 1952 to 1964–1965, is shown in Table 8-4.

TABLE 8-4. Distribution of Capital Outlay Allotted to State and Local Governments for 1952 to 1964–1965

	1952	1957	1962	1964–1965
		(PERCENTAGE)		
Allotted to education	23.0%	25.8%	23.9%	24.4%
Local schools	19.1	21.5	18.0	17.0
Institutions of higher education	3.6	4.1	5.7	7.0
Other	.3	.2	.2	.4

SOURCE: *Public Facility Financing*, Vol. 2, Washington, D.C., U.S. Govt. Printing Office, Dec. 1966, p. 56.

During the 20-year period, FY 1946 through FY 1965, the construction of elementary and secondary school facilities multiplied many times; $111 million was spent in 1946 and $3.5 billion was spent in 1965. There has been constant construction to meet the needs of increased enrollment and to replace obsolete facilities. The increases in construction were most rapid immediately after World War II and as the postwar babies entered school in the early 1950's. Since 1956, the number of classrooms constructed each year has ranged between 65,000 to 72,000 with the 10-year average being 68,000. Some of the fluctuation in the rooms constructed and expenditures is caused by the construction of large secondary schools, which take more than one year to complete. Consequently, the rooms are usually reported in the year of completion, which is not necessarily the year when the debts or expenditures are incurred.

Sources of Financing Capital Outlays (1946–1965) for Public Schools

Most of the financing (about 80 per cent) during the period of FY 1946 through FY 1965 has been by local school systems. Most of this has been by the sale of bonds (87.6 per cent in FY 1966). In the late 1940's, states began to recognize the financing problems and made some significant contributions in the area of financing school construction. It must be noted that nearly half the state contributions have been in the form of loans or advances, with the burden of repayment still on the local school systems.

School building authorities have accounted for nearly $200 million a year of public elementary and secondary school construction. Approximately another $200 million a year has been coming from current taxes and accumulative building funds. The items of gifts and private construction appear to be insignificant in the total picture; however, they undoubtedly may be very significant to the individual school systems involved.

TABLE 8-5. Capital Outlay and Tax-Exempt Bonds Sold for Public Elementary and Secondary School Facilities for the United States, 1946–1966 (Dollars in Millions)[a]

Fiscal Year	Classroom Units Con- structed	Expendi- tures	State	Public Author- ity	Local School District	Federal Grant P.L. 815	Tax- Exempt Bonds Sold
Totals							
1946–65	1,089,674	$44,794	$5,421	$2,956	$35,373	$991	$34,927
1946	(3,900)[b]	111	N.A.	N.A.	(110)	—	302
1947	(7,000)	205	N.A.	N.A.	(200)	—	395
1948	(13,500)	412	N.A.	N.A.	(400)	—	476
1949	(21,000)	664	N.A.	N.A.	(650)	—	370
1950	(30,900)	1,014	43	N.A.	(950)	—	854
1951	(38,900)	1,316	124	21	1,167	4	986
1952	(44,600)	1,563	194	66	1,260	43	957
1953	(55,100)	1,995	208	218	1,451	118	1,451
1954	(58,800)	2,200	180	204	1,711	105	1,667
1955	60,005	2,310	163	130	1,896	121	1,634
1956	63,283	2,607	196	211	2,111	89	1,804
1957	68,660	2,982	247	334	2,334	67	1,870
1958	72,070	3,062	327	242	2,424	69	2,420
1959	69,453	2,539	324	(200)	1,941	74	1,948
1960	69,400	2,823	370	161	2,226	66	2,195
1961	72,214	2,864	(370)	(120)	2,315	59	2,357
1962	72,089	2,987	372	125	2,448	42	2,568
1963	65,300	2,700	(372)	240	2,035	53	2,274
1964	69,300	3,116	526	177	2,391	22	2,569
1965	(65,200)	(3,524)	(705)	(257)	(2,533)	29	2,823
1966	(69,000)	(3,800)	(700)	(250)	(2,820)	(30)	(2,967)

[a] Includes only schools operated by local school districts. Items are taken from various reports and publications in the Office of Education.

[b] Items in parentheses are estimates.

N.A. = not available.

Source: *Public Facility Needs*, Vol. 1, Washington, D.C., U.S. Govt. Printing Office, Dec. 1966, p. 354.

Prospective Capital Outlays for Public Schools

Although the growth rate of new educational facilities in the 1965–1975 decade is likely to be considerably below that of the 1946–1965 period when the backlog of needs was particularly large, it is still expected to exceed the average growth rate for state and local construction as a whole. Capital outlay requirements for public elementary and secondary schools during the decade of 1965–1975 reflect three components. The components and the estimated dollar requirements (in billions) are as follows:[5]

Replacement of outmoded and unsafe facilities and reduction of overcrowding (400,000 classrooms)—	$20.6
Accommodation of new enrollment, including an allowance for migration (350,000 rooms)—	16.2
Improvement of education programs and extension of opportunities for disadvantaged pupils—	5.0
TOTAL:	$41.8

In the above summary, facility needs have been translated into dollar expenditures by assuming an average cost of $49,000 per classroom. It will be necessary to allow for a higher cost if there is further increase in construction costs beyond the recent rate of about 3 per cent per year; or if the construction of a substantial proportion of the needed facilities must be postponed to the latter part of the decade. For several reasons, including the long planning time required for effective rehabilitation of urban systems, it seems likely that some postponements will occur.

The capital outlay expenditures given include requirements for all vocational-technical education facilities during the 1965–1975 decade. Requirements for vocational-technical education total 2,860,000 student work stations, based on the prediction of a very sharp increase in vocational student enrollments from about 5.4 million in 1965 to about 14 million in 1975. It is assumed that each station will serve three students since the schools will operate three shifts—two during the day and one in the evening. At current estimated facility costs of about $1,850 per work station, the capital outlay required to meet those projected needs would be approximately $5.3 billion. However, the recent trend in cost of vocational facilities shows an increase of at least 3 per cent per year. If this trend continues, the average cost during the decade will be in the neighborhood of $2,200 per work station and a national total expenditure of approximately $6.3 billion.

[5] *Public Facility Needs, op. cit.,* p. 355.

Relative to the distribution of capital outlays by size of community, it appears that each of three sectors should account for about one-third of the school building activity during the decade: the urban fringe areas are expected to grow most rapidly; on the other hand, needs for replacement of facilities are generally greatest in the central cities and, to a lesser extent, in communities outside of standard metropolitan statistical areas.

The overwhelming majority of projected capital outlays will be expended by cities, counties, towns, and other local districts responsible for operation of public schools. A small proportion—perhaps as little as 6 per cent—will be expended by school building authorities.

Nonrevenue Receipts

Nonrevenue receipts of governmental agencies consist of amounts received that either incur an obligation that must be met at some future date, or change the form of an asset from property to cash and therefore decrease the amount and value of school property. Money received from loans, sale of bonds, sale of property purchased from capital funds, and proceeds from insurance adjustments are nonrevenue receipts.

Whether a receipt is a revenue or a nonrevenue receipt is determined from the standpoint of the school system receiving the money. If a state floated a bond issue and loaned the proceeds to local systems, the receipt would be classified as nonrevenue since ultimate repayment would lie with the local systems. However, if the bond-issue proceeds were granted to the local systems, the receipts would be classified as revenue since the systems' assets were increased without the imposition of an obligation to repayment.

The most important nonrevenue receipts for school districts are the proceeds of municipal bond issues. A discussion of municipal bonding is the substance of this chapter.

Municipals

The word *municipal* is defined as relating to the internal affairs of a nation or other political units. The term *municipal bonds* is applied to a group of tax-exempt bonds issued by state and local governments and their political subdivisions. These bonds are often referred to as municipals or tax exempts, since interest on such bonds is exempt from federal and often from state income taxes.

State and local governments and their subsidiaries have grown steadily in importance as borrowers of funds. In the first postwar year of 1946, a total of 3,319 new issues of municipal bonds with a value of $1.2 billion were brought to the market. Over the next two decades after 1946, this activity was increased until 6,059 issues valued at $11.1 billion were brought to the market in 1965.[6]

Another measure of the activity of state and local units in the financial markets is the volume of outstanding debt. Table 8-6 presents annual data on

TABLE 8-6. Privately Held Outstanding Public Debt,[a] 1946–1965 (Dollars in Millions)

STATE AND MUNICIPAL				U.S. INTEREST-BEARING			
YEAR	AMOUNT	YEAR	AMOUNT	YEAR	AMOUNT	YEAR	AMOUNT
1965	$92.0	1955	$37.5	1965	$210.8	1955	$197.6
1964	85.1	1954	32.4	1964	211.6	1954	194.5
1963	78.9	1953	27.3	1963	211.7	1953	191.6
1962	72.4	1952	24.5	1962	208.5	1952	189.6
1961	64.0	1951	22.3	1961	202.4	1951	188.9
1960	59.0	1950	19.8	1960	201.5	1950	199.0
1959	54.6	1949	17.3	1959	201.2	1949	193.1
1958	49.9	1948	15.4	1958	193.4	1948	192.9
1957	45.8	1947	13.6	1957	189.9	1947	200.4
1956	41.9	1946	12.8	1956	192.7	1946	215.2

[a] Includes U.S. interest-bearing securities not held by U.S. Government investment accounts and Federal Reserve banks; also state and local securities not held by federal agencies and trust funds; Federal Reserve banks; and state and local sinking funds, trust funds and investment funds.
SOURCES: *The Daily Bond Buyer* and the *Treasury Bulletin:* U.S. Treasury Department, and as reported in *Public Facility Financing*, Vol. 1, Washington, D.C., U.S. Govt. Printing Office, Dec. 1966, p. 107.

the amount of privately held municipal, state, and federal government debt from 1946 to 1965. The federal debt has remained relatively stable at $200 billion, whereas state and local debt has increased from $13 billion to $92 billion over the same time interval.

Coupled with the improved and increased tools and functions of brokers, the large increase in outstanding municipal debt has increased the liquidity of municipal bonds. The market for outstanding securities has been increased, too, by the large increase in outstanding municipal debt. These are important considerations in assessing the ability of the market to absorb additional securities.

There are four types of municipals: (1) general obligation bonds, which are backed by the full faith and credit of the issuer, usually including the unlimited taxing power of the issuer; (2) revenue bonds, which are secured

[6] *Public Facility Financing, op. cit.,* p. 105.

by revenue from the facility or facilities owned by the issuer; (3) limited tax bonds, which usually are backed only by the overall tax revenue of the jurisdiction that issued them; and (4) public housing authority bonds, secured by pledges of funds by the Public Housing Authority of the Department of Housing and Urban Development. Only the first two types will be discussed in detail in this chapter.

General Obligation Bonds

General obligation bonds are those to the payment of which is pledged the full faith and credit of the issuer and which are payable from and primarily secured by ad valorem taxes upon all of the taxable property within the boundaries of the issuer, subject to taxation by the issuer, without limitation of rate or amount.

Prior to World War II, practically all state and municipal long-term financing was through the medium of general obligation bonds. The next largest volume of municipal financing (prior to the financial crisis of 1929) was through bonds payable from assessments on property specially benefited from the improvements constructed from the bond proceeds. About 9 per cent, or about $2 billion of outstanding municipals in the early 1930's, went into default. This fact, and the high delinquencies in tax and assessment collections, resulted in increased interest costs to issuers and a reduction in public borrowing.

During World War II, a Capital Issues Commission was established and maintained regional offices to govern public financing. Except to provide services for rapidly growing populations in defense areas, public borrowing was limited to purposes associated with health and safety. Bond issues were at a minimum, and the total amount of outstanding general obligation bonds at the end of the war approximated the total outstanding in 1930.

As stated earlier, the curtailment of construction of public facilities during the 1930's and to the end of World War II led to a tremendous backlog of postponed requirements. After lifting the restrictions upon the creation of new debt, the federal government permitted local and state governments to initiate plans to construct postponed facilities and to issue municipals. However, it was not until 1946 that the volume of tax-exempt bonds brought to market showed a substantial increase, jumping from 1,876 new issues in 1945, aggregating $818 million, to 3,319 new issues in 1946 aggregating $1,203 million. The delay in the market impact was caused by the preliminary work prior to the issue of bonds, such as the employment of architects, preparation of plans and specifications, selection of building sites, and the like. Since

1946, the ratio of general obligation bonds issued to the total amount of tax-exempt financing in each year has declined. In 1946, general obligation issues were 82.9 per cent of the aggregate amount, while in 1965, the percentage was 67.8.[7]

The elements accounting for the declining percentage of general obligation bonds issued include demand and interest costs, authorities, and debt limitations. For example, the public bodies will turn to financing that does not require a vote of the electorate or an increase in ad valorem taxes to pay bonds when the demand for tax-exempt bonds and the resulting spread in interest costs between general obligation and revenue bonds is relatively narrow. In addition, quasipublic authorities issue bonds, which generally are payable from income-producing facilities. Finally, general obligation indebtedness limitations in the form of constitutions, statutes, and homerule charters have been in effect for generations and have been found difficult and almost impossible to change, with few exceptions.

Relative to debt limitations, the traditional constitutional debt limit is expressed as a percentage of the assessed valuation of the taxable property within the boundaries of the issuer, as indicated in Table 8-7. This method was adopted when practically all the revenues of the states and their subdivisions was derived from ad valorem taxes. However, it can be argued now that debt limitations based upon ad valorem taxes are no longer the true measure of ability to pay since the advent of a wide variety of taxes. The State of Delaware and the Commonwealth of Puerto Rico have abandoned the traditional percentage of assessed value limitation and have adopted a limitation based upon a ratio of debt service to gross revenues experienced in prior years. Many investors, however, feel that there is a danger in possible recessions over an extended period, and that the only true measure of security is the value of the real property behind the debt.

Debt limitations probably have not seriously prevented general obligation borrowing except in cases where the percentage is so low as to be unrealistic in the modern era. With a 2 per cent constitutional debt limit, Indiana is an example of a state in which local public agencies have circumvented the limitation by means of authorities and lease-purchase agreements.

Revenue Bond Financing

Revenue bond financing by municipalities enjoyed only a limited acceptance prior to World War II, although municipal public utility revenue bonds had been known since the turn of the century. Public authority revenue financing received an impetus from decisions of the federal courts affirming the status

[7] *Ibid.*, p. 150.

TABLE 8-7. Constitutional Limitations on Long-Term General Obligation Debt Imposed on School Systems (Percentage of Assessed Valuation of Taxable Property)

STATE	DEBT LIMITATION	STATE	DEBT LIMITATION
Alabama	None	Nebraska	None
Alaska	Vote required; no limit	Nevada	None
Arkansas	Prohibited	New Hampshire	None
California	Vote required; no limit	New Jersey	None
Colorado	Vote required	New Mexico	6%; vote required
Connecticut	None	New York	Cities under 125,000,
Delaware	None		5%; higher if voted;
Florida	20%		no limit other
Georgia	7%; vote required		systems
Hawaii	None	North Carolina	Vote required; no limit
Idaho	None; vote required	North Dakota	5%; 5% extra by vote[a]
Illinois	5%	Ohio	None
Indiana	2%	Oklahoma	10%; vote required
Iowa	5%	Oregon	None
Kansas	None	Pennsylvania	2%; 5% extra if voted
Kentucky	—	Rhode Island	None
Louisiana	10%; parishwide dis-	South Carolina	8%;[b] vote required
	tricts, 25%; vote	South Dakota	10%; vote required
	required	Tennessee	None
Maine	None	Texas	None; vote required
Maryland	None	Utah	Vote required; no limit
Massachusetts	None	Vermont	None
Michigan	None; vote required	Virginia	Vote required; no limit
Minnesota	None	Washington	1.5%; extra 8.5% by
Mississippi	None		vote
Missouri	10%; vote required	West Virginia	5%; vote required
Montana	5%	Wisconsin	10%
		Wyoming	10%; vote required

[a] Proposed amendment authorizes state debt if authorized by popular vote. Another proposed amendment raises the subdivision debt limit to 15%.

[b] If 2 or more subdivisions cover same territory, total debt is 15%.

of the Port of New York and Triborough Authorities as political subdivisions entitled to exemption from federal income taxation of interest on their bonds.[8]

Again, because of the depression and war, public officials were faced with a backlog of needs for public improvements and turned to revenue bond financing to raise capital without a corresponding rise in the tax level and without a corresponding drain on the general funds or (in most cases) a charge against the debt limit.

[8] *Commissioner of Internal Revenue v. Shamberg's Estate* (1944), 144 F 2d 998, Cert. denied, 323 U.S. 792; and *Commissioner of Internal Revenue v. White's Estate et al.* (1944), 144 F 2 1019, Cert. denied, 323 U.S. 792.

There still is no uniformity in the state court decisions relative to the exemption of revenue bonds from constitutional debt limits. However, a majority of the states have adopted the so-called special fund theory by which revenue bonds are not considered debt within the meaning of constitutional limitations. Fifteen states rejected the theory in whole or in part; those that have rejected it in part permit the exclusion of bonds payable from the revenues of the facility constructed from the proceeds of the bonds, but do not permit the exclusion if revenues from the existing facilities that were being added to or extended are also pledged.

A development in revenue bond financing during the period 1946–1966 was the increased use of advance refunding. Refunding of revenue bonds is not new. Bond resolutions and trust indentures ordinarily provide for the issuance of bonds to refund outstanding revenue bonds when subject to redemption. During a five-year period in the early 1960's, issuers were anxious to replace outstanding high-interest bonds with more moderately priced obligations. In addition, some issuers felt the need to modify or eliminate restrictive conditions in outstanding bond resolutions, particularly with respect to the issuance of additional bonds. In many cases, the bonds to be refunded were callable for several years. Accordingly, advance refundings were developed whereby the issuer sold refunding bonds and placed the proceeds in escrow pending the redemption of the outstanding bonds on the first-call data. Where the resolution securing the outstanding bonds contained adequate defeasance provisions, the placing of sufficient funds in escrow to retire the outstanding bonds on the redemption date had the effect of discharging the outstanding bond resolution or indenture. Where such provisions were absent, interest on the refunding bonds was paid from investment income until the outstanding bonds could be redeemed and the old resolution discharged. This method of advance refunding, which could be justified either because it offered savings in overall interest cost to the issuer or because it aided in removing onerous bond restrictions that prevented additional financing of public improvements, reached its peak in 1963 and accounted in part for the record volume of revenue bond issues in that year.[9]

There have been important changes since 1946 in revenue bond security requirements contained in bond resolutions, trust indentures, and similar instruments securing the issuance of revenue bonds. These changes reflect an increased market for revenue bonds, particularly among institutional investors and fiduciaries, and this expanding market has resulted in a greater demand for reasonable assurance against falling off of revenues, which might lead to a default on the bonds. Debt service coverage requirements are

[9] *Public Facility Financing, op. cit.*, pp. 158–159.

stricter; both reserves for debt service and for repairs and replacement of the facility being financed are being required; and earnings tests governing the issuance of additional revenue bonds that are pari passu with outstanding bonds are stricter today as to the earnings base and the required ratio or coverage of net earnings over debt service.

Lease Rental and Authority Financing

Lease-rental financing has been used primarily for two major purposes: (1) For construction of school buildings; and (2) for constructing other public buildings. School buildings have been built under lease-rental plans in the states of Georgia, Indiana, Kentucky, Maine, and Pennsylvania.

Under a lease-rental arrangement, a nonprofit corporation is created, a schoolboard conveys a site to the corporation, and the corporation then constructs the desired school building, sells bonds to pay for the construction, and simultaneously leases the building to the schoolboard for only one year at a time—at such rentals, if renewed from year to year, as would amortize the bonds and still not cause the schoolboard to exceed its budget in any year. It is agreed that after the bonds are retired, the building will be deeded back to the schoolboard.

The following is a list of the specific steps for the creation of a nonprofit school-building corporation in the State of Indiana:

1. A committee of interested school patrons (people with leadership qualities) should be formed to work with school officials in preliminary investigating and planning.

2. Committee and school officials should determine the extent of school building needs, probable costs of needed construction, and whether it is necessary and desirable to form a nonprofit school-building corporation.

3. After decision to form such a corporation has been made, the cooperating group should secure information and advice on procedure and planning from attorneys, bankers, commercial bond purchasing concerns, and the Superintendent of Public Instruction.

4. Stock subscription list is prepared and circulated, and subscription to common stock of at least $1,000 is obtained, of which at least $500 must be paid in before the building corporation may be formed. (Attorney should be retained.)

5. Meeting of subscribers is held to approve articles of incorporation, to designate incorporators, and to elect directors.

6. Articles of incorporation are filed with the Secretary of State.

7. Directors hold first meeting to elect officers, adopt by-laws and approve issuance, and plan further sales of common stock to public.

8. Trustee (usually a local bank) is selected to act as the business agent for building corporation, and a trust agreement is entered into.

9. Proper corporation officers and committees should confer fully with school officials to develop preliminary agreements on general plans for classrooms to be constructed.

10. An architect should be employed and authorized to prepare plans and specifications for the school building or buildings to be constructed.

11. While the architect is preparing plans (or before, if there is a question as to outcome), the signature of at least fifty school patrons (preferably as many as possible) must be obtained for a petition asking governing body of the school district to enter into a contract to lease the school building to be constructed. This petition is filed with the governing body of the school district, which investigates the need for the proposed school building. Before the lease may be negotiated, there must be a finding by the governing body, approved by the State Superintendent of Public Instruction, that need for the construction does exist, and that the school district is unable from its own resources to finance the needed construction.

12. The building corporation must acquire absolute title to the land on which the building is to be constructed.

13. Plans and specifications are submitted to the school district, the State Superintendent of Public Instruction, the State Board of Health, the State Board of Tax Commissioners, and the State Fire Marshal. Approval must be obtained from all these agencies before a lease can be executed.

14. The building corporation receives bids and awards the construction contract, subject to cancellation if the necessary financing cannot be arranged.

15. The building corporation and the school district agree upon terms and enter into a lease agreement, following notice and public hearing by the governing body of the school district.

16. Published notice of the lease execution is given by the school district. Ten or more objecting taxpayers may appeal to the State Tax Board, which after a public hearing issues a decision as to the necessity for the lease and whether rental is fair and reasonable. (Any legal action contesting the lease must be instituted within thirty days of the notice of the execution or decision of the State Tax Board.)

17. The building corporation adopts the proper resolutions for the issuance of first mortgage bonds and offers bonds after published notice at a public sale. (Information should be sent in advance to interested investment houses.)

18. If the bonds are sold, construction may proceed.

As reported earlier in this chapter, school building authorities have accounted for nearly $200 million annually of public elementary and secondary school construction. This approximates 6 per cent of the public school construction outlay for each of the recent years, and it is anticipated that authorities will continue to finance this same percentage of outlay between now and 1975.

State Credit Aid for Public Facilities

As of 1966, 17 states had credit assistance programs to aid local government in the financing of public facilities. The varieties of credit assistance included (1) direct loans, wherein the state government loaned money to the local jurisdiction, enabling the local unit to avoid private lenders and obtain favorable interest rates and repayment schedules; (2) guarantees of debt service payment, wherein the state pledged to pay principal and interest on local bond issues should the local unit be unable to do so; and (3) grants to cover debt service, wherein the state contributed in part or in whole to the local payment of debt service. The latter is, in effect, a variation of a grant-in-aid, whereby the payment was made over the life of the bond issue rather than during the period of construction.

Assistance was granted most often for the construction and repair of public school buildings and facilities. Eleven states—California, Indiana, Maryland, Minnesota, New Hampshire, North Carolina, North Dakota, Ohio, Pennsylvania, Rhode Island, and Wyoming—provided credit aid for that purpose.

Between 1947 and 1966, states provided the aggregate sum of $2,008,095,850 to aid local governments in financing school construction. Of this amount, the major portion of $1,329,700,000 was authorized by California between 1953 and 1966. Amounts provided in other states ranged from $325,402,150 in Pennsylvania and $190,024,000 in Maryland to $1,469,294 in Wyoming.

The number of states undertaking credit assistance programs for school construction increased steadily from the inauguration of Maryland's program in 1950 to the most recent enactment—Rhode Island in 1961. California and Pennsylvania programs, which developed into the largest, began in 1953. Programs also were initiated in North Dakota in 1954; Indiana in 1956; New Hampshire, Ohio, and Wyoming in 1957; and Minnesota in 1959. All these were preceded by the Hawaiian territory program in 1947.

The average annual spending by the states in five-year periods was $50,315,195 from 1951 to 1955, $153,280,087 from 1956 to 1960, and $196,445,887 from 1961 to 1965. It is probable that credit assistance programs in the states will increase as demands for public school construction outstrip the amount of money available for local government school construction.

TABLE 8-8. State Credit Aids for Construction
of Public Schools, 1946–1965

STATE	TOTAL AID
California	$1,329,700,000
Indiana	25,737,016
Maryland	190,024,000
Minnesota	24,047,557
New Hampshire	9,423,000
North Dakota	12,882,685
Ohio	81,000,000
Pennsylvania	325,402,150
Rhode Island	8,410,148
Wyoming	1,469,294

SOURCE: *Public Facility Financing*, Vol. 2,
Washington, D.C., U.S. Govt. Printing Office,
Dec. 1966, p. 101.

Brief descriptions of state credit aid for public schools in California,
Indiana, and Maryland are as follows:

CALIFORNIA

   Purpose: Acquisition, construction, and purchase of equipment for schools;
   school construction (school building aid law, 1952).

   Type of credit assistance: Direct loan.

   Eligible borrowers: School districts.

   Maximum interest rate: Interest rate has ranged from a low of $2\frac{1}{8}$ per cent
   to a high of 4 per cent since 1952; rate in 1966 was $3\frac{1}{2}$ per cent.

   Repayment period: 30 years; repayment of loans made for multipurpose
   facilities is extended for an additional 10 years.

   Maximum loan-to-value ratio: Up to 100 per cent.

   Other conditions: Any school district that has exhausted its legal bonding
   capacity and has unhoused pupils by a prescribed formula is eligible for
   assistance.

INDIANA

   Purpose: School construction (Burns Indiana Statutes Annotated 28-163).

   Type of credit assistance: Direct loan.

   Eligible borrowers: Local school corporations.

   Maximum interest rate: 4 per cent.

   Repayment period: 20 years.

   Other Conditions: In order to qualify for an advancement under the provisions of this act, the consolidated school corporation is required to

raise, either by a bond issue or by a cumulative fund tax levy, or by both, a sum of money equivalent to not less than 2 per cent of the adjusted assessed valuation of its geographical district; advancement must not exceed the sum of $2,000 per pupil accommodated in the new structure less the sum of any money raised by and made available to the corporation.

MARYLAND

Purposes: Public school construction (ch. 1, acts of 1949; ch. 609, acts of 1953; ch. 80, acts of 1956; ch. 86, acts of 1958; ch. 25, acts of 1962; ch. 542, acts of 1963; ch. 635, acts of 1965).

Type of credit assistance: Direct loan.

Eligible borrowers: Counties and mayor and city council of Baltimore.

Maximum interest rate: 5 per cent per annum.

Repayment period: 15 years.

Other conditions: The amount of state funds that can be loaned to any district is limited to the amount that could be amortized by 90 per cent of the total funds distributed to districts under provisions of state laws relating to income tax, racing tax, recreation tax, amusement tax, license tax, and incentive fund for school construction.

Municipal Bond Underwriting

Underwriting of municipal bonds is the process by which an investment banker (security dealer or a dealer bank who underwrites securities) purchases bonds from the issuing city or other governmental unit and, in turn, distributes them to the ultimate investor. The vast preponderence of new municipal bond issues are distributed through the underwriting efforts of investment dealers.

The investment banker performs his primary function by purchasing bonds from the municipality and selling them in turn to his investor clients He is responsible for obtaining the best terms possible for both the buyer and seller, and his business success is dependent on this ability. He may also act at different times as a dealer in the secondary market, buying and selling bonds for his own account; as a broker, buying and selling for the account of investors and being compensated by fee; or as a financial consultant.

Because the municipal market is almost exclusively an over-the-counter market, the services of the hundreds of dealers operating on a nationwide basis assure the marketability of bonds—the ready conversion of bonds to cash and vice versa—which is so vitally important to all investors.

Operating in the primary market as an underwriter, the investment banker provides a necessary service to municipalities. He stands ready to risk his capital in bidding for bonds offered in blocks by the issuer and distributes the bonds to his clients who are seeking profitable investments. It is thus through his efforts that the hundreds and thousands of investors of all sizes and types funnel their resources to school systems, for example.

The municipal market is intensely competitive, and the difference between the winning and second bids is normally a minute fraction of 1 per cent of the principal amount of the bonds being offered for sale and in which the margin of gross profit—from which all of the dealer's costs must be paid—is usually in the range of 1 to 2 per cent of the price of the merchandise.

Assuming that a $1-million bond issue will mature in 25 years and bear interest at 4 per cent, a dealer might bid par ($1,000 per bond), hoping to offer the bonds at a price of 101 ($1,010 per bond), making a gross profit of 1 per cent or $10,000. At the proposed offering price the bonds would yield approximately 3.94 per cent to the investor. Should the dealer find that investors are unwilling to purchase the bonds unless the yield is 4 per cent, then the dealer would have to cut his offering price to that level or down to $1,000 per bond—a price equal to his own cost. His loss would equal those costs that he could not avoid.

The system of syndicate bidding, or syndication, has grown in the municipal bond industry. By means of the syndicate arrangement dealers of all sizes and all geographical locations may be brought together in a group to participate in bidding for and offering bond issues of all sizes and types. At any one time a dealer may be a member of as many as 10 to 20 syndicates that, depending upon market conditions, may have undistributed balances varying from a few bonds to several million dollars worth of bonds.

The syndicate compensates the member who actually sells the bonds through a mechanism called the "takedown concession." If it is assumed as a typical case that the gross spread expected by the syndicate is $10 per $1,000 bond, a portion of this amount will be considered as underwriting profit and a portion selling profit. Assuming an offering price of $1,010 per bond, a bid of $1,000 per bond, and a gross spread of $10 per bond, $5 of this spread may be determined as selling compensation or takedown. The selling dealer, then, would withdraw bonds from the syndicate account at the offering price less the takedown, or at $1,005, and in selling the bond (at $1,010) will be compensated to the extent of $5 per bond. Of this amount, the syndicate member may reallow a portion—say, $2.50 per bond—to other dealers who are not members of the syndicate but who nevertheless may wish to sell bonds to their own investor clients. In this event, the syndicate member would sell the bond to the nonmember at $1,007.50, retaining $2.50 as his selling compensation, and the nonmember would earn $2.50 upon selling the bond to his client at $1,010.

After all the bonds have been withdrawn (or taken down) by syndicate members or otherwise sold by the manager for the benefit of the syndicate, there remains in the syndicate the difference between the gross spread and the takedown. This amount, less syndicate expenses, is distributed by the manager to the various syndicate members in proportion to their participations in the account as underwriting compensation.

The purchase of a new issue of municipal bonds from the issuer by an investment banker and the resale of the bonds by the investment banker constitutes the primary or new issue market. Any subsequent sale of the bonds by an investor or dealer is in the secondary market.

Like any other security, there are times when the municipal bond must be disposed of before maturity. Heirs sell, institutions have different securities needs, and commercial banks see deposits and commercial loans rise and fall cyclically, and so on. A change in money rates often will see an underwriting syndicate forced to break up and divide the unsold bonds among its members. Whatever the reason, the bond returns to the market to be offered to the investigating public for the second time. Hence, the term *secondary market* was created. The secondary market is almost without exception far more voluminous at any given date than the primary or new issue market.

The "Blue List" is published every business day, carrying most of the current offerings of all dealer subscribers. The offerings (with prices) are listed under the general headings of each of the states with subheadings for certain special bonds. Thus, the "Blue List" is a central listing of all available municipal bonds that dealers are publicly offering, and it also carries advertisements of new issues.

The "Daily Bond Buyer," also published every business day, serves a similar purpose in presenting detailed information regarding proposed bond issues and the results of sales of new issues of municipal bonds, together with other statistical information regarding interest rates on municipal and U.S. Government bonds. The "Daily Bond Buyer" has also offered on a subscription basis a wire service called "Munifacts." Via a private teletype circuit it helps to keep traders as well as underwriters advised on current news of pertinent importance in the municipal bond market.

Municipal Bond Ratings

Ratings for municipal bonds are basically an outgrowth of corporate bond ratings. The first ratings for corporate bonds appeared in 1909 when Moody's began rating railroads. In 1914, Moody's expanded its services to cover public utilities and industrials. In 1922, Poor's began rating all industries; Standard

Statistics and Fitch followed in 1924. Thus, four ratings were available for most large issues from 1924 through March 1941, when Poor's was merged with Standard Statistics.

Moody's began rating municipal bonds in 1919; Standard and Poor's not until 1950. Until the Great Depression, Moody's rated most issues *Aaa* or *Aa*. Large numbers of defaults (2.5 per cent of a total of 160,000 local governmental units in the 1930's) during the depression years caused Moody's to re-evaluate standards and adopt a more conservative approach, principally because 48 per cent of the number of defaulting issues in the 1930's were rated *Aaa* or the highest quality.

Agency ratings are long-run appraisals of the intrinsic quality of bond issues and reflect the ability of the issue to withstand default and capital loss over long periods of time in the future. Although agencies do not divulge in detail the particular factor and weights used in assigning the individual ratings, it does appear that attention is given to matters such as earnings, coverage, lien, position, capital structure, and growth and stability of earnings.

Moody's does not rate issues of less than $600,000 nor obligations of enterprises without established earnings records, projects under construction, or issues where current financial data are lacking. More than 16,000 public bodies and 20,000 issues were included in the 1966 Moody's Municipal and Government Manual.

Standard and Poor's rated 7,000 issues in 1966 but does not publish a comprehensive volume of data like Moody's prepares. Standard and Poor's rates governmental bodies having at least $1 million of outstanding debt.

TABLE 8-9. Municipal Bond-Rating Schedule

MOODY'S RATING	STANDARD AND POOR'S RATING	SIGNIFICANCE OF THE RATING
Aaa	AAA	Prime—highest grade
Aa	AA	High grade
A	A	Upper medium grade
Baa	BBB	Medium grade—the lowest group in which investment characteristics predominate
Ba	BB	Lower medium grade—these bonds move with interest rates but not enough to be significant as investments
Nonrated bonds	B, CCC, CC, and C	These ratings denote various degrees of risk and denote speculative issues
Nonrated bonds	DDD, DD, and D	Defaults—the higher ratings reflect a greater possibility of recovery

Other agencies that either rate municipal bonds or provide detailed information on municipal credits include Dun and Bradstreet, Inc., Fitch Investor Service, the North Carolina Municipal Advisory Service, the Texas Municipal Advisory Council, and the Oklahoma Municipal Advisory Council.

So attuned are investors to ratings that almost automatically the rating will determine, within rather broad limits, the interest rate the issuer must pay on its bonds. When a bond is not rated, it becomes the task for the underwriter to evaluate the credit and convince his market that the bond is, in fact, comparable to one that has received a particular rating. However, in 1964 holdings in the unrated category amounted to over one-half of all state and local issues for banks with deposits of less than $5 million. The small local bank is aware of local needs and conditions and is the traditional source of credit for small borrowers both private and public.

In general, there is the greatest demand for those issues rated *A* or better. Unrated issues are preferred to those rate *Ba* or lower since unrated issues usually carry higher yields than those rated issues believed to be comparable.

Security, or safety, remains as the principal, almost the sole ingredient of the ratings. Although statistics are used, great weight is given to numerous economic and nonfinancial factors that can affect the long-term future performance of the bonds.

The significance of ratings to school districts is evident by data given in Table 8-10. For example, the net average interest cost in October, 1967, ranged from 3.99 per cent for bonds rated *Aa* to 4.80 per cent for those rated *Baa*, or a difference of $42,525 in interest payments on a $500,000 bond issue maturing serially over a 20-year period.

Rating services expect effective school management, for example, to be a good public relations group. Management is appraised by how well its reports tell the story as well as by the story itself. Thus, the ratings and corresponding net average interest costs given in Table 8-10 depend upon school management to tell its story through school system records, histories, and statistics, as well as all documents relating to the proposed bond issue School authorities must furnish figures on such things as assessed value of realty, personal property, net direct debt, tax collections over a period of time, etc. From this data, the rating services attempt to answer questions such as the following:

1. Is the population already present, or is it only hoped for?
2. Is the total debt supportable by the present inhabitants under any foreseeable business conditions?
3. What additional financing is to be expected, either from the unit under consideration or from any other unit taxing the same properties?

TABLE 8-10. Average Net Interest Cost of Bonds Sold on the Primary Market for Public Schools: Annually 1959–1960 to 1966–1967 and Monthly November 1966 to November 1967

| | GENERAL OBLIGATION BONDS (PERCENTAGE) | | | | | | | REVENUE BONDS (PER-CENTAGE) |
| | BY MOODY RATINGS | | | | | | NON-RATED | |
PERIOD	Aaa	Aa	A	Baa	Ba	ALL		
			Annual					
1959–1960	3.26	3.63	3.77	4.21	4.55	3.84	4.03	4.21
1960–1961	2.82	3.34	3.33	3.75	3.97	3.48	3.58	3.87
1961–1962	2.84	3.23	3.19	3.51	3.93	3.27	3.43	3.55
1962–1963	2.64	2.86	2.99	3.29	3.72	3.03	3.25	3.42
1963–1964	2.88	3.07	3.17	3.43	3.80	3.21	3.40	3.50
1964–1965	2.93	3.11	3.16	3.44	3.76	3.21	3.40	3.40
1965–1966	3.26	3.48	3.56	3.86	4.01	3.62	3.83	3.83
1966–1967	3.56	3.79	3.86	4.17	4.69	3.94	4.23	4.24
			Monthly 1966					
November	3.83	3.93	4.03	4.38	—	4.10	4.40	4.34
December	—	3.81	3.99	4.34	4.70	4.04	4.41	4.54
			Monthly 1967					
January	3.25	3.67	3.68	3.96	4.50	3.76	4.00	3.54
February	3.13	3.38	3.60	4.14	—	3.65	4.01	3.98
March	—	3.47	3.57	3.90	—	3.71	4.03	3.89
April	3.42	3.50	3.63	3.87	3.99	3.70	3.87	4.03
May	3.54	3.73	3.73	4.15	4.75	3.86	4.11	4.42
June	3.64	3.89	4.05	4.36	4.58	4.07	4.25	4.39
July	—	3.87	4.10	4.56	4.81	4.38	4.41	4.47
August	—	3.88	3.98	4.37	4.82	4.15	4.43	4.85
September	3.71	4.08	4.16	4.43	—	4.17	4.36	5.00
October	—	3.99	4.26	4.80	—	4.10	4.48	4.63
November	—	4.14	4.38	4.67	4.99	4.42	4.62	4.81

SOURCE: *American Education*, Washington, D.C., U.S. Govt. Printing Office, Feb. 1968, p. 28.

4. Are securities payable from unlimited taxes on all property in the community, or are there limitations that might prove troublesome at some future date?

5. Is there heavy dependence on a single plant or a single industry?

6. How vulnerable is the community to economic unsettlement?

7. Are there nearby towns in which the residents can find work?

8. Are industries likely to migrate, and if so are there factors that suggest the attraction of replacements?

9. Has the attitude of the administration been prodebtor or procreditor?

10. Do the laws and traditions lend themselves to debt evasion?

Municipals and the Availability of Credit

The prospective capital outlay of $41.8 billion for public elementary and secondary schools during the decade of 1965–1975 does not truly represent the capital requirements of the public education sector. Rather than need, the determining factor of the volume of new facilities that will be created is somebody's ability and willingness to finance new facilities and somebody else's ability and willingness to service the debt.[10] Facilities are expensive, and many citizens believe taxes are already high. Construction on credit, too, costs vastly more than pay-as-you-go construction.

Taxpayer resistance to financing school construction was evident in 1967 when only 64 per cent of the dollar value of bonds voted on was approved. The dollar value of bonds proposed to the voters fell off in the first 11 months of the year to only 80 per cent of the amount for the same period in 1966.[11]

However, total sales of school bonds for the first 11 months of 1967 were $3 billion, topping the previous annual high of $2.9 billion recorded in 1965. State and local governments together issued $13.1 billions worth of bonds in that 11-month period, exceeding the volume in the first 11 months of 1966 by 29.4 per cent.

Uncertainties in the municipal bond market appeared in November, 1967, probably because of the British devaluation of the pound, the rise in the Federal Reserve rediscount rate, a continued deficit in foreign dollar balance of payments, an overload of tax-exempt industrial revenue bonds, and other unfavorable factors. Bond yields moved up 15 basis points to 4.42 per cent— the highest rate, as measured by the index since the 1930's.

History shows that all yields tended to rise from 1900 to 1921. They then fell most of the time until 1946, rose most of the time until 1960, stabilized for five years, and then started to rise again.

Municipal yields almost always fluctuated in the same direction as corporate bond yields, but between 1930 and 1955 the municipal yield fluctuations were much larger than the corporate yield fluctuations. This was undoubtedly because of the growing effect of the tax structure. The bull market in municipals far exceeded the bull market in corporates in the 1940's, and after 1946 the bear market in municipals far exceeded the bear market in corporates. However, the two markets have fluctuated similarly since 1955.

Early in the century when there was little or no income tax, the municipal yields were about the same as the corporate yields and for a time around 1913

[10] *Ibid.*, p. 276.
[11] *American Education*, Washington, D.C., U.S. Govt Printing Office, Feb. 1968, p. 28.

rose to be slightly higher than the corporate yields. During World War I, when corporate income tax rates rose to 12 per cent and individual top bracket rates to 75 per cent, a spread developed in favor of corporate yields, and by 1930 the municipal-corporate yield ratio had declined to 90 per cent. The ratio has never been higher since that time.

During World War II, the municipal-corporate yield ratio fell to 41 per cent. In the postwar years the volume of net new municipal financing grew from below zero to over $4 billion a year. As early as 1947 the flood of new municipal issues swamped the new funds of high-bracket private investors. Bond dealers had to seek lower bracket investors and especially institutions. By 1948 the municipal ratio was up from 40 per cent to above 62 per cent, and this equated to the prevailing 38 per cent corporate tax rate, the point of indifference for fire and casualty insurance companies and banks. This was not enough to attract a large enough volume of such institutional funds into the municipal market, and municipal prices continued to plunge much faster than corporate bond prices. By 1954 the ratio had reached 79 per cent, and this large differential from the 48 per cent corporate tax residual was enough. Municipals were then (as now) a bonanza for all corporate taxpayers and for many medium bracket private investors. Medium-grade municipals were attractive even to low-tax-bracket life insurance companies.

TABLE 8-11. Net after Tax Yield of Prime New Corporate Bonds and Municipal Bonds to Various Investor Groups in February 1966

	GROSS YIELD OF CORPORATES (PERCENTAGE)	TAX BRACKET (PERCENTAGE)	NET YIELD OF CORPORATES (PERCENTAGE)	NET YIELD OF MUNICIPALS (PERCENTAGE)
Top-bracket private investors	5%	70%	1.50%	3.60%
Corporate bracket (commercial banks, fire and casualty insurance companies, business corporations)	5	48	2.60	3.60
Medium-bracket investors	5	40	3	3.60
Low-bracket private investors	5	28	3.60	3.60
Low bracket (many life insurance companies, many savings institutions, many small private investors)	5	20	4	3.60
Nontaxpayers (pension funds, public retirement funds, foundations, endowment funds, political agencies)	5	0	5	3.60

SOURCE: *Public Facility Financing*, Vol. 2, Washington, D.C., U.S. Govt. Printing Office, Dec. 1966, p. 270.

Several groups that used to buy municipals have become net liquidators in recent years—that is, retirement funds, savings banks, and life insurance companies—because municipals now yield less than corporates to these investors. Commercial banks have come to dominate the municipal market. Changes since 1962 in the maximum rates payable on time and savings

TABLE 8-12. Ownership of State and Local Government Securities, 1965 (Dollars in Billions)

INVESTOR GROUP	AMOUNT HELD	PERCENTAGE DISTRIBUTION
Individuals	$35.0	35.8
State and local funds	5.3	5.4
Commercial banks	36.6	37.4
Mutual savings banks	.4	.4
Life insurance companies	4.7	4.8
Nonlife insurance companies	10.9	11.1
Pension funds	1.8	1.8
Other	3.1	3.2
TOTAL	$97.8	100.0

SOURCE: *Public Facility Financing*, Vol. 2, Washington, D.C., U.S. Govt. Printing Office, Dec. 1966, p. 331.

deposits under provisions of regulation Q and the consequent increases in bank funds also played a part in influencing the buying policies of banks' municipal bond departments. As a result of an inflow of high cost deposits, commercial banks were under pressure to examine all avenues of asset acquisition, and investment in tax-exempt bonds offered one possible way of preserving or improving after tax income in spite of higher costs. All indications are that over the next ten years, commercial banks will continue to be a major force in the municipal market. It has been projected that by 1975 the total loans and investments of commercial banks will range between $475 and $525 billion, while their state and local government bond holdings will reach $100 to $115 billion.[12]

Since most of the institutional investor groups in the United States have little or no interest in tax-exempts, it is fortunate for the municipal yield structure that the net volume of new municipal financing during recent years has not been very large. Each year the gross of new municipal issues sets a record and it is spoken of in the press as enormous, but, in fact, considering the size of our capital markets, our economy, and our municipal expenditures,

[12] *Public Facility Financing, op. cit.*, p. 350.

net municipal capital requirements as shown in Table 8-13 can be called modest.

Borrowing for school construction is not painless, as almost every real estate taxpayer knows. Uncle Sam can borrow and refund at maturity and, thus, carry a constantly rising debt provided it does not rise too fast. States and municipalities, including school systems, on the contrary usually sell serial issues and start repaying principal the next year. These principal repayments may come to 3 per cent or 5 per cent of the new debt, and total debt service may thus run 6 per cent to 9 per cent a year on the sum borrowed. Thus, a new school costs taxpayers dearly, and they know it. No doubt, this explains why school capital debt has not grown much faster than it has and why it probably will not soar.

TABLE 8-13. Principal Net Demands for Credit in the United States (Dollars in Billions)

	1960	1961	1962	1963	1964	1965
Real estate mortgages	$14.8	$18.9	$24.9	$30.2	$30.2	$29.4
Corporate bonds	5.0	5.1	4.9	5.6	6.6	8.1
Term loans	.9	1.0	1.4	2.0	2.8	5.3
State and local bonds	4.0	5.0	5.3	6.3	5.6	6.8
Foreign and international bank bonds	.6	.5	.9	1.0	.7	.9
TOTAL long-term demands	$25.3	$30.5	$37.4	$45.1	$45.9	$50.5
Other bank loans	5.1	4.6	8.6	9.1	10.8	15.0
Treasury and agency debt (publicly held)	−2.7	5.8	6.1	2.5	3.2	.5
GRAND TOTAL of demands	$27.7	$40.9	$52.1	$56.7	$59.9	$66.0

SOURCE: *Public Facility Financing*, Vol. 2, Washington, D.C., U.S. Govt. Printing Office, Dec. 1966, p. 274.

A significant development regarding municipal financing occurred in March, 1968, when the U.S. Treasury called a halt to the rising flood of tax-exempt municipal bonds that have provided private corporations with tax-free financing for billions of dollars worth of new industrial plants. The Treasury issued regulations canceling the tax exemption for interest paid on new issues of the so-called industrial development bonds, or IDB's. The action did not affect the tax exemption of any bonds issued before March 15, 1968, and provided exemptions and exceptions in cases where the cities or corporations concerned had made financial or other binding commitment.

The plans issued by the Treasury brought a storm of protest by congressmen and municipal officials from cities that have used this financing device. The Treasury invited comments, complaints, or suggestions within 30 days and announced that a hearing would be held in Washington in May, 1968, before the regulations became final.

The Treasury estimated that between $2 billion and $2.5 billion in industrial development bond issues had been voted or planned for in 1968, most of which would be cut off because of the new ruling. The volume of IDB's had been doubling each year.

Congress could overthrow the Treasury's decision. The Senate Finance Committee had recommended an amendment to the Excise Tax Extension Bill which would bar the Treasury from eliminating the IDB tax exemption by administrative action.

The Treasury described the swiftly expanding output of IDB's as an abuse of the tax-exemption privilege, which originally was intended to help states and municipalities obtain low-interest financing for needed waterworks, schools, and other public facilities. However, by 1968, 42 states permitted municipal and other governments to use the device to finance the construction of plants which were then leased to private firms. Bonds were paid off from the rentals paid by the companies, and therefore—in the Treasury's view—the municipality simply made its federal tax exemption available to a private corporation.

Provision for IDB's meant a revenue loss to the Treasury unofficially estimated at more than $75 million in 1967. More importantly, the outpouring of IDB's had the effect of glutting the market for municipal issues, forcing interest rates up, and making it harder for cities, school districts, and other units to float bond issues for normal public activities.

Regarding municipals in general, calculations by the U.S. Treasury and others indicate that the tax revenues foregone because of the present tax-exemption of the initial income of state and local obligations considerably exceed the interest cost savings enjoyed by these units. Bills introduced in the Congress recently propose that the federal government subsidize 33 per cent of the interest cost on state and local obligations that voluntarily give up their tax-exempt status. Issuing governments would be free to choose between issuing their securities on a tax-exempt basis as they now do, or issuing them on a taxable basis and receiving the subsidy.

Another proposed form of federal government assistance is the guaranteeing of debt service on state and local obligations to be financed by insurance fees. Such a proposal would virtually eliminate the default risk to investors on insured obligations, make them homogeneous in terms of investment quality (thus eliminating the need for individual bond ratings), and would enhance their marketability.

It appears that the current proposals would not constitute a revenue bonanza for the Treasury but rather would entail a net cost to the federal government. The net cost would be effected primarily because of the cost of the subsidy as well as in higher direct borrowing costs, since guaranteed taxable state and local obligations would be more competitive with U.S. government and federal agency issues.

CHAPTER 9

STATE-LOCAL SYSTEMS OF PUBLIC SCHOOL FINANCIAL SUPPORT

Introduction

Although each state is individually responsible for the development, adoption, and support of its own financial program, two principal types of plans for public school support may be conceptualized as (1) total centralized financing by the state, or (2) total decentralized financing through local governments. It is between these two polar positions that state practices are actually defined, but the decentralized program is dominant as shown by two statistics. First, it is estimated that for Fiscal Year 1967, 52.1 per cent of revenue receipts of school districts were received from local sources, while 39.9 per cent were received from state sources. Secondly, it is estimated that within only 15 states did state sources provide 50 per cent or more of the public school receipts. The range of state support was from a low percentage of 5.4 in Nebraska to a high of 76.8 in Delaware, as presented in Table 9-1.

217

TABLE 9-1. Percentage of Local Public School Revenue Receipts from the States

0–10%:	30–40%:	50–60%:
Nebraska (5.4)	Kansas (30.9)	Tennessee (50.2)
New Hampshire (9.8)	Maryland (31.9)	Mississippi (50.5)
10–20%:	Missouri (32.0)	Kentucky (52.3)
South Dakota (15.2)	Connecticut (34.4)	Utah (52.8)
Iowa (15.3)	Minnesota (38.3)	Alaska (53.3)
20–30%:	Indiana (38.8)	Nevada (54.0)
Illinois (22.2)	Virginia (38.8)	Washington (57.5)
Massachusetts (23.2)	40–50%:	South Carolina (58.7)
Wisconsin (25.1)	Wyoming (40.7)	Georgia (58.8)
Ohio (25.2)	Ariznoa (40.8)	60–70%:
Vermont (26.1)	Idaho (41.7)	New Mexico (62.3)
Oklahoma (26.2)	Pennsylvania (43.9)	Hawaii (62.5)
Colorado (26.3)	Arkansas (45.0)	North Carolina (63.8)
North Dakota (26.5)	New York (45.7)	Louisiana (63.7)
Oregon (27.0)	Florida (46.5)	Alabama (64.3)
Montana (28.7)	Michigan (47.7)	70–80%:
New Jersey (29.9)	Texas (49.3)	Delaware (76.8)
Maine (29.9)	West Virginia (49.5)	

SOURCE: *Estimate of School Statistics 1966–67*, Research Report, 1966–R20, Washington, D.C., National Education Association, 1966, p. 32.

Total state support of the public schools would place full program and financial responsibility for general educational requirements and services upon state legislatures, thereby reducing direct local influence on the content of the school program. Delaware and North Carolina have not had total state support for public schools but consistently have had proportionately more state funds than any other states.

Although decentralized plans have existed for a long period of time and at the moment are the dominant type, pressure for greater state and federal support to reduce so-called heavy local tax requirements, as described in Chapter 7, is likely to result in a new arrangement between those who propose completely centralized or completely decentralized school support. Thus, school finance programs in Iowa, Nebraska, New Hampshire, and South Dakota are particularly due for a more equitable state-local school finance structure.

Agreements and Disagreements on Basic or Foundation Programs

A foundation program is defined as the basic program of education that the state guarantees to every public school child in the state. This program is expressed in terms of the amount of money considered essential or basic for each unit of educational need. The cost of the basic program is shared between the state and the local school systems.

Because some school systems have more taxable wealth for each school child than do others, without a foundation program the wealthier systems could provide the cost of a basic program with a low tax rate, while poorer systems would have to levy a higher tax rate to provide a comparable program. Therefore, a foundation program law provides generally that, in order to participate, each school system must levy a required rate as its share, and the balance of the cost of the basic program is provided from state funds. The poorer systems thus receive proportionately more of the cost of the basic program from state funds than do the wealthier ones.

The development of an adequate foundation program plan for school support begins with the identification of educational services to be included for all public schools in a state. The services are then translated into terms of the dollar amounts required.

It is recommended that state statutes define the actual education program only in general terms in order to allow budget and program flexibility, but specify precisely the dollar amounts that will purchase the desired education program. However, care must be exercised to be certain that the dollar amount specified in the statutes will continue to purchase the desired program. A cost adjustment factor that reflects this changing purchasing power of the educational dollar would be helpful to legislatures and school officials.[1]

An adequate program of education has some major characteristics that have been identified in a recent report concerning development of a foundation program:

1. It must be effective in developing attitudes, habits of mind, skills, and the kinds of knowledge and understanding that will become instrumental in assuring continuous change and growth for every student.

2. It must facilitate the development of the human resources of the state in order to assure continuing improvement in the economy, institutions, and people.

3. It must assure high quality educational provisions for all but be adaptable to meet the needs and develop the competencies of each.

4. It must provide for all services needed for effective education: competent and skillful teachers, administrators, supervisors, clerical staff and other personnel, adequate housing and equipment, transportation, and other essential services.

5. It must be sufficiently flexible that adjustments can be made readily to meet emerging needs.

[1] Albert R. Munse, *State Programs for Public School Support*. Washington, D.C., U.S. Govt. Printing Office, 1965, p. 5.

6. It must be adequately financed on the basis of public recognition and acceptance of the fact that expenditures for a high quality program of education constitute an investment in people who will contribute to further progress in the state.[2]

A foundation program law for a state school system is based on the fundamental philosophy that every child needs and deserves a good educational program. A number of characteristics or basic principles of foundation programs have been agreed upon by authorities:

1. A foundation program should be designed to assure that a high quality program of education can be provided for every child regardless of where he lives, the color of his skin, his creed, his intellectual level, his parents' economic status, or any other factor.

2. The plans and provisions for a foundation program should place major emphasis on local leadership in the organization, administration, and operation of effective schools, and thus provide strong encouragement for the development and exercise of local leadership and responsibilities.

3. A foundation program should provide for a joint effort involving financial resources and other resources of both the state and the local community.

4. A foundation program should make provisions for the required local financial participation in public school programs to be calculated on a fair and equitable basis in relation to local financial resources as compared to those of other local school districts.

5. In order to ensure an adequate equalized opportunity for every child, provisions should be included in a foundation program to require local school districts to meet their required effort.

6. A foundation program should provide to the local school district the opportunity, encouragement and incentive to go beyond the required local effort.

7. A foundation program should include all essential school costs that determine the level of quality to be achieved under the program. Those costs are (a) instructional salaries, (b) other current expenses, (c) capital outlay, and (d) transportation.

8. The formula for determining the ability of any funds to be provided by a local school district should be included in the foundation program and based on measurable factors that are common to all school districts in the state.

9. A foundation program must allow a reasonable degree of leeway and flexibility in order to provide for changing needs, desires, and resources. Evaluations of major aspects should occur periodically.

[2] *Beyond the Minimum—A New Dimension for Kentucky's Foundation Program for Education.* Louisville, The Kentucky Education Association, Jan. 1967, p. 29.

10. A foundation program should be designed to encourage sound and efficient organization, administration, and operation of school districts and schools.[3]

Authorities have isolated two basic approaches and an option to combine elements of the two approaches in the development of a foundation program. In one approach, an amount per pupil or per classroom unit is guaranteed, while in the second approach incentives for a kind of educational program are included in the formula, and the amount guaranteed depends on the degree of compliance with the type of program for which incentives are offered. The latter approach or a combination of the basic two appear to be the trend in the more recently adopted foundation laws.

A foundation program that guarantees a given amount per pupil or classroom unit is often called the "unit cost" method and is based on the principle that the state is guaranteeing the program of education that a given amount of money per unit will buy. Advocates of this method stress the discretionary power of local school systems in that a local system might budget state money for salaries, instructional supplies maintenance, etc., or for any other purpose the school personnel decide suits their community best. Because state funds are distributed under this approach without regard to the kind of educational program being provided in the schools, the degree of equality of educational opportunity provided by the schools throughout the state will depend on the strength of local administrative units, local standards, and soundness of local budgets. However, other state laws pertaining to education can be utilized to control the program.

In the second or incentive approach, the state defines the incentives that it wishes to guarantee in order to improve the quality of the educational program. For example, the program the state wishes to guarantee might include reasonable class size, more highly trained teachers with more experience, longer terms, adequate-sized school units, etc. The state would then pay more money as an incentive for local systems to provide a program meeting state goals.

Distribution of funds under an incentive plan usually is on a classroom or teacher unit basis. Costs are determined frequently by a salary schedule based either on training or experience of teachers or both, plus a fixed amount per unit for other operating expense. Additional services such as supervision can be included by giving extra units for these purposes. The foundation program laws usually stipulate that a teacher must be employed for each unit for which aid is given.

[3] *Ibid.*, pp. 33–36.

Relative to the criterion of equity, those who are opposed to incentives contend that it is unfair to give different amounts of state aid per unit to schools with the same assessed valuation per pupil. Proponents of incentives counteract this criticism with the proposal that communities with the same wealth and the same quality of program (expressed in terms of the incentives) receive the same amount per unit.

Support for the incentive plan comes from those who believe that state funds should be distributed in such a way as to improve the quality of the education program. For example, on the premise that the quality of the educational program is improved with better trained and more experienced teachers, and because the cost of employing such teachers is greater, contention is that the state should offer an incentive in the form of more state aid to local units employing better qualified teachers.

Opponents of incentives for teacher training and experience in the foundation program often argue that because the basis of state distribution usually is well below the "going rate" for teachers' salaries, disparity between poorer and richer districts is increased. Poorer districts do not have sufficient local funds to permit them to employ teachers with higher qualifications, and the benefit of the incentives goes to the wealthier districts. However, it has been shown that employment of teachers with more training and experience is not necessarily related to the wealth of the school system, but is more likely to depend on whether the system is rural or urban.

Opponents of the incentive law maintain that schools should not be rewarded for employing teachers with long experience, because it is impossible and impracticable for all schools to do so. The counter-argument is that experienced teachers provide a better quality of education and that offering incentives for experience encourages career teachers and cuts down on turnover, thereby improving the educational program. In addition, because it costs the schools more to employ teachers with longer experience under the salary schedules of local schools, claim is that as a simple matter of economics this fact should be recognized in the formula.

Incentives are often included relative to the length of the school term. Those who favor an incentive for a longer term feel that if it is omitted those schools trying to improve the education of children through longer terms are penalized. Those against inclusion of such an incentive in the formula contend that the state should approve a law stating what the length of term should be and not leave this decision to local school systems as a discretionary matter. Contention is, too, that again it is the wealthier systems that benefit, because the state aid in itself is insufficient to provide the longer term, and the poorer systems cannot raise the remainder of the money locally to support a longer term. Somehow it seems that adequacy of the state support may be a factor in the wealthy-versus-poor argument pertaining to incentive plans.

Some authorities contend that recognizing any service in the foundation program formula—such as kindergarten, vocational, or special education—is a form of state control. Argument is that schools may then start these services solely to obtain state money and not because the services may be desired. Belief is that if there are state mandates, either the state should guarantee sufficient money to meet the mandates or help support them directly; otherwise, either the tax rate will have to be excessive or the quality of other program phases will suffer.

Because most states have laws regarding length of term, minimum salary schedules, curriculum requirements, compulsory attendance, etc., certain authorities hold that the state-versus-local control argument is largely theoretical. Furthermore, since education is the responsibility of the state, the state has ultimate control anyway.

Most authorities who oppose other types of incentives and special aids do not oppose those given to stimulate school system reorganization. Reduction of the number of school systems from 21,000 to 10,000 by the early 1970's has nearly unanimous support.

Many of the arguments advanced for or against either of the two foundation approaches—that is, unit cost or incentive—are really reflections of basic differences in political or economic philosophy. Those who believe that the state has the greater responsibility tend to favor a high level of state support. They also tend to favor the inclusion of incentives in a foundation program as a further means of strengthening educational standards in all school systems of the state. Moreover, those who favor incentives in any program of state support also tend to favor the state's contribution of a larger share of the school dollar.

Conversely, those who stress the importance of greater financial responsibility at the local level tend to favor a lower percentage of state support and few, if any, incentives in a foundation program. Those who oppose incentives in a formula may not necessarily be opposed to the end to be achieved by the incentive; they simply do not want the meeting of such standards as a prerequisite for state aid, because they believe local responsibility is thereby weakened.

Closely allied to theoretical differences over whether local or state financial responsibility is of prime importance is the question of what kinds of taxes one tends to favor. Thus, those who favor relief from so-called high local property taxes are more likely to favor a higher percentage of state support; those who are concerned about higher nonproperty state taxes are likely to favor a higher percentage of local financial effort, whether the revenue be from property or nonproperty sources.

Among those supporting incentives, the kind of incentive that any person or group favors is likely to reflect the importance that is attached to a particular phase of the educational program. Where fund limitations necessitate a choice between kinds of incentives, groups naturally tend to give priority in importance to the particular incentive that is "closest to their hearts."

There are a few people, of course, who believe that education should be financed wholly from local tax sources and therefore oppose state aid in any form, through a foundation program or otherwise. There are others who believe that state aid should be distributed only in very unusual circumstances and therefore oppose on principle foundation programs, which by their nature are a means for statewide distribution of state funds for educational purposes.

Those who favor the idea of a foundation program should keep in mind these points in their own evaluation of any program: Does it meet their desired objectives, whether they pertain to equalization, incentives, broadening the tax base, or shifting the tax burden, etc.? If so, are the means of achieving the desired objective or objectives (method of distribution) the best ones for the purpose? Is the division of financial responsibility between state and local funds equitable, and do the state and local funds come from the proper sources in equitable proportion to the ability of these sources to produce revenue? Finally, are the state and local levels of support specified by the foundation program adequate to achieve the objectives of the program?

Development of the Foundation Program

As discussed in Chapter 7, every state provided significant aid to local schools by 1900, but most did so with a bewildering variety of techniques. There was no common denominator until the publication of a study by Cubberley in 1905.[4] Cubberley brought order to the varied practices then in existence, and during the decades since Cubberley's publication professional educators have labored hard to explore the possibility of articulating general principles to govern state support to schools. Cubberley summarized the ends of state aid as follows:

> Theoretically all the children of the state are equally important and are entitled to have the same advantages; practically this can never be quite true.

[4] Ellwood P. Cubberley, *School Funds and Their Apportionment*, New York, Teachers College, Columbia University, 1906.

The duty of the state is to secure for all as high a minimum of good instruction as is possible, but not to reduce all to this minimum; to equalize the advantages to all as nearly as can be done with the resources at hand; to place premium on those local efforts which will enable communities to rise above the legal minimum as far as possible; and to encourage communities to extend their educational energies to new and desirable undertakings.[5]

Cubberley was concerned not so much with the form of state taxes but more with the extension of educational opportunity in the form of secondary education, kindergarten, vocational education, physical education, and evening classes. He encouraged state support of pioneer programs at the local system level and eventual inclusion of new programs as part of the state-mandated minimum requirements for school systems.

Cubberley was impressed with the extreme inequalities in school programs and in local financial ability to provide school programs. He examined data from California, Indiana, Kansas, Missouri, Washington, and Wisconsin plus New England, and concluded that inequality of program and financial ability existed throughout the United States.

The need for general school aid from the state along with a need to extend educational programs was espoused by Cubberley. Among other methods of distributing funds, Cubberley considered (1) apportionment on the basis of the amount of taxes paid; (2) distribution on the basis of total population of school systems; (3) distribution based on a school census; and (4) distribution based on ADM (average daily membership). These alternatives he considered to be unsatisfactory because they favored urban over rural areas and offered little program improvement incentives.

Determination by Cubberley was that the best plan of state general aid would be based on a combination of ADA (aggregate daily attendance multiplied by length of term) and of the number of teachers employed. Cubberley stated that the combination plan distributed aid on the basis of "effort and need." Because the plan placed no restriction on the type of work performed by an employed teacher, state aid would be provided for those districts offering programs such as kindergarten, vocational education, and physical education. In addition, districts lengthening the school year would not be penalized, nor would rural systems with low pupil-teacher ratios.

Cubberley's proposal, which was being implemented by at least a quarter of the states in 1960, included provision for a very modest program of equalization aid.[6] Equalizing grants were to be made from a reserve fund,

[5] *Ibid.*, p. 17.

[6] Paul R. Mort, Walter C. Reusser, and John W. Polley, *Public School Finance*, 3rd ed. New York, McGraw-Hill, 1960, p. 258.

which might amount to 5 per cent of the total state educational apportionment. As stated by Benson, "It is a cruel measure of equalization, moreover, that offers aid only when a district cannot provide a 'minimum' of services at a 'maximum' tax rate."[7] However, Cubberley's plan included a general

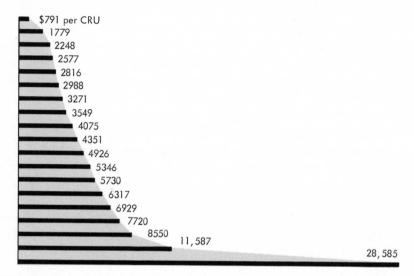

$791 per CRU
1779
2248
2577
2816
2988
3271
3549
4075
4351
4926
5346
5730
6317
6929
7720
8550
11,587
28,585

FIGURE 9-1 Comparison of Revenues Raised per Classroom Unit (CRU) by Colorado School Districts Through a 15-Mill Levy.

SOURCE: Frank S. Miles, *Understanding Colorado School Finance*, Boulder, Colorado: The Colorado Association of School Boards, 1968, p. 8.

requirement that a school system was to make the maximum tax effort allowed by law and still be unable to meet the minimum demands set by the state before applying for equalization aid. Result was that those states implementing the plan gave a favorable weighting to those systems with highly qualified personnel; but it was the rich districts who would benefit most because they were able to hire the trained and experienced teachers in the first place and who would use additional state support to hire additional teachers partially financed by the poorer districts who could not afford the local share of the cost of additional teachers.

Conceptualization of the modern practices in equalization were developed by George D. Strayer and Robert M. Haig in two pages of the Educational Finance Inquiry Commission report relative to the Commission's study for

[7] Charles S. Benson, *The Economics of Public Education*. Boston, Houghton Mifflin, 1961, p. 200.

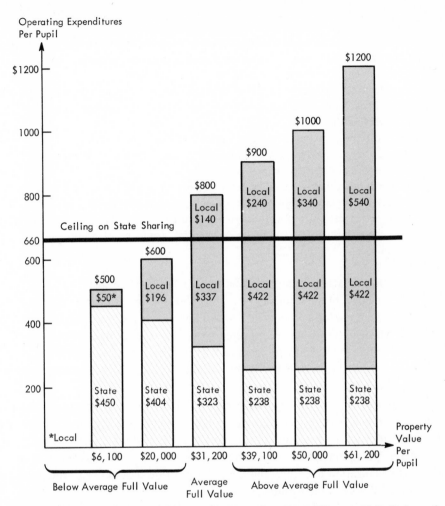

FIGURE 9-2 Relationship Between Operating Expenditures, Full Value of Taxable Real Property, State Aid, and Local Taxes in New York State.

SOURCE: *Understanding Problems in School Finance*, Albany, New York: The University of the State of New York, The State Education Department, September, 1967, p. 11. Mimeographed.

New York State (1921–1924).[8] The Strayer–Haig formula, commonly called the foundation program plan, provided:

> ... The essentials are that there should be uniformity in the rates of school taxation levied to provide the satisfactory minimum offering and that there be

[8] George D. Strayer and Robert M. Haig, *Financing of Education in the State of New York*. A report reviewed and presented by the Educational Finance Inquiry Commission under the auspices of the American Council on Education. New York, 1923, pp. 173–174.

such a degree of state control over the expenditure of the proceeds of school taxes as may be necessary to insure that the satisfactory minimum offering shall be made at a reasonable cost. Since costs vary from place to place in the state, and bear diverse relationships to the taxpaying abilities of the various districts, the achievement of uniformity would involve the following:

(1) A local school tax in support of the satisfactory minimum offering would be levied in each district at a rate which would provide the necessary funds for that purpose in the richest district.

(2) This richest district then might raise all of its school money by means of the local tax, assuming that a satisfactory tax, capable of being locally administered, could be devised.

(3) Every other district could be permitted to levy a local tax at the same rate and apply the proceeds toward the costs of schools, but—

(4) Since the rate is uniform, this tax would be sufficient to meet the costs only in the richest districts and the deficiencies would be made up by state subventions.[9]

Thus, if a satisfactory minimum offering in a certain state cost $700, and if the richest district in the state had an assessed valuation per pupil in ADA of $50,000, then a levy at a 14-mill rate would finance the offering in the richest district. All districts would be expected to tax themselves at a 14-mill rate minimum. State aid would vary from district to district but would amount in each case to the difference between the 14-mill rate and $700, the cost of the minimum offering.

A weakness of the Strayer–Haig formula is that it gave proportional tax burdens among rich and poor districts alike, but only at the amount of the foundation program. In addition, the same number of dollars may buy quite a different program from one district to another. Strayer and Haig also stressed equalization over incentives, a polar position that in itself brought a decided weakness to the formula.

Paul Mort advanced a number of refinements in the Strayer–Haig plan with his associates and disciples at Columbia University. Among them were (1) the key-district concept; (2) the adaptability principle; (3) the weighted-pupil measure; and (4) local tax leeway. Mort proposed the idea of using the "largest wealthy district" as the key district for determining the local contribution rate. Otherwise, for example, a small district with 50 pupils and a $1-million assessed valuation per pupil according to the Strayer–Haig plan could be the wealthiest district, and the local contribution rate would be unusually low for the remainder of the districts. Thus, there would be an unproportionately high rate of state support, thereby probably weakening

[9] *Ibid.*, pp. 174–175.

local educational effort in general. Mort proposed that basing a foundation program on the adaptability principle would emphasize the dynamic aspect of the work of school districts. Without such an emphasis, programs would be built on either the average level of expenditure over the entire state or the level of expenditure in districts of average income and freeze the level of performance of a district for all time in an economy free of inflation.

Mort used state and national norms in determining unusual costs to be included in a modified Strayer–Haig plan. Thus, allowances were made for the extra costs involved in secondary education, small districts with low teacher-pupil ratios, and sparsely settled regions with high transportation costs.

The concept of local tax leeway provided for a downward adjustment of the rate of local contribution so that almost all districts would receive some state aid. Also, the local district would have the discretionary power to tax itself beyond the required local contribution rate in order to purchase its own unique program, presumably one of a quality beyond the so-called state-mandated minimum.

Categories of Modern Foundation Program Support

Figure 9-3 includes a summary of the general patterns of state plans used to support state-local programs for public elementary and secondary schools in Fiscal Year 1967, according to a quasimodern classification of state distributions. Support plans were classified as "fixed grant" if they provided state support on the basis of a fixed amount per unit of educational need. Other categories were "variable-equalizing" and a combination of "fixed and variable-equalizing." The variable-equalizing plan provided for a distribution wherein the per-pupil or per-classroom unit amount of the state grant received by school districts was greater for the financially less able districts.

The most direct and the simplest of the state procedures for providing an amount for school support is shown by *A* in Figure 9-3. Theoretically, a state having this support pattern had only to determine the amount per unit of education need it considered essential and distribute the appropriate amount to each of the school systems of the state. Local taxes generally did not enter into the calculation for determining the amount of state funds.

An example of the fixed-grant plan was that in Connecticut in Fiscal Year 1967 when the state legislature established a per pupil aid fund, from which was distributed an amount to pay the operating or tuition expenses for resident public school pupils. The amount of per-pupil grant depended on the number of resident pupils in ADM in grades K-12 during the preceding year and

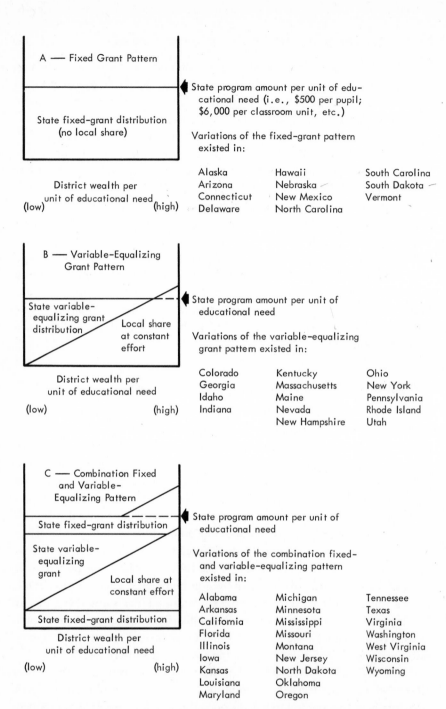

FIGURE 9-3 Patterns of Foundation Program Support, Fiscal Year 1967.

SOURCE: Figure 9-3 is a slight modification of Chart I included in: Albert R. Munse, *State Programs for Public School Support*, Washington, D.C.: U.S. Government Printing Office, 1965, p. 4.

230

ranged from $175 per pupil for towns having lower than 301 pupils to $97,500 plus $120 per pupil in excess of 600 per town having more than 600 pupils in ADM. In addition, towns received $20 per pupil for the increase in ADM over a 10-year period that ended with the preceding year.

Besides Connecticut, Alaska was another example of a state using the number of pupils in a system to establish a correction for size, while Alaska, Delaware, Hawaii, North Carolina, and South Carolina used state salary schedules for determining the amount to be used for the allotted teachers employed. Nebraska used a multifund plan in which the distribution bases in turn included the proportion of children 5 to 18 years of age in the school census; the counties' proportion of the state population and redistribution within the counties in proportion to ADA; and the counties themselves (an equal amount to all school systems).

The variable-equalizing grant states listed adjacent to *B* in Figure 9-3 provided for state recognition of differences in the ability of the communities to support public schools. The per-pupil amount of local revenue varied generally according to the per-pupil valuation of local taxable property. When this varied amount was subtracted from the standard state program amount, a correspondingly variable difference resulted as the state's share. A program of this kind provided a widely varying amount of state assistance per pupil or per classroom unit. Local receipts in excess of the established local contribution were retained locally, except in Utah where such an amount was forwarded to the state and became part of the state money distributed to local school systems.

In FY 1967, 25 states employed a combination of fixed-grant and variable-equalizing grant distribution procedures as listed in *C* of Figure 9-3. Fixed grants were combined sometimes with a variable grant by distributing the fixed grant to each system and then including such amount in the calculation of the variable-equalizing grant distribution. In other instances, fixed grants were added on top of the state program amount specified for the variable-equalizing grant.

Variable-equalizing grant distributions may be structured to obtain results similar to those for the combined fixed and variable-equalizing grant distributions. For example, the state-local program could be designed so that even in the most wealthy system in the state the amount to be locally derived from a standard tax would be less than the amount required to finance fully the state-defined program. Since the state would pay the difference between the amount for the defined state program and the amount from a standard local tax effort, all districts in a state, including the most wealthy, would participate and receive state money under this kind of provision.

Another modification of the variable-equalizing grant plan to obtain results comparable to a fixed grant added to the variable-equalizing grant distribution could be effected simply by the state specifying a minimum amount per unit, such as $100 per pupil, and indicating that every local system would receive at least this amount.

General and Special Purpose Factors

Legislative enactments establish support levels, such as an allowable amount per pupil or per classroom unit. Steps to be followed are spelled out in great detail, and state officials responsible for the administration of the program apply objective measures to assure equal consideration for each school system.

TABLE 9-2. General-Purpose Distribution Factors Used to Determine State Program Amounts for Public Schools for FY 1963

FACTORS	NUMBER OF DISTRIBUTIONS USING EACH FACTOR
Teacher, classroom, or similar unit	35
Pupil units	
Average daily attendance	25
Census	19
Average daily membership	15
Enrollment	6
Aggregate days attended	5
Full-time students	3
Other units or measures	
Amount budgeted or expended	11
Amount per district or county	5
Taxable value of district property	2
Pupil grade level	33
Size, type, or density of district	30
Salary schedule	22
Geographical location	3

SOURCE: Albert R. Munse, *State Programs for Public School Support*, Washington, D.C., U.S. Govt. Printing Office, 1965, p. 9.

Factors used to determine state program amounts for general operating expenses vary, as may be observed in Table 9-2, which lists factors identified among the 106 major general-purpose distributions for FY 1963 in the latest published analysis of state support programs by the U.S. Office of Education. It is probable that the factors used in FY 1968 were similar to those used in

FY 1963. Although the average number of general-purpose distributions was slightly over two in the latter year, the number ranged from one to five.[10]

About half of the general-purpose distributions employed only one of the Table 9-2 factors in determining the program amount. When only one factor was specified, the most frequently used were school census, average daily attendance, and the amount budgeted or expended.

Some of the factors named simply "weighted" another factor. For example, pupil grade level typically described the fact that a larger pupil allowance was provided for high-school pupils than for elementary-school pupils. Salary schedules were used to allow higher program amounts for the better trained and more experienced teachers.

Factors most often used in one combination or another in determining program amounts were teacher or classroom units; pupil grade level; size, type, or density of district; average daily attendance; salary schedule; census; or average daily membership.

Determination of program amounts for special-purpose distributions, such as vocational education and special education, was also based on generally identifiable basic measures in FY 1963. The following list includes the most common factors used in determining state program amounts for various relatively common special purposes and illustrates the tailoring of the state support plan through the use of measures appropriate to each special purpose:

Special education for exceptional children
    Approved expense
    Kind of exceptionality
    Number of pupils, teachers, or teacher units
Vocational and adult education
    Approved expense
    Number of pupils, teachers, or teacher units
Pupil transportation
    Approved expense
    Transported pupils per square mile, or areas served
    Number of buses, bus miles, size of bus, or number of bus drivers
Administration and supervision
    Number of pupils, teachers, or teacher units in the county, district, or school
    Amount per county
School construction or debt service
    Approved expense for school facilities
    Pupil capacity of needed facilities
    Number of pupils, teachers, or teacher units in district

[10] Munse, *op. cit.*, p. 9.

Payment of tuition for orphans and pupils residing on state tax-exempt property
  Number of tuition pupils
  Average expenditure per pupil from local revenue
Payment in lieu of taxes for special categories of property excluded from local
    taxation
  Value
  Local school tax rate
  Amount per acre of exempted land
Textbooks
  Number of pupils, total or by grade level
Contingencies
  Amount needed to meet the deficit
Driver education
  Approved expense
  Number of pupils completing course
Teacher or curriculum improvement
  Approved expense
Increased district attendance
  Increased number of pupils
School lunch
  Number and type of meals served[11]

Approved expense, to compensate districts for the additional expense
required for special services, was a frequently used base for determining state
program amounts for special education, vocational education, pupil transportation, capital outlay and debt service, driver education, and teacher or
curriculum improvement. However, this measure was generally limited to
maximum allowances.

Many states combined special- with general-purpose calculations. Tabula-
tion for the 49 states (Tennessee did not provide data for FY 1963) as shown
in Table 9-3 indicates those special purposes which states handled as separate
distributions and those which were included with the general-purpose calculation to determine a total program amount. Twenty-eight of the 106 general-
purpose distributions included additional allowances for an average of nearly
three of the listed special purposes. Most frequently included were education
of exceptional children, and vocational and adult education including evening
schools, pupil transportation, and administration and supervision.[12]

Authorities in school finance generally have preferred both state and federal
general-purpose grants over special-purpose ones. Their rationale is that local

[11] *Ibid.*, p. 10.
[12] *Ibid.*, pp. 10–11.

authorities need the flexibility offered through the general-purpose type in order to meet the unique needs in a community. In addition, belief is that special-purpose aid is likely to interfere with programs of equalization since wealthier school districts are more prone to respond to offers of state and federal funds.

TABLE 9-3. Separate Special-Purpose Factors and Combined General-Special Purpose Factors Used to Determine State Program Amounts for Public Schools, FY 1963

PURPOSE	FREQUENCY AS A SEPARATE DISTRIBUTION	FREQUENCY OF BEING COMBINED WITH GENERAL-PURPOSE DISTRIBUTION
Programs for exceptional children	63	17
Vocational and adult education	61	14
Pupil transportation	48	22
Administration and supervision	38	15
Capital outlay and debt service	34	3
Payments in lieu of taxes	24	—
Textbooks	16	—
Financial contingencies	15	—
Driver education	11	—
Increased pupil attendance	8	4
Teacher or curriculum improvement	8	0
School lunch	7	0
Tuition payments	5	2
Library books	4	0
Other	18	3

SOURCE: Albert R. Munse, *State Programs for Public School Support*, Washington, D.C., U.S. Govt. Printing Office, 1965, p. 10.

The concept of equalization supposedly has led to a more equitable sharing of the financing of the states' public educational systems and continues to receive even more consideration than the concept of adequacy in the establishment of financial programs. Admittedly, the concept of equalization has assisted legislatures in facing up to the fact that they are responsible for providing comparable educational opportunities throughout their respective states. Fanatics of equalization have persisted to effect equalization even within a local school system. However, the latter policy is not sound educationally when $1,000 per pupil may be needed to educate pupils in a slum school, while only $500 per pupil may be needed to meet the needs of students from another socioeconomic background in the same system.

Calculation of State Contributions

Having calculated the amount for the state program for each participating school district, the state must then determine its proportionate share of the cost. This determination is made generally in one of three ways:

1. The state pays the total of the calculated state program amount.

2. The state pays only a standard percentage of the calculated state program amount, such as 50 per cent of the allowable amount, with the balance to be paid locally from other receipts.

3. The state pays the difference between the calculated state program amount and some local share other than in 2 above. Typically, this kind of program specifies an allowable amount and subtracts an amount raised locally through a standard local tax rate to establish the state payment.[13]

In the Strayer–Haig formula as it is commonly used, $r = N_i u / Y_i$. A local tax rate equal to r must be levied prior to a school system's qualifying for state general-purpose aid, and the rate is computed by multiplying the number of pupils (N_i) in the largest wealthy system of the state by the "foundation program" in dollars (u) and dividing this product by Y_i, the taxable property in the largest wealthy system in the state. Thus, the value of u is the minimum expenditure allowed per pupil in all school systems in a state; all systems participating in the state program are mandated to tax at a minimum but same tax rate; the relative state and local contributions are calculated according to the respective distributions of resources per pupil in the systems; and increases in the amount of the minimum program will result in increases of both state and local support.

Under a *fixed-unit equalizing grant*, then, the amount of state support received by a school system is the difference between a dollar estimate of needs and a dollar estimate of the reasonable local contribution for schools. The needs figure is a product of a measure of attendance—average daily attendance (ADA), for example—and a state-mandated per-pupil expenditure. If a system has 1,000 pupils in ADA, and if it is determined by the state that per-pupil expenditure shall be a minimum of $600, the needs estimate of the system will be 1,000 × $600, or a total of $600,000. The estimate of the local contribution is then the product of a tax rate (r) times the tax base in the system (Y_i) or a contribution of $r Y_i$.

Assuming that a school system has a local tax base of $10 million and that the state-mandated rate of local contribution is 10 mills, then the state grant

[13] *Ibid.*, p. 11.

would be 1,000 pupils × $600 − (.01 × $10,000,000) = $500,000. Of the $600 per-pupil program, $500 would be provided by the state and $100 by the local school system. In another system with a student population of 1,000 pupils and a property tax base of $30 million, the state grant would be 1,000 pupils × $600 − (.01 × $30,000,000) = $300,000, with a $300 per-pupil contribution each from the state government and the local school system.

The above two examples included the same fixed unit of need, which was $600 per pupil, and varying contributions of state and local governments, dependent upon the local property tax base. Equalization is accomplished theoretically by equalizing programs (in the form of per-pupil costs) and by equalizing the qualifying tax rates in those school systems who choose to participate in a state's basic or foundation program.

Under a *variable-unit equalizing-grant system*, computations are similar to that under a fixed unit equalizing grant, except that the dollar unit of need varies. Ordinarily, the variability is accounted for according to the caliber of teacher hired system by system. Thus, in Florida an instructional unit for a certified teacher who was a college graduate and on an annual contract rather than a tenure contract has been evaluated at $5,300, while a certified tenure teacher with ten years of satisfactory service in a school system has been evaluated at $6,500. Most systems would have a mixture of beginning and experienced teachers and of teachers with or without advanced degrees. However, the range of this mixture can vary considerably within a state and results in varying amounts of dollars per educational unit. Ordinarily, there is a maximum number of teachers that a system can count for state aid purposes, generally one for each 25 to 30 students.

The *percentage equalizing grant* is receiving a great deal of verbal support from finance experts, and results of the implementation of this plan in Wisconsin, Rhode Island, New York, and Maryland are being studied eagerly. The prime feature is that the state pays a share of locally determined school expenditures in a given school system, not only pertaining to the foundation program but to a so-called quality program as well. Wisconsin has developed the most open-ended program, and it will be described in more detail later in this chapter. It is believed that the open-ended program developed at the local level, but subject to approval by responsible officials at the state level, will lead to more dynamic instructional and administrative systems plus a better implementation of the concept of leeway for diversity.

In determining the state's share for a particular system, it is first necessary to calculate the ratio of the tax base per pupil in the ith system, y_i, to the state tax base per pupil, y. Thus, the relative economic position of the ith system is established in the form y_i/y. This ratio is then multiplied by a constant, x (local share or percentage), which has a value between 0 and 1. The product of x times the relative economic position of the ith system— that is, $x(y_i/y)$—is subtracted from the numeral l. The resulting figure is the state percentage of support for the ith system. The lower the value of y_i/y in a system, the higher will be the state's share in financing a program, and the converse would apply to relatively wealthy systems.

The fundamental percentage-equalizing formula is:

$$S.A. = \left[1 - \left(\frac{xy_i}{y}\right)\right] \cdot u$$

when the code is as follows: $S.A.$ = state aid; x = local percentage of educational expenditures; y_i/y = relative wealth of a system; and u = the dollar cost of the program to be financed.

For example, in a system with 1,000 pupils, an equalized valuation per pupil of $20,000 (which also is average for the state), an expenditure level of $600 per pupil, and location in a state that agreed to meet 50 per cent of school costs in a system of average wealth, the state's share would be calculated as follows:

$$S.A. = \left[1 - \left(.5\,\frac{\$20,000}{\$20,000}\right)\right] \cdot \$600,000 = \$300,000$$

The state's share would be $300,000, or 50 per cent of expenditures.

In a relatively poor system—that is, a system with 1,000 pupils, an equalized valuation per pupil of $10,000 and an expenditure level of $600 per pupil—located in the same state as in the previous example, the state's share of expenditures would be:

$$S.A. = \left[1 - \left(.5\,\frac{\$10,000}{\$20,000}\right)\right] \cdot \$600,000 = \$450,000$$

The state's share should be 75 per cent of expenditures.

In the two examples above each of the systems could provide a program at a cost of $600 per pupil and at the same local tax rate—$1.50 per $100 of assessed valuation.

Descriptions and Calculations of Modern State Financial Programs

The state-local support programs of Wisconsin, Maryland, and a proposed California program are described in detail in this section. In addition, brief descriptions, primarily in worksheet form showing the computation of state aid for local schools in Ohio, Massachusetts, Georgia, Colorado, Arkansas, and Utah are included to exemplify program variety in scattered sections of the country. Finally, a model support program developed by the Advisory Commission on Intergovernmental Relations (ACIR) is outlined.

The Wisconsin program was a forerunner of the incentive type with an open-ended provision for state support of quality education. In addition, certain districts in Wisconsin qualify only for flat aid. This one description enables the reader to become oriented to a mixed package of support, parts of which exemplify patterns in many other states.

The Maryland program was included because it is a variation of the Wisconsin program, and because it was created as late as 1964 as a revolutionary change in support for Maryland's schools. A unique feature is that per capita income is used as a factor in determination of the relative fiscal capacity of local school systems.

The California program included was one proposed to the 1967 state legislature. Reasons for including it in this text are its newness, the specifics of the program descriptions including variable costs for meeting needs of different kinds of students, and its comprehensiveness.

ACIR's fiscal model was created for equalizing educational opportunities for economically and socially deprived children. It consists of (1) a basic program, (2) an educational-improvement program, (3) a special-needs program, and (4) a state program to assist local systems in matching federal funds.

Wisconsin's Educational Finance Program

In qualifying for state aid, Wisconsin's school systems must place a minimum levy upon the equalized valuation of property in the system. Elementary systems offering kindergarten or grades 1 through 8 and union high schools must levy at least 3 mills, and in school systems offering grades kindergarten through 12 or grades 1 through 12 the minimum levy must be at least 5 mills.

For state aid purposes, school systems are classified as qualifying for state aid on a basic level or an integrated level. School systems qualifying for state aids on an integrated level provide a better quality educational offering for children. Teachers are better qualified to teach in their respective positions. The course of study includes more subjects in more fields and better facilities in which to teach. The areas of music, art, and kindergarten are a regular part of the offering. The high school must employ more than five teachers, and the high school must provide a good offering in the vocational field as well as the academic areas of science, mathematics, English, and social studies.[14]

The state aid for elementary and high schools in Wisconsin as determined under the statutes in Section 40.67 through 40.71 may be either a flat or an equalization aid.

Flat aid. Flat aids are very simple to compute. Two basic factors are involved: (1) the number of children in average daily membership; and (2) the flat-aid amount set forth in the statutes. Table 9-4 will illustrate flat aid in terms of statutes in 1966.

TABLE 9-4. Flat-Aid Schedule, State of Wisconsin

TYPE OF AID CLASSIFICATION	1959–1960 THROUGH 1963–1964		1964–1965 AND 1965–1966		1966–1967	
	ELEMEN- TARY	HIGH SCHOOL	ELEMEN- TARY	HIGH SCHOOL	ELEMEN- TARY	HIGH SCHOOL
1. Basic elementary	$30.00	—	$30.00	—	$30.00	—
2. Basic union high school	—	$40.00	—	$40.00	—	$40.00
3. Basic elementary and high school	30.00	40.00	30.00	40.00	30.00	40.00
4. Integrated elementary	40.00	—	42.00	—	44.00	—
5. Integrated district high school	—	53.00	—	55.00	—	57.00
6. Integrated elementary and high school	40.00	53.00	42.00	55.00	44.00	57.00

SOURCE: *School Aids—Flat and Equalization.* Madison, Wisconsin State Department of Public Instruction, Aug. 16, 1966, mimeographed.

Let us assume that a school district offering kindergarten through grade 12 has been classified as a school system qualifying for state aid on an integrated level. The system has 500 elementary resident children in average daily membership and 200 high-school students in average daily membership. The equalized valuation totals $28,000,000, or $40,000 per resident child. Since this is greater than the guaranteed valuation per child of $38,000 for integrated K-12 systems, the system qualifies for flat aids. Since the flat aid schedule provides a state aid for resident elementary children in average daily membership of $44, the state aid for the elementary children would total 500 × $44,

[14] This paragraph as a description of quality education plus computations of the Wisconsin program were included in a mimeographed handout of the Wisconsin State Department of Public Instruction entitled *School Aids—Flat and Equalization*, Aug. 16, 1966.

or $22,000, while the high-school portion of state aid would represent 200 × $57, or $11,400. The total state aid to this system would be $33,400. The difference of $13 between the flat aid for elementary and high-school students is a result of the fact that the cost of education per high-school student is greater than the cost per elementary-school child.

Equalization aid. The basic factors that produce equalization rather than flat aid are the equalized valuation of a school district and the number of resident children in average daily membership. For example, for tax purposes a local school system has a certain amount of equalized valuation and a certain number of children in resident average daily membership. The system used in the flat-aid illustration had $28,000,000 of equalized valuation. The statutes require that the minimum valuation "back of each resident child" in integrated K-12 districts should not be less than $38,000. The equalized valuation per resident child is obtained by dividing the equalized valuation of the system by the resident average daily membership. In the flat-aid example, $28,000,000 divided by 700 equaled $40,000. The valuation back of each child exceeded the requirement by $2,000 per child.

As an introduction to the computation of equalization aid, it is important to note that the valuation per resident pupil in integrated K-12 grade systems on the basis of the 1965 equalized valuation in Wisconsin varied from a low of $8,292 in one system to a high of $132,811 in another. The districts exceeding $38,000 qualified only for the flat-aid portion of general-purpose state support.

Assuming that the flat-aid system used in the earlier example lost $9,800,000 of its equalized valuation and had only $18,200,000 in back of 700 children, the result would be an equalized valuation per pupil of $26,000, or $12,000 less than the guaranteed valuation set forth in the law. It would be necessary to determine the net operating cost per pupil so that a required operating levy rate for current operations might be established as a beginning in determining state and local support. Assuming that the net operating cost (locally determined) is equal to $456 per pupil (this will vary from system to system), the required operating levy rate would be equal to $456 divided by $38,000, or 12 mills, since the guaranteed valuation is $38,000 per resident pupil in average daily membership. Since the system has $26,000 of equalized valuation per resident child, the system would produce $26,000 × 12 mills, or $312 of the amount needed, and the state would provide $12,000 × 12 mills, or $144 per resident pupil. Through the guaranteed valuation, the state and local system would have raised the $456 needed to meet the current operating cost of educating each pupil. The state aid paid would have been equal to 700 × $144, or $100,800.

The prime difference in the two illustrations—the one for flat aids and the other for equalization aids—is found in the local property tax base. The flat-aid system had $28,000,000, or $40,000 per resident pupil, and the equalization aid system had $18,200,000, or $26,000 per resident pupil. The state aid paid to the flat-aid unit would equal $33,400, and the state aid paid to the system receiving equalization aid would total $100,800. The flat-aid system receiving less state dollars would be operating at a lower local tax rate. The pressure in the flat-aid system upon the local property tax would not be represented in the total per-pupil operating cost of $456. If the flat-aid average of $47.71 is deducted from $456, there would be a property tax load of approximately $408.29 on a local required tax effort of 10.2 mills.

An integrated level K-12 system was used in the illustrations because more than 75 per cent of the average daily membership in Wisconsin was included in this classification in 1966. The formula operates in a similar manner in the other five aid classifications, however. The variation in flat-aid and guaranteed valuations merely take into account the type of district organization, variation in the cost of education, and the incentive feature that tends to improve the quality of educational programs. The guaranteed valuations for the various aid classifications is given in Table 9-5. The illustrations applied to systems represented in line 6 of the valuation schedule.

TABLE 9-5. Guaranteed Valuation Schedule, State of Wisconsin

	GUARANTEED VALUATION PER RESIDENT PUPIL IN AVERAGE DAILY MEMBERSHIP		
CLASSIFICATION OF LOCAL SYSTEMS	1959–1960 THROUGH 1963–1964	1964–1965, 1965–1966	1966–1967
1. Basic elementary	$24,500	$24,500	$24,500
2. Basic union high school	55,000	55,000	55,000
3. Basic elementary and high school	24,500	24,500	24,500
4. Integrated elementary	28,000	28,500	59,500
5. Integrated district high school	70,000	72,000	75,000
6. Integrated elementary and high school	33,000	34,000	38,000

SOURCE: *School Aids—Flat and Equalization*. Madison, Wisconsin State Department of Public Instruction, Aug. 16, 1966, mimeographed.

A unique feature of the Wisconsin public education finance program is its open-endedness. School systems may establish educational programs at varied costs per pupil. The State Superintendent of Public Instruction is required to approve budgets of systems in which state aids exceed 50 per cent

TABLE 9-6. State-Aid Computation in Wisconsin—Kindergarten or 1–12 Grade System Classified on an Integrated-Aid Level

Average Daily Membership (ADM)	
Step 1. Elementary-school resident ADM	500
High-school resident ADM	200
Total resident ADM	700
Total nonresident high school ADM	0
Guaranteed valuation	
Step 2. Total resident ADM (not to exceed	
25 per teacher) 700 × $38,000 =	$26,600,000
Equalized valuation	
Step 3. 1965 Equalized valuation of system	$18,200,000
Current operating costs (use budget estimate for 1966–1967 school year)	
Step 4. Cost of operation and maintenance	$375,400
Deductions for receipts (use budget estimates for 1966–1967 school year)	
Step 5. Current receipts $56,200	
Step 6. High-school nonresident ADM 0 × $57 = 0	
Step 7. Total receipt deductions (Steps 5 and 6)	$56,200
Step 8. Net operating cost (Step 4 minus Step 7)	$319,200
Tax levy	
Step 9. Tax levy of system, 1966	$262,000
Aid Computation	
Step 10. Step 2 (guaranteed valuation)	$26,600,000
minus Step 3 (equalized valuation)	$18,200,000
equals net guaranteed valuation	$8,400,000
Step 11. Step 8 (net operating cost) divided by Step 2 (guaranteed	
valuation) equals required operating levy rate	12 mills
Step 12. Step 9 (tax levy of 1966) divided by Step 3 (equalized	
valuation) equals operating levy rate	14.4 mills
Step 13. Step 10 (net guaranteed valuation) times the lower rate in	
Steps 11 and 12 (not to exceed 17 mills) equals equalization aid	$100,800
Step 14. High-school nonresident ADM 0 × $57 = 0	
Step 15. Elementary school resident ADM 500 × $44 = $22,000	
High-school resident ADM 200 × $57 = $11,400	
TOTAL flat aid	$33,400
Step 16. State aid due system, either Step 13 (equalization) or	
Step 15 (flat aid), whichever is larger, plus Step 14	$100,800

of total receipts of the systems, and where excess state aid is required because of 17-, 20-, or 25-mill tax limitations, dependent on the organizational type.

In his evaluation of Wisconsin's general-purpose equalizing grant program, Burkhead used the criteria of stimulation, equity, efficient use of resources, and tax relief.[15] His conclusions were as follows: (1) Relative to stimulation, Wisconsin's educational expenditures rose 1.75 per cent for each 1.0 per cent increase in state personal income, as compared with a national average

[15] Jesse Burkhead, *Public School Finance.* Syracuse, N.Y., Syracuse University Press, 1964, pp. 225–227.

increase of 1.66 per cent in the period between 1947–1948 and 1957–1958. (2) Results in terms of equity were fairly startling in that for 121 equalization systems at that time, the coefficient of multiple correlation of equalized valuation per pupil and the size of the district on local tax rate for current school expenditures was .104, which was not significantly different from zero. It is not unusual generally to find simple correlation coefficients between per pupil support and valuation (or income) in excess of .8. (3) The number of school systems dropped drastically, and because integrated districts must meet a more stringent set of quality standards, an assumption is that there was an overall gain in the efficient use of resources. (4) The average local tax rate was stabilized, and the state's share of school support increased modestly but resulted in a form of local tax relief.

Maryland's Educational Finance Program

Legislation enacted by the Maryland General Assembly at its regular session in 1964 made the first major revision in the basic state aid-to-education program since 1921. In brief, this is what the new program provided in 1964:[16]

1. The foundation program guaranteed to every child was established as an amount ($340) to be expended annually per pupil for current costs.
2. The elements which made up the foundation program were raised to levels representing current average practice throughout the state as follows:
   a. A basic salary scale of $4,800–$7,000 (for teachers with bachelor's degrees);
   b. Staffing up to 45 professionals per 1,000 pupils plus an additional professional for each 1,000 of the first 5,000 pupils;
   c. An expenditure of $61 for every pupil enrolled plus an additional $30 for each additional pupil (from the previous year) enrolled "for other current expenses."
3. The state would pay the same percentage of the cost for providing professional staff beyond the number supported in the foundation program as it paid of the total cost of the foundation program for each subdivision. Thus the local subdivisions were encouraged to provide programs beyond the guaranteed minimum.

---

[16] *Financing Education for our Times in Maryland*, Baltimore, Maryland State Department of Education, May, 1964, Foreword. The Maryland support program for FY 1967, as reported by the U.S. Office of Education in its Maryland report in September, 1966, is basically the same as the one conceived in 1964.

4. For the first time, personal income as well as assessed valuation was
used to determine the local ability to support the foundation program.

The required local share for each subdivision was an amount equal to
1.228 per cent of the sum of its adjusted assessed valuation of real property
and its total net taxable ordinary income.

The incentive aspect of the Maryland plan is best exemplified in the current
expense incentive aid provision. For each professional staff member employed
by any subdivision above the number allowed under the foundation program,
and up to a maximum of 50 per 1,000 pupils enrolled, the state paid that
percentage of $6,200 that is the state percentage share of the total foundation
program for that subdivision. If, for example, the state share of the foundation
program for a county is 65 per cent, the county would receive 65 per cent of
$6,200, or $4,030, for each additional professional allowed beyond the basic
45 staff members. Each local system, therefore, regardless of wealth could
with the same additional effort percentagewise provide staffing beyond the
foundation program.

In addition to the foregoing, the State of Maryland pays to each system
the full cost of transporting pupils to public schools when such transportation
is approved by the State Superintendent of Schools. Also, to encourage
provision for adequate school facilities, the state provides a school constructive incentive fund and distributes $70 per enrolled pupil for the in-
creased enrollment of the preceding school year over the second preceding
school year and the difference between a required local levy of 5 cents per
$100 of local assessed property and $22 per child enrolled during a current
year.

California's Recommended School Support Program, 1967

The California Department of Education prepared a report entitled *Recommendations on Public Support*, and the recommendations were approved by
the California State Board of Education in March, 1967. The summary of
recommendations included the following provisions:

For elementary and high schools:
A. That the foundation program for school districts be defined to provide
   for the sharing by the state and school districts of the necessary expenses
   for the following:
   1. Salaries of certificated personnel
   2. Salaries of classified personnel

      3. Retirement, workmen's compensation, and the like connected with the employment of school personnel

      4. Instruction to bring instructional materials, textbooks, and other books to the classroom

      5. Special purpose augmentation made by the legislature

  B. That a single foundation program for kindergarten and grades one through twelve be established for unified districts.

  C. That the foundation program for each type of district be established so that it may be evaluated in terms of the actual expenditures of districts during the second preceding year.

  D. That the foundation program for each type of district be established as follows:

      1. Elementary districts: $370 per unit of average daily attendance

      2. High school districts: $550 per unit of average daily attendance

      3. Unified districts: $450 per unit of average daily attendance

  E. That the computational tax rates for each type of district be established as follows:

      1. Elementary districts: $1.00

      2. High school districts: $1.00

      3. Unified districts: $2.00

  F. That the following supplementary support programs be established for low-wealth districts:

      1. Elementary districts: $1.20 for each cent of tax in excess of the $1.00 tax rate up to $1.30 total rate and $36 minimum

      2. High school districts: $2.90 for each cent of tax in excess of the $1.00 tax rate up to $1.20 total rate and $58 maximum

      3. Unified school districts: $1.00 for each cent of tax in excess of the $2.00 tax rate up to $2.45 total rate and $45 maximum

For junior colleges:

  A. That the foundation program level of support be established at $620 per unit of average daily attendance and that a computational tax be established at 20 cents.

For additional state support for unified districts:

  A. That $15 per unit of average daily attendance be added to the foundation program established for unified districts as an incentive for the formation of unified districts.

For adult education:

	Present	Proposed	Computational Tax
High school	$320	$360	$.50
Junior college	490	530	.24

For special education:

  A. That maximum allowances for excess expense of special education programs be established as follows:

Program:	Maximum Allowances	
	Present	*Proposed*
Physically handicapped		
Regular classes	$910	$1,032
Remedial physical education	910	775
Remedial, other	910	2,150
Individual instruction	910	1,354
Mentally retarded	375	443
Severely mentally retarded	670	808

B. That excess expense allowances for the educationally handicapped be provided for each program group in the amount listed below:

Program group:	Maximum Allowances	
	Present	*Proposed*
Learning disability groups	$910	$1,880
Home and hospital instruction	910	1,590
Special day classes	910	1,140
Special consultation	—	10

C. That excess allowances for the mentally gifted be established at $40 for identification and $60 for program support, respectively. That the maximum statewide allowable support be based on 3 per cent rather than 2 per cent of the average daily attendance in grades one through twelve.

D. That allowances be computed on the basis of the average daily attendance of the current year rather than the preceding year.

For urban problems allowances:

A. Allocate $15 per unit of average daily attendance to all average daily attendance in kindergarten through twelve in unified districts in excess of 25,000 average daily attendance. Minimum allocation to each eligible district to be $15,000.

B. Provide $4,000,000 for school districts other than those specified in item A to be allocated on a project approval basis to cope with demonstrated urban problems.

C. The unified districts referred to in item A are those that contain or are a part of a city that was established before 1930 and which had in 1960 a population of 70,000 or more.

For kindergarten improvement:

A. That each school district maintaining elementary school be required to maintain kindergarten.

B. That the authority to establish waiting lists for kindergarten be abolished.

For local property tax relief:

A. Repeal all maximum statutory and permissive tax rate limits.

B. Return to the governing boards of school districts the actual power to reduce local property tax effort by making them responsible directly for local property tax effort over and above that required by the proposed program. Massive additional state support has as its primary purpose the shift from property taxes to state support a larger proportion of school expenditure. This objective is clear in the proposed program. The amount of shift, district by district, should be determined by the governing boards of the school districts on the basis of local educational objectives and needs rather than by a program of property tax rollback mandated by the legislature, a legislative mandated program applicable on a statewide basis will not serve to meet all educational needs and will result in more inequities in educational opportunity.[17]

A premise of those developing the California program was that if the purpose was to extend the concept of equalization, reliance on the assessed valuation per unit of average daily attendance of a district must be diminished. The purpose will be achieved to the extent that the foundation program level is established sufficiently high to meet the actual required expenditures supported through the foundation program. Any of these expenditures not covered by the foundation program are not equalized, and revenues to meet such expenditures must come from local property taxes.

Conclusion of the California Department of Education was that on the average, support through the foundation program should finance about 93 per cent of the total expenses at the elementary and high school level, and

TABLE 9-7. State of California Expense per Unit of Average Daily Attendance for Purposes Included in Definition of Foundation Program

PURPOSE OF EXPENSE	ELEMENTARY DISTRICT, 901 OR MORE ADA	HIGH SCHOOL DISTRICT, 301 OR MORE ADA	UNIFIED SCHOOL DISTRICT, 1,501 OR MORE ADA
Teachers' salaries	$258.49	$349.09	$292.27
Other certificated salaries	44.39	73.02	58.79
Certificated retirement	5.17	12.15	9.36
Classified salaries	53.33	87.97	73.88
Classified retirement	5.95	9.43	9.05
Other expenses of instruction	15.03	35.98	19.04
SUBTOTAL	$382.36	$567.64	$462.39
Special purpose augmentations			
Class size, grades 1–3	6.00	—	6.00
Additional for unified	—	—	15.00
TOTAL	$388.36	$567.64	$483.39

SOURCE: *Recommendations on Public School Support*, Sacramento, California Department of Education, March, 1967, p. 8.

[17] *Recommendations on Public School Support*, Sacramento, California Department of Education, March, 1967, pp. 1–4.

almost 100 per cent at the junior college level. The dollar support level was then determined by computing the expense per unit of average daily attendance (see Table 9-7), multiplying by .93 and then multiplying this product by the average annual change. The computations were as follows:

$$\text{Elementary} \quad \$382.36 \times .93 \times 1.0424 = \$370.67 \ (\$370)$$
$$\text{High school} \quad 567.64 \times .93 \times 1.0387 = \ 548.33 \ (\$550)$$
$$\text{Unified} \quad 462.39 \times .93 \times 1.0371 = \ 445.97 \ (\$450)$$

Basic Public School Support Programs in Massachusetts, Ohio, Georgia, Arkansas, Colorado, and Utah

Massachusetts. The computation of state aid for education under the provisions of Chapter 14, Acts of 1966, for the calendar year 1967, was made in accordance with the accepted legal and fiscal interpretation of Chapter 14, Acts of 1966, amending Chapter 70. The entitlements due each city and town as state aid for education were computed from the following basic formula:[18]

1. $\dfrac{\text{Average equalized valuation per school attending child local}}{\text{Average equalized valuation per school attending child state}} = \begin{matrix}\text{valuation}\\\text{percentage}\end{matrix}$
2. Valuation percentage multiplied by 65 per cent, subtract result from 100 per cent = school-aid percentage
3. Reimbursable expenditures multiplied by school-aid percentage = school aid

Example:

Shrewsbury School System   State of Massachusetts

1. Average equalized valuation per school attending child

$$\dfrac{\$18,186}{4509 \big/ \$82,000,000} \qquad\qquad \dfrac{\$20,554}{1,291,016 \big/ \$26,535,650,000}$$

2. Valuation percentage

$$\dfrac{\$18,186}{\$20,554} = 88.5 \text{ per cent} \qquad\qquad 100 \text{ per cent}$$

3. School-aid percentage

$$88.5 \text{ per cent} \times 65 \text{ per cent} = 57.5 \text{ per cent}$$
$$57.5 \text{ per cent} - 100 \text{ per cent} = 42.5 \text{ per cent}$$

4. School aid

$$\$1,837,518 \times 42.5 \text{ per cent} = \$780,945.15$$

[18] *School Aid to Massachusetts Cities and Towns*, Boston, Department of Education and Department of Corporation and Taxation, 1967, p. 6.

The maximum school-aid percentage is 75 and the minimum is 15. There are other limitations on the basic formula including: (1) a ceiling on the amount of the city or town's reimbursable expenditures that can be multiplied by the school-aid percentage; (2) if a city or town's reimbursable expenditures per child in net average membership fall below 80 per cent of the state average of reimbursable expenditures per child, then in computing the amount of school aid a figure equal to 80 per cent of the state's expenditures per child is used; (3) a ceiling on the amount of state aid that can be given to a city or town receiving substantial aid from the federal government—a community's state and federal aid together cannot be more than 75 per cent of its reimbursable expenditures and applied revenues received from the federal government; and (4) a requirement that every city and town receive in 1967 as state aid at least 115 per cent of the amount they received from the state in 1965 under Chapter 70 plus any grants and reimbursements paid under Chapters 69, 71, and 74.

After the Commissioner of Education certifies to the Comptroller and the State Tax Commissioner the amount of school aid to be paid each city and town, the State Tax Commissioner next determines the estimated amount of state aid to be distributed to each city and town from the sales tax revenue collected in the distribution year (January 1 to December 31) by determining the fraction the certified school aid bears to the total estimated sales and excise tax apportionment. The city and town's school aid entitlement represents a fraction of this distribution. Thus, the computation in the case of the Shrewsbury School System is as follows:

1. $\dfrac{\text{Estimated sales and excise tax receipts for school aid}}{\text{Total state school aid entitlement}}$ = Estimated per cent of distribution

2. A city or town's school aid entitlement multiplied by the estimated per cent of distribution equals the estimated distribution of school aid to the city or town.

Example:

State—$\dfrac{\$\ 97,228,919}{\$173,709,732}$ = 56.0852 per cent

Shrewsbury School System—$780,941.15 × 56.0852 = $437,994.81

Ohio. The 107th General Assembly in Ohio significantly changed the level of state support, the concepts of distribution, and also increased state taxes for support of public schools after a high percentage of levy-question failures, both additional and renewals, throughout the state. The cost factors of the basic program are common to each public school system and consist of the following: (1) Teacher salaries; (2) retirement and sick leave; (3) classroom (noncertificated employees') salaries; and (4) pupil transportation operation.

Calculation of state support is first made by classifying the certificated employees of a system according to their training level. The number of such employees in each training category is then multiplied by the base salary for that classification plus the total allowable years of experience of all employees in that category, multiplied by the annual experience increment for that training level. As can be seen in Table 9-8, allowances are then made in turn for extended service, retirement and sick leave (13 per cent of the certified salary allowance and extended service), classroom operation (the number of classroom units multiplied by $2,425), and transportation. The "charge-off" amount, equal to 17.5 mills times the total value of the district tax duplicate, is then subtracted from the basic program cost. This charge-off is the amount of expected local funds used to pay basic program costs.

The total amount of state support is the larger of (1) the formula calculation, (2) the minimum-per-classroom calculation (the number of approved classroom units multiplied by $3,050 plus an amount for retirement and sick leave), or (3) guarantee calculations, including a guarantee that no system shall receive less than the amount provided by the formula in effect during 1966–1967 plus $600 times the approved units calculated during 1967–1968 for the year 1968–1969.

Georgia. For FY 1967, approximately 85 per cent of the state grants for public schools in Georgia was allocated for foundation program support for teachers' salaries, transportation expenses, other current expenses, and instructional materials. Allowances for teachers' salaries ranged from $4,200 to $5,607 for teachers with a bachelor's degree; from $4,480 to $6,216 for teachers with a master's degree; and from $6,360 to $7,224 for teachers with the six-year certificate.

All the state support for public education was derived from legislative appropriation. There were no state taxes earmarked for the schools, and there was no permanent endowment fund income.

Required local effort (RLE) for participation in the state foundation program was determined by multiplying the percentage that the equalized adjusted school property tax digest of each system was of the total equalized adjusted property tax digest for the state as a whole by that portion of the cost of the state foundation program to be paid by local funds. Each county was required by the state constitution to levy a tax of 5 mills for public school support. A maximum levy of 20 mills could have been imposed by action of the county board of education.

Statewide, 17 per cent of the cost of the calculated foundation program

TABLE 9-8. Sample Form for Calculation of State Support of City District, Ohio State Department of Education, Division of School Finance Form SF-12 for Fiscal Year (19— Calculation)

	ADM	Approved Classroom Units Legend	Divisor	Number of Units
1.	573	Kindergarten pupils	60	9.55
2.	6,800	Grades 1–12	30	226,67
2A.		1 and 2 teacher schools		
3.	40	Vocational units		6.00
4.	18	Deaf, blind, emotionally disturbed, crippled		3.00
5.	30	Slow learning units		2.00
6.		Speech and hearing units		3.00
7.		Child study units		2.00
8.		Total		252.22
9.	Administrative and special instruction, line 8/8			31.53
10.	Supervision, line 8, 1st 50/50, excess of 50/100			3.02
11.	7,461	Total aim and approved classroom units		286.77

State Support Calculations

	Certificated Employees A Number Employed	B Calculation Based On	Training	Minimum Salary	Experience Credit Cumulative Years	
12.	80.00	80.00	Masters	$5,500+	800.00 × $250	$640,000.00
13.	63.50	63.50	5, W/O MA	5,200+	504.00 × 225	443,600.00
14.	133.00	133.00	Bachelors[0]	5,000+	650.00 × 200	795,000.00
15.	23.50	10.27	Less than B[0]	4,300+	80.00 × 180	58,561.00
16.	300.00	286.77	Total allowance for certified employees			$1,937,161.00
17.	Line 16 × 13%					251,830.93
18.	Approved extended service + 13%					7,910.00
19.	Line 16, column B × $2425					695,417.25
20.	Transportation					35,000.00
21.	Total—Lines 16, 17, 18, 19, and 20					2,927,319.18
22.	17.5 mills on tax valuation of $115,392,792					2,019,373.86
23.	Basic state support—Line 21 minus line 22 + $1000 × units in lines 3, 4, and 5					918,945.32
24.	Line 16, column B × $3,050 + $1000 × units in lines 3, 4, and 5					885,648.50
25.	$600 guarantee					908,495.23
26.	Other guarantees					905,594.20
27.	Total State support—Largest of lines 23, 24, 25, and 26					$918,945.32

Source: *The Ohio Law for State Support of Public Schools*, Revised 1967, Columbus, Ohio State Department of Education, 1967, p. 21.

amount was to be provided locally. By 1969–1970 the amount will be 20 per cent. Receipts for P.L. 874, federal assistance to federally affected areas, were not included in the local-share requirement. Also, a share of the cost of statewide school education television service was charged to local districts and deducted from the state money calculated for the foundation program.

The allotment sheet for the Ocmulgee school system is shown in Table 9-9.

TABLE 9-9. Allotment Sheet, 1967–1968, Georgia School System, Ocmulgee, Georgia

I. Foundation items		R.L.E.[a] index percentage: .00794983	
1. Number of teachers			
Section 11: 331, Section 20: 12 @ $5,792.19		TOTAL $1,986,721.17	
Section 12: 45, @ $7,360.30 (salary and supplement)		TOTAL $331,213.50	
	TOTAL	STATE	LOCAL
Salaries	$2,317,934.67	$1,936,708.27	$381,226.40
2. M & O (Sec. 13) @ $798.60	273,919.80	229,481.05	44,438.75
3. Sick leave (Sec. 13) @ $50	17,150.00	14,367.69	2,782.31
4. Textbooks (Sec. 14)	42,711.60	34,360.20	8,351.40
Library books (Sec. 16)	12,339.36	10,309.31	2,030.05
5. Transportation (Sec. 18)	139,194.00[b]	114,154.98	25,039.02
6. Travel (Sec. 19)	5,491.00	4,110.11	1,380.89
7. Isolated schools (Sec. 17)			
Required local effort for mid-term			
adjustments, transportation, isolated			
schools, travel when not shown above			
	1,745.83		1,745.83
TOTAL foundation items	2,810,486.26	2,343,491.61	466,994.65
II. Nonfoundation items			
1. Capital outlay (Sec. 24)			
1st Program	101,300.00	101,300.00	—
2nd Program	76,436.00	76,436.00	—
Other building programs	79,289.94	79,289.94	—
2. County and regional librarians			
(Sec. 25) salaries and travel	64,895.00	64,895.00	—
Materials	35,949.32	35,949.32	—
TOTAL nonfoundation items	357,870.26	357,870.26	—
GRAND TOTAL	$3,168,356.52	$2,701,361.87	$466,994.65

[a] Required local effort.
[b] Includes funds ($50 times allotted bus drivers), which must be transferred to sick leave fund.

Arkansas. Revenue for school support was obtained through legislative appropriation except for less than a half of one per cent of the total state grant money distributed for the public schools. About 84.8 per cent of the state money granted to the school systems in FY 1967 provided foundation program support at (1) 106 per cent of the amount of state aid provided in 1963–1964 for a foundation program level of $114 per weighted pupil in average daily attendance, plus (2) a teacher's salary expenditure adjustment, which ranged from $20 to $80 per pupil in ADA, not weighted, dependent on the amounts paid for teachers' salaries and the local tax and assessment rates, and an amount to guarantee an increase of $500 per teaching position and/or an average salary of $4,250. Required minimum local support was calculated from an index of taxpaying ability.

Act 259 of 1967 provided that the amount of additional funds received by each school district for the 1967–1968 school year should be not less than $500 per teacher. The application for minimum foundation program aid for 1967–1968 by the Little Rock School District of Pulaski County included the following:

1. Minimum foundation program aid received in 1966–1967: $2,449,641
2. Number of teacher positions in 1966–1967: 1,103
3. 1,103 (item 2) multiplied by $500:   551,500
4. Tentatively approved minimum foundation program aid
   for 1967–1968 (items 1 plus 3): $3,001,141

Item 4 was to be increased or decreased, then, dependent on the 1967–1968 revenue collections by the state and made available to the Public School Fund as provided by the Revenue Stabilization Act of 1967.

Colorado. In 1962, the Colorado General Assembly adopted a minimum equalization program still in effect in 1968, encompassing the concept that the ability of people to pay property taxes depended also on the collective income of people who reside within a county. Two base measures to determine taxpayer ability were thus combined: the assessed valuation per child in a county, and the adjusted gross income per child in a county. Through the minimum equalization program, $5,400 was provided for FY 1968 for the support of each classroom unit (25 ADA per classroom unit) and, for "low-income counties," an additional $200 was provided.

The operation of the minimum equalization plan was as follows:

1. County-required support—$200 for the support of each classroom unit in the county was raised through a county mill levy.
2. County-state shared support—$5000 was provided for the support of each classroom unit through the combined resources of a county mill levy and state appropriation. The share each must provide was computed as follows:
   a. The total assessed valuation of property in a county was divided by the number of classroom units in the county.
   b. The total adjusted gross income of people residing in the county was divided by the number of classroom units in the county.
   c. The resultant computations of (a) and (b) were added together, then multiplied by the factor .0057. The product was the amount to be raised

by the county for the support of each classroom unit (CRU).

   d. State share = $5000 minus county share. By subtracting the county share of support per classroom unit from $5000, the state share for each classroom unit was determined.

3. State-required support—$200 for the support of each classroom unit was provided by the state, regardless of other state fund entitlements.

4. The state provided an extra $200 per classroom unit to those counties wherein the adjusted gross income per CRU was less than $100,000.[19]

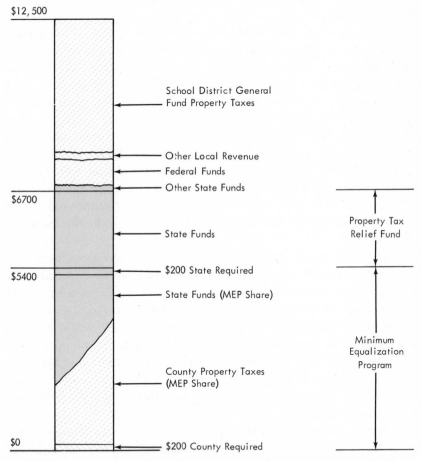

FIGURE 9-4 Financing One Classroom Unit in a Typical Colorado School District Spending $500 per Pupil, or $12,000 per Classroom Unit (CRU).

SOURCE: Frank S. Miles, *Understanding Colorado School Finance*, Boulder, Colorado: The Colorado Association of School Boards, 1968, p. 4.

[19] Frank S. Miles, *Understanding Colorado School Finance*, Boulder, The Colorado Association of School Boards, 1968, p. 10.

To provide for excess growth, the Colorado program provided that a school system must assume the total burden for the first 5 per cent of growth, but would receive state aid in the amount of $5,200 per CRU for all units in excess of 5 per cent.

In 1965, the Colorado General Assembly passed a law establishing a "property tax relief fund" (PTRF) and providing $40 per pupil in average daily attendance during the last completed school year. In 1967, the General Assembly amended a provision of the PTRF to increase, from $40 per pupil to $52 per pupil, the amount to be distributed to schools beginning in the 1968 calendar year.

Utah. The State of Utah school finance program was divided into three main categories in 1967: (1) The basic program; (2) state supported leeway; and (3) the state supported voted leeway. Under the basic program all school systems were required to levy 16 mills on the assessed valuation in their system, and if the money raised from this local levy did not reach a sum as established by the legislature for each distribution unit plus transportation in that system, the state would make up the difference from the uniform school fund. The basic unit for 1967–1968 was guaranteed at $7,400 and for 1968–1969 was guaranteed at $7,700. If a school system raised more with a 16-mill levy than was required to meet the basic distribution amount, the excess was to be turned in to the state to help meet the state's cost of the program. In 1967, only one system (San Juan) raised sufficient money to be affected by the provision.

Under the state-supported leeway program, a school system might levy from 1 to 12 mills at the discretion of the local board, but for each mill levied there was a guarantee of $140 per distribution unit. That is, if a 1-mill levy in a school system did not raise an amount of money equal to $140 times the number of distribution units that the system had, the state would make up the difference from the uniform school fund. This would make it possible for every system in the state who desired to levy the 12 mills to have a guaranteed program of $1,680 per distribution unit beyond the distribution unit and amount in the basic program. In 1967, only two districts were not levying the full 12 mills under the provision.

The state-supported voted leeway provided that a local system could by a vote of the people in the system levy an additional mill levy not to exceed 10 mills. In this provision, as in the state supported leeway provision, there was a guarantee of $110 per distribution unit per mill.

Two supplemental parts of the finance program provided $500,000 to be allocated to the Utah State Board of Education for distribution to local school systems for the improvement of library services, and a sum of $800,000 for distribution to local systems for an extended year or small school program.

In 1967, another innovation was added to the finance program. Provision was that the local districts were to use not more than $20 per distribution unit of the state funds distributed under the main three provisions of the act for the implementation of a professional certification salary differential. Basically, a distribution unit was allowed for each 27 pupils in average daily attendance in grades 1 through 12.

A Critique of State-Local Systems of School Financial Support

In a democratic society dedicated to the proposition that all persons should have an equal chance to develop their potentialities to the fullest, equality of educational opportunity for attainment is of critical importance. This objective becomes an urgent one as technological advancement causes employment opportunities to become progressively more limited to persons with professional and technical skills.

The assumption of responsibility for high-quality education has thus far been hampered by a reluctance to marshal all the state's fiscal resources, including the local property tax, in support of a total state educational program. Intercommunity disparities in educational opportunity will persist until each state revamps its school grant formulas to provide an adequate educational level below which no community may fall, to build in factors designed to measure as accurately as possible local tax effort and diverse community educational requirements, and to reflect such measurements in the allocation of aid.

Under provisions of a recommended program developed by the Advisory Committee on Intergovernmental Relations (ACIR), continuing state responsibility to support local expenditures for education would be emphasized, not only at the minimum level but well above it, to achieve equality of educational opportunity. Legislation would provide the following four-phase plan:

1. A "basic program" at an adequate expenditure level ($700 per pupil, for example) financed jointly at the state and county levels. Funds would come from the levy of a required countywide property tax rate based on equalized assessed value and from state appropriations in inverse proportion to each county's relative ability to support the basic program.

2. An "educational improvement program" in which states and localities participate in accordance with each local community's relative need for state

aid to supplement the basic program in order to raise expenditure per pupil up to a maximum of twice the basic program level ($1,400 per pupil, for example).

3. A "special-need program" to identify those segments of the state pupil population necessitating extraordinary costs over and above those required for the average pupil and to provide funds to meet such special requirements until such time as they become integral parts of the regular school program.

4. A "state program" to provide funds to districts for federal programs requiring local matching contributions or local outlays that will be federally reimbursed. The objective is to give all school systems equal access to federal aid that is now expanding into an ever-increasing variety of programs, regardless of local ability to meet the matching or funding requirements.

The proposed basic program would require that property throughout the state contribute equally to the basic school program through a state-mandated local property tax rate levied in each county, and that collections in excess of local needs be transferred to the state for redistribution to less wealthy counties. Variations in the property tax bases would be submerged for purposes of this program in the interest of obtaining equal distribution of the property tax resource behind each pupil.

The present inadequacies of school-aid legislation to achieve equal educational opportunity for attainment on a statewide basis and the desirability of establishing a multifaceted program with built-in flexibility to respond to emerging needs make suggested legislation along the lines presented a timely subject for state consideration. In addition, the growth of national and state programs in education demonstrates increasing citizen recognition that the vagaries of political boundaries, the variations in local property tax bases, and the unwillingness of local rate-making bodies to underwrite education are no longer acceptable reasons for wide differences in educational opportunity.

Focus on present state support programs is being centered upon the inequitable treatment to urban districts. Legal action is being contemplated or effected. In the case of the Philadelphia, Pennsylvania, school district a suit directed at the state demanding adequate support of urban schools is included in a proposed report to the Philadelphia Commission on Human Relations, while the Detroit, Michigan, Board of Education has already filed suit against the State of Michigan and its Treasurer.[20]

[20] See *A Desegregation Plan for the School District of Philadelphia*, Proposed Report to the Pennsylvania Commission of Human Relations, prepared as a staff report to the Board of Education, School District of Philadelphia, Draft of August 25, 1968.

The Philadelphia complaint includes reference to "municipal overburden" and "educational overburden." By municipal overburden is meant that a disproportionate relative share of municipal taxes must be spent for police, fire, sanitation, and other noneducational costs. The following facts are illustrative:

—The 37 largest cities in the country had noneducational outlays of $232 per capita in 1965, all $100 greater than their suburban counterparts.
—In 1965, all local taxes in Philadelphia were 6.5 percent of per capita income; for nonfarm Philadelphia suburbs, all local taxes were only 4.7 percent of per capita income.
—Philadelphia's educational expenditure was 30.7 percent of total general expenditures of funds from federal, state, county, and local sources in 1965, up from 29 percent in 1958, while the nonfarm suburbs were spending 60.7 percent of their total for education, up from 52 percent in 1958.
—Because the market value of real estate per pupil in Philadelphia is higher than the average in the state, the school district gets less than the average grant under the base formula.[21]

Further illustration is that the state equalization formula assumes that market value of real estate is a fair index of ability to pay for education, ignoring other local wealth (nonproperty wealth) which may be greater in suburban areas.

By educational overburden is meant the high cost of educating handicapped and disadvantaged children who are concentrated in the cities. Some federal and state funds are allocated in an effort to overcome this factor, but the scale is "miniscule in relation to the need."

Suggestions advanced for correcting the present disparities include:

—additional state or federal subsidies for municipal overburden and to provide for tax leeway;
—a regional tax for educational purposes, allocated on the basis of need, to the various communities in the area;
—a suit directed at the state demanding adequate support of urban schools.[22]

The Board of Education of Detroit filed suit on February 2, 1968, in Wayne City, Michigan against the State of Michigan alleging that the state, through its system of allocating funds among the various school districts, has denied plaintiffs equal protection of the law as guaranteed by the 14th Amendment to the United States Constitution. The plaintiffs contend that it has levied

[21] *Ibid.*, Appendix B (1).
[22] *Ibid.*, Appendix B (3).

the maximum taxes allowable but that as a result of the method of apportioning state funds "substantial disparities in the financing of public education and, therefore, in the quality and extent of availability of educational services and facilities, exist among the several school districts of the state." Thus, the plaintiffs allege that the School Aid Act and particularly its formula for the apportionment of state funds among the several school districts, is unconstitutional because:

1. The apportionment of funds does not relate in any way to the variety of educational needs of the several public school districts of the state, nor does it take into account any factors which would tend to equalize the educational opportunities made available in public schools in different parts of the state;

2. The Act fails to correct marked differences in the equality of public school buildings, equipment and other facilities, which exist among the various school districts as a result of past inequitable distribution of state funds under the Act;

3. The Act fails to take into consideration the substantial differences in the level of school construction costs, salaries of teachers, administrators and other public school employees which prevail in different areas of the state; and

4. The Act fails to take into account the added costs incurred in providing substantially equal educational opportunities to those children who live in the extremely disadvantaged urban areas of the state, predominantly in Detroit, and who consequently lack the preschool background and extra-curricular educational experiences enjoyed by most of the children attending public schools in other districts of the state.[23]

Thus, the Philadelphia and Detroit cases are examples of a prevailing financial situation which needs to be remedied by state and local governments. Not only do state and local governments need to change school support programs, but it is in the national interest, let alone morally sound, that the revolution in providing equal educational opportunity for attainment be won through substantial federal fiscal support of public schools.

[23] *Ibid.*, Appendix B (4).

CHAPTER 10

FEDERAL FISCAL
SUPPORT OF
PUBLIC EDUCATION

Although the history of education in the United States has consistently reported public education as the responsibility of the states and local communities, the federal government has shown a considerable interest in the educational welfare of the nation. The federal government has engaged in two types of educational activities: (1) aiding the states and territories in financing and promoting education; and (2) operating its own educational programs.

Federal Financing and Promotion of Education

Even prior to the founding of the nation, the federal government initiated a policy in 1785 that eventually led to the setting aside of 175 million acres of public lands for the endowment of schools in the territories and later on in the states. The Ordinance of 1787 provided for the establishment of an administrative and governmental structure in the Northwest Territory. In

261

Article 3, it contained a sentence that is accepted as the charter of public education in the United States: "Religion, morality, and knowledge being necessary to good government and the happiness of mankind, schools and the means of education shall forever be encouraged." Thus, the federal government may be regarded as the founder of the public school systems operating in many of the states.

The "general welfare" clause (Article 1, Section 8, of the Constitution of the United States) has served as a warrant and guide for the development of federal educational programs:

> The Congress shall have Power To lay and collect Taxes, Duties, Imposts and Excises, to pay the Debts and provide for the common Defence and general Welfare of the United States; but all Duties, Imposts and Excises shall be uniform throughout the United States . . . .
>
> To make all Laws which shall be necessary and proper for carrying into Execution the foregoing Powers, and all other Powers vested by this Constitution in the Government of the United States, or in any Department or Officer thereof.

Prior to the adoption of the Constitution, the antifederalists repeatedly expressed the fear that in one way or another the new government would destroy the sovereignty and even the autonomy of the states. This was the line of attack selected by Patrick Henry, who led the antifederalist forces in Virginia, and by Luther Martin in Maryland. The argument had several variations but a prime one was that the "necessary-and-proper" clause, as quoted above as a part of Article 1, Section 8, was a grant of plenary legislative authority in disguise, and that the federal government would be able to use it to usurp the powers of the states. Another pointed out the vast size of the new nation, the distance of the new capital from its sources of authority, the people, and the consequent probability of abusing the grant of authority by usurpation. And still another pointed to the broad powers of taxation possessed by the new government and warned that these could be used to drain the states' sources of revenue and thus reduce them to impotence.

These arguments the federalists met in various ways. In the Virginia convention Madison explained that the new government was not altogether national and was in some respects "federal," for the states were still given direct representation in one branch of the legislature. As for fear of the new government's taxing powers, the federalists were able to point out the disastrous financial record of the Confederation, the failure of the requisition system, and the necessity of guaranteeing the new government an adequate revenue.

The antifederalist and federalist arguments are still alive, but the federal government has determined through time that it was "necessary and proper" for it to provide financial support for public education through programs of grants-in-aid and shared revenues.

Federal grants for education prior to 1860 were generally for the broad purpose of establishing and supporting programs of education, as exemplified in the land-grant program as provided in the Ordinance of 1785 and in succeeding legislation. In 1862, the Congress initiated a policy of giving aid to the states for special purposes in contrast to the land-grant general purpose aid. The Morrill Act of 1862 established the land-grant colleges, and federal financial aid was provided to stimulate development of the specialized fields of agriculture and the mechanical arts. The Morrill Act and supplemental acts introduced the following changes in federal educational policy: (1) some control by specifying programs; (2) annual appropriations for programs in addition to the original land grants; and (3) reimbursement of the state after federal authorities were assured that money had been spent for the purpose designated by law.

Federal programs for the promotion of vocational education have included nautical education since 1874; in-service training of federal government personnel at least since 1876; vocational education in the public schools since 1917; vocational education of physically disabled persons since 1920; apprentice training since 1934; and aeronautical education since 1939. Implementation of the Federal Employment Act of 1946 is heavily dependent upon the success of the Vocational Education Act of 1963 and the Manpower Development and Training Act (MDTA) of 1963.

During the economic depression of the 1930's, several federal emergency agencies carried out extensive educational activities as measures of relief to the states and localities. Fear developed that one relief program—the NYA—might develop into a national school system, but the program was repealed in the early 1940's.

In 1918, the Congress provided for the vocational education of disabled veterans of World War I. The Vocational Rehabilitation Act of 1943 (Public Law 16) made a similar provision for disabled veterans of World War II. The Servicemen's Readjustment Act of 1944 (Public Law 346) authorized an educational program of unprecedented scope for almost all veterans of World War II.

In 1906, the federal government began activities in the field of international education. Activities since have included (1) bilateral programs of educational cooperation with other countries, (2) educational activities participated in by the federal government as a member of international organizations, and

(3) programs for the re-education of defeated nations in the ways of democracy.

Some other activities indicative of the evolution of federal policies in education have been (1) since 1879, the financial support given to Howard University (primarily devoted to the education of Negroes); (2) since 1918, promotion of education for citizenship; (3) since 1933, aid for the provision of lunches in elementary and secondary schools—a program, which for many years could have been designated as one to rid the nation of agricultural surpluses rather than as federal aid to education; and (4) intermittently since 1941, aid to local communities for the construction, maintenance, and operation of schools in areas adversely affected by federal activities. In the latter category, Public Laws 815 and 874 (SAFA, i.e. School Assistance to Local Educational Agencies in Federally Affected Areas) provided nearly $4 billion to 5,250 school systems in the 1950–1966 period.

The National Defense Education Act of 1958 (NDEA, Public Law 85-864) has touched every level of education, public and private, and from the elementary school through graduate school. Congress has extended the Act through seven amendments since enactment in 1958. The law authorized originally over $1 billion in federal aid through the following ten titles:

Title I   —General provisions
Title II   —Loans to students
Title III   —Financial aid for strengthening instruction
Title IV   —Fellowships
Title V   —Guidance, counseling, and testing
Title VI   —Language development
Title VII   —Research in uses of TV, radio, movies, etc.
Title VIII—Area vocational education
Title IX   —Science information service
Title X   —Improving statistical service in state departments of education

In order to participate in the NDEA program, as in other federal programs, the states had to have authorization from their legislatures to receive federal funds before they could initiate a program for using the funds. Twenty-nine states already had the legislative authority to receive and administer federal grants-in-aid; but the other 19 had to wait until such authority was forthcoming. Conditions were further complicated for the states by the fact that they had to match the federal funds dollar for dollar, and they were unable to meet this requirement until state legislatures appropriated the money.

Moreover, before any state could receive payments under a particular title, it had to submit its plan for using the federal funds to the U.S. Commissioner

TABLE 10-1. Revenue Receipts for Public Elementary and Secondary Schools, By Source, United States, 1919–1920 to 1966–1967

SCHOOL YEAR	TOTAL	FEDERAL GOVERNMENT	STATE GOVERNMENTS	LOCAL SOURCES[a]
		AMOUNTS		
1919–20	$970,120,000	$2,475,000	$160,085,000	$807,561,000
1929–30	2,088,557,000	7,334,000	353,670,000	1,727,553,000
1939–40	2,260,527,000	39,810,000	684,354,000	1,536,363,000
1949–50	5,437,044,000	155,848,000	2,165,689,000	3,115,507,000
1951–52	6,423,816,000	227,711,000	2,478,596,000	3,717,507,000
1953–54	7,866,852,000	355,237,000	2,944,103,000	4,567,512,000
1955–56	9,686,677,000	441,442,000	3,828,886,000	5,416,350,000
1957–58	12,181,513,000	486,484,000	4,800,368,000	6,894,661,000
1959–60	14,746,618,000	651,639,000	5,768,047,000	8,326,932,000
1961–62	17,527,707,000	760,975,000	6,789,190,000	9,977,542,000
1963–64	20,544,182,000	896,956,000	8,078,014,000	11,569,213,000
1965–66[b]	24,900,000,000	1,900,000,000	9,600,000,000	13,400,000,000
1966–67[c]	26,822,778,000	2,148,908,000	10,690,851,000	13,983,019,000
		PERCENTAGE DISTRIBUTION		
1919–20	100.0%	0.3%	16.5%	83.2%
1929–30	100.0	.4	16.9	82.7
1939–40	100.0	1.8	30.3	68.0
1949–50	100.0	2.9	39.8	57.3
1951–52	100.0	3.5	38.6	57.9
1953–54	100.0	4.5	37.4	58.1
1955–56	100.0	4.6	39.5	55.9
1957–58	100.0	4.0	39.4	56.6
1959–60	100.0	4.4	39.1	56.5
1961–62	100.0	4.3	38.7	56.9
1963–64	100.0	4.4	39.3	56.3
1965–66[b]	100.0	7.6	38.6	53.8
1966–67[c]	100.0	8.0	39.9	52.1
Increase, 1955–1956 to 1966–1967:				
Amount	$17,136,101,000	$1,707,466,000	$6,861,965,000	$8,566,669,000
Percentage	176.9	386.8	179.2	158.2
Annual rate	9.7%	15.5%	9.8%	9.0%

[a] Includes relatively minor amounts from gifts, tuition, and transportation fees from patrons, which accounted for 0.4 per cent of revenue receipts in 1963–1964.

[b] Estimated from 1963–1964 data. It is assumed that federal contributions increased by about $1 billion (because of Elementary and Secondary Education Act of 1965) and that receipts from state and local sources rose at approximately the same rate as between 1961–1962 and 1963–1964.

[c] Data from *Financial Status of the Public Schools, 1967*, Washington, D.C., National Education Association, 1967, pp. 47–48.

SOURCE: *Progress of Public Education in the United States of America, 1966–1967*, Washington, U.S. Govt. Printing Office, Table 13, p. 16.

of Education. A state was not irrevocably bound to its first outline of a plan
but could make revisions as time passed and circumstances changed.

The NDEA represents again the role of the federal government in serving
as an agent of change for the American public school systems. The law came
about originally because of glaring inadequacies of science, mathematics, and
modern foreign language programs and facilities. In later amendments, the
NDEA was extended to the fields of the humanities and social sciences.
Through an offer of matching funds, the federal government encouraged
local and state governmental units to participate in the improvement of their
own educational programs.

The NDEA represented the usual type of legislation approved by a
Congress in a period of emergency. Precedents had included important
educational legislation during the emergency periods of the Civil War,
World War I, the Great Depression, and World War II. Sputnik served as
the instigator of an emergency, which prompted Congress to approve NDEA
in a lopsided vote; Senate approval was 62 to 26, while the House approval
was 212 to 85.

Supply- and equipment-starved teachers throughout the nation overcame
their hunger by flooding businesses with orders to be financed with NDEA
funds. Teachers were taught how to spend money by representatives of supply
and equipment dealers in submitting NDEA proposals.

The inclusion of provision for money under a matching provision to
acquire films had been effected by an ad hoc lobby, which large educational
film producers with huge inventories were able to assemble through their
friends in high places. Firms such as these were active in legislation again
when President Johnson began to seek an identity as "the education
President," and particularly when it appeared that an Elementary and
Secondary Education Act was a possibility that would far outstrip NDEA
in its economic consequences. Specific effects of such lobbying may not be
clear, but one of the lobbying educational corporations received 85 per cent
of its gross revenues from one kind of federal money in 1966.

Federal Government's Own Educational Programs

From "general instruction" provided in the Army under the Von Steuben
regulations of 1779, federal activities in education for national defense and
war have grown to include instruction in practically all subject fields. These
training programs have covered all educational levels, from teaching illiterates
to read and write to postgraduate courses at the nation's leading universities.

The Military Academy at West Point was established in 1802. An act in July, 1866, marked the beginning of the long-lived post school system for enlisted men. The Army Medical School was established in 1893 and the Army War College in 1901. The National Defense Act of 1916 as amended in 1920 established the Reserve Officers' Training Corps at four-year universities and colleges. This marked a new policy in federal activities in education involving close working relationships with civil educational institutions.

Under the Army Specialized Training Program established during World War II, many thousands of soldiers were sent to the best universities in the country. Since that war, the Army has provided training for some of its military personnel in civilian educational institutions, and it has also established the Army Information, Strategic Intelligence, Counter-Intelligence, and Army Security Schools.

The Naval Academy at Annapolis was established in 1845. In the 1850's, the Navy initiated shore-based schools for specialists—an educational system later enormously expanded. The Naval Academy Preparatory School and the Marine Corps Institute were established in 1920, and the Naval Reserve Officers' Training Corps in four-year colleges and universities in 1925.

In August, 1942, Joseph W. Baker, Special Assistant to the Secretary of the Navy, reported: "The Navy itself has become one huge school. No officer or enlisted man ever ceases to go to school in the Navy. For every man, from the lowest apprentice to the Commander-in-Chief, schools are in session all the time." Following World War II, the Navy rapidly reduced its educational programs but is currently expanding them as the world faces new threats to peace.

Under an act of April, 1939, the Army Air Corps was authorized to institute its own educational system. By provision of the National Security Act of 1947, the Army Air Forces became the autonomous United States Air Force, which has since carried on its educational programs principally through the Air Training Command, the Air University, and the USAF Institute of Technology.

During World War II, the federal government carried out or promoted a number of educational activities designed to prepare the civilian population for more effective support of the war effort. Besides adapting some of its established educational program to wartime needs, the federal government initiated a variety of new activities, such as vocational training for war production workers; food-production war training; training in engineering, science, and industrial management; education for civilian defense; and a comprehensive educational program in support of the production of strategic materials.

In Project 100,000, the Department of Defense is currently developing a program to make useful and productive men of those previously unqualified for military service. The goals of the services in Project 100,000 are to develop capabilities not only for military duties, but also to build background for civilian pursuits after the subject leaves military service.

Throughout its history, the federal government has made various provisions for the education of persons residing in areas under its special jurisdiction. Federal provisions for education in the District of Columbia date from 1804, in Alaska from 1824, and in the Canal Zone from 1905.

Federal Aid Versus Federal Control

In the Ordinances of 1785 and 1787, the Continental Congress insisted that state constitutions provide for common schools, and the Congress contributed an endowment from the sale of public land for these schools. The operation of the schools and the subject matter taught were left to the states.

The trend toward restricting federal aid began with the Morrill Act of 1862. Congress deliberately prescribed that aid could be used only to support instruction in agriculture, mechanical arts, and military tactics. The Second Morrill Act of 1890 added an additional restriction:

> ... That no money shall be paid out under this act to any state or territory for the support and maintenance of a college where a distinction of race or color is made in the admission of students, but the establishment and maintenance of such colleges separately for white and colored students shall be held to be a compliance with the provisions of this act if the funds received in such State or Territory be equitably divided as hereinafter set forth. ...

In rudimentary form, the Morrill Acts established a pattern for providing needed resources in exchange for acceptance of certain national standards. This type of aid came to be known as categorical grants.

During the one hundred years in which Congress has created special laws for education, there have been many attempts at more general legislation. The Hoar and Blair bills in the 1870's and 1880's appear to have been radical proposals by Republicans intending to establish continuous federal funding of the common schools. On separate occasions, George Hoar of Massachusetts got his bill through the House and the Senate, but each time it was voted down in the opposite house.

In the 1930's, the Democrats proposed grants to combat the poverty of local school systems, but there was heavy criticism, and the New Deal spirit was channeled instead toward such programs as the NYA and the CCC.

Federal involvement in the education of youth was allowed to increase as long as it did not require fiscal intervention.

By 1957, there was evidence that the aid to federally impacted areas entailing a great deal of fiscal intervention had caused no ill will in the affected communities. Although the government was in one sense "sitting on the school board," there were no incidents of attempts to tamper with curriculum. With this in mind, the Senate and House considered legislation to extend school construction aid to more communities. Some of the proposals involved matching provisions, others credit assistance, purchase of obligations, etc., and the final law was a combination.

The Elementary and Secondary Education Act of 1965 was a breakthrough toward a general-type of assistance to both public and private schools. Under Title I of the Act funds were distributed to 58,000 schools—public and private—hopefully benefiting nearly 14 million children in 1966 at a cost of $1.06 billion.

Every current federal act includes the following statement about federal control:

> ... Nothing contained in this act shall be construed to authorize any department, agency, officer or employee of the United States to exercise any direction, supervision or control over the curriculum, program of instruction, administration or personnel of any educational institution or school system.[1]

This clause puts limitations on federal control. The question of federal control arises when the federal departments develop guidelines and regulations to implement programs. The guidelines arising from the administration of federal aid illustrate this contention.

The Smith–Hughes Act of 1917 (which was the first federal fiscal support for local schools), the Library Service Act of 1956, and the Vocational Education Act of 1963 required the states to submit to the U.S. Commissioner of Education for his approval a plan to be supported with details. Since few states had experience with vocational programs, many of them followed the outlined suggested by the federal administrating agency.[2]

The Vocational Act of 1963, along with the requirement for a state plan, required a minimum qualification for teachers and other personnel, set forth essential fiscal controls to ensure proper disbursement and provided for making reports to the Commissioner.

[1] Paul E. Smith, "Schoolman Worry: Will Federal Education Laws Do More Harm Than Good in the Long Run?" *Nation's Schools*, Feb. 1966, p. 48.
[2] Genevieve Dane, "Grant Programs for Fiscal 1966," *American Education*, Washington, D.C., U.S. Govt. Printing Office, July–August, 1965, p. 5.

State laws have been by-passed by some federal aid. Relative to the School Lunch Act of 1946, for example, in states where the educational agency was prohibited by law from disbursing public funds to nonpublic schools, payments were made directly to these schools by the Secretary of Agriculture.

The federal government in its administration of the Elementary and Secondary Education Act, of 1965, Title I, is demanding that evidence be submitted on the effectiveness of these programs. Title I requires that "effective procedures, including provisions for proper objective measurements of educational achievement, will be adopted by evaluating at least annually the effectiveness of the programs in meeting the special educational needs of educationally deprived children."[3] The law also requires under Section 205 (a) (6) that the local educational agency will make an annual report on educational achievement to the state educational agency and under Section 206 (a) (3) that:

> ... the state educational agency will make to the Commissioner (a) periodic reports (including the results of objective measurements required by section 205 (a) (5)) evaluating the effectiveness of payments under this title and of particular programs assisted under it in improving the educational attainment of educationally deprived children . . . .[4]

These guidelines drawn up for the administration of federal aid to education cause alarm among some educators. However, the federal requirements for minimum standards and fiscal control are inevitable. When the federal legislation such as Title II of ESEA states that "the director is authorized to prescribe such additional criteria for programs carried on under this part as he shall deem appropriate," then guidelines necessarily follow.

The stipulations, restrictions, conditions, fiscal policies, and auditing procedures of the federal educational aid programs are all part of the government's policy of following the practices of big business. The policy makers in Washington have programmed action for national needs. The ability, the "know-how" of federal policy makers, is encouraging educational institutions to use modern auditing and evaluation methods. Harold Howe, the Commissioner of Education, stated at an AASA meeting in Atlantic City in 1966, that when Congress spends $3.3 billion it wants to know if it is getting any returns for its investment. The argument often presented is that responsible educators already evaluate the effectiveness of dollars invested in local programs of instruction.

[3] *Guide to Evaluation of Title I Projects*, Draft Information Copy, Washington, Office of Education, October, 1966, p. 3.
[4] *Ibid.*, p. 4.

It is evident today that the federal government has undertaken a humani-tarian reconstruction program. Federal educational programs definitely have prescribed some direction for state programs of education.

Local and state initiative has been guided in areas where federal policy deems it necessary for the national interest. The issue of federal control is still being debated. The fact remains that education is a national problem, and the federal partner in education views education as an instrument to bring about social and economic reforms.

The federal relation to education in the future will result in selecting programs and creating new policies to explore many new avenues of solving social and economic needs. National needs, changing technological innova-tions, social injustice, changing social conditions and values, and the world crises, have urged the federal government to increase the currency in the power house where changes take place—education—and a new kind of intergovernmental relationship is developing.

Cooperative Federalism[5]

At the Constitutional Convention in 1787, as discussed earlier, the question before the delegates was whether to form a weak federal government with strong sovereign states or to form a strong federal government with some control over the states in the hierarchies of defense and law. The Randolph Plan, backed by Madison, was adopted, and the ideology of sovereign states was rejected. Madison and his followers maintained that a strong national government would ensure private rights and guarantee harmony among the states.

The question of federalism has been debated for many years. However, the ideology adopted by the Constitutional Convention of 1787 still prevails. Tensions between state powers and federal powers exist, but appear to be diminishing gradually (except in isolated areas), and a new role has emerged whereby the states, local governments, and the federal government are developing an intergovernmental and cooperative arrangement. Prior to the present decade, conceptualization has been that the total amount of power in the federal system remains constant so that when one governmental unit assumes a greater percentage of power, another governmental unit in turn loses the same percentage. However, the concept of cooperative or creative federalism does not provide for a constant power total, but creates oppor-

[5] An excellent description of the concept of cooperative federalism appears in an article entitled, "Creative Federalism and the Great Society," by M. Ways in *Fortune*, Jan. 1966, p. 225.

tunities for each governmental unit to increase its power and influence without necessarily borrowing or stealing power from other units.

Cooperative federalism is being formalized, and particularly in the field of education there is an increasing federal government participation in providing incentives for educational innovations. Federal innovative leadership at all levels of educational, social, and economic concerns has been the result of the persistent demands by citizens for needed action. This action has been the result of the following:

1. Many state constitutions, which restrict the scope, effectiveness, and adaptability of state and local action.
2. Congress has been more oriented toward urban problems than have been state legislatures. Local political expedience has precluded minority groups from gaining action to alleviate their needs except through help from the federal government.
3. There is greater fiscal rigidity at the state and local level.
4. Federal programs can be applied all over the nation with less time and with more efficiency than each of the 50 states could adopt and expedite a needed program.
5. Federal lawmakers have less pressure from their constituents in voting on national programs than do local legislators who meet pressures almost immediately.

Cooperative federalism is likely to become more of a reality with the development of a tax-sharing plan that will bring federal resources to the state-local setting where the domestic problems are being faced currently with limited resources and so-called federal red tape.

Tax-Sharing

The theory of revenue redistribution or tax-sharing appears to have originated with Thomas Jefferson, who said in 1805 that "liberated revenue" might "by a just repartition among the states . . . be applied in time of peace to rivers, canals, roads, arts, manufactures, education and other great objects within each state."

Long years have worked surprisingly little change on the politics and motivations of a plan used by the Republican Whigs in an attempt to deflate Andrew Jackson in 1836 through a revenue redistribution and a current plan to effect a tax-sharing program. The parallelism of the 1830's and 1960's pertaining to revenue-sharing other than the concept introduction itself is that Presidents Jackson and Johnson suggested the program and then had second thoughts about it and turned against it. Both presidents were attacked by the opposition party for allegedly manipulating the Treasury for maximum political advantage, and critics of both administrations claimed that administrative disapproval of distribution was that it took money out of their control that they wanted for political-managing and electioneering purposes. Opponents of the plan emphasized that it would be dangerous to relieve the politicians who spend the money (state officials) of the responsibility of raising it and answering for it.

The Republican Whigs slipped revenue redistribution in at a rear door in the 1830's when some $35 million in federal funds were merely to be deposited in state depositories but in reality turned out to be distributions to the states. The federal government made three of its scheduled four deposits to the states, and the treasury surplus was exhausted. In all, the states collected $28 million, which was largely squandered, but the U.S. Treasury Department ledgers still reflect $28 million on deposit with the states.

Dozens of tax-sharing bills were introduced into the Congress during 1967. The popularity of such financial means was that it offered hope to governors, mayors, and county supervisors as "a way out" in resolving fiscal problems. These officials have felt hemmed in by fiscal resources they considered to be inadequate at the state and local level. Beset by an increasingly complex grant-in-aid structure at the federal level, they have been urging congressional action to return a share of federal revenues to state and local governments for unrestricted use. Expansion or the creation of direct federal programs designed to relieve social welfare expenditure pressures on state and local governments also were suggested—for example, income maintenance, family allowance, or negative income tax programs.

Many variations of the original Heller Plan, which will be discussed later, have been under consideration, including tax-sharing with the states without strings; tax-sharing with the states with a required channeling of specified funds to local governments; tax-sharing with state and local governments separately; and tax-sharing conditioned wholly or in part on the constitutional and statutory modernization of state and local governments.

A subcommittee of the Advisory Committee on Intergovernmental Relations has been conducting a study on intergovernmental fiscal problems and has listed its assumptions as follows:

1. That it is most appropriate to maintain our system of decentralized government in good working order because our nation continues to manifest:
   a. significant regional, social, and economic diversity—despite growing economic and cultural interdependence.

  b. remarkable tenacious support for "grass roots" government and con-
     siderable uneasiness about "big government" despite (or perhaps because
     of) the centralizing trends of the last three decades.
2. Because of our social diversity and political traditions, progress in domestic
   affairs will require the active and innovative support of state and local
   government.[6]

A basic concern for the subcommittee was:

  Our federal system of government tends to lose its integrity when the con-
  stituent members can no longer maintain fiscal balance and are forced to lean
  heavily on the central government for ear-marked funds. Four current developments indicate the presence of potentially serious kinds of fiscal imbalances:
    1. The growing superiority of the national government's fiscal position in
       relation to the state-local systems.
    2. The emergence of relatively rich and poor jurisdictions within the same
       metropolitan economic community as the earlier relatively balanced
       municipal tax jurisdiction becomes a casualty of suburbanization.
    3. The existence of hard-core poverty areas and regions—e.g. Appalachia—
       despite narrowing of interstate per capital income differentials.
    4. Growing state and local reliance on federal grants with expenditure strings
       attached as Congress becomes more assertive in its efforts to stimulate
       and direct state and local spending.[7]

There is growing awareness of the national government superiority from a
revenue-yield standpoint. Collection trends and revenue projections clearly
indicate that the revenue response of the national tax system to economic
growth is far more impressive than the state-local performance. The yield of
each tax responds differently to changes in the GNP, and the concept that
measures the degree of automatic responsiveness is called income elasticity.
If an increase of 8 per cent in the GNP is accompanied by an 8-per-cent rise
in the proceeds of a particular tax (with no change in rate), the tax is said to
have an income elasticity of one. If the percentage change in yield is less than
the percentage change in the GNP, the tax is inelastic (the ratio of the
percentage changes has a value of less than one). If the reverse is true, the tax
is elastic (income elasticity is greater than one). An expenditure elasticity of
1.7 and a revenue elasticity of 0.9 or 1.0 leave a financing gap that is the
perennial fiscal problem of the states. At the federal level the situation is
entirely different. The GNP elasticity of federal expenditures appears to be

  [6] *Congressional Record*, Washington, D.C., Proceedings and Debates of the 90th
Congress, First Session, Vol. 113, No. 19, Feb. 8, 1967, p. 1.
  [7] *Ibid.*

considerably less than that of state expenditures. The elasticity of federal receipts by all indications appears to be in the same neighborhood as the elasticity of expenditures—1.1 or 1.2.[8]

In addition, in spite of its flaws, the federal income tax appears to conform far more closely to ability to pay, especially as state and local governments are forced to make more intensive use of property and consumer taxes, and as demands for property tax relief mount. The massive federal income tax was built largely during times of great national "crisis-consensus" in 1917–1919, 1933–1936, and 1941–1944. State and local tax increase action must be taken continuously in the absence of widespread agreement—hence, fear of political mortality. Also, limited jurisdictional reach coupled with growing economic interdependence is reflected in great sensitivity to adverse economic effects of tax competition.

In striking contrast to the favorable long-term outlook for "elbow room" in the U.S. budget, there is no prospect of any decline in state and local expenditures. From 1955 to 1965, state and local expenditures rose 125 per cent, while federal outlays rose only 65 per cent. In 1965, the state and local share in total spending for civilian purposes was 77 per cent; the federal share, only 23 per cent. Even if grants-in-aid were to be treated as federal rather than state or local expenditures, the ratio in 1965 was about two-to-one in favor of the states and localities. In 1964, the ratio of federal taxes to total national production was 14.4 per cent, representing the lowest ratio since World War II. Further justification for tax-sharing is the growing acceptance of federal deficits as a tool of fiscal policy since the 1930's, in contrast with the political and legal necessity for maintaining balanced operating budgets at the state and local level.

The Heller Plan calls for the federal government to send a fixed portion of the individual tax revenues collected by the Treasury back to the states. Originally, the Heller plan contemplated unconditional grants to the states, but fears that funds might be wasted have led its advocates to propose that money be dispersed in block grants tagged for specific purposes, such as education. Every state would get a share of each grant, but the plan could be altered to give relatively bigger portions of funds to the poorer states.

Another sharing scheme provided for enlarged federal tax credits on payments of state income taxes, which would benefit only those 35 states levying a broad-based personal income tax. In effect, the states would be getting back funds in strict proportion to what they pay. The suggestion was that a credit

[8] *Revenue Sharing and Its Alternatives: What Future for Fiscal Federalism?* Volume I: Lessons of Experience, Washington, D.C., U.S. Govt. Printing Office, July, 1967, pp. 228–233.

against federal personal income tax liability be given for up to 40 per cent of state income taxes paid. Criticisms of the tax credit device are that (1) tax credits would provide more help to rich than to poor states; (2) the proposal does not provide direct aid to cities; and (3) the plan adds to state revenues only when and if the states react to initiate or raise rates on income taxes.

Either system could be designed to provide funds directly to the cities as well as to the states, but there are significant differences between the two. The tax-credit approach appears superior. It would create pressure for adoption of state income taxes by an additional 15 states, which would automatically strengthen the fiscal position of the states.[9] In addition, those states which already have income taxes would be encouraged to rely on them more heavily. Even more important, it would establish a direct link between spending and taxing. Under the tax-credit plan, states initiating new spending programs would still have to finance them, but under the block-grant plan, the federal government would pay the bill, which means it would face constant pressure to step up its dividends to the states.

The per-capita method of distributing the grants has been given considerable support because it is the best available index of state fiscal capacity and need. It would allocate more money to the populous states, but at the same time distribute relatively more to the poor states than to the rich. For example, a $25-per-capita distribution would amount to 10 per cent of the budget of a state that can afford to spend $250 per capita, and only 5 per cent of the budget of a state that can afford to spend $500 per capita. More equalization could easily be provided if, for example, a small part of the fund—say, 10 per cent—could be allocated to the poorest third of the states. Tax effort could be given some weight in the formula, thereby encouraging states to maintain or increase tax collections out of their own sources and penalizing those that might yield to the temptation of reducing state taxes. The range of tax efforts by the 50 states to support public elementary and secondary schools in terms of percentage of personal income for the 1967 fiscal year is included in Figure 10-1.

Several methods can be used to calculate the amounts to be set aside annually for revenue-sharing. The most important criteria are that (1) the amounts should grow more than in proportion to the growth of the economy, and (2) the changes that might be required with the passage of time should be

---

[9] AUTHOR'S NOTE: It is significant that not a single state adopted a personal income tax between 1937 and 1960, a period during which 12 states adopted general sales taxes. Although five new state income taxes have been adopted since 1960, approximately 95 per cent of collections from this source in 1965 went to states that enacted such taxes before 1938. See *ibid.*, p. 234.

held to a minimum. The first criterion would be satisfied by any one of a number of growing bases—for example, total federal revenues, total income tax revenues, and the individual income tax base. The second would be satisfied best by the individual income tax base (i.e., taxable income), which is changed only rarely. The income tax base has declined only twice since the end of World War II—by 4 per cent in 1949 and by less than one-tenth of 1 per cent in 1958.

The federal government would expect states to pass tax-sharing funds through to the local governments in an equitable manner. This may be less of a problem than most people might suppose, since state grant-in-aid systems for local governments are much more highly developed than is the federal grant system. In the aggregate, transfers from state to local governments account for more than a third of state expenditures and about 30 per cent of local general revenues. Thus, even without any specific requirements, the local governments would receive at least a third of any general funds the states might receive from the federal government.

Under the tax-sharing plan proposed by Congressman Laird of Wisconsin, 5 per cent of the revenue from the federal tax on personal incomes would be returned to the states. During 1967, the total distributed would have been $3.1 billion.

The Laird plan would distribute 90 per cent of the money to the states on the basis of population and tax effort. States in which the total of state-local taxes is high in relation to people's income would get larger per-capita grants from the sharing portion than states in which taxes are low in relation to income. In 1967, about 10 per cent of the funds, or about $310 million, would have gone to the 17 states with the lowest levels of personal income as an additional or equalization allowance.

Under the Laird plan, the national average of federal tax-sharing would have been $16 per capita in 1967, and the range in shares would have been from $11.18 in Alaska to $24.25 in Mississippi. Belief is, however, that the Laird plan and other tax-sharing proposals will be dead issues in 1968 except for campaign purposes.

In order to suggest a different perspective of the possible impact of the tax-sharing plan and a possible minimal effect relative to a state problem, the following case is given. If one were to assume that 50 per cent of Florida's $84.5 million tax-sharing receipt was to be alloted to education, or a total of $42.25 million, and that the money was designated for teacher-salary increases, the state's 55,000 teachers would have received an additional $800 each on an across-the-board increase basis. According to the Laird formula, Florida's tax effort was approximately average for the nation. Chances are

FIGURE 10-1 Current Expenditure per Pupil in Average Daily Attendance—Public Elementary and Secondary Day Schools, 1967, and Per Cent of Personal Income Devoted to Local and State Revenue for Schools, 1967.

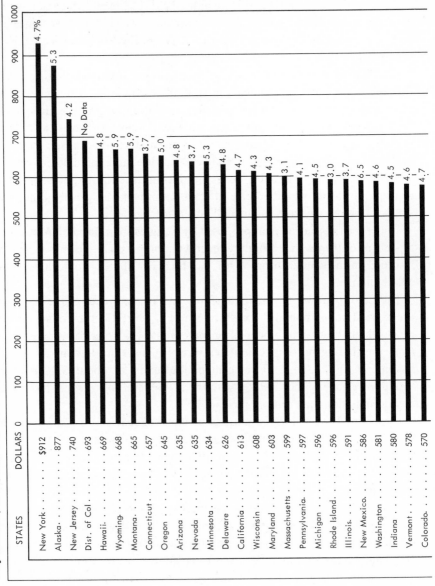

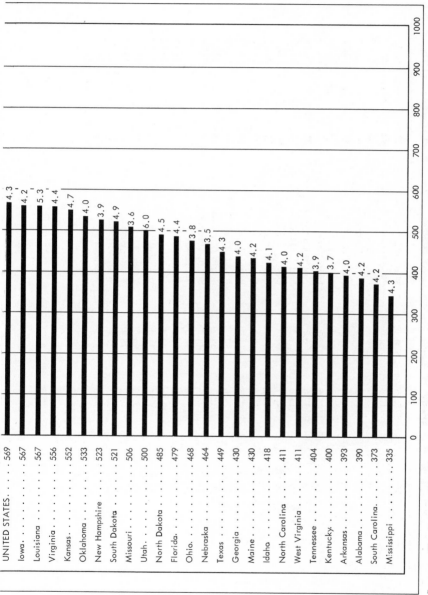

	0	100	200	300	400	500	600	700	800	900	1000
UNITED STATES. 569							4.3				
Iowa. 567							4.2				
Louisiana 567							5.3				
Virginia 556							4.4				
Kansas. 552							4.7				
Oklahoma. 533							4.0				
New Hampshire . . .523						3.9					
South Dakota 521						4.9					
Missouri 506						3.6					
Utah. 500						6.0					
North Dakota 485					4.5						
Florida. 479					4.4						
Ohio. 468					3.8						
Nebraska 464					3.5						
Texas 449					4.3						
Georgia 430					4.0						
Maine 430					4.2						
Idaho 418					4.1						
North Carolina 411					4.0						
West Virginia 411					4.2						
Tennessee 404				3.9							
Kentucky. 400				3.7							
Arkansas. 393				4.0							
Alabama. 390				4.2							
South Carolina. 373				4.2							
Mississippi 335				4.3							

SOURCE: Chart prepared by Department of Commerce, Bureau of the Census. Data are from the Department of Health, Education and Welfare, Office of Education; and reported in *Statistical Abstract of the United States, 1967*; and in *Financial Status of the Public School, 1967*; Washington, D.C.: Committee on Educational Finance, National Education Association 1967, and Table 27, p. 53.

279

TABLE 10-2. The Laird Tax-Sharing Proposal, 1967

STATE	RANKING AMONG 50 STATES AND D.C. FOR "TAX EFFORT"	GRANT PER CAPITA	TOTAL GRANT (MILLIONS)	STATE	RANKING AMONG 50 STATES AND D.C. FOR "TAX EFFORT"	GRANT PER CAPITA	TOTAL GRANT (MILLIONS)
Alabama	37	$20.15	$70.2	Montana	10	$16.43	$11.6
Alaska	51	11.18	3.0	Nebraska	42	12.89	18.8
Arizona	6	16.95	26.7	Nevada	25	14.60	6.3
Arkansas	41	20.05	38.9	New Hampshire	43	12.85	8.6
California	8	16.59	305.3	New Jersey	46	12.36	83.8
Colorado	13	16.11	31.4	New Mexico	9	22.55	22.9
Connecticut	44	12.75	36.1	New York	7	16.73	303.0
Delaware	32	13.76	6.9	North Carolina	31	20.28	100.1
District of Columbia	50	11.48	9.2	North Dakota	3	23.20	15.1
Florida	26	14.57	84.5	Ohio	48	12.02	123.1
Georgia	33	19.52	85.7	Oklahoma	27	20.13	49.3
Hawaii	19	15.40	10.9	Oregon	22	15.14	29.4
Idaho	12	16.15	11.2	Pennsylvania	38	13.20	152.9
Illinois	47	12.28	130.7	Rhode Island	30	13.90	12.4
Indiana	29	13.93	68.2	South Carolina	35	20.43	52.1
Iowa	14	16.04	44.3	South Dakota	2	23.90	16.4
Kansas	20	15.28	34.3	Tennessee	34	19.93	76.7
Kentucky	40	19.42	61.6	Texas	36	18.89	200.0
Louisiana	11	22.54	80.2	Utah	17	15.83	15.7
Maine	18	21.25	21.0	Vermont	1	23.74	9.6
Maryland	39	13.14	46.5	Virginia	49	11.80	52.1
Massachusetts	24	14.62	78.4	Washington	21	15.17	45.1
Michigan	23	14.65	121.8	West Virginia	28	20.56	37.3
Minnesota	4	17.20	61.3	Wisconsin	5	17.19	71.2
Mississippi	15	24.25	56.0	Wyoming	16	15.98	5.3
Missouri	45	12.68	57.0				

NOTE: A number of States, in which major tax increases have been too recent to show up in these rankings, would be entitled to larger grants in any future sharing.

SOURCE: *U.S. News and World Report*, March 20, 1967, p. 118. Copyright 1967 U.S. News and World Report, Inc.

280

that the nation's teachers on the average would have received a similar salary increase as hypothetically granted in Florida and that Florida's teachers would continue to receive a below-average salary. Receipts under the Laird plan would not appease Florida's underpaid professionals and would not resolve serious educational finance problems.

Current Federal Support for State and Local Governments by Function [10]

By sharing the resources derived from a growing economy, federal aid enables vital national goals to be pursued in such areas as education, health, welfare, and urban development. In addition, jointly administered programs have the following results:

1. Make it possible to pursue broad national objectives in a way that recognizes the diversity of local conditions and needs;
2. Spread creative innovation in public services from one jurisdiction to another; and
3. Preserve a fair and equitable total tax system, by relieving some of the pressure on those states and local tax sources that are less closely related to ability to pay than income taxes.

In response to the diversity of problems confronted, the emphasis of federal-aid programs has shifted from time to time. Highlights of the aid program for Fiscal Year 1968 were as follows:

1. Total federal aids to state and local governments were estimated to be $17.4 billion—an increase of $2.1 billion over the previous year.
2. Public assistance and highway programs together were to constitute one-half of the total federal aid.
3. The fastest-growing grants were those to advance the war on poverty and to upgrade elementary and secondary educational opportunities available to children of low-income families. Grants administered by the Office of Economic Opportunity and those for the new elementary and secondary education program will have increased by $1.3 billion and $1.4 billion, respectively, between fiscal years 1965 and 1968.
4. Metropolitan or urban area federal aid increased from $3.9 billion in 1961 to an estimated $10.3 billion in 1968.

[10] This section borrows heavily from "Special Analysis J: Federal Aid to State and Local Governments," *Special Analyses, Budget of the United States*, 1968, pp. 145–161.

TABLE 10-3. Percentage of Distribution of Federal Aids to State and Local Governments by Function[a]

FUNCTION	1950	1955	1960	1965	1968 ESTIMATE
Agriculture and agricultural resources	5%	7%	3%	5%	3%
Natural resources	2	3	3	3	3
Commerce and transportation	21	19	43	40	25
Housing and community development	1	4	4	5	7
Health, labor, and welfare	69	57	41	40	46
Education	2	8	5	6	14
Other	1	2	1	1	1
TOTAL	100	100	100	100	100

[a] Excludes loans and repayable advances.
SOURCE: "Special Analysis J," *Special Analyses, Budget of the United States*, Fiscal Year 1968.

As a proportion of federal outlays, federal aid has risen from 5 per cent of total federal outlays in 1957 to an estimated 10 per cent in 1967. Relative to domestic programs, about one-fifth of federal payments will have taken the form of grants to state and local governments in 1968.

Local government expenditures declined relative to those of the states between 1900 and the early 1950's. However, the three levels of government— local, state, and federal—have shown a remarkable stability in the proportionate costs they have incurred directly for domestic programs over the past decade.

In early 1964, the number of major federal assistance programs exceeded 115. Two years later the number of programs had grown to 162. In many

TABLE 10-4. Percentage of Distribution of Federal, State, and Local Direct Spending for General Domestic Programs[a]

FISCAL YEAR	FEDERAL	STATE	LOCAL	TOTAL
1965	34%	23%	43%	100%
1960	36	22	42	100
1955	38	21	41	100
1950	46	19	35	100
1944	60	12	28	100
1936	49	15	36	100
1902	28	9	62	100

[a] Direct general expenditures, excluding those for defense, space, and international programs. Excludes trust funds and government-operated enterprises.
SOURCE: "Special Analysis J," *Special Analyses, Budget of the United States*, Fiscal Year 1968.

TABLE 10-5. Number of Federal Aid Authorizations in Effect at Specified Dates

Functional Category	April 1, 1964	January 4, 1965	January 10, 1966
National defense	11	11	11
Agriculture and agricultural resources	12	12	15
Natural resources	33	41	54
Commerce and transportation	23	25	37
Housing and community development	17	23	32
Health, labor, and welfare	94	114	153
Education	37	42	82
Veterans benefits and services	1	3	3
General government	11	12	12
Total number of authorizations	239	283	399
Total number of major programs	(116)	(135)	(162)

Source: "Special Analysis J," *Special Analyses, Budget of the United States*, Fiscal Year 1968.

cases a given program had several different grant authorizations. The total number of such authorizations rose from 239 in 1964 to 399 in 1966, as shown in Table 10-5.

Current Federal Support for Elementary and Secondary Schools

One hour before adjournment of the first session of the 90th Congress on December 15, 1967, the Congress passed the largest school assistance bill in the nation's history, the Johnson Administration's Elementary and Secondary Education Amendments of 1967 (HR 7819). The bill authorized appropriations of $9,249,860,644 in Fiscal Year 1969–1970 and added $132,884,000 to existing authorizations for Fiscal 1968. The House had approved the conference report (H Rept 1049) earlier on the afternoon of December 15 by a 286 to 73 roll-call vote, and then one hour before adjournment the Senate approved the conference report by a 63 to 3 roll-call vote.

An estimated $2.7 billion in Fiscal Year 1969 and $2.9 billion in Fiscal Year 1970 were authorized for disadvantaged children under Title I of the Elementary and Secondary Act (P.L. 89–10). In Fiscal Year 1969–1970, innovative education programs under Title III were slated to receive $1.1 billion, while school systems in which there were federal installations were slated to receive $1.3 billion in Fiscal Year 1968–1970.

One of the most revolutionary provisions of HR 7819 was that Congress was authorized to vote appropriations for FY 1970 as well as FY 1969. Both local and state education officials had been complaining that school years had been budgeted for and underway prior to their receipt of information concerning anticipated federal receipts during the respective school

TABLE 10-6. Federal Funds—State Allotments for Funded Projects, Fiscal Year 1968

| | ELEMENTARY AND SECONDARY EDUCATION | | | |
| | EDUCATIONALLY DEPRIVED CHILDREN (ESEA I) | | SCHOOL LIB. MATERIALS (ESEA II) | SUPPL. CENTERS AND SERVICES (ESEA III) |
STATE	BASIC GRANTS	ADMINISTRATION		
TOTALS	**$1,177,009,192**	**$13,990,808**	**$99,234,000**	**$187,876,000**
Alabama	37,773,357	377,734	1,767,887	3,424,541
Alaska	1,816,482	150,000	124,897	452,588
Arizona	9,976,695	150,000	816,510	1,661,909
Arkansas	23,491,781	234,918	906,017	1,936,210
California	85,936,416	859,364	9,337,909	16,449,141
Colorado	9,672,195	150,000	1,064,689	1,977,876
Connecticut	9,062,813	150,000	1,400,476	2,676,143
Delaware	2,535,307	150,000	260,120	658,430
Dist. of Columbia	5,933,620	150,000	336,897	857,785
Florida	32,933,155	329,332	2,648,847	5,245,934
Georgia	37,681,381	376,814	2,152,555	4,223,564
Hawaii	2,430,762	150,000	386,217	858,244
Idaho	3,095,753	150,000	360,311	848,919
Illinois	47,499,842	474,998	5,337,276	9,565,795
Indiana	15,973,553	159,736	2,534,729	4,624,411
Iowa	15,674,581	156,746	1,448,999	2,669,953
Kansas	10,495,541	150,000	1,115,859	2,213,590
Kentucky	32,871,586	328,716	1,505,814	3,071,760
Louisiana	32,673,571	326,736	1,902,770	3,551,093
Maine	3,605,865	150,000	506,785	1,078,491
Maryland	15,482,996	154,830	1,830,047	3,397,502
Massachusetts	17,914,276	179,143	2,658,619	4,835,193
Michigan	34,269,334	342,693	4,634,860	7,885,320
Minnesota	20,020,502	200,205	1,979,521	3,470,610
Mississippi	39,559,828	395,598	1,173,309	2,388,011
Missouri	24,417,125	224,171	2,236,998	4,126,703
Montana	3,666,149	150,000	371,750	851,654
Nebraska	6,029,159	150,000	742,427	1,501,013
Nevada	963,372	150,000	218,847	584,322
New Hampshire	1,438,907	150,000	334,087	794,968
New Jersey	25,471,868	254,719	3,214,941	6,078,962
New Mexico	10,494,933	150,000	585,437	1,184,497
New York	121,097,330	1,210,973	8,122,336	15,596,196
North Carolina	53,123,825	531,238	2,353,748	4,705,505
North Dakota	4,467,399	150,000	331,096	806,364
Ohio	35,843,674	358,437	5,357,489	9,489,272
Oklahoma	18,106,545	181,065	1,211,458	2,341,021
Oregon	8,426,612	150,000	998,243	1,931,407
Pennsylvania	49,346,231	493,462	5,590,970	10,273,043
Rhode Island	3,693,961	150,000	423,153	966,799
South Carolina	32,410,715	324,107	1,286,889	2,603,012
South Dakota	5,815,575	150,000	377,371	833,672
Tennessee	34,417,670	344,177	1,774,313	3,647,737
Texas	77,122,017	771,220	5,322,514	9,893,210
Utah	3,181,914	150,000	582,833	1,165,174
Vermont	1,765,195	150,000	208,063	562,265
Virginia	29,146,020	291,460	2,076,258	4,175,918
Washington	11,965,941	150,000	1,589,629	2,868,147
West Virginia	17,464,443	174,644	858,758	1,840,104
Wisconsin	15,343,592	153,436	2,277,841	3,960,810
Wyoming	1,601,175	150,000	174,290	504,969
Outlying areas[3]	31,806,653	310,136	2,420,341	4,546,244

STRENGTHENING STATE ED. DEPTS. (ESEA V)	PROGRAMS FOR HANDICAPPED (ESEA VI)	EQUIPMENT AND MINOR REMODELING (NDEA) III			GUID., COUNS AND TESTING
		GRANTS[1]	LOANS[2]	ADMINSTR'N.	(NDEA V-A)
$25,287,500	**$14,250,000**	**$75,680,000**	**$6,469,091**	**$2,000,000**	**$24,500,000**
497,350	263,547	1,918,412	31,736	36,897	463,990
171,871	100,000	105,239	2,391	10,000	50,000
300,954	103,733	774,785	34,222	16,782	211,036
328,124	137,460	1,000,044	12,618	19,234	241,872
1,895,749	1,106,581	5,273,406	415,539	177,666	2,234,188
347,190	131,656	812,768	45,789	20,077	252,472
386,662	170,519	718,891	117,872	26,820	337,272
192,381	100,000	163,493	20,170	10,000	65,045
206,022	100,000	172,293	25,334	10,000	83,354
652,801	339,800	2,266,713	94,348	54,369	683,699
577,997	314,971	2,253,042	27,628	45,633	573,845
213,704	100,000	298,618	31,355	10,000	94,918
217,211	100,000	360,587	9,750	10,000	94,436
1,013,556	687,167	3,056,685	564,469	102,071	1,283,562
610,586	343,940	1,946,443	140,520	49,541	622,990
402,486	199,790	1,130,606	103,815	27,395	344,499
354,128	156,308	898,884	54,583	22,338	280,900
417,806	235,368	1,610,633	94,829	32,184	404,727
476,462	263,453	2,009,273	151,035	38,966	490,008
236,260	100,000	447,007	36,710	10,000	121,900
464,535	227,938	1,304,710	143,768	35,824	450,499
581,783	346,508	1,553,953	273,304	49,579	623,472
955,682	585,544	3,390,149	352,160	87,856	1,104,807
482,274	255,057	1,570,349	175,693	37,165	467,363
380,091	184,471	1,330,738	19,787	25,594	321,853
533,910	296,211	1,639,964	178,566	42,491	534,336
214,585	100,000	339,695	21,986	10,000	93,954
275,106	100,364	591,630	60,319	14,368	180,682
190,404	100,000	115,302	4,206	10,000	53,000
200,831	100,000	262,364	36,614	10,000	81,909
679,227	400,066	1,792,228	315,069	63,066	793,072
255,743	100,000	598,278	28,678	11,763	147,918
1,450,692	1,075,982	4,203,741	895,787	161,727	2,033,751
622,127	371,623	2,578,830	20,839	50,920	640,335
206,396	100,000	341,302	21,604	10,000	87,691
1,078,054	701,492	4,080,409	415,830	104,331	1,311,989
387,284	169,344	1,038,377	21,412	23,180	291,500
337,476	128,794	745,215	36,134	19,157	240,903
1,034,524	771,722	4,036,521	640,847	108,853	1,368,843
211,259	100,000	286,848	56,112	10,000	102,627
404,942	207,146	1,454,248	16,060	27,970	351,727
214,536	100,000	361,319	24,950	10,000	91,063
497,987	273,483	1,912,391	33,268	38,238	480,854
1,175,595	737,950	5,073,135	159,155	109,811	1,380,889
264,277	100,000	560,955	6,404	11,533	145,027
182,331	100,000	185,766	18,547	10,000	50,591
549,649	304,744	1,974,056	58,696	44,292	556,981
449,344	208,605	1,100,863	59,745	29,656	372,927
316,091	144,955	928,179	18,259	18,353	230,791
504,462	288,659	1,729,885	271,950	42,300	531,926
181,253	100,000	150,938	4,205	10,000	50,000
505,750	415,049	1,229,840	64,424	32,000	392,000

(continued)

TABLE 10-6 (*continued*)

STATE	SCHOOL ASSISTANCE TO FEDERALLY AFFECTED AREAS		VOCATIONAL EDUCATION ACT OF 1963		VOCATIONAL EDUCATION	
	OP'NS. (PL 874)	CONSTR'N. (PL 815)	STATE GRANTS	WORK-STUDY	GEORGE-BARDEN AND SUPPL. ACTS	SMITH-HUGHES ACT
TOTALS	$395,390,000	$24,772,498	$198,225,000	$10,000,000	$49,990,823	$7,161,4
Alabama	8,955,406	92,000	4,589,666	197,787	1,140,849	143,3
Alaska	9,762,046	821,000	243,040	15,881	259,576	30,0
Arizona	6,285,722	545,000	1,842,665	83,735	279,450	51,7
Arkansas	1,953,560	29,000	2,475,963	105,390	797,790	85,1
California	60,978,019	4,142,498	14,917,026	919,639	2,549,008	534,0
Colorado	10,290,723	55,000	1,992,977	101,059	434,455	66,7
Connecticut	2,616,498	—	2,183,680	132,821	461,753	92,5
Delaware	2,350,131	—	399,998	25,024	232,631	30,0
Dist. of Columbia	4,618,402	—	543,244	31,280	228,058	—
Florida	12,953,787	681,000	6,196,204	272,860	967,146	187,5
Georgia	12,330,086	710,000	5,815,882	247,836	1,291,071	172,4
Hawaii	6,857,193	2,174,000	779,107	43,311	230,196	31,6
Idaho	2,418,106	—	858,478	38,980	335,250	39,4
Illinois	9,983,678	220,000	8,266,810	503,371	2,130,336	360,3
Indiana	3,039,259	596,000	4,781,770	246,873	1,440,031	193,4
Iowa	1,787,388	114,000	2,846,311	140,039	1,327,878	122,5
Kansas	6,196,140	804,000	2,326,685	114,534	784,270	91,3
Kentucky	6,040,371	1,004,000	4,089,596	175,651	1,324,728	143,1
Louisiana	3,001,338	333,000	4,585,248	198,269	912,068	134,2
Maine	2,661,479	27,000	1,173,870	51,011	310,383	48,1
Maryland	18,746,284	679,000	3,350,943	185,275	666,815	118,6
Massachusetts	10,412,223	111,000	4,492,554	251,686	833,089	179,4
Michigan	4,981,623	4,000	7,778,655	427,817	1,798,634	297,7
Minnesota	1,706,172	—	3,641,294	180,944	1,312,235	141,9
Mississippi	2,478,037	184,000	3,137,749	137,633	1,163,305	107,3
Missouri	5,221,005	121,000	4,535,632	216,555	1,390,638	173,6
Montana	3,228,800	19,000	802,261	38,018	299,881	38,6
Nebraska	3,802,700	490,000	1,474,594	71,223	642,728	64,2
Nevada	2,719,033	90,000	326,107	19,249	228,058	30,6
New Hampshire	1,859,828	155,000	697,660	32,724	228,058	34,0
New Jersey	7,904,435	797,000	5,330,872	320,983	876,457	201,9
New Mexico	7,912,906	1,181,000	1,267,614	57,748	245,693	43,1
New York	21,055,954	22,000	13,539,820	819,542	2,700,384	575,3
North Carolina	9,344,737	1,275,000	6,647,542	283,447	2,032,505	221,7
North Dakota	2,359,730	365,000	811,763	35,611	434,085	42,7
Ohio	9,660,120	186,000	9,903,582	516,364	2,201,568	369,3
Oklahoma	8,932,441	1,111,000	2,969,877	126,083	735,384	96,2
Oregon	1,945,923	—	1,991,915	100,578	508,946	73,6
Pennsylvania	7,313,773	—	11,164,872	552,457	2,343,066	437,7
Rhode Island	2,638,017	—	861,074	43,792	231,350	37,9
South Carolina	6,682,898	179,000	3,639,695	158,326	973,362	114,7
South Dakota	3,446,992	87,000	817,192	36,093	436,475	42,9
Tennessee	4,915,534	285,000	4,881,629	204,525	1,426,595	159,3
Texas	20,904,631	2,179,000	12,676,680	563,525	2,357,417	359,6
Utah	4,505,686	304,000	1,184,139	54,861	228,854	38,4
Vermont	122,508	—	480,096	20,693	228,058	33,3
Virginia	24,455,489	222,000	5,430,470	243,023	1,294,292	173,1
Washington	10,549,718	543,000	2,955,581	161,213	723,517	113,3
West Virginia	465,327	—	2,369,947	103,465	604,758	91,3
Wisconsin	1,669,789	—	4,136,678	207,893	1,364,517	162,2
Wyoming	1,304,017	—	341,187	17,324	228,058	30,6
Outlying areas[3]	7,064,338	1,836,000	3,677,106	165,979	1,815,109	—

[1]Includes Arts and Humanities grants to States.
[2]Includes Arts and Humanities loans to nonprofit private schools.
[3]Includes funds transferred from Department of the Interior, Bureau of Indian Affa technical services, and reserves.

SOURCE: Joe G. Keen, "State Allotments for Funded Projects, Fiscal Year 1968," *Ameri‹ Education*, Washington, D.C., U.S. Govt. Printing Office, April, 1968, pp. 32–33.

terms. In spite of the new advanced funding provision, it is possible that appropriation committees will not approve advanced funding, and that the President will find it a political disadvantage to add $2 billion to his budget ahead of time.

As an incentive feature of the ESEA amendments, it was provided that, beginning in FY 1969, the states that spent a larger proportion of total resources for education than was the national average were to be allocated additional grants for Title I. Provision was that no state was to receive more than 15 per cent of the total incentive grants.

Title III included a requirement that 75 per cent of the funds for innovative education centers were to be distributed in a block-grant to the states in FY 1969 and that in FY 1970 all the funds under this title would be in block-grant form. Prior to this amendment, the U.S. Office of Education distributed Title III funds on a project basis through local school systems.

Congressman Quie (Republican, Minnesota), a member of the House Education and Labor Committee, led a movement by Republicans to attempt to substitute block grants to states for the traditional direct categorical grants which bypassed the states. Under the Quie amendments, ESEA Titles I, II, III, and V funds would have been distributed by the states in FY 1969. Agreement on this arrangement for Title III was effected through the leadership of Congressman Edith Green (Democrat, Oregon), who remained neutral on the Quie amendment but led Republicans and Southern Democrats in development of a modest compromise.

The U.S. Chamber of Commerce, the Chief State School Officers, the Republican governors of several states (Colorado, Massachusetts, Montana, Nevada, Minnesota, South Dakota, Washington, and Wisconsin), and the State School Superintendents of Arkansas, Florida, Colorado, Kansas, Minnesota, North Dakota, and Pennsylvania, supported the Quie proposal. Opposition included the National Education Association, the American Federation of Teachers, Citizens for Educational Freedom, the National Association for the Advancement of Colored People, the United States Catholic Conference, and City School Superintendents from New York, Chicago, Detroit, Atlanta, Baltimore, Cleveland, Minneapolis, and San Francisco, among others.

The "child-benefit" approach and provision for specialized rather than general purpose aid under the Elementary and Secondary Education Act of 1965 permitted private-school youngsters to enjoy the benefits of the Act since 1965. Catholic church leaders feared that laws in many states would keep parochial pupils from federal-aid programs under Quie's plan. Congressmen feared the Quie amendment would create a new holy war between parochial and private schools, the old one having kept federal general purpose aid from becoming a reality in the 1950's and early 1960's.

The amendments approved in December, 1967, did not include the Senate authorization for taxpayers to bring suits challenging the constitutionality of federal aid to church-related school systems. Senator Sam Ervin, Jr. (Democrat, North Carolina) as usual led the movement to bring sufficient standing to individuals allowing them to challenge federal law. In 1923, the Supreme Court (*Frothingham v. Mellon*) ruled that it would not hear a challenge to federal law by individual taxpayers on grounds that the taxpayer was being unduly deprived of property. The Court stated that the Constitution charged it to hear only real cases and controversies and that individual taxpayers did not have sufficient standing to provide such a case or controversy. However, in 1968 the Supreme Court ruled in an action (Flast v. Gardner) to enjoin use of federal funds to finance guidance services in religiously operated schools and to prevent expenditure of federal funds for purchase of textbooks and other instructional materials for use in such schools that the plaintiff did have standing to bring this action.

Those city-school superintendents who opposed Quie's proposal for block-grants feared that rural-oriented legislatures would distribute an unproportionate share of funds to rural areas. The superintendents preferred to receive funds directly from the federal government.

Passage of the ESEA amendments resulted partially from a compromise statement by John Gardner, Secretary of Health, Education and Welfare, that educational funds would not be deferred because a school system was not complying with the Civil Rights Law unless adequate warning had been given. Title VI of the Civil Rights Act of 1964 states:

> No person in the United States shall, on the ground of race, color, or national origin, be excluded from participation in, be denied the benefits of, or be subject to discrimination under any program or activity receiving federal financial assistance.

The amendments stipulated that a school system was in compliance with Title VI if it was complying with a court desegregation order.

Other provisions of the new legislation required (1) that 15 per cent of Title III funds be used for special programs for the handicapped; (2) establishment of state advisory councils to plan and evaluate Title III; (3) establishment of a National Advisory Council on Supplemental Centers and Service to evaluate programs and report annually to the President and Congress; and (4) that 40 per cent of Title V funds not reserved for the Commissioner

(5 per cent reserve) be allocated equally among states, and that 60 per cent be allotted according to the relative number of pupils in each state.

President Johnson declared unconditional war on poverty in America in 1964, and the Economic Opportunity Act of 1964 was the beginning of a coordinated assault on the roots of poverty: joblessness, poor education, bad housing, family disintegration, and discrimination. In spite of formidable opposition to the war on poverty during the First Session of the 90th Congress, the Johnson Administration achieved a notable victory, and the Congress passed the Economic Opportunity Act Amendments of 1967 late in the session.

TABLE 10-7. Elementary and Secondary Education Act, Amended, 1967 (Dollars in Millions)

PROGRAM	NEW AUTHORIZATION, 1968	TOTAL AUTHORIZATION		
		1968	1969	1970
Title I, Disadvantaged		$2,563	$2,726	$2,862
Title I, Special incentive			50	50
Title II, Libraries and textbooks		155	167	206
Title III, Supplemental centers and services		515	528	567
Title V, Part A, State education departments	$15	65	80	80
Title VI, Handicapped				
Resource centers	7.5	7.5	7.75	10
Deaf-blind	1.0	1.0	3.0	7
Recruitment	1.0	1.0	1.0	1
Captioned films	3.0	8.0	8.0	10
Grants to states		154	167	206
Title VII, Information				
Rural areas	1.5	3.5	3.7	4
Impacted areas				
Construction	62	62	66	66
Operation-maintenance	15.9	477	510	545
Adult		60	70	80
School bus safety			.15	
Bilingual education				
Aid to districts	15	15	30	40
Teacher training	11	11	10[a]	10
Dropouts, New demonstration projects			30	30
Mental retardation				18

NOTE: Figures over $20 million were rounded out.

[a] $275 million for fellowships for FY 1968; 195 million for fellowships for FY 1969; 240 million for fellowships for FY 1970; 50 million for fellowships for NDEA training institutes in FY 1968.

SOURCE: *Congressional Record—Appendix*, Dec. 27, 1967, pp. A6348–A6349.

As finally approved by the Congress, the OEO amendments of 1967 continue the poverty programs through FY 1968 and FY 1969. They authorized appropriations of $1.98 billion in 1968 and $2.18 billion in 1969.

An important amendment pertained to drawing public officials in a community into the effort to overcome poverty conditions. Local governments were authorized to assume administrative power over community-action programs no later than February 1, 1969. The community-action program committee is to have no more than 51 members in each case: one-third of the membership shall be public officials; one-third shall be democratically elected as representatives of poverty areas; and one-third shall be representatives of business, labor, civil, and charitable organizations.

Authorizations for regular poverty programs included (1) $950 million for community action, including Headstart, and $25 million to feed the hungry; (2) $295 million for the Job Corps; (3) $476 million for Neighborhood Youth Corps and other work-training programs; (4) $60 million to attract business to ghettos; (5) $20 million for rural loans; (6) $27 million for migrant workers; (7) $10 million for small business loans; (8) $25 million for day-care centers; (9) $70 million to train welfare recipients for jobs; (10) $30 million for VISTA; and (11) $16 million for administration expenses.

Another key aspect of the poverty program was the extension of Public Law 90-35 (Teacher Corps) for three years through FY 1970. The purpose of the Corps is to send teams of teachers and student interns into urban slums and impoverished rural areas to upgrade the standards of education. Congress authorized $135 million for Fiscal Years 1968–1970 for that purpose.

The law additionally authorized $435 million in Fiscal 1969–1970 for graduate fellowships for elementary and secondary school teachers and grants to colleges and universities for improvement of their graduate education facilities.

Four new programs were authorized for beginning in 1969: (1) grants to attract qualified persons to the field of education; (2) grants to assist local education agencies to carry out programs to attract and qualify teachers and teacher aides; (3) grants for advanced training and retraining for persons serving in elementary and secondary school programs; and (4) fellowships and other training for college and university teachers and administrators.

A proviso in Public Law 35 specified that the recruitment, selection, and enrollment of Corps volunteers is to be carried out by local education agencies and the colleges and universities. This ensures that local decisions will determine how the Teacher Corps programs are to be implemented and administered at the local level.

The Vocational Rehabilitation Amendments of 1967 can be considered as part of the strategy in attacking poverty. Public Law 66-236, approved in 1920, was the federal government's first assistance to the handicapped. In 1943, Public Law 78-113 expanded rehabilitation programs. The 1943 law authorized state rehabilitation agencies to provide to handicapped persons with limited medical and vocational diagnoses to determine their rehabilitation potential and aid them in realizing it, in addition to the occupational training and counseling programs that existed under authority of the original act. In 1954, Congress continued and expanded these programs with Public Law 83-565.

In 1965, Congress enacted Public Law 89-333, which increased the number of physically and mentally handicapped persons to be rehabilitated annually from 120,000 to 200,000. Intent of the law was to expand services available and to place special emphasis on rehabilitation of the mentally retarded and severely handicapped.

The 1967 amendments further expanded vocational rehabilitation programs and provided 90 per cent federal reimbursement for such services to disabled migratory farm workers. This the Congress did in Public Law 90-99. The new law also provided for the establishment of a new National Center for Deaf-Blind Youths and Adults, which will coordinate efforts to train these handicapped persons for employment.

Authorizations were made for $500 million in 1969 and $600 million in 1970 for grants to the states for basic vocational rehabilitation services. For comparison, authorizations were $350 million and $400 million in 1967 and 1968, respectively.

The new law raises the number to be rehabilitated in 1969 to 247,000 and in 1970 to 278,000. However, the number of disabled Americans needing rehabilitation training was 4 million in 1968, with an annual increase of 400,000.

The year 1967 marked not only the centennial of the Office of Education, but also the golden anniversary of the first national vocational education act. President Woodrow Wilson signed into law on February 23, 1917, the Smith–Hughes Act, which became the first to provide federal funds for local schools.

Approximately $1.7 billion has been made available to the states, the District of Columbia, and outlying areas, under the Smith–Hughes and other vocational education acts for vocational and technical education during the fifty years.

Allotments to the states under the Smith–Hughes Act total over $7.1 million for education in agriculture, trades and industry, and home economics, and training of teachers in these subjects, ranging from $30,000 in four states

(Alaska, Delaware, Nevada, and Wyoming) to $575,316 in New York and $534,067 in California.

Under the George–Barden and supplemental acts more than $49.9 million was allocated in FY 1968 for education in agriculture, distributive occupations, home economics, trade and industry, fishery trades and industry (Title I), practical nurse training (Title II), and technical education (Title III).

Under the Vocational Education Act of 1963, $198.2 million was allotted for general vocational activities (section 4) and $10 million for the vocational work-study program (section 13) during FY 1968. Allotments for general vocational activities ranged in the 50 states from $243,040 in Alaska and $326,107 in Nevada, to $14,917,026 and $13,539,820 to California and New York, respectively.

Determining State Shares of Federal Programs

Most current federal-grant programs for education, as well as for other federal grant programs, have two distinct but coordinate provisions to determine state shares of grant funds. The first is an apportionment formula, which specifies the proportion of total federal grant funds for which each state is eligible. The second provision, a matching formula, specifies to what extent a participating state must share in the costs of the program.

Apportionment formulas vary considerably but most often incorporate one or more of the criteria embraced by the so-called "PFN" formula: population, financial ability, and need for the program. Program need is usually measured by the total population or the relevant population group. Financial ability is typically measured by relative per-capita income. This is the case, for example, in grants for school lunches.

Matching requirements—that is, requiring states to share in program costs —are common elements of most grants. The matching or cost-sharing requirements are of two kinds: variable matching, which takes account of the differing abilities of the states to support their aided functions; and fixed ratio matching, under which each state is required to share in the same proportion of program cost.

By writing such formulas into legislation, the Congress makes sure that federal aid goes where it is most needed. Under Public Law 89-10, distribution of Title I funds in 1968 was based on the number of children in families with income below $2,000, and the state's average per-pupil expenditure, or the national average expenditure, whichever was higher. However, it was provided that beginning in FY 1969, the states which spent a larger proportion of total resources for education than was the national average were to be allocated additional grants for Title I, as described earlier. Under the Vocational

Education Act of 1963, the formula is based on population and per-capita income, which means that a state with a large population between the ages of 15 and 65 and lower per-capita income gets proportionately more funds than a state with a smaller population and a higher per-capita income.

Under Public Laws 874 and 815, which provide assistance to areas affected by federal programs, the formula is based on the number of children who live on or who live with a parent employed on federal property. Under Public Law 874, the rate of payment is based on expenditure from local revenue for current operating expenses by a comparable community in the same state.

An important factor to consider in the allocation of federal resources is the effect on the geographic distribution of income. As shown in Table 10-8, some types of federal programs have a far stronger tendency to act as "income equalizers" among the different regions than others. Specifically, farm price supports and federal aid to education demonstrate this characteristic to a very strong degree. In contrast, defense and space contract awards tend to be received by those highly industrialized states that also have above-average income levels.

Redistribution effects of federal aid are sometimes assessed by comparing the total amount of assistance to each state's total personal income. There has been criticism of this type of analysis on several grounds. One is that income equalization is necessarily a secondary and an irrelevant criterion in some respects when applied to the operating results of the complex of existing programs. Considering the grant structure as if it were a unified whole, any redistributional or income-equalizing effects are incidental and not a product of explicit congressional design.

Insofar as there is a common focus of existing grants, it is on service standards and not on personal incomes. Any important contribution to equalization is in the form of assured support everywhere for nationally defined minimum standards in designated public services. The Advisory Commission on Intergovernmental Relations found that as recently as 1961–1962 the correlation between federal grants and state personal incomes, though slightly negative, was not statistically significant. Grants disbursed on an equalized basis, also taken as a group, exhibited a moderately low—rather than the expected high—inverse relationship to personal incomes. Staff studies for the Commission indicate that since 1962 there has been no significant change in the relationship between state personal incomes and federal grants.[11]

[11] Advisory Commission on Intergovernmental Relations, *The Role of Equalization in Federal Grants* (1964), p. 63. For all grants in the study ($7 billion), the coefficient of correlation was −.041. For equalized grants ($1.3 billion), the coefficient of correlation was −.389. The point is discussed also in the Commission's report now in preparation, *Fiscal Balance in the American Federal System*, Chap. V.

TABLE 10-8. Regional Shares of Population, Income, and Selected Federal Expenditure Programs, 1963 Percentage of Distributions

REGION	POPU- LATION	PER- SONAL INCOME	DE- FENSE	COM- POSITE NON- DEFENSE	NASA	RECLA- MATION	HIGH- WAYS	VET- ERANS	PUBLIC ASSIST- ANCE	CORPS OF ENGI- NEERS	EDU- CATION	FARM SUBSI- DIES
Low income, TOTAL	29.7%	22.9%	17.8%	36.2%	21.8%	22.4%	31.1%	32.8%	37.1%	38.7%	45.1%	52.9%
Southeast	21.7	16.1	11.2	24.6	18.8	—	21.8	23.9	26.2	21.4	34.6	30.9
Southwest	8.0	6.8	6.6	11.6	3.0	22.4	9.3	8.9	10.9	17.3	10.5	22.0
Average income. TOTAL	36.3	37.7	32.1	33.9	15.8	48.2	39.9	35.4	31.9	28.6	28.0	42.5
Rocky Mountain	2.4	2.3	4.2	3.2	.4	35.4	5.8	2.5	2.8	.3	1.8	1.6
Plains	8.3	7.9	6.3	13.8	9.6	12.8	9.5	8.9	8.7	21.1	8.9	31.7
Great Lakes	19.8	21.0	12.6	13.0	3.3	—	19.6	17.2	14.5	5.8	14.2	9.2
New England	5.8	6.5	9.0	3.9	2.5	—	5.0	6.8	5.9	1.4	3.1	—
High income, TOTAL	34.0	39.4	50.1	29.9	62.4	29.4	29.0	31.8	31.0	32.7	26.9	4.6
Mideast	21.4	24.6	22.0	12.9	11.8	—	15.1	20.1	15.9	10.1	17.6	.3
Far West	12.6	14.8	28.1	17.0	50.6	29.4	13.9	11.7	15.1	22.6	9.3	4.3

NOTE: The education program was for fiscal year 1966.

SOURCE: *U.S. Economic Growth to 1975: Potentials and Problems*, Washington, U.S. Govt. Printing Office, 1966, Table 18, p. 45.

TABLE 10-9. Federal Grants to State and Local Governments, in Amounts Per Capita, by Major Function, as Related to Personal Income Levels in Three Groups of States—Fiscal Year 1966 and Comparisons with 1957

PROGRAM OR OTHER CATEGORY	TOTAL, 50 STATES AND D.C.	17 HIGHEST-INCOME STATES	17 MIDDLE-INCOME STATES	17 LOWEST-INCOME STATES
Federal grants to state and local governments, Fiscal Year 1966				
Average amount per capita, all grants	$63.90	$56.88	$62.56	$82.80
Public assistance	18.12	17.80	15.31	23.21
Employment security	2.40	2.77	2.07	1.75
Health services	2.24	1.78	2.47	3.43
Other welfare services	8.49	7.69	7.62	12.90
Education	7.92	6.27	7.65	12.08
Highway construction	20.47	16.50	23.47	24.31
All other	4.27	4.07	3.97	5.12
Percentage of all grants, Fiscal Year 1966				
Public assistance	28.4%	31.3%	24.5%	28.0%
Employment security	3.8	4.9	3.3	2.1
Health services	3.5	3.1	3.9	4.1
Other welfare services	13.3	13.5	12.2	15.6
Education	12.4	11.0	12.2	14.6
Highway construction	32.0	29.0	37.5	29.4
All other	6.7	7.2	6.3	6.2
Personal income per capita (annual average during calendar years 1963–1965)				
Median state	$2,457	$3,044	$2,457	$1,949
Range of state averages:				
Highest in group	3,535	3,535	2,611	2,191
Lowest in group	1,510	2,639	2,217	1,510

SOURCE: I. M. Labovitz, *Federal Assistance to State and Local Governments*, a paper presented at the Tax Institute of America Symposium, Washington, D.C., Nov. 29, 1967, p. 37, Table 4.

In Table 10-9, Labovitz pointed out that in his comparison of federal grants per capita in 1966 and 1957, grants per capita were substantially higher in low-income states as a group than in middle- and high-income states. Only in the low-income states was the average amount per capita above the nationwide average, not only in total for all grants, but also for the separate categories of public assistance, other welfare services, education, and all others.

In 1957, the largest federal assistance for education was in selective payments to federally affected school districts. By 1966, grants under the Elementary and Secondary Education Act of 1965 were important. Aids for higher education also had been substantially enlarged. One result was a sharper rise in education aid per capita in the lowest-income states.

Proportionately, the grants increased most in high-income states as a group. The greatest amount of increase for these states was in highway construction and public assistance, but the rate of increase was faster for other welfare services and education.

Among low-income states as a group, the absolute increase in grants per capita was greater than in the rest of the nation, but the percentage increase was less. The greatest amount of increase for these states was for highway construction, but the next largest increment was for education.

Studies establish clearly that regional income trends between 1929 and the early postwar years involved a shift of income away from four northern and eastern regions to four southern and western regions, as can be seen in the shift of per-capita personal income shown in Table 10-10. However, there was

TABLE 10-10. Changes in the Geographic Distribution of Per-Capita Personal Income by Regions, Selected Years

REGION	PER-CAPITA PERSONAL INCOME (PERCENTAGE OF THE UNITED STATES)			
	1929	1948	1957	1966
United States, TOTAL	100%	100%	100%	100%
New England	125	104	110	110
Mideast	138	115	116	113
Great Lakes	114	112	110	109
Plains	81	101	91	96
Southeast	52	69	72	77
Southwest	67	83	87	85
Rocky Mountain	85	99	94	91
Far West	129	120	117	115

SOURCE: *Survey of Current Business*, Washington, D.C., U.S. Department of Commerce, Office of Business Economics, April, 1967, p. 16.

still a serious gap in per-capita personal income by states as listed in Table 10-11. The per-capita personal income in Mississippi was $1,751 in 1966, while it was $3,678 in Connecticut. Current expenditures per pupil in 1967 were $335 in Mississippi and $657 in Connecticut, as shown in Figure 10-1.

Of the ten low-spending states relative to current expenditures per pupil in average daily attendance, eight were located in the Southeast (North Carolina, West Virginia, Tennessee, Kentucky, Arkansas, Alabama, South Carolina, and Mississippi), while the remaining two were Idaho and Maine. Among the ten high-spending states, two were located in the Mideast (New York and New Jersey), one from New England (Connecticut), two from the Rocky

Mountains (Wyoming and Montana), two from the Far West (Oregon and Nevada), one from the Southwest (Arizona), and the remaining two were Alaska and Hawaii.

Methods and Agencies Involved in Allocation of Federal Funds

The term *federal aid* has become identified with Economic Opportunity, Educationally and Economically Deprived Children, Area Vocational Centers, Manpower Training, Community Action, Work-Study, and Migrant programs. Many federal programs involving elementary and secondary education have not originated from the United States Office of Education, and even some of those that have originated from the Office of Education are not administered through the state education departments.

In its 1966 edition of the *Federal Aid Handbook*, the Division of Educational Finance in the New York State Education Department described allocation methods as follows:

Method A—Allocation of federal funds directly to state educational agency from U.S. Office of Education but amount of local educational agency's allocation is not available for use by another local agency but returned to the federal government. This particular allocation method was used under Title I of the Elementary and Secondary Education Act.

Method B—Allocation of federal funds directly to the state educational agency from the U.S. Office of Education but amount of local educational agency's allocation is not specified by the federal agency. The unused portion of the local educational agency's allocation is available for use by another local agency. This allocation method was used under Title II of the Elementary and Secondary Education Act; Title III of the National Defense Education Act; Title V-A of the National Defense Education Act; the Vocational Education Act; Title I of the Library Services and Construction Act; the National School Lunch Act and Title II-B of the Economic Opportunity Act.

Method C—Allocation of federal funds not directly to the state educational agency but to the local educational agency from the U.S. Office of Education was based upon individual federal projects. Federal funds for the project, however, were channeled through the state educational agency. The unused portion of the local educational agency's allocation was not available for use by another local agency or project. This method was used under the Manpower Development and Training Act and Title II of the Library Services and Construction Act.

Method D—Allocation of federal funds was not directly to the state educational agency but to the local educational agency from the U.S. Office of Education based upon individual federal projects. Federal funds for the

TABLE 10-11. Per-Capita Personal Income, by States and Regions, 1948–1966

State and Region	1948	1949	1950	1951	1952	1953	1954	1955	1956	1957	1958	1959	1960[a]	1961[a]	1962[a]	1963[a]	1964[a]	1965[a]	1966[a,b]
United States	$1,430	$1,384	$1,496	$1,652	$1,733	$1,804	$1,785	$1,876	$1,975	$2,045	$2,068	$2,161	$2,215	$2,264	$2,368	$2,455	$2,579	$2,746	$2,940
New England	1,494	1,452	1,601	1,779	1,865	1,921	1,905	2,030	2,152	2,241	2,258	2,338	2,425	2,496	2,618	2,698	2,843	2,995	3,223
Maine	1,235	1,174	1,185	1,297	1,411	1,422	1,417	1,551	1,635	1,679	1,742	1,780	1,844	1,830	1,904	1,961	2,122	2,277	2,438
New Hampshire	1,285	1,259	1,323	1,497	1,557	1,616	1,652	1,765	1,829	1,729	1,957	2,084	2,143	2,204	2,300	2,347	2,428	2,547	2,761
Vermont	1,134	1,073	1,121	1,275	1,323	1,375	1,464	1,464	1,586	1,646	1,650	1,739	1,841	1,877	1,980	2,013	2,130	2,312	2,590
Massachusetts	1,500	1,470	1,633	1,793	1,866	1,910	1,893	2,026	2,146	2,247	2,287	2,373	2,459	2,544	2,659	2,746	2,910	3,050	3,217
Rhode Island	1,493	1,437	1,606	1,765	1,803	1,879	1,866	1,961	1,993	1,999	2,042	2,154	2,211	2,281	2,425	2,507	2,652	2,823	2,980
Connecticut	1,713	1,660	1,875	2,138	2,263	2,346	2,294	2,414	2,603	2,712	2,642	2,695	2,807	2,892	3,040	3,118	3,234	3,401	3,678
Midwest	1,648	1,618	1,756	1,912	1,985	2,068	2,054	2,153	2,283	2,378	2,387	2,494	2,565	2,612	2,728	2,806	2,948	3,108	3,310
New York	1,797	1,749	1,873	2,015	2,067	2,139	2,167	2,283	2,396	2,518	2,518	2,661	2,746	2,795	2,901	2,978	3,127	3,278	3,480
New Jersey	1,689	1,663	1,834	2,028	2,133	2,247	2,231	2,306	2,443	2,536	2,516	2,634	2,708	2,765	2,889	2,965	3,069	3,237	3,414
Pennsylvania	1,431	1,401	1,541	1,697	1,773	1,870	1,804	1,889	2,032	2,137	2,130	2,196	2,242	2,257	2,371	2,441	2,588	2,747	2,951
Delaware	1,721	1,854	2,131	2,208	2,293	2,379	2,329	2,519	2,755	2,641	2,610	2,712	2,757	2,759	2,882	3,013	3,121	3,392	3,563
Maryland	1,467	1,456	1,602	1,769	1,888	1,964	1,888	1,994	2,126	2,198	2,205	2,269	2,343	2,464	2,573	2,675	2,828	3,001	3,220
District of Columbia	1,957	2,107	2,221	2,377	2,457	2,363	2,424	2,483	2,660	2,701	2,818	2,928	3,017	3,065	3,249	3,370	3,527	3,708	3,969
Great Lakes	1,603	1,517	1,666	1,864	1,937	2,062	1,983	2,095	2,198	2,248	2,203	2,322	2,383	2,405	2,521	2,619	2,766	2,985	3,198
Michigan	1,560	1,520	1,700	1,874	1,962	2,161	2,031	2,183	2,214	2,229	2,149	2,251	2,324	2,299	2,438	2,587	2,772	3,010	3,219
Ohio	1,558	1,474	1,620	1,848	1,927	2,028	1,961	2,081	2,171	2,227	2,148	2,276	2,334	2,328	2,427	2,509	2,641	2,829	3,027
Indiana	1,451	1,361	1,512	1,694	1,766	1,930	1,795	1,894	1,991	2,028	1,998	2,119	2,188	2,222	2,359	2,471	2,599	2,846	3,061
Illinois	1,815	1,685	1,825	2,015	2,078	2,186	2,154	2,243	2,416	2,488	2,466	2,581	2,650	2,720	2,826	2,915	3,050	3,280	3,511
Wisconsin	1,419	1,366	1,477	1,697	1,756	1,787	1,722	1,816	1,927	1,991	2,018	2,152	2,175	2,221	2,330	2,374	2,534	2,724	2,935
Plains	1,444	1,298	1,428	1,547	1,624	1,642	1,677	1,681	1,749	1,860	1,970	1,990	2,067	2,119	2,241	2,315	2,395	2,624	2,820
Minnesota	1,432	1,310	1,410	1,548	1,592	1,665	1,671	1,729	1,783	1,874	1,990	2,020	2,116	2,193	2,254	2,372	2,440	2,666	2,871
Iowa	1,589	1,316	1,485	1,577	1,652	1,598	1,723	1,608	1,694	1,869	1,921	1,949	1,986	2,082	2,177	2,303	2,392	2,676	2,931
Missouri	1,389	1,338	1,431	1,555	1,656	1,728	1,715	1,802	1,884	1,922	2,023	2,101	2,115	2,166	2,269	2,358	2,458	2,663	2,845
North Dakota	1,402	1,129	1,263	1,315	1,217	1,243	1,254	1,379	1,437	1,479	1,700	1,537	1,715	1,504	2,156	2,003	1,991	2,279	2,400
South Dakota	1,497	1,092	1,243	1,438	1,272	1,377	1,398	1,293	1,364	1,604	1,668	1,469	1,782	1,772	2,001	1,908	1,877	2,213	2,355
Nebraska	1,509	1,303	1,491	1,571	1,668	1,612	1,681	1,595	1,628	1,876	1,963	1,976	2,110	2,114	2,247	2,277	2,383	2,629	2,819
Kansas	1,334	1,287	1,443	1,578	1,782	1,722	1,762	1,732	1,795	1,883	2,073	2,075	2,161	2,251	2,343	2,398	2,488	2,639	2,814
Southeast	984	953	1,022	1,141	1,213	1,267	1,256	1,343	1,423	1,467	1,507	1,585	1,610	1,664	1,749	1,837	1,950	2,089	2,256
Virginia	1,130	1,108	1,228	1,387	1,470	1,488	1,502	1,571	1,635	1,652	1,684	1,770	1,841	1,898	2,017	2,095	2,264	2,419	2,581
West Virginia	1,120	1,033	1,065	1,192	1,258	1,282	1,232	1,326	1,491	1,610	1,549	1,584	1,594	1,634	1,698	1,781	1,891	2,027	2,195

STATE AND REGION	1948	1949	1950	1951	1952	1953[a]	1954[a]	1955	1956	1957	1958	1959	1960[a]	1961[a]	1962[a]	1963[a]	1964[a]	1965[a]	1966[a,b]
Kentucky	990	933	981	1,143	1,228	1,292	1,272	1,329	1,417	1,466	1,496	1,552	1,574	1,668	1,751	1,837	1,887	2,045	2,205
Tennessee	944	927	994	1,081	1,137	1,229	1,222	1,281	1,368	1,419	1,448	1,532	1,543	1,620	1,696	1,776	1,874	2,013	2,199
North Carolina	973	940	1,037	1,139	1,181	1,223	1,239	1,313	1,377	1,369	1,436	1,510	1,561	1,626	1,726	1,804	1,918	2,041	2,235
South Carolina	891	850	893	1,071	1,160	1,199	1,119	1,181	1,210	1,236	1,259	1,334	1,377	1,429	1,531	1,580	1,696	1,846	2,027
Georgia	968	947	1,034	1,167	1,241	1,288	1,259	1,375	1,446	1,469	1,519	1,609	1,639	1,678	1,775	1,879	2,004	2,159	2,311
Florida	1,180	1,191	1,281	1,358	1,443	1,526	1,520	1,620	1,723	1,768	1,827	1,936	1,950	1,970	2,051	2,145	2,285	2,423	2,576
Alabama	866	815	880	1,006	1,071	1,124	1,100	1,233	1,304	1,371	1,404	1,465	1,488	1,508	1,580	1,676	1,777	1,910	2,039
Mississippi	789	691	755	830	886	923	908	1,020	1,026	1,040	1,128	1,203	1,205	1,268	1,309	1,436	1,485	1,608	1,751
Louisiana	1,032	1,085	1,120	1,205	1,279	1,346	1,346	1,396	1,500	1,614	1,613	1,666	1,655	1,687	1,748	1,843	1,936	2,067	2,257
Arkansas	875	799	825	927	992	1,035	1,044	1,142	1,194	1,207	1,279	1,377	1,372	1,487	1,546	1,627	1,740	1,845	2,015
Southwest	1,187	1,256	1,297	1,431	1,513	1,555	1,570	1,629	1,713	1,783	1,836	1,899	1,922	1,978	2,023	2,095	2,191	2,324	2,492
Oklahoma	1,144	1,169	1,143	1,284	1,391	1,467	1,445	1,507	1,580	1,641	1,762	1,805	1,861	1,910	1,925	1,992	2,111	2,289	2,456
Texas	1,199	1,291	1,349	1,469	1,544	1,583	1,611	1,667	1,752	1,823	1,851	1,913	1,925	1,984	2,026	2,105	2,208	2,338	2,511
New Mexico	1,084	1,116	1,177	1,305	1,366	1,386	1,412	1,504	1,593	1,702	1,827	1,917	1,890	1,951	2,014	2,053	2,090	2,193	2,310
Arizona	1,274	1,269	1,331	1,567	1,662	1,653	1,623	1,677	1,767	1,803	1,863	1,948	2,032	2,070	2,171	2,220	2,272	2,370	2,528
Rocky Mountain	1,419	1,360	1,457	1,659	1,727	1,699	1,661	1,742	1,821	1,919	2,001	2,064	2,108	2,154	2,284	2,324	2,379	2,536	2,678
Montana	1,616	1,385	1,622	1,760	1,786	1,779	1,729	1,852	1,892	1,944	2,059	2,010	2,037	1,973	2,272	2,265	2,255	2,438	2,615
Idaho	1,316	1,249	1,295	1,443	1,588	1,508	1,503	1,539	1,667	1,720	1,800	1,872	1,849	1,914	2,033	2,048	2,131	2,395	2,441
Wyoming	1,595	1,606	1,669	1,911	1,867	1,893	1,819	1,857	1,939	2,054	2,143	2,234	2,263	2,304	2,386	2,421	2,429	2,558	2,686
Colorado	1,433	1,405	1,487	1,744	1,830	1,767	1,719	1,814	1,887	2,022	2,115	2,196	2,275	2,343	2,425	2,483	2,559	2,710	2,872
Utah	1,240	1,244	1,309	1,492	1,541	1,578	1,553	1,625	1,707	1,794	1,831	1,926	1,968	2,040	2,163	2,215	2,268	2,355	2,500
Far West	1,715	1,689	1,801	1,985	2,103	2,144	2,117	2,239	2,335	2,400	2,433	2,567	2,622	2,693	2,811	2,910	3,038	3,174	3,385
Washington	1,600	1,569	1,674	1,821	1,919	2,001	2,001	2,038	2,093	2,170	2,231	2,318	2,349	2,455	2,593	2,622	2,714	2,906	3,280
Oregon	1,621	1,573	1,620	1,789	1,875	1,868	1,821	1,928	2,015	1,995	2,082	2,191	2,235	2,275	2,374	2,472	2,600	2,761	2,938
Nevada	1,814	1,822	2,019	2,250	2,431	2,462	2,437	2,549	2,500	2,588	2,651	2,767	2,856	2,929	3,242	3,243	3,232	3,311	3,330
California	1,752	1,730	1,852	2,044	2,167	2,204	2,172	2,313	2,419	2,489	2,511	2,651	2,710	2,776	2,886	2,997	3,133	3,258	3,449
Alaska	—		2,385	2,835	2,614	2,493	2,302	2,275	2,446	3,325	2,357	2,509	2,846	2,714	2,775	2,862	3,082	3,187	3,272
Hawaii	1,407	1,354	1,387	1,580	1,747	1,796	1,802	1,837	1,900	1,944	1,987	2,156	2,369	2,485	2,538	2,647	2,775	2,879	3,143

[a] Total includes Alaska and Hawaii, 1960–1965, but not in earlier years.
[b] Preliminary.
SOURCE: U.S. Department of Commerce, Office of Business Economics.

300   MODERN PUBLIC SCHOOL FINANCE

projects were not channeled through the state educational agency. The unused portion of the local educational agency's allocation was not available for use by another local agency or project. This allocation method was used under the Cooperative Research Act; Title III of the Elementary and Secondary Education Act until amended in December, 1967; Public Laws 815 and 874; and Title V of the Higher Education Act.

Method E—Allocation of federal funds was made not to the state educational agency or local educational agency from the U.S. Office of Education but directly to the state educational agency from another federal governmental agency other than the Office of Education. The unused portion of a local educational agency's allocation was available for use by another local agency. This allocation method was used under portions of Title III-B of the Economic Opportunity Act.

Method F—Allocation of federal funds was not to the state educational agency or the local educational agency from the U.S. Office of Education but directly to the local educational agency from another federal governmental agency other than the Office of Education based upon individual federal projects. Federal funds were not channeled through the state educational agency. The unused portion of local educational agencies was not available for use by other local agencies or projects. This allocation method was used under Title I-B of the Economic Opportunity Act; Title II-A of the Economic Opportunity Act and portions of Title III-B of the Economic Opportunity Act.[12]

Federal aid was described by a division of the New York State Education Department "at times to have no sense of direction, no point of reference, and no respect for the traditional boundaries of public education."[13]

Criteria for Evaluating Federal Education Programs

It is generally recognized that a comprehensive evaluation of existing federal fiscal programs in education is required in order that reasonable rational intergovernmental planning can be effected. The evaluation is not an easy task because it involves input-output or cost-benefit analyses. Difficulty of the task is exemplified in deciding what evidence is needed and what criteria will be used for assessing merits of the individual or collective federal programs. Lindman suggested three basic questions that must be answered:

1. Is the purpose of the program worthy and appropriate to the federal government?

2. Are the administrative arrangements effective and conducive to sound federal-state-local relationships?

[12] *Federal Aid Handbook*, Albany, The University of the State of New York, The State Education Department, Division of Educational Finance, 1966, pp. xiv and xv.
[13] *Ibid.*, p. xiii.

3. Does the combined effect of all federal programs promote the development of adequate public schools in the states?[14]

Two major efforts have been made by the federal government for establishment of educational program criteria. President Hoover's National Advisory Committee on Education issued a report in 1931 declaring that there was justification for using the federal tax system for education provided that the federal government did not control the social purpose or specific processes of education. Emphasis was also given to advantages of general grants.

In 1938, President Franklin Roosevelt's United States Advisory Committee stated that grants should be made available to the states for "all types of current operating expenses for public elementary and secondary schools;" that the states be permitted to use part of federal funds for books, transportation, and scholarships for children attending both public and nonpublic schools; and that general purpose grants be given in preference to categorical aids.

In spite of the recommendations of the two committees for general aid, there has been a proliferation of federal programs since. As a result, many individuals and groups claim that there is a threat of federal control, primarily through a fiscal mechanism.

Criteria for the review of existing and proposed federal grant programs for public schools were included in a statement by the NEA Legislative Commission and the Committee on Educational Finance Joint Task Force on Federal Support.[15] The criteria were based on a point of view that balances the need for general aid and special aid, and the need to preserve state and local control of education. The criteria emphasized that federal general aid for elementary and secondary education should be available to all pupils and programs as determined by local and state plans for improving educational opportunity of attainment. Special grants would be limited in number and comprise a small portion of the total federal aid. Justification for special purpose grants would center upon financing the research, development, and demonstration phases of special educational problems or in meeting the federal government's obligation as a landowner and employer for payments in lieu of local property taxes. Another criterion was that at the federal level all federal education programs would be administered by the U.S. Office of Education.

[14] Erick L. Lindman, "Criteria for Evaluating Federal Education Programs," *The Challenge of Change in School Finance*. Washington, D.C., National Education Association Committee on Educational Finance, 1967, p. 24.

[15] *Ibid.*, pp. 29–30.

The Major Purpose of Federal Aid to Education

Historically, the amount of federal aid granted to states and to local school systems has been extremely meager. However, with the passage of the Elementary and Secondary Education Act in 1965, Congress expressed a growing national interest in public education for reasons cited throughout this text, and appropriated an increase in funds that led to a doubling of the percentage of federal support for public elementary and secondary education. Both in the past and in the present, the purpose of federal aid remains the same— that is, to improve the quality of public education throughout the nation.

Beginning with the Morrill Act and continuing through the period of the second session of the 90th Congress, the federal government has been able to use the time of emergency periods to influence public education primarily through programs of categorical aids. Federal programs have broadened both university and public school educational opportunities, they have opened local and state educational systems to the rest of the nation and vice versa, and they have helped to bring a new accommodation among the three basic levels of government.

As was stated so well by Sufrin, "education is far too important to have any of its aspects conform to the values and ideals of the moment, or to some pressure groups whose interests lie not so much in education as in allocation of public funds and energies away from education in order to keep the tax rate at some 'reasonable' level or to pay for some other social benefit."[16] The value of local autonomy is more dear to some citizens than to others, and the same is true concerning the values of learning, compassion, states' rights, national interests, social mobility, and the right to learn. There is no clear-cut hierarchy of values for the present and the future. No one aspect of the so-called American value system should be controlling, particularly if the promotion of differences is an ultimate goal of public education.

Certain news or mass media and a great number of ambitious politicians continue to manufacture strawmen in order to sell their products or to promote a political future. The federal government has been a perennial strawman pertaining to public education, but its influence continues to be positive in raising national educational standards. If the author's assumption that political consensus at the local and state levels generally will effect development of mediocre educational programs is valid, it is imperative that human and material resources at the national level be tapped to assist in the development of quality programs, if that is a national objective.

[16] Sidney C. Sufrin, *Issues in Federal Aid to Education.* Syracuse, N.Y., Syracuse University Press, p. 54.

CHAPTER 11

A QUESTION OF
COMMITMENT

Introduction

Progress involves a judgment of values and implies that a stream of history flows generally in a desirable direction. As an idea from the concept of history, as a genetic process, or as an evolutionary process, it requires that criteria must be established for determination as to whether the movement of history is in a desirable direction, and to serve as a guideline for man to make present and future choices to accelerate the movement to the good. The criterion of national progress that could be considered most basic is the effectiveness of government to protect individual freedom, to maintain social justice, to furnish a variety of public services, and to provide a system of laws that permits the functioning of a free market economy based on private property.[1]

Educators have argued persistently that only through a relatively big investment in public education could a nation achieve the goals such as those listed above and thereby effect progress. The United States Commissioner of

---

[1] Otto Eckstein, *Public Finance*. Englewood Cliffs, N.J., Prentice-Hall, 1964, p. 1.

303

Education reported that if he were an educator from another planet visiting
the earth in 1966, part of this report would include the following:

> Around 65 per cent of Earth's inhabitants have been exposed to some form of
> organized education but there is little opportunity for the remaining 35 per cent
> to become literate, although Earth has reasonably modern systems of com-
> munication and large unused resources which could be turned to educational
> purposes. In general, education is reserved for people with economic and social
> power. Exceptions are in the United States, Canada, and Russia, countries
> that try to provide education for all their citizens . . . .
>
> Again in general, persons with white skin have more educational opportunity
> than those with black, brown or yellow skin, although enough individuals in
> the latter groups succeed in advanced education to validate the assumption that
> skin color has nothing to do with educational capacity . . . .
>
> It must be recognized that the U.S.A. has gone far beyond most Earth
> countries in the development of its schools. Almost all its children are involved
> in learning and more and more of its citizens are moving toward high
> education . . . .[2]

There are encouraging signs that the American schools are becoming
accommodating agents as exemplified by the fact that a larger proportion of
young people are graduating from high school than ever before. For every
1,000 children in the fifth grade in 1959–1960, there were an estimated 721
high school graduates in 1967. This may be compared with 621 graduates in
1960, with 505 in 1950, and with 455 in 1940 for each 1,000 pupils in the fifth
grade eight years earlier. Thus, within a single generation the proportion of
pupils who were graduated from high school has risen by more than one-
half.[3]

Even more impressive is that 40 per cent of the former fifth-graders now
enter college, as contrasted with only 16 per cent just prior to World War II.
By 1971, it is anticipated that about 20 per cent of our young people can be
expected to earn a bachelor's degree in college. This figure may be compared
with the 7 per cent who were graduated from college in the early 1940's.[4]

Magnitude of Projected Educational Responsibility

In spite of the favorable outputs just discussed, and in spite of growing public
and private investments in education, the nation is far from solving the

[2] Harold Howe II, "A View from Afar," *American Education*, Washington, D.C.,
United States Office of Education, Sept. 1966, Editorial.
[3] W. Vance Grant, "School Retention Rates," *American Education*. Washington, D.C.
U.S. Govt. Printing Office, Dec. 1967–Jan. 1968, inside back cover.
[4] *Ibid.*

serious complex problems of American education. The tremendous demands on the educational systems are exponential in form because of dramatic social, economic, and technological changes, characterized by population growth, urbanization, growing wealth and production, and the rising expectations on the part of all citizens to share in prosperity.[5]

American schools must provide better and more educational opportunities for all who seek them, and they must reach out to large minority groups who have been ignored in the past. They must adapt to the changing role and meaning of education, and the services they provide must reach upward, downward, and throughout the whole age range of the nation's population. They must foster and provide life-long learning opportunities and become oriented to leisure time and cultural pursuits, and they must become increasingly involved in the affairs of the local and worldwide community.

Most of our cities' schools are in difficulty in numerous ways—economically, socially, and culturally. In both city and rural areas, however, there are numerous unmet educational needs.

Teachers' salaries range generally from $3,500 to $9,500 with the national average being $6,821 in 1966–1967. Capable, imaginative, and enthusiastic individuals will not be attracted generally to the teaching profession when male beginning teachers with bachelor's degrees will have beginning salaries averaging $5,850 in 1968–1969, while male graduates with bachelor's degrees will have average salaries of $8,280 in fields other than teaching, as recorded in Table 11-1. Over $2 billion annually would be needed to raise the national average teaching salary to $8,100, the California average.

One out of ten school-age children in the United States has a mental or physical handicapped condition that requires special educational attention. In 1967, there were only 60,000 teachers and other professional personnel available in the field of education of handicapped children, and by 1973 more than 300,000 professionals will be needed in this area. At a cost of $5,400 per person, $150 million would be required to prepare the required number of personnel to meet the educational needs of handicapped children.

Almost 50 per cent of the nation's elementary school children attend schools without libraries or with substandard libraries. About $1 billion would be needed to bring school library book collections up to standards.

Quality preschool opportunities are necessary for disadvantaged children

[5] See the *Congressional Record—House*, October 24, 1967, p. H13922, for an excellent statement by Wilbur J. Cohen, Secretary of Health, Education, and Welfare, concerning unmet educational needs and the matter of revitalizing the schools. A summary of Mr. Cohen's statements comprises a major portion of the next several paragraphs in this section.

TABLE 11-1. Starting Salaries: Teaching vs. Private Industry (Men)

| | Average Starting Salaries, School Year | | | |
| | 1965–1966 | 1966–1967 | 1967–1968 | 1968–1969 [a] |
Group				
Beginning teachers with bachelor's degree (school systems with enrollments of 6,000 or more)	$4,925	$5,142	$5,519	$5,850
Male graduates with bachelor's degree:				
Engineering	7,584	8,112	8,772	9,168
Accounting	6,732	7,128	7,776	8,172
Sales-marketing	6,276	6,744	7,044	7,512
Business administration	6,240	6,576	7,140	7,464
Liberal arts	6,216	6,432	6,780	7,332
Production management	6,186	7,176	7,584	8,076
Chemistry	7,032	7,500	8,064	8,460
Physics	7,164	7,740	8,448	8,844
Mathematics-statistics	6,672	7,260	7,944	8,316
Economics-finance	6,600	6,732	7,416	7,584
Other fields	6,360	7,044	7,644	8,100
Total, all fields (weighted average)	$6,792	$7,248	$7,836	$8,280

[a] Average beginning salary for teachers in 1968–1969 is an advance estimate made by NEA Research Division and subject to revision. Average salaries for other personnel are based on offers made in November, 1967, to men who will graduate in June, 1968.

Source: *NEA Research Bulletin*, Washington, D.C., National Education Association, March, 1968, p. 8.

if they are ever to have the hope of succeeding in regular classroom situations. Yet only 710,000 of the 2 million children aged 3 to 5 from poor families received preschool training in 1966 in Head Start programs. To expand the program to remedy the background deficiencies of 2 million children would cost $405 million a year.

About 2 million school children between the ages of 6 and 15 are underachievers and need compensatory education. The present $1.4 billion programs are reaching only about one-fourth of these children.

Approximately 80 per cent of the students enrolled in the fifth grade of elementary school will not complete a four-year degree program; more than 1 million students a year do not complete high school. By 1972, an estimated 18 million individuals will be in need of vocational education, but only 11.4 million will be enrolled in current programs unless new ways are found to meet the special needs of disadvantaged youth and school dropouts.

Underemployment is disproportionately concentrated among the disadvantaged, the unskilled, the less educated, and the young. The situation is particularly acute for Negroes; in 1966, the proportion of Negroes who were temporarily working part-time for economic reasons was twice as great as the proportion of whites, and the proportion permenently working part-time was four times as great.[6]

The likelihood of being underemployed or unemployed varies inversely with educational attainment, as demonstrated in Table 11-2. In March, 1966, 15 per cent of those with no formal schooling were unemployed or on short workweeks for economic reasons. About 5 per cent of those with four years of high school—about the average attainment in America today—were unemployed or underutilized. In contrast, less than 1.5 per cent of the workers with five years or more of college work were unemployed or underemployed.

TABLE 11-2. Underemployment and Unemployment Rates, by Years of School Completed, March, 1966 (Civilian Labor Force Age 18 Years and Over)

Years of School Completed	Number (000's)	Percentage Under- employed or Unemployed	Total	Usually Work Full- time	Usually Work Part- time	Unem- ployed
			Total			
Total	71,958	5.8%	2.1%	1.1%	1.0%	3.7%
No school	393	15.3	7.9	2.3	5.6	7.4
Elementary						
1–4 years	1,984	10.6	5.2	2.5	2.7	5.4
5–7 years	5,381	9.9	4.9	2.1	2.8	5.0
8 years	8,187	7.8	3.1	1.9	1.2	4.7
High school						
1–3 years	13,640	8.1	2.8	1.6	1.2	5.3
4 years	26,130	4.7	1.6	.8	.8	3.1
College						
1–3 years	7,760	3.9	.9	.4	.5	3.0
4 years	5,248	1.6	.5	.2	.3	1.1
5 years or more	3,235	1.4	.3	.1	.2	1.1

UNDEREMPLOYED[a] (PERCENTAGE)

[a] Prefer full time but working part-time for economic reasons.
SOURCE: Claire C. Hodge and James R. Wetzel, "Short Workweeks and Underemployment." *Monthly Labor Review*, Vol. 90, Sept. 1967, p. 32.

Occupational attachment, which tends to vary directly with educational attainment, is an important factor in the extent of the underutilization. Workers in high-paying, high-status jobs frequently report substantial amounts of overtime. In contrast, nearly 15 per cent of the nation's skilled workers in 1966 were either unemployed or underemployed, as listed inTable 11-3.

[6] Claire C. Hodge and James R. Wetzel, "Short Workweeks and Underemployment." *Monthly Labor Review*, Vol. 90, Sept. 1967, p. 30.

TABLE 11-3. Underemployment and Unemployment Rates, by Occupation, 1966 (Civilian Labor Force Age 14 Years and Over)

OCCUPATION	NUMBER (000's)	MEDIAN EDUCATIONAL YEARS OF FORMAL SCHOOLING ATTAINMENT[a]	PERCENTAGE UNDEREMPLOYED OR UNEMPLOYED	UNDEREMPLOYED (PERCENTAGE)			
				TOTAL	USUALLY WORK FULL-TIME	USUALLY WORK PART-TIME	UNEMPLOYED
White-collar	34,012		3.0%	1.0%	.5%	.5%	2.0%
Professional and technical	9,446	16.3	1.9	.6	.3	.3	1.3
Managers and officials	7,481	12.6	1.6	.6	.4	.2	1.0
Clerical workers	12,193	12.5	4.0	1.2	.5	.6	2.8
Sales workers	4,892	12.5	4.7	2.0	.7	1.3	2.7
Blue-collar	28,370		7.5	3.3	2.2	1.1	4.2
Craftsmen and foremen	9,878	11.9	4.9	2.1	1.5	.5	2.8
Operatives	14,511	10.7	7.4	3.1	2.4	.8	4.3
Nonfarm laborers	3,981	9.5	13.9	6.6	2.9	3.7	7.3
Service	10,146		9.1	4.6	1.1	3.5	4.5
Private household workers	2,334	8.9	12.9	9.3	.9	8.4	3.6
Other service workers	7,812	11.4	8.0	3.2	1.1	2.1	4.8

[a] Data apply to employed persons age 18 years and over in March, 1966.

[b] Prefer full-time employment, but working part-time for economic reasons.

SOURCE: Claire C. Hodge and James R. Wetzel, "Short Workweeks and Underemployment." *Monthly Labor Review*, Vol. 90, Sept. 1967, p. 33.

The problem of the underemployed is not amenable to a single solution; however, enlightened manpower policies, rapid economic growth, and generally high employment have made substantial inroads on the problems. Between May, 1965, and May, 1966, the number of underemployed wage and salary employees was reduced by 300,000 with practically the entire reduction falling in the $40-or-below earnings per week category. In effect, the tangible boost in general job opportunities increased opportunity for those previously unable to find full-time work.

The disadvantage of reduced workweeks falls not only upon the worker but upon the economy generally, in the loss of goods and services that would have been produced if all the employed had been able to secure as much work as they desired. The educational implications of underemployment and unemployment center not only around the need to provide general educational and technical training, but the necessity of investing a huge amount of resources in continuing education.

As referred to in Chapters 7–10, indications are that current educational programs can be financed readily according to projected public revenues and expenditures, assuming that adequate administrative, political, and psychological changes can be made relative to intergovernmental arrangements. In other words, the results of macropolicy analysis, as it has been applied to educational finance and including the balance of total expenditures and resources, is very encouraging. However, the analysis included definition of conservative educational needs and did not include provision for meeting the unmet needs outlined in this chapter, the cost of which would be from $15 to $18 billion annually between 1968 and 1975.

United States Economic Growth to 1975

It has been estimated that the United States economy has a potential for a rate of economic growth of between 4 and 4.5 per cent per year between 1965 and 1975. This is between one-third and one-half above the rate prevailing in the first two-thirds of this century, and is substantially above the 3.5 per cent prevailing over the 17 years from 1948 to 1965. This higher rate of growth will not be achieved automatically, but will require improvements and adjustments in economic policies, both public and private, if it is to be achieved in a manner that does not generate undesirable inflationary by-products.[7] This statement summarizes the results of a year-long study undertaken by the Joint Economic Committee staff at the request of the Sub-

[7] *U.S. Economic Growth to 1975: Potentials and Problems*. Washington, D.C., U.S. Govt. Printing Office, 1966, p. 1.

committee on Economic Progress at the federal level of government to determine the most probable range of the potential economic growth of the United States economy over the next decade.

The distinction between progress and growth in economics is a familiar distinction between ends and means. Progress relates to an increase in the welfare of the people of the nation as a whole, while economic growth concerns itself with an increase in the economy's ability to provide the material means to satisfy individual or collective desires for different kinds of goods and services. Thus, in the end, economic growth contributes to the nation's ability to progress, if this is what the nation decides to do with its increase in means.[8] Economic growth does not guarantee an increase in wealth, in the skills and abilities or the nation's people, or in the quality of life.

The Joint Economic Committee staff listed a variety of questions of long-term economic policy that are likely to arise during the coming decade and indicated many of the difficult interrelationships:

1. What are the major alternative methods of attaining the economic growth rates projected in this report, and what are the implications involved in selecting among these methods?
2. What are likely to be the policy reactions to the rising supply of potential workers as indicated by projections of the labor force age group?
3. How can the projected relatively rapid rates of economic growth be reconciled with the fairly moderate estimates of future increases in the aggregate price level?
4. What are the alternative methods of encouraging additional manpower training and, again, what are the implications involved in selecting among them?
5. What are likely to be the major effects of alternative wage policies?
6. What are likely to be the major choices among alternative tax and other fiscal policies?
7. What are the major economic considerations involved in the changing composition of federal government expenditure programs?
8. What are likely to be the major effects of the alternative methods of federal aid to state and local governments?
9. How do the various Great Society programs influence regional income distribution and economic development?
10. What are the alternate means of promoting public and private investment, consumer spending, and a rising standard of living?[9]

One level of choice involved in achieving a high and rising level of economic activity is the selection of emphasis among the major sectors of the national economy. The choice of sector emphasis also implies decisions as to (1)

[8] *Ibid.*   [9] *Ibid.*

whether the economy will become more or less oriented to private versus public needs and desires; (2) whether the major national concern is with the acceleration of the rise in the standard of living or with the enhancement of the nation's productive capacity; and hence (3), whether the main thrust of the economic policies are of a relatively short-run or long-run nature.

Another type of future economic choice involves the nation's policy reaction to the growing potential productive capacity, particularly as indicated by the rising labor force age group. The numbers of those in the 18-to-24 age group, whose unemployment rates have been much above average, are anticipated to increase at double the national average. The effects of varied decisions as to the most desirable methods of responding to the increased potential supply of workers and their effects on other aspects of the American economy are illustrated in Table 11-4.

TABLE 11-4. Adjustments to Rising Labor Force Age Group

NATURE OF ADJUSTMENT	TYPES OF OTHER EFFECTS				
	ON OUTPUTS	ON LEISURE	ON PRODUC-TIVITY	ON PRICES	ON INTER-NATIONAL COMPETI-TIVENESS
Increase employment via:					
Economic growth	Expansion	Neutral	Mixed	+ Pressure	Mixed
Reduced standard work-week	Reduction	Expansion	Mixed	Mixed	+ Pressure
More holidays, vacations, sabbaticals	Reduction	Expansion	Mixed	+ Pressure	+ Pressure
Lower minimum wage law for new entrants	Mixed	Reduction	Mixed	− Pressure	− Pressure
Reduce participation rates:					
More schooling	Long- and short-term differences	Short-term expansion	Long-term expansion	Mixed	− Pressure
More retirement programs	Reduction	Expansion	Neutral	− Pressure	Mixed
Rising unemployment	Reduction	Expansion	Mixed	− Pressure	Mixed

SOURCE: *U.S. Economic Growth to 1975: Potentials and Problems.* Washington, D.C., U.S. Govt. Printing Office, 1966, p. 33.

Table 11–5 indicates some of the possible alternative methods of tax adjustments.

A number of recent studies have pointed out a possible "fiscal mismatch" between needs and resources, as was pointed out in an earlier chapter. Under nonwar conditions, the supply of readily available federal revenues appears to

TABLE 11-5. Choices Among Alternative Tax Policies

POSSIBLE TAX CHANGES	SOME FACTORS TO BE CONSIDERED
Across-the-board changes in rates	Effects on equity among taxpayers
Corporate taxes:	Effects on income distribution
Depreciation practices	Effects on GNP growth rate
Investment credits	Effects on allocation between consumption
Basic rates	and investment
Individual taxes:	Effect on built-in stabilizers
Emphasizing upper brackets	Effect on relative emphasis between saving
Emphasizing lower brackers	and investment
Exemptions	
Deductions	
Capital gains treatment	
Pension trusts	
Excises:	
General	
Selective	
Estate and gift taxes	
User charges	

SOURCE: *U.S. Economic Growth to 1975: Potentials and Problems.* Washington, D.C., U.S. Govt. Printing Office, 1966, p. 41.

rise faster than current demands on the federal purse, but the state-local situation is the reverse; expenditure demands on state and local governments rise faster than readily available revenue supply, although Tax Foundation projections outlined in Chapter 7 were optimistic in contrast to the usual projections to 1975.

Methods of utilizing the potential increase in federal revenues include block

TABLE 11-6. Alternate Methods of Utilizing Potential Increases in Federal Revenue to Aid State and Local Governments

METHOD	FEDERAL ROLE IN ECONOMY	FEDERAL INFLUENCE ON STATES	INCOME EQUALI- ZATION	TAX PROGRES- SIVITY	BUILT-IN STABI- LIZERS	ROLE OF CITIES
Direct federal programs	+	0	+	0	0	0
Tied grants	0	+	+	0	0	0
Block grants	−	0	+	0	0	−
Tax credits	−	0	−	0	0	−
Tax sharing	−	0	0 or +	−	−	+
Federal tax reduction	−	0	0	−	−	0

NOTE: Increase = +; no change = 0; decrease = −.
SOURCE: *U.S. Economic Growth to 1975: Potentials and Problems.* Washington, D.C., U.S. Govt. Printing Office, 1966, p. 43.

grants to states, expanded program or tied grants, tax-sharing, individual
federal tax credits for state and local taxes paid, and new direct federal
activities in the various localities. The methods and an outline of their effects
are included in Table 11-6.

Outright reductions in federal taxes would be an indirect way of aiding
state and local governments, since this would permit the latter to increase
their tax rates without increasing the total tax bill of the average citizen, but
this would introduce questions of interstate rivalry. In addition, the overall
national tax structure would become less progressive (as well as less anti-
cyclical), because the nation would be placing greater reliance on frequently
proportional and regressive state and local taxes.

The Joint Economic Committee staff projections of gross national product,
with major components, adjusted to illustrate an equilibrium full-employment
position are in Table 11-7. Projection A was based on an assumed 4.5 per cent
annual rate of growth for real GNP and 3-per-cent unemployment, while

TABLE 11-7. Projections of Gross National Product, with Major Components,
Adjusted to Illustrate an Equilibrium Full-Employment Position
(Dollars in Billions)

	ACTUAL 1966	ACTUAL 1967	PROJECTION A 1970	PROJECTION A 1975	PROJECTION B 1970	PROJECTION B 1975
Gross national product	$743.3	$785.0	$950.0	$1,310.0	$920.0	$1,205.0
Personal consumption expenditure	465.9	491.7	601.7	815.8	583.4	753.9
Durable goods	70.3	72.1	92.7	125.6	87.5	113.5
Nondurable goods	207.5	217.5	247.9	315.7	241.5	292.9
Services	188.1	202.1	261.1	374.5	254.4	347.5
Gross private domestic investment	118.0	112.1	142.9	201.4	137.5	183.5
Nonresidential fixed investment	80.2	82.6	87.4	113.0	85.0	105.5
Residential structures	24.4	24.4	46.0	72.7	44.3	66.0
Change in business inventories	13.4	5.2	9.5	15.7	8.2	12.0
Net exports of goods and services	5.1	4.8	9.2	10.8	9.3	12.1
Exports	43.0	45.3	52.1	69.2	51.0	66.2
Imports	37.9	40.6	42.9	58.4	41.7	54.1
Government purchases of goods and services	154.3	176.3	197.8	282.0	189.8	255.5
Federal	77.0	89.9	80.9	99.3	78.5	93.1
State and local	77.2	86.4	116.9	182.7	111.3	162.4

SOURCE: U.S. Department of Commerce, Office of Business Economics, and staff, Joint
Economic Committee.

TABLE 11-8. Percentage of Distribution of Real Gross National Product for 1965, 1970, and 1975 for Government

	ACTUAL	ASSUMPTION A		ASSUMPTION B	
	1965	1970	1975	1970	1975
Government purchases of goods and services	18.6%	18.1%	17.7%	18.2%	17.9%
Federal	9.4	7.8	6.7	7.9	7.0
State and local	9.2	10.3	11.0	10.3	10.9

SOURCE: *U.S. Economic Growth to 1975: Potentials and Problems.* Washington, D.C., U.S. Govt. Printing Office, 1966, p. 55.

Projection B was based on an assumed 4 per cent annual rate of growth for real GNP and 4 per cent unemployment.

A gross national product of $1.2 trillion in 1975 would be about $462 billion greater than in 1966 and $632 billion greater than in 1962. Increases of this magnitude would appear to be enormous enough to finance a major improvement in education. However, the nation's population is expected to increase by 22 million between 1966 and 1975, and there will be 18 million more persons in the civilian labor force. In addition, total enrollment of formal educational institutions—public and private—was projected to increase 6 million.

We are currently spending about 6.6 per cent of the GNP for public and private elementary, secondary, and higher education. In order to achieve educational goals such as those listed by the President's Commission on National Goals would require a spending of about 8 per cent of the gross national product for education by 1975.[10] Among the ways to narrow the gap between resources and aspirations in education, three appear to be the most obvious: (1) a change of priorities in the public sector; (2) the sharing of federal revenues with the states in addition to grants-in-aid for special purposes; and (3) a modest shift in priorities from private consumption to public services.[11] In the case of the latter, for example, a shift of 2.5 per cent of the projected personal consumption expenditures of $753.9 billion in 1975, as shown in Table 11-7 to public education would result in an additional $22 billion for education that one year. However, the monopolizing of the mass

[10] *Goals for Americans, The Report of the President's Commission on National Goals.* Englewood Cliffs, N.J., Prentice-Hall, 1960.

[11] See Leonard A. Lecht, "Strategic Variables in Planning," in *Designing Education for the Future, No. 3*, Edgar L. Morphet and Charles O. Ryan, eds. New York, Citation Press, 1967, pp. 12–14.

media by the private sector in advertising its wares gives the private sector an advertising or information advantage over the public sector that probably cannot be overcome.

The Internal Efficiency of Education

While macropolicy issues as related to educational finance relate to the balance of total expenditures and resources and involve projections of educational aspirations and revenues, and educational expenditures as a proportion of the gross national product and of the total public sector, micropolicy issues deal with specific revenue sources, the mixture of specific educational programs, and the internal efficiency of schools.[12] Although considerable attention has been given to specific revenue sources and to the link between educational outputs and the personal and societal benefits that ensue, this section will include a few promising efforts to achieve different educational outputs in accordance with given changes in inputs.

As pointed out previously, the inputs used in the educational systems are similar to those used in the private sector—the costs of personnel, supplies, equipment, etc. Educational systems have precise information of this kind primarily because of state requirements for accounting for revenues and expenditures by function and by object. However, an input that has been ignored generally in any internal efficiency analysis is that of the varying student characteristics of ability, motivation, prior learning, and time devoted to learning.

A second unique educational input is the professional commitment to use of a single salary schedule, which allows only minor salary variations because of conditions in the private market economy. Thus, if a male with a bachelor's degree in mathematics can earn a beginning salary of $8,500 in the private sector, a school system with a single salary schedule providing a beginning salary of $5,800 could not compete satisfactorily for the services of the new graduate. As a result, the school system is left with the choice of raising every teacher's salary in order to meet market conditions relative to a few teachers, or to use poorly qualified teachers in instructional areas where the demand for personnel is unusually high. Fear has been that a multiple-salary schedule adoption by a board of education would lessen educational productivity caused by a lowering of teacher morale.[13]

[12] See Jerry Miner, "Financial Support of Education," in *Designing Education for the Future, No. 2*, Edgar L. Morphet and Charles O. Ryan, eds. New York, Citation Press 1967, pp. 298–323.
[13] J. A. Kershaw and R. N. McKean, *Teacher Shortages and Salary Schedules.* New York, McGraw-Hill, 1962.

The Temple City Unified School District, Temple City, California, has been involved in an 18-month study grant from the Charles F. Kettering Foundation for the design of a differentiated teaching staff. Rationale for the study was that the revolution in education was all about challenging organizational equality. The project director summed up the rationale as follows:

... Teachers are not the same. We cannot successfully individualize instruction until teachers, too, are secure as individuals within an educational framework of inequality that permits its personnel to have strengths and weaknesses, vast differences in training and professional motivation, and varying responsibilities based upon the training.

Once we admit to the fallacy of teacher equality, the role of the principal as it is now constituted is threatened. Once we create an organization which can capitalize upon the collective talents within it, we create technical gaps between teachers themselves, and between teachers and principals that cannot be submerged. The roles must change. The first hallowed notion which goes is the idea of the principal as "*the* instructional leader." Although regnant in administrative handbooks and textbooks, the viability of this concept rests wholly upon an undifferentiated teaching staff. As long as teachers are lumped together in one homogeneous mass, doing the same things with the same skills, it is conceivable that somebody with a little more training can be technically more competent. However, once specialization and differentiation creep into the schools, the principal's expertise is easily surpassed.

... Outstanding characteristics of the proposed model [Figure 11-1] are that all personnel above the Academic Assistant level function in part or wholly as teachers in the schools; subject and skill area "self-renewal" is a built-in feature; excellent teachers can be promoted as teachers without being locked in by degrees, units or years of experience; and that certain teacher roles earn more salary than many administrative roles, including that of the school principal. In addition, the evaluative responsibilities of the school principal have been reshaped so that it is no longer his sole judgment as to the competence of instruction in any subject or skill area of the curriculum.[14]

Through Kettering Foundation support, the Temple City school unit hopes to make a complete changeover on a systematic basis within a five-year period. The ability of the school system to support the differentiated staffing model after the transition period has been anticipated in preliminary studies.

The model provides for two salary schedules; the basic salary schedule for certificated and noncertificated would be continued as at present. Staff

[14] Fenwick English, *The Secondary Principalship Today: Changing Roles and Relationships*, a paper presented at the National Association of Secondary School Principals, 52nd Annual Convention, Atlantic City, N.J., Feb. 13, 1968, mimeographed.

members participating in the study model would be placed upon special schedules adopted for the professional position they occupy in the model. Persons participating in the study model would be volunteers.

	TENURE	TENURE	NONTENURE	NONTENURE
				Teaching Curriculum Research Associate Doctorate or Equivalent
			Senior Teacher M.S. or Equivalent	
		Staff Teacher B.A. Degree and Calif. Credential		
Associate Teacher A.B. or Intern				
100% Teaching	100% Teaching Responsibilities	3/5's Staff Teaching Responsibilities	2/5's Staff Teaching Responsibilities	
$6,500 — 9,000*	10-Months $7,500 — 11,000*	10-11 Months $14,000 — 18,500*	12-Months $16,000 — 20,000*	
Academic Assistants A.A. Degree or Equivalent $6,000 — 7,500*				
Educational Technicians $4,000 — 7,500*				
Clerks $5,000 — 7,500*				

*SALARIES ARE TENTATIVE

FIGURE 11-1 Temple City Unified School District—A Model of Differentiated Staffing.

SOURCE: *A Preliminary Proposal for the Implementation of a Differentiated Teaching Staff in the Temple City Unified School District, Temple City, California,* presented to The Charles F Kettering Foundation, January, 1968, p. 15.

One of the key functions of the Teaching Curriculum Research Associate (salary range of $16,000 to $20,000) would be to bring promising and research-tested ideas directly into the instructional program in each subject area. "Self-renewal" is thus incorporated into the school system.

Faith is that experimental programs of individualized instruction will bring eventually greater internal efficiency (same achievement in less time or more achievement in the same time) in public schools. In the first attempt to compare the cost of Traditionally Administered Instruction (TAI) with Computer Administered Instruction (CAI), Kopstein and Seidel concluded that CAI does not pose an immediate economic threat for TAI in public education.[15] Kopstein and Seidel assumed equal effectiveness of TAI and CAI, but found the hourly costs of TAI to be $.33 to $.34 on the average in the United States in 1965–1966, while the CAI cost per student hour in elementary and secondary education amounted to $3.73. Unless CAI could be shown to be at least ten times more effective or efficient than TAI, a replacement did not seem warranted. Hardware costs alone amounted to $3.63 per student hour.

Systematic approaches to individualizing instruction are being developed at such schools as UCLA's University Elementary School and the Oakleaf School in suburban Pittsburgh, the latter a project of the Learning Research and Development Center at the University of Pittsburgh. Leading officials in the U.S. Office of Education are convinced that IPI (Individually Prescribed Instruction) programs are the nation's present hope to meet individual and collective educational goals. It is estimated that instructional costs are likely to increase $25–$100 per pupil under an IPI program because of the added use of audiovisual equipment and supplies.

Input-output relationships will be clarified partially through the use of program budgeting by school systems. However, program budgeting or the more sophisticated Planning-Programming-Budgeting System (PPBS) are just now being introduced at all levels of educational government, and present record systems still emphasize input rather than output.

The few input-output studies that have been completed offer no generally consistent findings.[16] School and nonschool determinants of educational performance have been isolated, and socioeconomic characteristics of pupils accounted for much of the explained variations in school outputs. The controversial Coleman report, for example, concluded that an individual's educational attainment related to his personal background, whether because of heritage or environment much more than to the characteristics of the school he attends.

Belief by many leaders is that prior to any further input-output analyses of education at the national level, there is need for a national educational

---

[15] Felix F. Kopstein and Robert J. Seidel, *Computer Administered Instruction Versus Traditionally Administered Instruction: Economics*. Washington, D.C., Human Resources Research Office, The George Washington University, April, 1967, p. 20, prepublication draft.

[16] See Jesse Burkhead, *Input-Output Relationships in Large City High Schools*, Syracuse, N.Y., Syracuse University Press, 1967; and *Achievement Norms for New York State Schools by Type of Community and Socio-Economic Level*, Albany, The University of the State of New York, 1963.

assessment. The instigation of such a movement has brought about one of the most potentially significant and actively debated issues in American education.

National Assessment of Educational Progress (NAEP)

When Francis Keppel was serving as the U.S. Commissioner of Education, he encouraged the Carnegie Corporation of New York to explore the matter of the assessment of American education with private funds. In 1964, the Carnegie Corporation appointed an Exploratory Committee on Assessing the Progress of Education, with Dr. Ralph W. Tyler, Director of the Center for Advanced Study in the Behavioral Sciences, Stanford, California, serving as chairman.

In its developmental work, the Exploratory Committee determined that a national assessment would not be very meaningful unless separate measures were obtained for populations within the total country, which varied among themselves and presented different degrees and kinds of progress and different problems to be solved. Thus, plans were to assess a probability sample for each of 192 populations defined by the following subdivisions: boys and girls; four geographic regions; four age groups (9, 13, 17, and adult); three divisions by urban, suburban, rural classifications; and two socioeconomic levels.

The assessment exercises would differ from current achievement tests in many respects. Because the assessment would not require that all participants be in classes, the exercises to be used would not be limited to the usual test items. Although an achievement test is used to measure individual differences among pupils taking the test, assessment exercises at each age level would be developed such that approximately one-third would represent achievements characteristic of most of those in the population of an age level, one-third would represent achievements characteristic of about half of those at the age level, and one-third would represent the achievements characteristic of the most advanced—that is, the top 10 per cent—of the age level.

Justification for the national assessment has been compared with the need for data on progress in other American spheres of life. For example, out of the need information about the progress of the economy particularly during the economic depression in the 1930's grew the Gross National Product, an index of production. In addition, the Consumer Price Index was created as a useful measure of the changes in the cost of living and inflation. Similarly, an index of gross national educational product could be used in guiding educational development.

Fears are that (1) if national tests do not reflect the local and state educational objectives, pupils and teachers would be deflected from their work; (2) assessment will enable the federal government to control the curriculum; and (3) the project would stultify the curriculum by not allowing changes over the years in instructional methods and educational goals.

A lively clash of ideas among leading educators arose at the White House Conference on Education in July, 1965, when Panel 2-B ("Assessment of Educational Performance") chose to discuss the question of national assessment. Some of the comments were as follows:

> We have two monsters now, College Entrance Examinations and Merit Scholarship Exams, keeping youngsters from developing intellectual creativity.
> . . . .
> Assessment is going on all the time, not only by teachers but by parents, voters, employers, legislators, and others. I question our ability to construct any valid system of central assessment. The divisive effect of any effort to quantify our strengths and weaknesses may not be worth the gain.
> . . . .
> Can we assess student achievement without encouraging conformity?
> . . . .
> What are we afraid of? We compare people on physical fitness, color blindness, mental retardation, and other traits. Why not compare them on academic achievement? The NEA assesses states on their treatment of teachers and applies sanctions to those which fail to measure up.
> . . . .
> What objection is there to an assessment that seeks to collect data on the condition and progress of education in the several states? The only objections we have heard are hints that if we get more significant information someone might be tempted to misuse it. Isn't that somewhat irrelevant?
> . . . .
> Fact-finding we need; new tests we need; testing the tests we need. But we do not need to hang a sword of Damocles over the head of the child by instituting ruinous pressure of competition.
> . . . .
> We need not more tests but fewer interruptions of learning. At Sarah Lawrence or anywhere else, when you abolish tests you get more learning. Europe, the Middle East, and the Far East illustrate the paralysis of education produced by standard tests linked with government assessment. Let's abolish all tests and concentrate on teaching and learning.[17]

The debate goes on, but there has not been a national assessment. However, quantitative information available does not satisfy policy-makers. Certain

[17] See *National Educational Assessment, Pro and Con*, Washington, D.C., National Education Association, 1966, 56 p.

politicians clamor for efficiency in the schools and build positive images with such noise.

Even though critical evaluation of programs and their administration is clearly needed, a call for evaluation of programs already launched can too easily become a means for avoiding future action. A valid national, state, or even local assessment will not be accomplished within the next five to ten years. In the meantime, "hold-the-line" tax or educational policy at any level of government could result in ultraconservative forces gaining control of educational sectors, thereby slowing to a halt a train of new educational instruments heading the nation toward an objective of real social progress as measured according to criteria of increased human dignity and opportunity.

A Matter of Commitment—Matching Educational Needs and Expenditures

Public education is in the midst of the resolution of issues involving the bomb, the pill, the spread and improvement of cities, the spread of crime, the elimination of poverty, and the continuing extension of freedom and equality. Partisan schoolboard elections are even decided by how the voter feels about the Vietnam War, the price of groceries, and the balance of trade. There is rich opportunity for the participation of the increasing numbers of the formally educated electorate in public educational matters, which are not isolated matters, and it is likely that educational money problems will motivate them as much as the resolution of other public issues.

Educators, who subsidized the development of the American public educational systems through their relatively low economic status for college graduates, are primed to contend for a place in the hierarchies of American power and influence. Aggravated by economic and political second-class citizenship and tired of using only indirect influence, they will be on the political frontlines not only to improve their economic welfare but also to influence educational policy-making, in which all things are considered negotiable. They will be using the "Sock it to 'em, teach" approach and working to eliminate the Greyhound bus theory of "you educators do the teaching and leave the decisions to us."

Resentment of the educators' growing power as perceived by vested political and economic interests can be understood. However, the emergence of a powerful profession is the healthiest development that could occur in the society and will sharpen up political debate, heat up processes of allocating resources in budget-making sessions, affect intergovernmental relations,

322

create a more highly cultured society, and improve the American form of democracy.

In 1968, the State of Florida was the scene of a sorry example of a state's power structure failing to respond to the needs of public education. In the nation's first statewide walkout of teachers, approximately 35,000 of Florida's 58,000 teachers stayed away from classes on February 19, 1968, after "hold-the-line" legislative sessions since 1959, during which period Florida's average teacher salary fell to $400 below that of the national average. Improved teacher welfare was a prime motivation of the teachers, but so was the need for general improvement of the state's teaching and learning conditions.

The dramatic walkout by teachers was based on the hope that the general public would respond positively to the plea of the professionals for greater state financial support and an opportunity to be successful rather than being doomed to failure in their teaching endeavors. However, public apathy, a general news blackout of the walkout effectiveness during a three-week period, and a continuing lust for power by certain unenlightened business interests, school board members, educational administrators (Florida had elected superintendents in 58 of 67 counties in 1968) and legislators, minimized the immediate walkout benefits in behalf of quality education. The American Federation of Teachers (AFT) seized the opportunity to provide another lobbying channel for frustrated Florida teachers and claimed enrollment of 2,000 new Florida members by June, 1968. In the meantime, the Florida Education Association came out of its 1968 spring convention with a major increase in dues and an enthusiastic membership ready to win a long-term war for quality education.

If Florida is any example for the remainder of the nation, it is clear that public education will be in serious difficulty if image-building politicians who are not problem-solvers are supported by powerful economic interests at any cost to the society, if policy-makers are not informed as to the relationship of educational finance to public finance, to redistribution of income, to full employment, to economic stabilization, to adequate economic growth, and to social and labor mobility. "Hold-the-line" or "protection of the tax rate" has characterized educational affairs for several decades. In contrast to this political strategy, until the strategy of "returns equal to or greater than the investment" is understood, educational needs will remain unmet, and the world's greatest social innovation destroyed bit by bit.

The nation has the resources to finance quality education but is not yet committed to cooperation among its governments rather than competition between governments; classifying education as an investment in human capital rather than merely as an expenditure of "money down the drain" (spending for construction of a tavern is termed an investment); creating an educational climate through the mass media by promoting learning relatively more than entertainment; promoting learning for the sake of learning; accepting schools as centers of inquiry rather than mere disseminators of information; encouraging the development of each student's intellect and accepting the results rather than trying to program the results; accepting the fact that results of a free dialogue between teachers and students and among students are unpredictable and become the heart of the educational processes; defending public schools and their personnel against the smear attacks of extremists who appeal to the mass, especially the bigoted and those with pugilistic tendencies with terms such as *unionists*, *federal bureaucrats*, and *educrats* for political advantage; participating in, improving, and helping to restore confidence in local school and civil government; remembering that important American values in addition to local autonomy and states' rights are compassion, pluralism, and learning; and eliminating the myth that the nation can continue to recruit qualified teachers with beginning salaries $2,400 below that of beginning salaries in other professions.

Elimination of the dual system of education by race must be accomplished as rapidly as possible. Relative to this problem in the cities and to other metropolitan area problems, the Advisory Commission on Intergovernmental Relations found startling fiscal disparities in metropolitan areas during a comprehensive fiscal study in 1966 and 1967:

1. An increasing fiscal disparity between central cities and suburbs 'particularly in the Northeast and Midwest.

2. The paradox of central city poverty in the midst of metropolitan plenty, strikingly illustrated by the fact that metropolitan areas account for 65 per cent of the population, 70 per cent of taxable assessed valuation, three-quarters or more of federal personal income tax collections, and 80 per cent of bank checking accounts; but these areas also account for most of the nation's poverty, crime, delinquency, and civil disorder.

3. A concentration of "high cost citizens"—children in school, the elderly, welfare recipients—in the central city, with the prospect that this concentration will increase in the future.

4. Central city educational expenditures lower than in the suburbs, not only on a per capita basis, but also on a per pupil basis. Where the need is greatest the support dollars are fewest.

5. A local tax burden in the central cities, measured against income, more than one-third greater than in the suburbs. Growth in state and federal aid has not been sufficient to counteract growing disparities in per capita tax revenues between the central city and suburbia.[18]

[18] *Ninth Annual Report*, Washington, D.C., Advisory Commission on Intergovern-mental Relations, Jan. 31, 1968, p. 19.

Among the recommendations of the Commission was a broadened fiscal mix and greater fiscal flexibility in federal aid to states and localities. Congress and the President were to be asked to reduce the number of separate authorizations for federal grants—as a general goal, a reduction by at least half the present number starting with a consolidation in the field of vocational education. In addition, Congress and the Administration were to be requested to adopt a flexible combination of federal financial assistance to states and localities to consist of categorical grants-in-aid, general functional block grants, and per-capita general support payments.

In the meantime, there has been teacher unrest in Florida, Oklahoma, New Mexico, South Dakota, Pennsylvania, Michigan, and New York in 1968, accounted for by something other than militancy. The teaching profession has been challenging the society's value system that permits an expenditure yearly of $29 billion each for recreation, the Vietnam War, and automobiles, and only the same $29 billion annually to educate 43.7 million elementary and secondary students. Is there any question as to which $29 billion is giving the nation the most return on its investment?

Public education, the very phenomenon that made a rising living standard possible, is being undermined by it. American adults are committed to a rising standard of living in materialistic terms. An advertising economy that continuously creates needs results in expenditures for refrigerators, freezers, automobiles (first, second, and third), television sets, stereo units, costlier houses (first and second), liquor, tobacco, trips to Europe, cosmetics, sports events, and a general good time. Added to these expenditures are those for a vast defense network, and the result is a commitment to mediocre education for millions of youngsters and adults. The nation's value system is showing and should embarrass most thinking citizens.

In addition, the group most strategic for social change in the society is the teaching profession, which has been shaped by certain political and economic forces into a very vulnerable association because of its potential influence in changing the status quo and in reconstructing the society. If teachers with keen perception and vision had been allowed to teach as they knew best and allowed to bargain and argue with schoolboard members concerning allocation of resources over the past decades, efficiency would have resulted and quality education for most could have become a reality. Instead, the profession has been left relatively powerless and vulnerable because of a weak individual and collective economic posture.

The private sector, with a rapidly emerging elite of education enterprises which are primarily mergers of electronic and publishing companies, is promising instant learning with "curriculum packages." Rest assured that the

curriculum packages will probably assist in the teaching of what is a predictable and safe outcome. The content will be salable because of its maximum
acceptability in being shiny but conservative in content. In the meantime,
there will be a limited promotion of differences among people, and the unpredictable outcomes of an open system providing exciting dialogue between
teachers and students will be sacrificed for the sake of efficiency in teaching
the predictable and effecting predictable results.

Faith is that political rationality is still the most valid process in educational decision-making and in allocating resources. However, how will
anyone know about such rationality if its results are not advertised through
the mass media? The problem is that the mass media has space and time
primarily for advertising commercial products, including commercial educational products. That is the dilemma of American public education. Its
tremendous story of the promotion of human dignity, in correcting the
American democracy, and in promotion of social and labor mobility has not
been told fairly and adequately. The result may be a gradual switching of the
educational function from the public to the private sector under the guise of
the promotion of efficiency for the benefit of those who see profits in the
commercialization of mass education, the nation's biggest growth industry.

A

EXPENDITURE PROJECTIONS AND ELEMENTS OF TREND FITTING

Introduction

Theory and practice are two different worlds in educational budgeting at all levels of government. Emphasis in Chapters 5 and 6 in this text, for example, was that a sound budgeting system is effected by a sequential order of educational programming, costing, and financing. Practice generally appears to have been that the tail (revenue) has been wagging the dog (program). In effect, the money available has been determined first, and program has been adjusted accordingly.

A perennial criticism in all public sectors has been the lack of long-term planning. Long-term budgets represent the most concrete form of long-term planning, since implication is that differentiated and abstract programs have been converted into a means of comparability—dollars.

For making projections of enrollments and expenditures, even the most sophisticated school systems have used simple regression methods whenever a trend could be established. Where no consistent series was available, or the data were too irregular to establish a trend, a constant based on the last observation or an average of the last two or three observations was used.

For a trend, observations in the ten most recent years could probably be justified as could extrapolations for ten years into the future. Rapid changes in economic and social conditions are likely to prevent valid projections beyond the ten-year period.

Straight-line projections have been used since the invention of the straight edge. Straight lines fitted by the least squares technique to a ratio (for example, of enrollment to population) as a dependent variable and time in years as the independent variable have been used. Rationale for using the straight line has been that the long-range time curve of relationships would be likely to yield a straight line over any portion covering only a ten-year span. An advantage, too, in using the straight lines is their additive property, which simplifies projections of components.

What is new is the use of projections using something other than a linear function. Curve-fitting is an attempt to represent data in a form that permits past data to have some meaningful effect on projections and, consequently, on decision-making. It is a process that assists in refining decision-makers' judgments and intuition. Its potential has not been explored thoroughly. However, a reasonable assumption seems to be that for long-term projections for budgeting purposes, the use of nonlinear functions for curve-fitting offer as tangible a process as now exists.

Data presented in this chapter have been compiled in a heuristic study by Dr. Dan Lee, Assistant Professor at Florida State University, at the local school system level in Florida, designated as School Systems A and B. Lee's work was an attempt to apply mathematical tools or so-called scientific tools in effecting more valid long-term educational programming and decision-making.

The centuries are full of the ways in which man has attempted to predict or to project future events. It is significant that science had made no impact on the problem of prediction until the advent of the digital computer.[1]

In this chapter, the intent is to present the use of still another tool whose judicious application may assist persons in projecting the future of a system, whether it be school or nonschool. The method is to derive from data an equation, $y = f(x)$, which expresses the functional relationship between x and

[1] C. M. Berners-Lee, ed., *Models for Decision*. London, English University Press, 1965, p. v.

y. The stress is on application and the method of deriving the equation, rather than on theory. For those interested in the theory, footnotes suggest sources for further study.

The fundamental purpose of projection is not the projection itself, but rather its assistance in initiating or modifying a course of action. The most accurate projection technique is of no value if it does not in some way assist in making better decisions. Thus, the central problem is the use of estimates to determine action in such a way that the future of a system is as near as possible to the desired one.[2]

Ideally, projection is a by-product of the quantitative understanding of a situation or physical model.[3] The laws of classical physics lead to very accurate projections. Newton's laws of motion enable astronomers to project the movement of the planets. The laws of dynamics and elasticity enable the engineers to project the structural requirements for bridges and buildings. These models are deterministic and can project with a high degree of accuracy. Thus, a model is said to be deterministic if it does not contain any random variables.

A stochastic model does contain random variables. Therefore, the idea of a definite projection would be replaced by a probability distribution of future values conditioned by the knowledge of the system's environment and past activity. The educational systems operate in environments that are changing continuously, and in which the plurality of governmental, economic, and human factors influence the conditions in which the systems operate. Obviously, there will be uncertainty in the models developed for an educational system. As always, there is no substitute for knowledge of the system, just as there is no substitute for good judgment in the use of any tool.

Extending the curves of $y = f(x)$, which have been fitted to the data, and predicting values of y from this extension is called *extrapolation*. An assumption of one using the process of extrapolation is that the rate of change that has occurred will continue to occur. The fault in this assumption lies not so much in the assumption that the rate of change will continue, but in the ignorance as to what it is that remains at the same rate. Having found this fault with extrapolation, Whittle noted: "It must be admitted that sometimes one can hardly do better. One recognizes regularities in a series, but has not the information needed to construct a model."[4]

The problem still remains to predict the future in such a way that the right

[2] P. W. Whittle, *Prediction and Regulation*. Princeton, N.J., Van Nostrand, 1963, p. 106.
[3] *Ibid.*, p. 1.
[4] *Ibid.*, p. 2.

decision can be made to meet changing circumstances in the desired way. Such decisions can be valid if not only the changing circumstances can be predicted, but also the behavior of the system as the conditions alter.

By considering what the system has done in the past, combining this with a knowledge of the system itself, and fitting a curve to the quantitative data thus obtained, there can be assembled another model designed to equate foresight with hindsight, which hopefully will assist in making decisions.

Characteristics and Selection of Typical Fitting Curves

Characteristics of curves influence the selection of a curve for fitting data. Selection of the most appropriate curve for data is not always deterministic, and a large number of uncontrollable variables as well as unknown variables make curve-fitting dependent on prior knowledge of the system that produced the data. Part of this prior knowledge is concerned with the behavior of the curves that are to be used.

In the selection of a curve to express the trend of a time series, data should first be plotted on arithmetic paper—that is, graph paper whose scales both vertically and horizontally have a constant interval length. If the data appear to lie on a straight line, a first degree equation (linear function) is indicated. The first degree form is $Y = a + bX$.

In the event $a = 0$, and $b = 1$, the equation becomes $Y = X$. Even this elementary curve has the characteristic of all first-degree equations. That is,

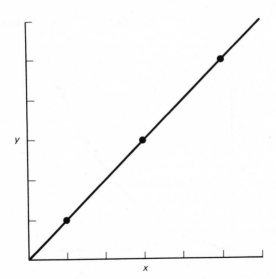

FIGURE A-1 First-Degree Equation Form.

for a uniform variation in X, the independent variable, there is a constant first difference between the Y values, or between values of the dependent variable.

$$Y = X$$

If X Is	Then Y Is	
1	1	
		2
3	3	
		2
5	5	
		1st difference

If the data appear on the arithmetic paper to be a single-bend curve, then a second degree curve may be the most appropriate. The second degree form is $Y = a + b + cx.^2$

In the event $a = 0$, $b = 0$, and $c = 1$, the second-degree polynomial reduces to $Y = X^2$, which has the characteristics of any second-degree polynomial; that is, second differences are equal.

If X Is	Then Y Is		
1	1		
		8	
3	9		8
		16	
5	25		8
		24	
7	49		8
		32	
9	81		
		1st difference	2nd difference

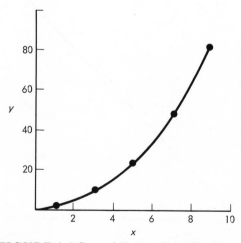

FIGURE A-2 Second-Degree Equation Form.

Notice that as the value of X increases, the value of Y increases rapidly. In particular, the larger the X value the greater the Y increase. For forecasting purposes, this means that the farther the curve is projected into the future, the greater the interval change.

In case the data appear to be increasing more rapidly than a second-degree polynomial, or in case the data have an inflection point (a point at which the rate of change changes), a third polynomial seems to be indicated. The third-degree form is $Y = a + bx + cx^2 + dx^3$.

In the event $a = 0$, $b = 0$, $c = 0$, and $d = 1$, then $Y = X^3$.

IF X IS	THEN Y IS	1st difference	2nd difference	3rd difference
1	1			
		26		
3	27		72	
		98		48
5	125		120	
		218		48
7	343		168	
		386		
9	729			

Compare the first difference of the third-degree form with the first difference of the second-degree form. The implication for curve fitting is that a cubic

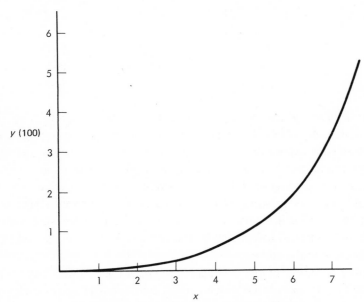

FIGURE A-3 Third-Degree Equation Form.

must be used as a predictive function with caution. Even though some data may fit a cube up to the present, the explosive increase in extrapolating a cubic should be justified by expert knowledge of the system producing the data. On the assumption that few school systems will continue such rapid development, the discussion of the polynomial function will end with the cubic.

There are other functions that have great utility in curve-fitting and projecting. They are the exponential, the modified exponential, the second-degree exponential, the Gompertz, and the logistic.

The exponential curve will be recognized by some as the compound interest curve, one of the more deterministic applications of curve fitting. In order to anticipate the use of the exponential, the data should be plotted on semilog paper. On this paper, the exponential appears as a straight line. If the data were plotted on arithmetic paper, it would appear to be a parabola or cubic (see Figures A-2 and A-3).

In exponential form $Y = AB^x$, let $A = 1$ and $B = 2$. Then, $Y = 2^x$.

IF X IS	THEN Y IS		
1	2		
		6	$\frac{2}{8} = 4$
3	8		
		24	$\frac{8}{32} = 4$
5	32		
		96	$\frac{32}{128} = 4$
7	128		
		384	$\frac{128}{512} = 4$
9	512	1st difference	1st ratio

The first differences are not equal, but the first ratios are equal.

In the event data plotted on semilog paper have one bend, as in Figure A-4, a second-degree exponential is suggested. Care must be taken in the use of this logarithmic parabola or second-degree exponential because it changes directions. If it is going up, it has the possibility of coming back down. With some assurance as to what part of the curve is the present, there is the possibility of using it. Thus, this curve should be used for small interval forecast only. Limited forecasting by this curve is further emphasized by the rapid increase in the curve.

Another variation of the exponential curve is the modified exponential. The curve is the exponential with an added constant. The modified exponential equation is $Y = K + AB^x$—for example, $Y = 10 + 2^x$.

IF X IS	THEN Y IS		
1	12		
		6	$\frac{6}{24} = \frac{1}{4}$
3	18		
		24	$\frac{24}{96} = \frac{1}{4}$
5	42		
		96	$\frac{96}{384} = \frac{1}{4}$
7	138		
		384	Ratio of
9	522	1st difference	1st difference

Notice that the first differences are not equal, but the ratios of the first differences are equal. Figure A-4 shows that the graph of a modified exponential on semilog paper has the appearance of a second-degree exponential. By

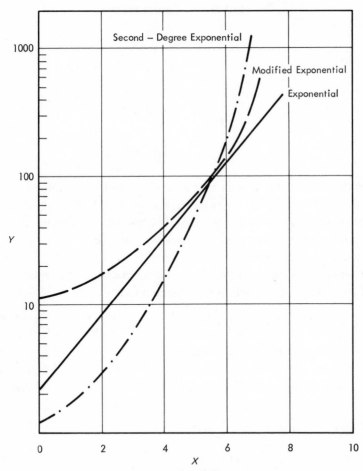

FIGURE A-4 Exponential Forms.

examining the ratios of the first differences, the two curves become distinguish-able.

The Gompertz and logistic curves are two growth curves that have applica-tion to biological growth phenomena. Both of these curves are used exten-sively in population projections. The Gompertz curve equation is $Y = kG^{B^x}$. If $k = 1$, $G = \frac{1}{2}$, and $B = \frac{1}{2}$, then

$$Y = (\tfrac{1}{2})^{(1/2)^x} = \frac{1}{(2)^{\frac{1}{2^x}}}$$

Careful notice should be taken of the denominator of this fraction. The $\frac{1}{2}$ is the exponent of 2, and x is an exponent of the 2 in the denominator of the exponent $\frac{1}{2}$.

IF X IS	THEN Y IS
-3	$\dfrac{1}{256}$
-1	$\dfrac{1}{4}$
0	$\dfrac{1}{2}$
1	$\dfrac{\sqrt{2}}{2}$
3	$\dfrac{\sqrt[8]{128}}{32^2}$

From the table it can be seen that as X gets smaller, the value of Y gets closer to zero. However, as X gets larger, the value of Y edges closer to one. Both zero and one are termed *asymptotes*. If k has some value other than one, then whatever value k has would be an asymptote. See Figure A-5 for the graph when $k = 1$ and when $k = 4$.

To examine the characteristics of the Gompertz curve, the ratios of the first differences of the logarithms must be compared.

Y	log Y	1ST DIFFERENCE	RATIOS OF 1ST DIFFERENCE
$\dfrac{1}{256} = .003906$	$7.5918 - 10 = -2.4082$		
		1.8061	
$\dfrac{1}{4} = .2500$	$9.3979 - 10 = -0.6021$		4.00
		0.4515	
$\dfrac{\sqrt{2}}{2} = .7070$	$9.8494 - 10 = -0.1506$		4.00
		0.1128	
$\dfrac{\sqrt[8]{128}}{2} = .9173$	$9.9622 - 10 = -0.0378$		

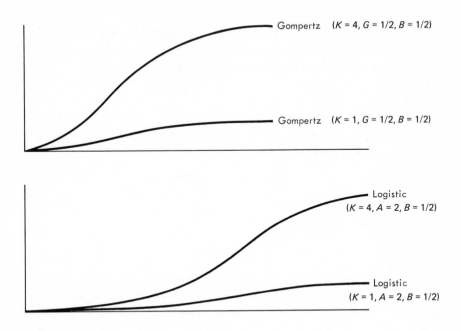

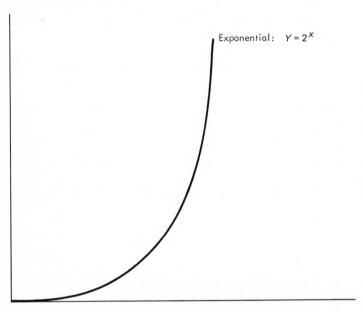

FIGURE A-5 Growth-Curve Forms.

From this chart, it is apparent that the ratios of the first differences of the logarithms are equal. In this example, the ratios of the logarithms themselves are 4.00 because the value of $k = 1$. However, regardless of the value of k, the ratios of the first differences of the logarithms remain equal.

Two forms of the logistic curve are as follows:

1. $Y = K/1 + 10^{a+bx}$
2. $1/Y = 1/K + AB^x$

For computation purposes, the second equation is the better one to use. If $K = 1$, $A = 2$, and $B = \frac{1}{2}$, then $1/Y = 1 + 2(\frac{1}{2})^x$

IF x Is	THEN Y Is
-5	$\frac{1}{65}$
-3	$\frac{1}{17}$
-1	$\frac{1}{5}$
0	$\frac{1}{3}$
1	$\frac{1}{2}$
3	$\frac{4}{5}$
5	$\frac{16}{17}$

This table demonstrates that K is the upper limit of the curve, and zero is the lower limit. In Figure A-5, the logistic curve is drawn for $K = 1$ and for $K = 4$, with $A = 2$ and $B = \frac{1}{2}$. The asymptotes of the logistic curve are K and 0. Characteristically, the ratios of the first differences of the reciprocals are equal. This is shown in the chart below.

x	Y	$1/Y$	1ST DIFFERENCES	RATIO OF 1ST DIFFERENCES
-5	$\frac{1}{65}$	65		
			48	
-3	$\frac{1}{17}$	17		4.00
			12	
-1	$\frac{1}{5}$	5		4.00
			3	
1	$\frac{1}{2}$	2		4.00
			$\frac{3}{4}$	
3	$\frac{4}{5}$	$\frac{5}{4}$		4.00
			$\frac{3}{16}$	
5	$\frac{16}{17}$	$\frac{17}{16}$		

Partial Summary

A suggested procedure for identifying the most appropriate curve with which to fit data is the following sequence of activities:

1. Plot the data on arithmetic paper. If the data appear to lie on a straight line, use a first-degree equation.

If the curve has one bend, try a second-degree polynomial (see step 2 also).

If the curve changes its rate of increase very rapidly, try a third-degree polynomial (see step 2 also).

2. Plot the data on semilog paper. The logarithm scale may be traced from the example in Figure A-4 if semilog paper is not available.

   If the data appear to lie on a straight line, an exponential curve is suggested.

   If the curve has a single bend, a second-degree exponential curve is suggested.

3. If plotting the data do not give some indication of an appropriate curve, put the data in a chart, as shown in Table A-1. The seven columns of the chart as indicated by numbers in parentheses are the key columns. If the numbers in any column are approximately equal, it means that the data fit the particular curve designated.

Values for X in Table A-1 were chosen with equal intervals between observations. This must be done if the chart is to be of help in the selection of a fitting curve. In case the data do not come in equal intervals, the data should be placed on an arithmetic scale graph and the plotted points connected with an estimated curve of good fit. From this curve, Y values for equal interval X values should be read. The Y values become the ones to use in the chart, as well as the calculations required to fit the curve to data.

Values for Y in the example represent no particular system of observations. Rather, the values in an increasing order were chosen arbitrarily. In other words, if the chart would show that a fitting curve were one of the seven curves, it would have been a coincidence. With this in mind, examination of the chart reveals that none of the seven columns contains approximately equal numbers. Figures in columns 4 and 6 suggest that either an exponential or a Gompertz would be the most appropriate.

After the data have been fitted with either of the two suggested curves, the curves should be plotted on arithmetic paper along with the original data. The curve that appears to fit the data most reasonably when using prior knowledge and expert judgment of the system should be used.

The judgment value at this point replaces what a statistician would call a goodness-of-fit test or analysis of variance. These statistical procedures have been omitted in this example in order to reduce further complications. For those so inclined, most statistics textbooks contain a discussion of the procedure.

TABLE A-1. Determination of Curve of Best Fit

X	Y	DIFFERENCE 1ST	DIFFERENCE 2ND	DIFFERENCE 3RD	Y	FIRST RATIO	RATIO OF 1ST DIFFERENCES	Log Y	Log Y 1ST DIFFERENCES	1/Y	1ST DIFFERENCES	RATIO OF 1ST DIFFERENCES
1	2				2			.3010		.5000		
		5				.2857	5		.5441		.3572	
2	7		6		7		.4545	.8451		.1428		4.0916
		11		−11		.3888	11		.4102		.0873	
3	18		−5		18		1.8333	1.2553		.0555		7.0000
		6		−3		.7500	6		.1249		.0139	
4	24		−8		24		.4285	1.3802		.0416		.9084
		14		8		.6315	14		.1996		.0153	
5	38		0		38		1.0000	1.5798		.0263		1.9615
		14		4		.7037	14		.1606		.0078	
6	54		4		54		.7777	1.7404		.0185		1.6595
		18					18		.1169		.0047	
7	72							1.8573		.0138		
	Polynomial			Exponential	Modified Exponential			Gompertz		Logistic		
(1)	(2)	(3)		(4)	(5)			(6)		(7)		

338

Computation of Curve Fitting

Straight Line—First-Degree Equation

From analytical geometry, the form of the equation for any straight line is found to be $y = a + bx$. If $a = 1$ and $b = 2$, then $y = 1 + 2x$.

	If x Is	Then y Is
C	0	1
D	1	3
E	2	5

Note that when $x = 0$, $y = a$, or in the equation, $y = 1$. The a value is the y intercept—that is, where the line intersects (intercepts) the y axis. The b value is the slope of the line; it represents the amount of change in y or Δy, compared to the amount of change in x or Δx. Thus, in Figure A-6, moving from C to D,

$$\Delta y = 1 - 3 = -2,$$

while $\Delta x = 0 - 1 = -1$,

$$\frac{\Delta y}{\Delta x} = \frac{-2}{-1} = 2, \qquad \text{the slope of the line.}$$

Notice: C to E

$$\frac{\Delta y}{\Delta x} = \frac{1 - 5}{0 - 2} = \frac{-4}{-2} = 2, \qquad \text{or the same slope.}$$

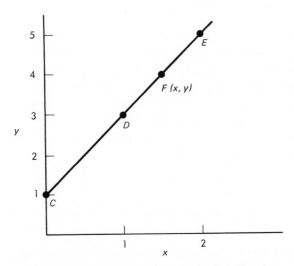

FIGURE A-6 First-Degree Equation Graph.

Using this idea, a straight line can be fitted to any two points, and its equation can be determined. Using the data from Figure A-6 and considering points C and D, choose another point on the line which passes through C and D; call it F. Since the x and y values of the point are unknown, let them be x and y.

Having shown that the slope between two points on a line is equal to the slope between any two points on the line, this means that the slope from C to F = the slope from C to D.

$$\frac{\Delta y}{\Delta x} = \frac{1-y}{0-x} \ (C \text{ to } F) \quad \text{and} \quad \frac{1-3}{0-1} \ (C \text{ to } D).$$

$$\frac{1-y}{0-x} = \frac{1-3}{0-1}.$$

Multiplying this equation by $(-1)(x)$ gives:

$$1 - y = x(1 - 3)$$
$$1 - y = -2x$$
$$-y = -1 - 2x, \text{ or multiply by } -1 \text{ and the result is:}$$
$$y = 1 + 2x, \text{ which is the basic straight-line equation.}$$

See if you can derive the equations of the straight lines that fit these data:

(a)		(b)		(c)		(d)	
x	y	x	y	x	y	x	y
0	0	0	0	0	3	0	−1
5	5	3	6	5	3.5	5	.5
10	10	5	10	10	4	10	2

Since only two of the points are used to fit the equation, the third one can be used to check your equation by substituting its value in your equation.

If the models with which one actually comes in contact were as deterministic as these, there would be no need for further discussion of projections. In practice, a straight line of best fit is found. This simply means that an average straight line of the data is determined.

To demonstrate the problem, data have been taken from Figure A-6 and changed slightly.

	IF x Is	THEN y Is
C	0	1
M	1	4
N	2	3

A glance at Figure A-7 indicates that there cannot be a straight line that passes through the three points. What is the predicted value of y where

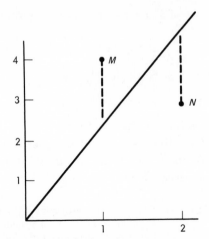

FIGURE A-7 Fitted First-Degree Equation Method of Least Squares.

$x = 5$? There is an average line that will assist one in predicting the value of y. The problem becomes that of finding the line of best fit.[5]

Recall that $y = a + bx$ is the general equation. The values of a and b can be found by the method of least squares (n equals the number of observations).

$$b = \frac{\sum (xy) - \frac{(\sum x)(\sum y)}{n}}{x^2 - \frac{(\sum x)^2}{n}}.$$

$$a = \bar{y} - b\bar{x}.$$

$\sum$ is read "sum of," and $\bar{x}$ and $\bar{y}$ are arithmetic averages.

x	y	xy	x^2
0	1	0	0
1	4	4	1
2	3	6	4
$\sum 3$	8	10	5

$$b = \frac{10 - \frac{(3)(8)}{3}}{5 - \frac{(3)^2}{3}} = \frac{10 - 8}{5 - 3} = \frac{2}{2} = 1.$$

$$a = \tfrac{8}{3} - (1)(\tfrac{3}{3}) = \tfrac{8}{3} - 1 = \tfrac{5}{3}.$$

[5] See F. E. Croxton and D. J. Cowdon, *Practical Business Statistics.* Englewood Cliffs N.J., Prentice-Hall, 1960, pp. 362–369.

Substituting these values of a and b in $Y = a + bx$ gives the linear equation of best fit:

$$y = \tfrac{5}{3} + 1x = \tfrac{5}{3} + x.$$

Thus, when $x = 5$, $y = \tfrac{5}{3} + 5$, which simplifies to:

$$y = \tfrac{20}{3} \qquad \text{or } 6\tfrac{2}{3}.$$

A reasonable prediction for y when $x = 5$ is $6\tfrac{2}{3}$.

The forecasting curves discussed in this chapter are based on a time sequence. For example, in education the growth of a total system might be estimated by its growth over the past years.

TABLE A-2. Data Base for Projecting Current Expenditures for School System A by Using First-Degree Equation

YEAR	x	y ($10,000)	xy	x^2
1957	-9	$265.1	-2385.9	81
1958	-7	283.1	-1981.7	49
1959	-5	286.8	-1434.0	25
1960	-3	339.4	-1018.2	9
1961	-1	407.6	-407.6	1
1962	1	407.5	407.5	1
1963	3	457.1	1371.3	9
1964	5	435.7	2178.5	25
1965	7	586.9	4108.3	49
1966	9	604.6	5441.4	81
	$\Sigma\,0$	$4073.8	6279.6	330

The computations in Table A-2 and in other examples to follow have been simplified by coding the years as positive and negative integers such that the intervals between coded values are all equal, and most important the sum of the coded values (x) is zero. If n (the number of years) is an even number, there is no one year that can be called the middle year, so $x = 0$ is halfway between the two middle years. Because the x values are integers, the two middle years are assigned values of -1 and $+1$. The interval thus established is 2, which means that all intervals must be 2. With ± 2 as the interval, the coded values are -1, -3, -5, and $+1$, $+3$, $+5$, etc., must be assigned to consecutive years. In particular, note that such assignment of values results in the $\Sigma x = 0$. In examples where there is an odd number of years, the middle year or x can be assigned a value of zero. Consecutive years are then given positive integral values on one side of the middle year and negative integral values on the opposite side of zero. Again, note that such assignment results in the sum of the x's being equal to zero.

Why all the concern about $x = 0$? Notice in both numerator and denominator of the formula for b that there is $(\sum x)^2$.

$$b = \frac{\sum (xy) - \frac{\sum x \sum y}{n}}{\sum x^2 - \frac{(\sum x)^2}{n}}$$

$$= \frac{\sum (xy) - \frac{(0)(\sum y)}{n}}{\sum x^2 - \frac{(0)^2}{n}}.$$

Therefore, by the judicious assignment of coded values as discussed, the calculations for b now become:

$$b = \frac{\sum (xy)}{\sum x^2}.$$

The line of best fit then is computed as follows:

$$y = a + bx.$$

$$b = \frac{6279.6}{330}, \qquad b = 19.029.$$

$$a = \bar{y} - b\bar{x} = 407.38 - b(0) \quad \text{when} \quad \bar{y} = \frac{\sum y}{n}.$$

$$= 407.38.$$

Thus, $y = 407.38 + 19.029x$ is the line of best fit.

PARABOLA—SECOND-DEGREE EQUATION

In the second type of computation for curve fitting, the parabola, or a second-degree equation, becomes the tool of projection. The form of the equation is $y = a + bx + cx^2$. To solve for the three unknowns of a, b, and c requires three equations.[6]

$$na + c \sum x^2 = \sum y. \tag{1}$$

$$b \sum x^2 = \sum xy. \tag{2}$$

$$a \sum x^2 + c \sum x^4 = \sum x^2 y. \tag{3}$$

[6] *Ibid.*

TABLE A-3. Data Base for Projecting Current Expenditures for School System A yb Using Second-Degree Equation

YEAR	x	x^2	x^4	y ($10,000)	xy	x^2y	t_2	t_2y
1957	-9	81	6,561	$265.1	$-2,385.9$	21,473.1	6	1,590.6
1958	-7	49	2,401	283.1	$-1,981.7$	13,871.9	2	566.2
1959	-5	25	625	286.8	$-1,434.0$	7,170.0	-1	-286.8
1960	-3	9	81	339.4	$-1,018.2$	3,054.6	-3	$-1,018.2$
1961	-1	1	1	407.6	-407.6	407.6	-4	$-1,630.4$
1962	1	1	1	407.5	407.5	407.5	-4	$-1,630.0$
1963	3	9	81	457.1	1,371.3	4,113.9	-3	$-1,371.3$
1964	5	25	625	435.7	2,178.5	10,892.5	-1	-435.7
1965	7	49	2,401	586.9	4,108.3	28,758.1	2	1,173.8
1966	9	81	6,561	604.6	5,441.4	48,972.6	6	3,627.6
	0	330	19,338	4,073.8	6,279.6	139,121.8		585.8

In equation (2), note that $b = \sum xy / \sum x^2$. This is the value of b in the first-degree equation. Thus, $b = 19.0291$. Substituting the values required in (1) and (3):

$$10a + 330c = 4073.8. \qquad (4)$$

$$330a + 19338c = 139,121.8. \qquad (5)$$

Solving equations (4) and (5) simultaneously determines the value of a to be 389.074, and the value of c to be .55473. The parabola of fit, then, is $y = 389.074 + 19.0291x + 0.55473x^2$.

CUBIC—THIRD-DEGREE EQUATION

The fitting of a cubic, or third-degree equation, to data has been rare. One method of fitting such data necessitates the solution of four equations and four unknowns, which is a very tedious task. Such difficulty can be avoided by using either orthogonal polynomials or computer curve-fitting programs.[7]

Using the orthogonal polynomial form, the problem just discussed of fitting a polynomial—$y = a + bx + cx^2 + dx^3$, etc.—can be reduced to fitting $Y = B_1 + B_1t_1 + B_2t_2 + B_3t_3$, etc., where t_i represents a function of the ith degree.[8] These functions have been computed for t's from t_1 to t_5, and for n from 3 to 52.

A few remarks about the general orthogonal polynomials will assist in developing the concept beyond what is designated in Table A-3. The form

[7] See Croxton, *op. cit.*, pp. 516–624; and Palmer O. Johnson and Robert W. B. Jackson, *Modern Statistical Methods*, Chicago, Rand McNally, 1959, pp. 397–401.

[8] R. A. Fisher and F. Yates, *Statistical Tables for Biological, Agricultural and Medical Research*, 5th ed. Revised and enlarged, New York, Hafner, 1957, Appendix.

$y = B_0 + B_1t_1 + B_2t_2 + B_3t_3$, etc., can be written, $y = \sum\limits^{n} B_rt_r$, where $r = 0$, and $B_r = \sum t_ry/\sum t_2r$ with $t = 1$ and $t_1 = x$ such that $\sum x = 0$. If n is even, x should take on values of $\ldots -3, -1, +1, +3$, etc., and if n is odd, x should be $\ldots -2, -1, 0, +1, +2$, etc.

$$B = \frac{\sum t_0y}{\sum t_20} = \sum \frac{y}{n} = \bar{y}.$$

$$B_1 = \frac{\sum t_1y}{\sum t_1^2}, \qquad B_2 = \frac{\sum t_2y}{\sum t_2^2}, \qquad B_3 = \frac{\sum t_3y}{\sum t_3^2}.$$

Therefore, the basic equation can be written $y = \bar{y} + B_1t_1 + B_2t_2 + B_3t_3$. In general, $t_r = t_1t_q - [q^2(n^2 - q^2)/4(4q^2 - 1)]$ with $q = r - 1$ Thus, when $r = 2$,

$$t_2 = t_1t_1 - \frac{1(n^2 - 1)}{4[4(1)^2 - 1]}.$$

$$= (x)(x) - \frac{(n^2 - 1)}{12}.$$

$$= x^2 - \frac{n^2 - 1}{12}.$$

In using data from Table A-4 for curve fitting, the computations for first-, second-, and third-degree equations are as follows:

Straight line:

$$y_1 = \bar{y} + \frac{\sum t_1yt_1}{\sum t_1^2}.$$

$$y_1 = \frac{4073.8}{10} + \frac{6279.6}{330}t_1.$$

$$y_1 = 407.38 + 19.029t_1.$$

Since $t_1 = x$ in (x, y) coordinates, $y = 407.38 + 19.029x$, as previously determined in discussion on the first-degree equation.

Parabola:

$$y_2 = \bar{y} + \frac{\sum t_1y}{\sum t_1^2}t_1 + \frac{\sum t_2y}{\sum t_1^2}t_2.$$

$$y_2 = 407.38 + 19.029t_1 + \frac{585.8}{132}t_2.$$

$$y_2 = 407.38 + 19.029t_1 + 4.438t_2.$$

TABLE A-4. Data Base for Projecting Current Expenditure for School System A by Using Orthogonal Polynomials

YEAR	t_1	t_2	t_3	y ($10,000)	$t_1 y$	$t_2 y$	$t_3 y$
1957	-9	6	-42	$265.1	$-2,385.9$	1,590.6	$-11,134.2$
1958	-7	2	14	283.1	$-1,981.7$	566.2	3,963.4
1959	-5	-1	35	286.8	$-1,434.0$	-286.8	10,038.0
1960	-3	-3	31	339.4	$-1,018.2$	$-1,018.2$	10,521.4
1961	-1	-4	12	407.6	-407.6	$-1,630.4$	4,891.2
1962	1	4	-12	407.5	407.5	$-1,630.0$	$-4,890.0$
1963	3	-3	-31	457.1	1,371.3	$-1,371.3$	$-14,170.1$
1964	5	-1	-35	437.7	2,178.5	-435.7	$-15,249.5$
1965	7	2	-14	586.9	4,108.3	1,173.8	$-8,216.6$
1966	9	6	42	604.6	5,441.4	3,627.6	25,393.2
$[t_r^2$	330	132	8,580]	[4,073.8	6,279.6	585.8	1,146.9]

Since $t_1 = x$ and $t_2 = (x^2 - 33)/8$ in (x, y) coordinates, $y_2 = 407.38 + 19.029x + 4.438 (x^2 - 33)/8$. Therefore, $y_2 = 407.38 + 19.029x + .5547x^2 - 18.31$ or $y_2 = 389.07 + 19.029x + .5547x^2$ as evolved in the previous discussion on parabolas.

Cubic:

$$y_3 = y + \frac{\sum t_1 y}{\sum t_1^2} t_1 + \frac{\sum t_2 y}{\sum t_1^2} t_2 + \frac{\sum t_3 y}{\sum t_3^2} t_3.$$

$$y_3 = 407.38 + 19.029t_1 + 4.438t_2 + \frac{1146.9}{8580} t_3.$$

$$y_3 = 407.38 + 19.029t_1 + 4.438t_2 + .1336t_3.$$

In (x, y) coordinates, since $t_1 = x$,

$$t_2 = \frac{x^2 - 33}{8}, \quad \text{and} \quad t_3 = \frac{5x^3 - 293x}{24},$$

$$y_3 = 407.38 + 19.029x + .5547x^2 + .1336 \frac{(5x^3 - 293x)}{24}$$

or

$$y_3 = 407.38 + 17.417x + .5547x^2 + .0275x^3.$$

Growth Curves

The polynomial curves discussed have a variable rate of change, while another family of curves has a rate of growth to time t dependent on the level attained at time t. The latter family includes exponential, second-degree exponential, modified exponential, Gompertz, and logistic curves.

The fitting of the exponential, the modified exponential, and the logistic curves will be discussed in detail.

EXPONENTIAL

The form of the exponential curve is

$$Y = AB^x. \tag{1}$$

The equation for computing the logarithm of (1) would be

$$\log Y = \log A + x \log B. \tag{2}$$

For computation, when x is coded so that $\sum x = 0$, equation (2) simplifies to

$$\log Y = \overline{\log Y} + x \log B. \tag{3}$$

Equation (3) is of the form $y = a + bx$, which is a straight line. Consequently, the fitting of the logarithm of the exponential is analogous to fitting any straight line. Again, using School System A data, the computational chart for fitting is Table A-5.

TABLE A-5. Data Base for Projecting Current Expenditures for School System A by Using Exponential Curve

	CODE						COMPUTED
YEAR	x	x^2	Y ($10,000)	$\log Y$	$x \log Y$	$\log Y_x$	Y
1957	−9	81	$265.1	2.42341	−21.81069	2.40965	256.8
1958	−7	49	283.1	2.45194	−17.16358	2.45047	282.1
1959	−5	25	286.8	2.45758	−12.28790	2.49128	309.9
1960	−3	9	339.4	2.53071	− 7.59213	2.53210	340.5
1961	−1	1	407.6	2.61023	− 2 61023	2.57292	347.0
1962	1	1	407.5	2.61013	2.61013	2.61373	410.9
1963	3	9	457.1	2.66001	7.98003	2.65455	451.4
1964	5	25	435.7	2.63919	13.19595	2.69536	495.9
1965	7	49	586.9	2.76856	19.37992	2.73618	544.7
1966	9	81	604.6	2.78147	25.03323	2.77700	598.4
	0	330	$4073.8	25.93323	6.73473	25.93324	4064.6

Thus, the equation for finding $\log B$ is $\log B = \sum (x \log Y)/\sum x^2$. Substituting values in (3), $\log Y = 2.593328 + (6.73473/330)x$ or

$$\log Y = 2.593328 + .020408x. \tag{4}$$

By taking the antilog of (4), $Y = 392(1.048)^x$, which is the exponential curve of School System A total current expenditures.

MODIFIED EXPONENTIAL

The form of the modified exponential curve is

$$Y = K + AB^X. \tag{1}$$

The exponential equation $Y = AB^X$ has been modified by adding K, which changes the properties of the exponential equation. Now the first ratios are no longer equal to B, but rather the ratios of the first differences have a constant value B. The limit of the modified exponential is K, an asymptote.

Although the method of selected points is to be used in fitting the modified exponential, it is of interest to note that (1) can be written in linear form

$$Y - K = AB^X \quad \text{or} \quad \log(Y - K) = \log A + X \log B. \tag{2}$$

The shape of a modified exponential depends on the values of K, A, and B. The four graphs in Figure A-8 not only depict the shapes of the modified exponential, but also the possible shapes of the exponential itself. The

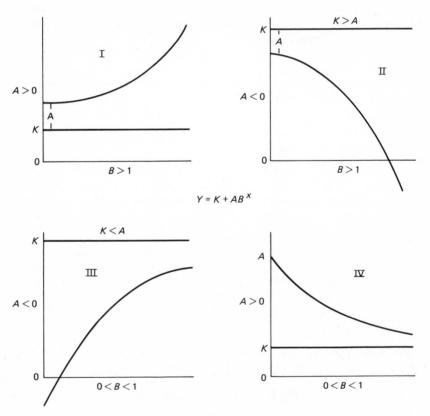

FIGURE A-8 Modified Exponential Forms.

discussion that follows will pertain to the curve of graph I where $K > 0$, $A > 0$, and $B > 1$.

Using the method of selected points, plot the School System A data on semilog paper. Draw an estimated straight line of best fit through the plotted data. From this line read three values of y which are equidistant in time. These values do not have to be observed values. Usually the chosen values will not be observed values since the line does not go through all points. For convenience in the example to be discussed, the values used are the observed values.

The formula for the trend constants used with the method of selected points are as follows:[9]

$$B^r = \frac{Y_2 - Y_1}{Y_1 - Y_0}$$

where $r = (n - 1)/2$.

$$A = \frac{Y_1 - Y_0}{B^r - 1}$$

and $K = Y_0 - A$.

School System A Current Expenditures

X		x	Y	
1957	Y_0	0	265.1	
1958				$B^4 = \dfrac{586.9 - 407.6}{407.6 - 265.1} = 1.2582$
1959				
1960				$B = 1.0591$
1961	Y_1	4	407.6	
1962				$A = \dfrac{407.6 - 265.1}{1.2582 - 1}$
1963				$A = 551.8977$
1964				
1965	Y_2	8	586.9	
				$K = 265.1 - 551.9$
				$K = -286.8$

Substituting in $Y = K + AB^x$, $Y = -286.8 + (551.8977)(1.0591)^x$.

LOGISTIC

Using the formulas for B, A, and K as just described, but placing Y's into the form of $1/Y$ and K's into the form of $1/K$, the fitting of the logistic curve can be computed.

[9] Croxton, *op. cit.*, p. 592.

School System A Current Expenditures

X		x	Y	$1/Y$	
1957	Y_0	0	265.1	.00377358	
⋮	⋮	⋮	⋮	:}5027	
1961	Y_1	4	407.6	.00245338	
⋮	⋮	⋮	⋮	⋮	$r = \dfrac{n-1}{2}$
⋮	⋮	⋮	⋮	⋮	
1965	Y_2	8	586.9	.00170386	$r = 4$

$$B^4 = \frac{\frac{1}{Y_2} - \frac{1}{Y_1}}{\frac{1}{Y_1} - \frac{1}{Y_0}} = \frac{.00170386 - .00245338}{.00245338 - .00377358} = .56773.$$

$$B = .868035.$$

$$A = \frac{\frac{1}{Y_1} - \frac{1}{Y_0}}{B^r - 1} = \frac{.00245338 - .00377358}{.56773 - 1.00000} = .00305412$$

$$\frac{1}{K} = \frac{1}{Y} - A = .00170386 - .00305412 = .00071948.$$

Substituting these values in $1/Y = 1/K + AB^X$ results in $1/Y = .00071948 + .00305412(.868035)^X$.

GOMPERTZ

The equation of the Gompertz curve is $Y = kG^{B^x}$ or

$$\log Y = \log k + B^X \log G.$$

If $\log G = A$, then $\log Y = \log k + AB^X$. Again, using the formulas discussed under the modified exponential curve section except for changing all Y's to log Y, and again, using selected points of the School System A current expenditure data, the Gompertz curve-fitting includes:

School System A Current Expenditures

X	x	Y		$\log Y_i$	
1957	0	265.1	Y_0	2.4234	
⋮	⋮	⋮	⋮	⋮	
⋮	⋮	⋮	⋮	⋮	$r = \dfrac{n-1}{2}$
1961	4	407.7	Y_1	2.6104	
⋮	⋮	⋮	⋮	⋮	$r = 4$
1965	8	586.9	Y_2	2.7685	

$$B^4 = \frac{\log Y_2 - \log Y_1}{B^4 - 1} = \frac{2.7685 - 2.6104}{2.6104 - 2.4234} = .845454.$$

$$B = .958898.$$

$$A = \frac{\log Y_1 - \log Y_0}{B^4 - 1} = \frac{2.6104 - 2.4234}{.8454 - 1} = -1.20957.$$

$$\log k = \log Y_0 - A = 2.4234 - (-1.20957) = 3.6330.$$

Substituting in the basic equation, $\log Y_x = 3.6330 - (1.20957)(.958898)^x$ and the antilog of this equation results in $Y = 4295/16.21(.958898)^x$.

As another example of fitting the growth curves, instructional salary data for School System B from 1958–1966 has been selected for data bases. Plot these data on semilog paper, then choose three points over equal intervals of time. With these three points and the formulas previously given in the growth curve sections discussed, complete the modified exponential, logistic, and Gompertz curve fittings.

School System B Instructional Salaries

X	x	Y
1958	0	327
1959	⋮	378
1960	⋮	481
1961	⋮	555
1962	4	637
1963	⋮	743
1964	⋮	947
1965	⋮	1058
1966	8	1164

Values read from line AB in Figure A-9 are:

x	Y	
0	327	Y_0
4	637	Y_1
8	1164	Y_2

Computing the trend constants requires the use of the following formulas:

$$B^r = \frac{Y_2 - Y_1}{Y_1 - Y_0} \tag{1}$$

where $r = (n - 1)/2$

$$A = \frac{Y_1 - Y_0}{B^r - 1} \tag{2}$$

$$K = Y_0 - A \tag{3}$$

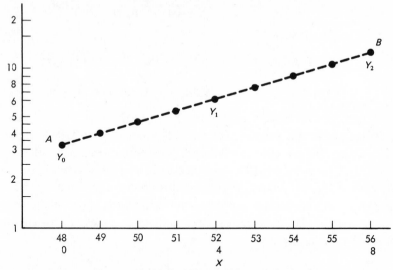

FIGURE A-9 Fitted Modified Exponential Methods of Three Points.

Substitution of the data in equation (1) results in

$$B^4 = \frac{1164 - 637}{637 - 327} = 1.700.$$

Using logs and antilogs, $B = 1.142$. Substituting in (2),

$$A = \frac{637 - 327}{1.7 - 1} = 442.8571.$$

Substituting in (3), $K = 327 - 442.8571$ or $K = -115.8571$. The trend equation is $Y = K + AB^x$, and substituting the values found for B, A, and K gives $Y = -115.8571 + (442.8571)(1.142)^x$. Comparing trend values with observed values indicates there may be another curve of better fit:

	1958	1959	1960	1961	1962	1963	1964	1965	1966
Observed Y	327	378	481	555	637	743	947	1058	1164
Computed Y	327	389	461	543	637	744	866	1005	1165
Difference	0	−11	20	12	0	−1	81	53	−1

The logistic curve is stated as $1/Y = 1/K + AB^x$. Again, the method of selected points is to be used. Choosing the three points that were used in fitting the modified exponential results in the following:

x	Y	$\dfrac{1}{Y}$
0	327	.00305810
4	637	.00156985
8	1164	.0085910

To find the trend constants:

$$B^r = \frac{\dfrac{1}{Y_2} - \dfrac{1}{Y_1}}{\dfrac{1}{Y_1} - \dfrac{1}{Y_0}} = .47757433.$$

$$A = \frac{\dfrac{1}{Y_1} - \dfrac{1}{Y_0}}{B^r - 1} = .00284825.$$

$$\frac{1}{K} = \frac{1}{Y_0} - A = .00020985.$$

If $B^4 = .4776$, using logs and antilogs results in $B = .8314$. Substituting in equation (1) results in $1/Y = .00020985 + (.00284825)(.8314)^x$. From this equation, values for $1/Y_x$ are obtained:

x	$\dfrac{1}{Y}$	Y OBSERVED	Y COMPUTED	DIFFERENCE
0	.00305810	327.0	327	0
1	.00257788	378.0	389	11
2	.00217863	459.0	481	22
3	.00184669	541.5	555	13.5
4	.00157071	636.7	637	.3
5	.00134126	745.6	743	−2.6
6	.00115050	869.2	943	73.8
7	.00099190	1008.2	1058	49.8
8	.00086004	1162.7	1164	1.3

The differences between the computed values and the observed values are all less than 7.5 per cent in error. Most computed values are less than 5 per cent in error. Only $x = 7$ exceeds the 5-per-cent error, and it is less than 7.5 per cent.

In computing the Gompertz curve, the basic data include:

X	x	Y	$\log Y$	
1958	0	327	2.5145	
1962	4	637	2.8041	$r = \dfrac{n-1}{2}$
1966	8	1164	3.0660	$r = 4$

$$B^4 = \frac{3.0660 - 2.8041}{2.8041 - 2.5145} = .9043.$$

$$B = .97517.$$

$$A = \frac{2.8041 - 2.5145}{.9043 - 1} = -3.02612.$$

$$\log K = 2.5145 - (-3.02612) = 5.54062.$$

Substituting these values in $\log Y_x = \log K + AB^x$ results in $\log Y_x = 5.54062 - 3.02612(.97517)^x$. Using the antilog results in

$$Y = \frac{34730}{106.2(.97517)^x}.$$

A summary list of curves for School System A comprises:

$$Y = 407.38 + 19.029x$$

$$= 389.07 + 19.029x + .5547x^2$$

$$= 407.38 + 17.417x + .5547x^2 + .0275x^3$$

$$= (256.83)(1.0958)^x \text{ (exponential)}$$

$$= -286.7977 + 551.8977(1.05911)^x \text{ (modified exponential)}.$$

$$\frac{1}{Y} = .00071948 + (.00305412)(.868035)^x \text{ (logistic)}.$$

$$Y = \frac{4295}{16.21(.9589)^x} \text{ (Gompertz)}.$$

A summary list of curves for School System B includes:

$$Y = -115.8571 + (442.8571)(1.142)^x \text{ (modified exponential)}.$$

$$\frac{1}{Y} = .00020985 + (.002848)(.8313)^x \text{ (logistic)}.$$

$$Y = \frac{34730}{106.2(.97517)^x} \text{ (Gompertz)}.$$

Computer Programs to Fit Polynomials

There are programs available that can fit polynomials. One program has been termed PRANK and has the capability of fitting a twentieth-degree polynomial. It is available from SHARE under the code name of G2*FSF by Roman and Martin.[10]

A University of California computer program entitled "Polynomial Regression" is a part of the Biomedical series. Its designation is BMDO5R, and it is programmed to run on the IBM7094. Output from this program is

---

[10] SHARE is an IBM library of programs for the IBM 7000 series equipment. SHARE is an acronym for the Society to Help Avoid Redundant Effort.

statistically oriented, but among the statistics are the equations that require untold hours to produce manually. In addition to the equations, the output consists of means, correlation coefficients, intercept and regression coefficients, analyses of variance, table of residuals, plot of observed and predicted values.

Limitations of the program are as follows: (1) the highest degree is 10; (2) the number of cases must be at least one greater than the degree of the final equation and less than 500; (3) the number of variable format cards is between one and two, inclusive.

TABLE A-6. Computer Program—Third-Degree Equation

Polynomial regression of degree 3
Intercept (A value)   7789.28659
Regression coefficients
  −434.41202   7.89065   −.04585
Standard error of regression coefficients
  188.90021   3.45066   .02090

ANALYSIS OF VARIANCE FOR THIRD-DEGREE POLYNOMIAL

SOURCE OF VARIATION	DEGREE OF FREEDOM	SUM OF SQUARES	MEAN SQUARE	F VALUE
Due to regression	3	129877.46689	43292.48896	322.72227
Deviation about regression	15	2012.21732	134.14782	
TOTAL	18	131889.68421		

FINAL ANALYSIS OF VARIANCE FOR THIRD-DEGREE POLYNOMIALS

SOURCE OF VARIATION	DEGREE OF FREEDOM	SUM OF SQUARES	MEAN SQUARE
Linear term	1	126800.39474	127800.39474
Quadratic term	1	1431.64153	1431.64153
Cubic term	1	645.43062	645.43062
Deviation about regression	15	2012.21732	134.14782
TOTAL	18	131889.68421	

Output is exemplified in Table A-6, from which it can be determined that the third-degree equation is $Y = 7789.28659 - 434.41202x + 7.89065x^2 - .04585x^3$. Both observed and computed values can be plotted by the computer programs.

Summary

There still remain many deficiencies in man's ability to project data for decision-making that must be accomplished in the future. The projection methods discussed show promise as projection instruments. However, each has relative strengths and weaknesses and must be used judiciously.

Most projections for educational budgeting continue to be straight-line in form. In some systems the straight line may be best, but in a growth situation, the straight-line extrapolation will project low. To emphasize this point, many new schools have been overcrowded with students the day the doors were opened.

The parabolic or cubic curves tend to overestimate. In a growth situation, the farther a projection extends beyond the present time, the faster a parabolic or cubic curve will be increasing for each unit of time. Thus, the projection will be increasing faster than the actual growth of an educational system, for example.

The logistic and the Gompertz curves overcome—although not completely —the error in short- or medium-range projections effected by using polynomial and exponential extrapolations. The logistic and Gompertz forms both have asymptotes, and in their use for long-range projections an assumption would be a population maximum of K. There may be some justification for this assumption, but for most school systems, a limit can be considered to be something less than infinite.

"Something less than infinite" has a special implication for the use of the logistic or Gompertz curves. The point of inflection of both curves is that point at which growth changes directions. Under ideal growth conditions, this point is halfway between the asymptotes. This means that the other asymptote can be computed, or, in particular, the probable limit of the population can be determined.

Because the logistic curve is symmetrical about the point of inflection, the extrapolating properties of the logistic curve about its point of inflection is perfect. Of course, the problem becomes a twofold question: (1) does the logistic curve represent the system? and (2) where is the point of inflection?

With the assumption that population growth is represented by a logistic curve, a second assumption is that the point of inflection is at the present time. By using this point as the inflection point, a whole family of logistic curves can be formed by using the three-point selection method. The three points are point A from the data; point B, the inflection point, and point C, by symmetry of A about B. Thus, if the data consist of 20 observations, there would be 19 logistic curves. One of these 19 would fit best the 20 points of data. This curve then should be given primary consideration as the extrapolating curve.

Without further development in methods of projecting educational expenditures, long-term budgeting such as included in planning-programming-budgeting systems will be a hazardous enterprise. Without satisfactory projections, educational programs and their costs cannot be valid bases for budgeting. It is likely, then, that budgeting will remain on a crisis-to-crisis, short-term basis, and emphasis will continue to be on determining "what the traffic will bear" prior to program determination. Thus, the tail (revenue) will continue to wag the dog (program).

APPENDIX B

CHRONOLOGICAL OUTLINE OF FEDERAL LEGISLATION[1]

The following list of actions on the part of the federal government is intended to provide a larger view of the background to Federal Aid to Education as it presently exists. Necessarily omitted from the array are many legislative proposals that were defeated, and the cited instances of temporary or permanent enactments of programs or policies are not represented as being complete or all-inclusive.

1777   Establishment of a policy of instruction for military personnel.

1783   Proposals for the Settlement of the Ohio Territory. Article VII recommended the establishment of schools and academies supported by the disposal of surplus public lands.

1785   The Ordinance of 1785. Reserved Lot Number 16 of each township for school usage. Extended aid to Territories (later to States) by the endowment of schools with public lands.

[1] SOURCE: *Federal Aid Handbook*, Albany, The University of the State of New York, The State Education Department, Division of Educational Finance, 1966, pp. 1–5.

1787 Endowment of certain public institutions of higher education with public lands.

1800 Founding of the nucleus of the Library of Congress with the first congressional appropriation for books.

1802 The Enabling Act for Ohio. The agreement of Ohio at entering the Union to the land-grant conditions of the Ordinance of 1785.

1802 Establishment of the Military Academy at West Point.

1804 Initiation of Federal provisions for education within the District of Columbia.

1824 Establishment of the first Army Special Service School.

1830 Forty-seven million dollars spent by Andrew Jackson for the purpose of building classrooms.

1845 Establishment of the Naval Academy at Annapolis.

1857 The Morrill Act. Proposed land grants to states for agricultural and industrial education purposes. (Defeated)

1862 The Morrill Act. Enacted aid to States through land grants for colleges to further agricultural and industrial education.

1864 Establishment of the Freedmen's Bureau. Accepted the federal responsibility to educate Negroes freed from slavery.

1867 Establishment of the United States Department of Education.

1868 Reduction of the United States Department of Education to Bureau status; redesignated as Office of Education.

1870 The Hoar Bill. Proposed the compulsion of satisfactory school systems in all the states; a national school system. (Defeated)

1872 The Pierce Bill. Proposed a perpetual fund to be used to provide wages for teachers. (Defeated)

1879 Establishment of a Federal School for Engravers.

1879 The Burnside Bill. Proposed support for national colleges to advance scientific and industrial education and to train common school teachers. (Defeated)

1882 The Blair Bills. Proposed a matching aid to common schools payable in proportion to the rates of illiteracy of each State with regard to the rates of the United States. (Defeated)

1887 The Hatch Act. Established agricultural experimental stations.

1888 The Blair Bills. Continued to propose matching aid to common schools based upon illiteracy rates. (Defeated)

1893 Establishment of the Army Medical School.

1901 Establishment of the Army War College.

1907 The Davis Bill. Proposed a federal system of vocational schools. (Defeated)

1911   Established federal matching aid to states for nautical schools.

1912   The Page Bill. Proposed a federal system of vocational schools. (Defeated)

1914   The Smith–Lever Act. Appropriated federal funds to improve rural living by sponsoring investigative and information services relating to home economics and agriculture.

1915   Establishment of the Coast Guard Academy.

1916   Establishment of the Army Reserve Officers Training Corps.

1917   The Smith–Hughes Act. Established the promotion of vocational education at grades below the college level.

1918   The Smith–Sears Vocational Rehabilitation Act. Initiated training for the rehabilitation of disabled veterans.

1919   Origination of Federal Surplus Property Programs for the disposal of property surplus for the benefit of educational institutions.

1919   The Smith–Towner Bill. Proposed the return of the Office of Education to Department status and the payment of federal aid to the public schools. (Defeated)

1920   Establishment of the Graduate School of the Department of Agriculture.

1920   The Smith–Bankhead Act. Established a policy of federal and state cooperation for vocational rehabilitation, including people who had been disabled in industry.

1921   The Sterling–Towner Bill. Proposed Department status for the Office of Education and financial aid for public schools. (Defeated)

1923   The Sterling–Reed Bill. Proposed Department status for the Office of Education and financial aid for public schools. (Defeated)

1924   The Clark–McNary Act. Provided increased funds for the implementation of the Smith–Lever Act.

1926   Establishment of the Naval Reserve Officers Training Corps.

1928   The Capper–Kitchener Act. Provided further increased funds to extend the Smith–Lever Act.

1929   The George–Reed Act. Authorized additional funds for vocational education under the Smith–Hughes Act.

1933   Authorized work scholarships for students in universities under the Emergency Relief Administration.

1934   The George–Ellzey Act. Extended additional funds for vocational education under the Smith–Hughes Act.

1935   Organization of the National Youth Administration under the Works Progress Administration, which provided college and secondary school financial assistance for youth and auxiliary services such as guidance, testing, and work experience for youths out of school.

1935   The Bankhead–Jones Act. Provided additional funds to implement the Smith–Lever Act.

1936   The Harrison–Black–Fletcher Bill. Proposed general aid to public elementary and secondary schools. (Defeated)

1936   Established the entrance of the United States into international educational exchanges.

1937   Established the Civilian Conservation Corps, which sponsored programs of vocational educational exchanges.

1937   The George–Deen Act. Authorized additional funds for vocational education, including provision for distributive education benefits.

1938   The Harris–Thomas–Fletcher Bill. Proposed general aid to public elementary and secondary schools. (Defeated)

1939   The Civilian Pilot Training Act. Provided for the training of civilian pilots in cooperation with colleges.

1941   The Lanham Act. Provided for some school housing within housing measures sponsored for war-industry impacted areas.

1942   Establishment of the Armed Forces Institute.

1943   The Educational Finance Act of 1943. Proposed an apportionment of Federal funds to States by a formula based upon financial need and average daily attendance in public elementary and secondary schools. (Defeated)

1943   Establishment of the Army Specialized Training Program.

1944   The Servicemen's Readjustment Act. Provided for subsidized education and training for veterans.

1944   The Surplus Property Act. Provided a broad policy in the disposal of government surplus property for health, educational, and civil defense purposes.

1946   The National School Lunch Act. Provided funds for the establishment and operation of school lunch programs.

1946   The George–Barden Act. Provided additional funds with cooperative federal-state action in vocational education.

1946   The Atomic Energy Act. Provided fellowships for education under the direction of the Atomic Energy Commission.

1946   The Fullbright Act. Provided for international educational exchanges.

1946   Establishment of membership of the United States in the United Nations Educational, Scientific, and Cultural Organization (UNESCO).

1946   The Thomas–Hill–Taft Bill. Proposed general aid to public element-
        ary and secondary schools. (Defeated)

1948   The Smith–Mundt Act. Established an expanded program for
        international educational exchanges.

1950   Public Law 815. Provided Federal funds for public school con-
        struction in federally impacted areas.

1950   Public Law 874. Provided federal funds for public school operating
        expenses in federally impacted areas.

1950   The Housing Act. Provided the beginning of the college housing
        loans program.

1952   Establishment of the fellowship program of the National Science
        Foundation.

1954   Establishment of the Air Force Academy.

1956   The Library Services Act. Provided grants to the states for the
        improvement of public library services in rural areas.

1958   The National Defense Education Act. Established a broad program
        of financial assistance for the stimulation of a specific areas pertinent
        to the national interest.

1959   The Murray–Metcalf Bill. Proposed allocations for public school
        construction and teachers' salaries. (Defeated)

1961   The School Assistance Bill. Proposed allocations for public school
        construction and teachers' salaries. (Defeated)

1962   The Manpower Development and Training Act. Provided a program
        of training for unemployed or underemployed persons to enable
        them to become wage-earning citizens.

1962   The Public Welfare Act. Provided a program of literacy training for
        public welfare recipients.

1963   The Higher Education Facilities Act. Provided funds to higher
        education institutes to construct classrooms, laboratories, and
        libraries.

1963   The Vocational Education Act of 1963. Provided additional funds
        for vocational education designed to serve particular groups within
        the population.

1963   The Library Services and Construction Act. Provided funds to
        states for the extension and construction of public library
        facilities.

1964   The Economic Opportunity Act. Provided some educational pro-
        grams under the antipoverty program to rehabilitate chronic
        poverty groups.

1965   The Elementary and Secondary Act. Provided federal funds to local agencies by a formula based upon per-pupil expenditure and the number of children from families with low incomes.

1965 The Higher Education Act. Provided funds to strengthen the educational resources of colleges and universities and to provide financial assistance to students in postsecondary and higher education.

SELECTED

BIBLIOGRAPHY

BARR, W. MONFORT. *American Public School Finance.* New York: American Book Company, 1960.

BECKER, GARY S. *Human Capital: A Theoretical and Empirical Analysis, with Special Reference to Education.* Princeton, N.J.; Princeton University Press, 1964.

BENSON, CHARLES S. *The Cheerful Prospect: A Statement on the Future of American Education.* Boston: Houghton Mifflin Company, 1965.

BENSON, CHARLES S. *The Economics of Public Education.* Boston: Houghton Mifflin Company, 1961.

BURKHEAD, JESSE, *et al. Input and Output in Large-City High Schools.* Syracuse, N.Y.: Syracuse University Press, 1967.

BURKHEAD, JESSE. *Public School Finance.* Syracuse, N.Y.: Syracuse University Press, 1964.

CLARK, HAROLD F. *Cost and Quality in Public Education, The Economics and Politics of Education, 5.* Syracuse, N.Y.: Syracuse University Press, 1963.

CORBALLY, JOHN E., JR. *School Finance.* Boston: Allyn and Bacon, 1962.

DE YOUNG, CHRIS A. *Budgeting in Public Schools.* Garden City, N.Y.: Doubleday, Doran and Company, 1936.

ECKSTEIN, OTTO. *Public Finance.* Englewood Cliffs, N.J.: Prentice-Hall, Inc., 1964.

GALBRAITH, JOHN KENNETH. *The New Industrial State.* Boston: Houghton Mifflin Company, 1967.

GAUERKE, WARREN E., and CHILDRESS, JACK R. (editors). *The Theory and Practice of School Finance.* Chicago: Rand McNally and Company, 1967.

HILL, FREDERICK W., and COLMEY, JAMES W. *School Business Administration in the Smaller Community.* Minneapolis: T. S. Denison & Company, Inc., 1964.

JACOB, HERBERT, and VINES, KENNETH N. (editors). *Politics in the American States.* Boston: Little, Brown and Company, 1965.

JOHNS, ROE L., and MORPHET, EDGAR L. *Financing the Public Schools.* Englewood Cliffs, N.J.: Prentice-Hall, Inc., 1960.

KEPPEL, FRANCIS. *The Necessary Revolution in American Education.* New York: Harper and Row, 1966.

KERSHAW, JOSEPH A., and MCKEAN, ROLAND N. *Teacher Shortages and Salary Schedules.* New York: McGraw-Hill Book Company, Inc., 1962.

KNEZEVICH, STEPHEN J., and FOWLKES, JOHN GUY. *Business Management of Local School Systems.* New York: Harper & Row, 1960.

LIEBERMAN, MYRON, and MOSKOW, MICHAEL H. *Collective Negotiations for Teachers.* Chicago: Rand McNally & Company, 1966.

LINDMAN, ERICK. *The Federal Government and Public Schools.* Washington: American Association of School Administrators, 1965.

LINN, HENRY H. (editor). *School Business Administration.* New York: Ronald Press Company, 1956.

LOUGHARY, JOHN W. *Man-Machine Systems in Education.* New York: Harper and Row, 1966.

MCKEAN, ROLAND N. *Efficiency in Government Through Systems Analysis.* New York: John Wiley and Sons, Inc., 1958.

MORPHET, EDGAR L., and RYAN, CHARLES O. *Designing Education for the Future. No. 3, Planning and Effecting Needed Changes in Education.* New York: Citation Press, 1967.

MORT, PAUL R., REUSSER, WALTER C., and POLLEY, JOHN W. *Public School Finance.* New York: McGraw-Hill Book Company, 1960. 3rd ed.

MUSGRAVE, RICHARD A. *The Theory of Public Finance.* New York: McGraw-Hill Book Company, Inc., 1959.

MUSHKIN, SELMA J., and MCLOONE, EUGENE P. *Local School Expenditures: 1970 Projection.* Chicago: Council of State Governments, 1965.

National Education Association Committee on Educational Finance. *Local, State, Federal Partnership in School Finance.* Washington: National Education Association, 1966.

NETZER, DICK, *Economics of the Property Tax.* Washington: The Brookings Institution, 1966.

OVSIEW, LEON, and CASTETTER, WILLIAM B. *Budgeting for Better Schools.* Englewood Cliffs, N.J.: Prentice-Hall, Inc., 1960.

PIERCE, TRUMAN M. *Federal, State and Local Government in Education.* Washington: Center for Applied Research in Education, Inc., 1964.

ROBERTS, JOAN I. (editor). *School Children in the Urban Slum,* New York: The Free Press, 1967.

ROE, WILLIAM II. *School Business Management.* New York: McGraw-Hill Book Company, Inc., 1961.

ROSS, DONALD H. (editor). *Administration for Adaptability.* New York: Teachers College, Columbia University, 1958. Rev. ed.

SELAKOVICH, DANIEL. *The Schools and American Society.* Waltham, Mass.: Blaisdell Publishing Company, 1967.

SEXTON, PATRICIA CAYO. *Education and Income.* New York: The Viking Press, Inc., 1966.

SHULTZ, WILLIAM J., and HARRISS, C. LOWELL. *American Public Finance.* New York: Prentice-Hall, Inc., 1954. 6th ed.

THURSTON, LEE M., and ROE, WILLIAM H. *State School Administration.* New York: Harper and Row, 1957.

TIEDT, SIDNEY. *The Role of the Federal Government in Education.* New York: Oxford University Press, 1966.

United States Office of Education. *State Programs for Public School Support.* Washington: United States Government Printing Office, 1965.

Utah School Merit Study. *Report and Recommendations.* Salt Lake City: Utah School Merit Study Committee, 1958.

INDEX